Permanent Alliance?

PERMANENT ALLIANCE?

NATO and the Transatlantic Bargain from Truman to Obama

by
Stanley R. Sloan

continuum

2010

The Continuum International Publishing Group Inc
80 Maiden Lane, New York, NY 10038

The Continuum International Publishing Group Ltd
The Tower Building, 11 York Road, London SE1 7NX

www.continuumbooks.com

Library of Congress Cataloging-in-Publication Data
Sloan, Stanley R.
Permanent alliance?: NATO and the transatlantic bargain from Truman to Obama /
by Stanley R. Sloan ; forward by the honorable Lee H. Hamilton.
    p. cm.
Includes bibliographical references and index.
ISBN-13: 978-1-4411-5126-1 (hardcover : alk. paper)
ISBN-10: 1-4411-5126-5 (hardcover : alk. paper)
ISBN-13: 978-1-4411-3805-7 (pbk. : alk. paper)
ISBN-10: 1-4411-3805-6 (pbk. : alk. paper) 1. North Atlantic Treaty Organization–History.
2. United States–Foreign relations–Europe. 3. Europe–Foreign relations–United States.
I. Title.

UA646.3.S586 2010
355'.031091821–dc22   2009051363

978-1-4411-5126-1 (HB)
978-1-4411-3805-7 (PB)

Typeset by Newgen Imaging Systems Pvt Ltd, Chennai, India
Printed in the United States of America

Dedicated to the memories of my son, Scott Rawson Sloan, and my brother, Steven Dean Sloan, both of whom will always be part of my heart.

Contents

Foreword

Throughout my 34 years as a Member of the US Congress, and particularly during my service as Chair and ranking member of the House Committee on Foreign Affairs, the future of the North Atlantic Treaty Organization was a major priority on America's foreign policy agenda. It remains so today.

The responsibilities that the alliance has assumed in Afghanistan have put alliance capabilities and political unity to the test. The George W. Bush administration diverted US resources to the war in Iraq, neglecting the fight against Al Qaeda and the Taliban. Some of our allies in Afghanistan have been criticized for risk aversion on the ground and an insufficient commitment to Afghanistan's reconstruction. This has created divisions not just between the United States and some European allies but among the Europeans themselves—creating a "casualty differential," as Stan Sloan calls it, between those allies who have been willing to serve on the front lines of the conflict and those who have chosen important but less demanding and dangerous tasks.

Today, it has become clear that the goal of ensuring that Afghanistan does not once more become a base for Al Qaeda and other transnational terrorist groups will depend on a successful strategy in both Afghanistan and Pakistan. The challenge has become even more demanding for the United States and its NATO allies.

Many have speculated success or failure in Afghanistan could determine the fate of NATO. While NATO's performance there could affect the way that the allies coordinate action in the future, it would be too simplistic to pin failure on the alliance. Among the foreign powers active in Afghanistan, the United States, which initiated military operations, designed the strategy there, and is NATO's leading power, clearly holds the largest responsibility for the outcome. We have rediscovered the truth of the old adage that Afghanistan is easy to invade but difficult to pacify.

This, however, does not absolve the international community of responsibility for Afghanistan's future. The entire international community would suffer a defeat if the outcome in Afghanistan were to leave a vacuum that once again could be filled by extremist forces aiming to attack the United States and its allies around the world.

And this brings me back to the question of what the transatlantic relationship is all about. As this interpretive history of the alliance makes clear, NATO is about far more than military operations. In 1949, the United States and the West European democracies faced a real and imminent threat from the Soviet Union. Yet the North Atlantic Treaty names no enemy. It simply declares what values the signatories considered important and the interests they deemed worthy of defense. The preamble to the North Atlantic Treaty says it all. The allies affirmed that "They are determined to safeguard the freedom, common heritage and civilization of their peoples, founded on the principles of democracy, individual liberty and the rule of law." Those same values continue to sustain our democracy and that of our allies.

Even though the essence of the transatlantic alliance is captured in the preamble to the North Atlantic Treaty, the Atlantic community is a product of a complex set of historical, social, economic, political, and security factors that are reflected in a wide variety of multilateral and bilateral relationships. It has NATO at its security core, but that is only the start. The fact is that, even with all the differences and disagreements that are constantly debated across the Atlantic, neither the United States nor Europe could find more compatible, like-minded partners elsewhere in the world. The transatlantic relationship not only works for the interests of its members, it also often serves the interests of the international community. As we have discovered in recent years, dysfunction in the transatlantic relationship is to nobody's benefit.

The question raised in this volume's title is a provocative one. The transatlantic alliance has been sustained well beyond what anyone might have expected in 1949. Stan Sloan traces the development of this relationship, and skillfully recounts its ups and downs and the reasons for both the failures and successes of transatlantic cooperation.

The bottom line is that, particularly in democratic states, international commitments and responsibilities—like membership in NATO—must be revalidated by each generation of leaders and opinion-makers. New generations of American and Canadian leaders will have to be convinced that transatlantic cooperation should remain a priority. Their counterparts in Europe will have to decide whether or not cooperation with the United States and Canada still serves their vital interests.

The process of reaffirming such commitments will not happen without changes to the way things are done. The alliance has changed constantly since 1949, adapting to new international circumstances and evolving relationships among allies and inside the political systems of the member democracies. That process of change must continue. It may mean that NATO will look different down the road. It may mean that cooperation among the transatlantic allies will be enhanced, perhaps along the lines suggested in this book.

In any case, the requirement for revalidation and adaptation is what makes this book so valuable. Written in an elegant and accessible style, Stan Sloan tells the story of this alliance and examines its prospective future. Whether or not this is a "permanent alliance," it clearly is a persistent one, and one with a rationale rooted in the values and interests that it represents and defends.

Honorable Lee H. Hamilton
President and Director, Woodrow Wilson Center for Scholars
Vice-Chair, National Commission on Terrorist Attacks
upon the United States

Acknowledgments

Thinkers, researchers and writers all stand on the shoulders of those who have come before us. We learn from our predecessors and contemporaries alike, and try to add something worthwhile to the foundations already established. When in 1985 I published the first in a series of books on NATO I adopted the term "transatlantic bargain" from the man who first developed the concept. Ambassador Harlan Cleveland passed away in 2008, but the idea that the transatlantic bargain is a deal among the Europeans and between Europe and North America, remains a helpful prism through which to see Euro-Atlantic relations.

In 1985, I suggested that there was another partner to the bargain: the US Congress. From the beginning, the powerful American legislative body has played a major role in shaping, as well as critiquing, the deal. The roles played by the US House and Senate are indicative of the fact that the bargain is one made among states with democratic systems that respect individual liberty and the rule of law. As a result, the bargain is by no means static. Changes in the deal over the years have been validated by successive generations of leaders in the United States, Canada, and Europe, and will continue to require such validation.

The twists and turns of transatlantic relations have been traced and dissected by many commentators, historians and political scientists. However, at least for me, Lawrence S. Kaplan stands head and shoulders above the rest. Larry is widely regarded as NATO's leading historian, and I am privileged to know him as a friend and to have benefitted greatly from his guidance and encouragement over the years.

The 24 years that I spent at the Congressional Research Service (CRS) of the Library of Congress introduced me to another contingent of experts with broad shoulders, whose peer reviews of my work always required that I think more deeply and effectively. A few of my former colleagues still work at this marvelous institution, and they have been joined by new analysts who continue to produce the best objective and non-partisan research around. Fortunately for scholars, even though CRS regrettably resists putting its studies out in public after they have been delivered to the Congress, they are now quite readily available on several websites.

My years spent working for Congress left me with respect for the intended role of the institution and for many of its members. On the long list of Members of Congress for whom I provided research and analysis, Lee Hamilton stands out as a man of substance, principles, and common sense. I am therefore more than grateful that he agreed to contribute the foreword for this book.

For over 20 years now, I have been fortunate to have been invited regularly to lecture on transatlantic relations at the NATO Defense College in Rome. This little-known institution makes an important contribution to spreading awareness of what NATO is, and what it isn't, to ranking military officers and civilian defense and foreign policy officials of NATO countries, and now of partner countries ranging from

North Africa to the Middle East, and Asia. I appreciate the decisions of the College's many commandants, deans, and their staffs over the years to allow me to share in and learn from this experience.

Most recently, my work has been stimulated by many bright and capable students at Middlebury College, where I have had the privilege of teaching in the winter term for some six years. The challenge of trying to contribute to the education and world views of these valuable young people has, for me, been a stimulating learning experience. Guest lecturers and friends who have enriched the sessions for me and my students include Lawrence R. Chalmer, Marten van Heuven, and Leo G. Michel. In addition, the Rohatyn Center for International Affairs at Middlebury, under the leadership of Dr Allison Stanger and her excellent staff, made me feel welcome as a visiting scholar. The Center has additionally provided me with precious help from several excellent interns, including Middlebury students Brian Fung and, most recently, Daniel Sharon, who contributed invaluable research assistance and perspectives to this volume, particularly to Chapters 7 and 9.

I am overjoyed to have connected with Continuum Books, which, from the beginning, has enthusiastically welcomed this volume. Marie-Claire Antoine, acquisitions editor for politics and international relations, has been more supportive than anyone could hope for, and I knew from the very beginning of the process that I was in very good hands. The work of her colleagues at Continuum is greatly appreciated, as are the efforts of Mr. Muralidharan and his copy editing and production staff colleagues. Responsibility for any mistakes or roads not taken in this book is, of course, mine.

Finally, I wish to acknowledge most importantly my in-house critic, copy editor, and loving wife Monika. On many days of work on this volume she saw my eyes glued to a laptop screen, and understood when she spoke to me and, at times, found me lost in thought, or at least in a tangle of words and ideas that wouldn't fit together properly. My everlasting love and gratitude go out to the better half of our own "transatlantic bargain."

Stanley R. Sloan
Richmond, Vermont

Map 1: NATO Expansion Map

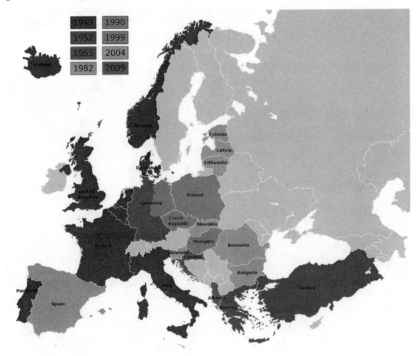

Source: Wikipedia. Image by Kpalian.

1949	Belgium	Luxembourg
	Canada	Netherlands
	Denmark	United States
	France	Norway
	Iceland	Portugal
	Italy	United Kingdom
1952	Greece	Turkey
1955	Germany	
1982	Spain	
1999	Czech Republic	Poland
	Hungary	
2004	Bulgaria	Romania
	Estonia	Slovakia
	Latvia	Slovenia
	Lithuania	
2009	Croatia	Albania

Map 2: The European Union

Source: CIA, *The World Factbook.*

List of Acronyms

ABM	Anti-Ballistic Missile Treaty
ACLANT	Allied Command Atlantic
ACO	Allied Command Operations [NATO]
ACT	Allied Command Transformation [NATO]
AFSOUTH	Allied Forces Southern Europe [NATO]
ANA	Afghan National Army
ANAAC	Afghan National Army Air Corps
ANP	Afghan National Police
ANSF	Afghan National Security Forces
ASOP	Afghan Social Outreach Program
AWACS	Airborne Warning and Control System
BENELUX	Belgium, the Netherlands, and Luxembourg
CAP	Common Agricultural Policy [EU]
CBRN	Chemical, Biological, Radiological and Nuclear Defence Batallion [NATO]
CDE	Conference on Security and Confidence Building Measures and Disarmament in Europe
CEE	Central and East European countries
CFE	Conventional Forces in Europe Treaty
CFSP	Common Foreign and Security Policy [EU]
CIS	Commonwealth of Independent States
CJTF	Combined Joint Task Force [NATO]
COMECON	Council for Mutual Economic Assistance
COPS(I)	(Interim) Political and Security Committee [EU] (French acronym)
CSCE	Conference on Security and Cooperation in Europe
CSTO	Collective Security Treaty Organization
DCI	Defense Capabilities Initiative [NATO]
DPC	Defense Planning Committee [NATO]
DSACEUR	Deputy Supreme Allied Commander in Europe [NATO]
EAPC	Euro-Atlantic Partnership Council [NATO]
EC	European Communit(y)(ies)
ECSC	European Coal and Steel Community
EDC	European Defense Community
EEC	European Economic Community
EFTA	European Free Trade Area
EMS	European Monetary System [EU]
EMU	European Monetary Unit [EU]

EPC	European Political Cooperation [EU]
ESDI	European Security and Defense Identity [WEU/EU]
ESDP	European Security and Defense Policy [EU]
ETT	Embedded Training Team [NATO, ISAF]
EU	European Union
EUMC	European Union Military Committee [EU]
EUMS	European Union Military Staff [EU]
EURATOM	European Atomic Energy Community
Euro	European Union currency unit
EUFOR	European Force [EU-Bosnia]
EUROCORPS	European Rapid Reaction Force [EU]
Eurogroup	Informal grouping of NATO European defense ministers dissolved in 1993
FSU	Former Soviet Union
FYROM	Former Yugoslav Republic of Macedonia
GATT	General Agreement on Tariffs and Trade
GDP	Gross Domestic Product
GWOT	Global War on Terror
ICS	Integrated Command Structure (ICS)
IED	Improvised Explosive Device
IEPG	Independent European Programme Group
IFOR	Implementation Force (for Bosnia) [NATO]
IGC	Intergovernmental Conference [EU]
INF	Intermediate-Range Nuclear Forces
ISAF	International Security Assistance Force [NATO]
KFOR	Kosovo Force [NATO]
LANDCENT	Allied Land Forces Central Europe [NATO]
LTDP	Long Term Defense Plan [NATO]
MAP	Membership Action Plan [NATO]
MBFR	Mutual and Balanced Force Reductions
MC	Military Committee [NATO]
MLF	Multilateral Force [NATO]
NAC	North Atlantic Council [NATO]
NACC	North Atlantic Cooperation Council [NATO]
NATO	North Atlantic Treaty Organization
NGO	Non-governmental organization
NPA	NATO Parliamentary Assembly (formerly NAA, North Atlantic Assembly)
NPG	Nuclear Planning Group [NATO]
NPT	[Nuclear] Non-Proliferation Treaty
NRF	NATO Response Force [NATO]
NSC	US National Security Council
OECD	Organization for Economic Cooperation and Development

OEF	Operation Enduring Freedom
OMLT	Operational Mentoring and Liaison Team [NATO, ISAF]
OSCE	Organization for Security and Cooperation in Europe
PARP	[Partnership for Peace] Planning and Review Process [NATO]
PFP	Partnership for Peace
PJC	NATO–Russia Permanent Joint Council [NATO]
PRT	Provincial Reconstruction Team
PSC	Political and Security Committee [EU]
RMA	Revolution in military affairs
SACEUR	Supreme Allied Commander, Europe [NATO]
SACLANT	Supreme Allied Commander, Atlantic [NATO]
SDI	Strategic Defense Initiative
SFOR	Bosnia Stabilization Force [NATO]
SHAPE	Supreme Headquarters Allied Powers, Europe [NATO]
SNF	Short-Range Nuclear Forces
STANAVFORMED	Standing Naval Force Mediterranean [NATO]
START	Strategic Arms Reduction Talks
TEU	Treaty on European Union, "The Maastricht Treaty" [EU]
UK	United Kingdom
UN	United Nations
UNDP	United Nations Development Program
UNPROFOR	United Nations Protection Force (in Bosnia)
US	United States of America
USSR	Union of Soviet Socialist Republics
WEAG	Western European Armaments Group
WEU	Western European Union
WMD	Weapons of mass destruction

PART I

Cold War Alliance

CHAPTER 1

The Bargain as a Framework for Analysis

The glue that has held the allies more or less together is a large, complex and dynamic bargain—partly an understanding among the Europeans, but mostly a deal between them and the United States of America.

—*Harlan Cleveland,* NATO: The Transatlantic Bargain[1]

Crafted in the late 1960s, Harlan Cleveland's description of NATO as a "transatlantic bargain" remains, in the early years of the twenty-first century, a helpful prism through which to analyze the North Atlantic alliance. Cleveland, a former US permanent representative to NATO, knew the alliance was far more than the sort of deal struck between business partners. Although the transatlantic bargain is based firmly on unsentimental calculations of national self-interest on both sides of the Atlantic, it also depends on some amorphous but vital shared ideas about man, government, and society. It is a "bargain," to be sure, but a bargain with roots in the hearts (and values) as well as in the minds (and interests) of the partners.

The United Kingdom's Lord Palmerston, a nineteenth-century British statesman, famously declared that "Nations have no permanent friends or allies, they only have permanent interests." Palmerston's observation stood up well through the mid-twentieth century. However, the persistence of the North Atlantic Treaty Organization—the leading component of the transatlantic bargain—seems to be challenging Palmerston's assertion.

From George Washington's warning in his farewell address that the United States should avoid permanent foreign alliances, particularly with European states, the United States followed his advice—until April 1949, when the North Atlantic Treaty was signed. As Lawrence S. Kaplan has observed, "The Europeans may have initiated the process, but bipartisan U.S. advocates brought it to a conclusion and terminated America's 149-year tradition of political and military non-entanglement with Europe."[2] Superficially, the treaty certainly looked like what Washington had warned against. However, both the circumstances and the alliance were in fact quite different than what Washington had considered.

This volume examines the origins and development of the transatlantic alliance with an eye on the major factors that have influenced its evolution and may offer clues about its future. Throughout NATO's history, the alliance has been said to be moving from one "crisis" to another, and its demise has frequently been projected by scholars and officials alike.[3] So far, they have been wrong. The question is: will they continue to be wrong?

What Was the Original Bargain?

The original transatlantic bargain, described in Chapter 2 of this book, was a bargain between the United States and its original European partners[4] with the militarily modest but politically important participation of Canada.[5] The first half of the deal was that the United States would support Europe's economic recovery from the war if the Europeans would coordinate their efforts to use the assistance most effectively. The second half pledged that the United States would contribute to the defense of Europe if the Europeans would organize themselves to help defend against the Soviet threat.

The European allies were quite successful in developing the first half of the bargain. In 1948, the Organization for European Economic Cooperation was created to coordinate utilization of Marshall Plan assistance from the United States and to promote European economic cooperation. The Europeans constructed a European Coal and Steel Community (1951) and then, through the 1957 Rome Treaties, the European Economic Community and the European Atomic Energy Community, the precursors of today's European Union.

The allies were not nearly so successful in the security area. As discussed in Chapter 2, France had proposed the creation of a European Defense Community to organize Europe's military contribution to the bargain. When that initiative failed in 1954, the arrangements adopted in place of the European Defense Community, considered in Chapter 3, left the transatlantic bargain highly dependent on US nuclear weapons and a substantial US force presence in Europe to give credibility to NATO's defense against the Soviet threat.

Throughout the Cold War, the alliance lived with the 1954 "revised" bargain and a persistent burden-sharing debate between the United States and its European allies as well as between successive US administrations and the US Congress.

Congress, given the crucial constitutional roles of the Senate in the process of ratifying treaties and the House of Representatives in legislating funding for government programs, participated actively in shaping and overseeing the US side of the transatlantic bargain. The involvement of Congress, judiciously sought by President Harry Truman's administration in the late 1940s, ensured a solid foundation for US participation in the transatlantic bargain. But it also guaranteed that senators and representatives would, for the life of the deal, closely inspect its terms and conditions. From the beginning, this inspection process has focused particularly on whether the costs of the deal were being fairly shared. For most of the history, they have found the sharing process lacking; this continues to be the case today, even under much-changed conditions.

In addition to the important congressional "clause" in the transatlantic bargain, there were many subordinate bargains that were more important to individual allies than to the United States. For example, France wanted the deal to ensure that it would not have to face a resurgence of German power on its own. The United Kingdom wanted US participation in European defense to provide an effective deterrent to Soviet expansionism so that some British military assets would be available to maintain its position as a global power. Canada wanted the bargain not only to be about military power, of which it had little, and more about political values, which it held high. When the Federal Republic of Germany joined in the bargain, it accepted constraints on its military capabilities in return for sovereignty over its internal affairs.

Every addition to the membership of the alliance brought new subordinate bargains as European states sought specific benefits from the alliance. Recent candidates for membership, starting with the Czech Republic, Hungary and Poland in the 1990s, have seen belonging to NATO and the European Union as the two key tokens of acceptance in the Western community of nations and as protection against external domination by Russia or any other power.

Factors that emerged in the transatlantic relationship over the course of the Cold War still resonate in relations among the allies today, as discussed in Chapters 4 and 5. The period of transition and new missions from 1989 through the first decade of the twenty-first century is examined though the prisms of NATO outreach and enlargement (see Chapter 6), NATO and Russia (Chapter 7), NATO's missions (Chapter 8), NATO in Afghanistan (Chapter 9), and the evolving relationship between European integration and transatlantic cooperation (Chapter 10).

Among all the changes and adjustments in the bargain over the years, the step-by-step development of European integration may be of the greatest importance. The allies were unsuccessful in fulfilling the original transatlantic bargain because Europe was not politically prepared for the degree of unity that would have been required to produce a coherent contribution to Western defense. Since the end of the Cold War, the process of European integration has made substantial progress, but does that suggest that transatlantic alliance has become unnecessary or unwanted? The future of the transatlantic bargain depends heavily on whether the European integration process is able to produce a more integrated Europe within the framework of continued cooperation with the United States and Canada, or if integration cannot develop inside the protective embrace of transatlantic alliance.

What Has NATO Become?

For now, NATO remains at the heart of the transatlantic bargain. However, the 9/11 terrorist attacks on the United States, followed by the US intervention in Iraq, have challenged relations within Europe and across the Atlantic, as discussed in Chapter 11. Looking toward the future, Chapter 12 asks: Is NATO necessary but not sufficient for the future security requirements of its members? Transatlantic security in the twenty-first century calls for the use of a wide variety of policy instruments extending well beyond the military cooperation that is part and parcel of NATO's mandate. Does the mandate need to be enhanced or do the allies need a new framework for cooperation on the non-military aspects of security? The question of whether or not the transatlantic alliance is becoming "permanent," or if it is on its last legs, as predicted by some observers, is addressed in Chapter 13.

In any case, NATO provides the starting point for any such venture, so it is important to consider where NATO's evolution has brought the alliance early in the twenty-first century. Today, more than 15 years after the Berlin Wall fell, many diverse views about what NATO is—or should become—remain. The discussion of NATO's essence recalls the Indian fable about the king who asked a group of blind men to feel various parts of an elephant and describe the elephant on the basis of the part they had touched.[6] Naturally, each blind man produced a different description of the elephant. This analysis starts from the premise that an objective assessment of NATO's purpose and mission can be based on several sources: on the provisions of the 1949 North Atlantic Treaty,[7] on the declared goals and intentions of its members, and on the fact that an organization is in many respects defined by its activities.

NATO has always been more than simply a defensive alliance. The North Atlantic Treaty provides a broad and flexible mandate through which to defend and promote allied interests and security. Moreover, preserving the attributes of a collective defense system, including an integrated command structure, a vital defense planning process, and thoroughgoing political and military consultations strengthens NATO's ability to play new roles and assume new missions that respond to the post-Cold War challenges to the values and interests of the members.

NATO Is a Community of Values

The North Atlantic Treaty was designed to counter Soviet expansion and military power. But the Treaty itself was based on common values, identified no enemy, protected the sovereign decision-making rights of all members, and was written in sufficiently flexible language to facilitate adjustments to accommodate changing international circumstances. British Foreign Secretary Ernest Bevin, one of NATO's "founding fathers," urged the creation of a "Western Union" in a speech to the British Parliament on January 22, 1948. He asserted that "our sacrifices during the war, our hatred of injustice and oppression, our party democracy, our striving for economic rights and our conception and love of liberty are common among us all." During the negotiation of the Treaty, the government of Canada argued the need to reflect "the ideological unity of the North Atlantic powers." US Secretary of State Dean Acheson subsequently maintained that "the central idea of the treaty is not a static one" and that "the North Atlantic Treaty is far more than a defensive arrangement. It is an affirmation of the moral and spiritual values which we hold in common." During the 1949 Senate hearings on the Treaty, Acheson and other Truman administration witnesses argued that what they were proposing was very different from previous military alliance systems.[8]

What made NATO different from previous military alliances was that the Treaty's preamble clearly articulated allied support for "democracy, individual liberty, and the rule of law." It is true that, during the Cold War, the values of democracy, rule of law, and individual freedom occasionally took second place when authoritarian regimes in NATO were tolerated in the interest of maintaining a militarily strong alliance. But NATO's survival beyond the end of the Cold War suggests that its value foundation and the inherent logic of Euro-Atlantic cooperation remain important ingredients in the glue that holds the alliance together. These same factors combined with the perceived need for a security link to the United States have made NATO membership so attractive to new European democracies.

NATO Is Based on a Broad and Flexible Mandate

The North Atlantic Treaty's relatively simple language does not spell out in great detail how its objectives should be implemented. There is no specified military strategy and no requirement for any particular organization or even military arrangements beyond the creation of a North Atlantic Council and a defense committee. This suggests substantial latitude for adaptation and adjustment to changing circumstances. The only limits on such changes are imposed by national interests, values, inertia, and other human and institutional factors, not by the Treaty.

NATO's flexibility was demonstrated, for example, by the military buildup and elaboration of an integrated command structure in the early 1950s that had not been anticipated when the Treaty was signed and that was judged necessary only after North Korea invaded South Korea. The alliance was adjusted again following the failure of the European Defense Community in 1954. In the mid-1960s, NATO was forced to adapt to France's departure from the Integrated Command Structure (ICS). In 1967, the allies revamped NATO's strategy with the doctrine of "flexible response" to a possible Warsaw Pact attack. That same year, they approved the "Harmel Report," which gave the alliance the mission of promoting détente as well as sustaining deterrence and defense. And, in the 1990s, the allies reoriented NATO's goals and activities to take into account the peaceful revolutions that brought democracy to eastern and central Europe and gave Russia, Ukraine, and other former Soviet republics the opportunity for independence and democratic reform.

NATO Is a Collective Defense System

At its founding, the most prominent aspect of the Treaty was its requirement for individual and collective actions for defense against armed attack. Article 3 of the Treaty provides that the allies "separately and jointly, by means of continuous and effective self-help and mutual aid, will maintain and develop their individual and collective capacity to resist armed attack." In Article 5, the Treaty's collective defense provision, the parties agreed that "an armed attack against one or more of them in Europe or North America shall be considered an attack against them all."

They specifically agreed that each party to the Treaty would "assist the Party or Parties so attacked by taking forthwith, individually and in concert with other Parties, such action as it deems necessary, including the use of armed force, to restore and maintain the security of the North Atlantic area."

During the Cold War, NATO's strategy and the way in which the United States, Canada, and the United Kingdom deployed their forces on the Continent gave Article 5 more substance in practice than suggested by the words in the Treaty. Beginning in the early 1950s, the United States deployed its military forces and nuclear weapons forward in Europe, mainly in Germany, in a fashion ensuring that a Soviet attack on the West would, in its early stages, engage US forces, thereby constituting an attack on the United States as well as on the host nation. In the mid-1950s, the United States threatened massive nuclear retaliation against the Soviet Union should it attack a NATO country. After massive retaliation's credibility was undermined by Soviet acquisition of long-range nuclear weapons, NATO adopted its "flexible response" strategy. Flexible response suggested that battlefield nuclear weapons might be used early in any European conflict. Such weapons were deployed well forward in West Germany to ensure that they were seen as part of NATO's first line of defense.

Today, the collective defense commitment still endows the North Atlantic Treaty with special meaning. It is a potential deterrent against would-be enemies of the allies and a source of reassurance should future threats develop. With no imminent Soviet-style threat currently facing the allies, they have been adapting NATO strategy and force deployments to fundamentally new circumstances. Most activities of the alliance have turned toward purposes of defense cooperation that lie beyond collective defense, even though the institutions and processes developed to implement collective defense, including the Integrated Command Structure, remain critically important to NATO's future. Article 5 still provides a continuing rationale for maintaining the Integrated Command Structure, and the day-to-day political and military consultation and planning that make NATO a unique facilitator of defense cooperation among the member states. They are now seeking to translate their commitment to cooperate against threats posed by terrorist operations and weapons of mass destruction into NATO strategy, force planning, capabilities, and operations.

NATO Is a Cooperative Defense Organization

NATO has been and always will be a political as well as a military alliance. In recent years, it has been increasingly common for observers to say that NATO would have to adapt to new circumstances by becoming "more political." In 2002, following the US failure to use NATO military structures to help conduct military operations in Afghanistan and the decision to intensify cooperation with Russia, many said that NATO was clearly in the process of becoming, for all intents and purposes, a political organization. But NATO's activities in the past and today make clear that its unique role is as an instrument of both political and military cooperation among member and partner states. The process involves consultations in the North Atlantic Council and its many subordinate bodies, practical coordination developed in the work of the Military Committee, and day-to-day collaboration in the Integrated Command Structure. In the 1990s, consultation and cooperation with partners, including Russia and Ukraine, became a critical part of NATO's role. The goals of such cooperation today, however, are more diverse and complex than during the Cold War.

NATO Creates Policy Options for Crisis Management

At the end of the Cold War, the allies questioned whether they still needed an elaborate system of political and military cooperation at a time when the Soviet threat had all but vanished. Their answer, in the November 1991 "new strategic concept," was that political consultation and defense cooperation, so essential in the Cold War, could be broadened to include other purposes. NATO cooperation was widely accepted as having facilitated an effective US-led coalition response to Iraq's invasion of Kuwait, and the experience had a significant influence on the directions taken in the 1991 strategic concept. Since that time, most of NATO's military activities have been focused on "non-Article 5" requirements, starting in the Balkans and continuing in Afghanistan and Iraq. The mandate for such activities is found primarily in Article 4 of the North Atlantic Treaty, which authorizes cooperation to deal with circumstances that threaten the security of one or more NATO members.

NATO remains an organization of sovereign nation-states in which no member can be compelled to participate in a military operation that it does not support. There is, as a consequence, no guarantee that the allies will respond to any given political or military challenge. But NATO can be used to build political consensus and create military options to implement political goals. The allies would have fewer credible military options if their military leaders and forces were not working together on a day-to-day basis, developing interoperability of those forces, planning for contingency operations, and exercising their military capabilities. This day-to-day routine develops political and military habits of cooperation that underpin the ability to work together under pressure and, more important, under fire.

The interests of the allies clearly will require the application of military force in defense of US and European interests for the foreseeable future. The political/military cooperation that is unique to NATO gives the allies the option of facing such circumstances as an effective coalition rather than as individual nation-states.

NATO Defense Cooperation Is a Burden-Sharing Tool

NATO can also be seen as a way to ensure that allies carry a fair share of the burdens of maintaining international peace. This is a role that can be seen as a glass half full or half empty. During the Cold War, some Americans saw NATO as a creator of burdens for the United States rather than as an instrument for sharing them. Some may still hold this view, particularly in light of the growing gap between US and European military capabilities, and the large gap between North American and continental European military contributions in Afghanistan. On the one hand, the US military presence in Europe, down to well under 100,000 troops on shore, is now increasingly oriented toward force projection and peace operations rather than toward defense of European territory. The NATO framework provides the United States with leverage to push for additional European defense efforts, presuming that the Europeans want the United States to remain involved in European security, which they apparently do. On the other hand, it could be argued that the habit of European security dependence on the United States is perpetuated by NATO, and that new means of cooperation, for example, by giving the European Union a homegrown role in defense, are needed to increase European self-reliance and reduce US burdens.

NATO Defense Cooperation Is an Instrument to Promote Political Change

NATO defense cooperation is now being used more prominently for political goals beyond its members' borders as well. Perhaps for this reason, some see NATO as becoming "more political." The Partnership for Peace (PFP) was established at the Brussels Summit in January 1994 to develop cooperation with non-NATO states. Through the PFP, Europe's new democracies have been learning how to develop systems of democratically controlled armed forces as well as habits of cooperation with NATO nations and neighboring partners. The partnership approach helped the Czech Republic, Hungary, and Poland meet the requirements for NATO membership in 1999 and remains the principal path through which other nations have prepared to enter the alliance. Countries that had been neutral during the Cold War are using the PFP to participate in NATO's efforts to promote stability in and around Europe.

The allies are also using political/military cooperation with Russia to try to change Russian perceptions of the alliance and, it is hoped, to change the political relationship between Moscow and NATO by gradually integrating Russia into a cooperative Euro-Atlantic security system. In a sense, the 1997 Founding Act with Russia, creating a NATO-Russia Permanent Joint Council, updated NATO's attempt to promote improved relations with Russia, a goal that was prominently advanced in the 1967 Harmel Report. The strengthening of that tie in 2002 sought to continue the process. If NATO succeeds, the defense cooperation relationship with Russia, which began with military cooperation in Bosnia, could leapfrog over the arms control accords that were designed during the Cold War to regulate relationships between parties that otherwise were in conflict with one another. Moving from a Russia-NATO relationship governed by arms control to one characterized by the transparent, predictable, and confidence-building nature of defense cooperation would mark a sea change in the European security system.

NATO Is an Open Organization

The drafters of the North Atlantic Treaty made it clear in Article 10 that accession to the Treaty would remain open to "any other European state in a position to further the principles of this Treaty and to contribute to the security of the North Atlantic area." This "open door" policy led to the membership of Greece and Turkey in 1952, Germany in 1955, and Spain in 1982. After the countries of central and Eastern Europe freed themselves from communism and began establishing democratic systems of government, NATO's rejection of their desire for membership in the alliance would have repudiated everything the North Atlantic Treaty stands for. Acceptance by the allies of the Czech Republic, Hungary, and Poland in 1999, Bulgaria, Estonia, Latvia, Lithuania, Romania, Slovakia, and Slovenia in 2004, and Albania and Croatia in 2009 highlights the fact that NATO is organized around transcendent values and goals that do not require an enemy to validate their continuing relevance.

NATO Is a Source of Stability

It is clear that NATO serves a variety of purposes for individual member states beyond these broadly stated goals. Many such secondary agendas help explain why current members of NATO want the alliance to continue and why the new central and east European democracies sought to join. Former members of the Warsaw Pact do not fear attack from today's Russia, but they do see NATO as a guarantee against falling once again into the Russian sphere of influence as well as an insurance policy against any future resurgence of a Russian threat. Most European governments hope that the process of European unification will lead to more intensive security and defense cooperation among European states. But they continue to see the transatlantic link as essential to their security.

Further, many Europeans believe that the US role in Europe, particularly as translated through NATO, provides an important ingredient of stability that facilitates cooperation among European states. For example, even though Germany is not seen as a threat by its neighbors, both Germany and its neighbors feel more comfortable with Germany's role in Europe thoroughly integrated within the framework of both the European Union and the transatlantic alliance. From the US point of view, NATO cooperation is a way to seek equitable sharing of the burdens of maintaining international stability with like-minded states.

NATO Is at the Center of a Cooperative European Security System

Finally, it is necessary to address the somewhat academic but politically important question of whether NATO is a collective security organization. The term "collective security" is widely and loosely used in today's discussion of NATO's future role. According to its classic definition, collective security is a system of interstate relations designed to maintain a balance of power and interests among the members that ensure peaceful relationships within that system. The League of Nations, established after World War I without US participation, is usually regarded as such a system.

From the outset, NATO was designed as a system of cooperation among member states to deal with challenges and problems originating outside that system, not within it. Granted, NATO has to some extent tried to promote peaceful settlement of problems within the system in support of its mission of defending against external threats. It is credited with having helped heal World War II wounds inflicted by Nazi Germany on its neighbors. NATO has served to mitigate conflicts between Greece and Turkey. Indeed, the requirements of collective defense promoted a degree of cooperation between these two NATO members that might not have been realized in NATO's absence. Today, several NATO activities support the goal of collective security. Russia-NATO cooperation, the PFP, and the Euro-Atlantic Partnership Council, for example, have helped maintain peaceful and cooperative relations among all states in Europe. Such efforts enhance collective security and make it less likely that any NATO country will be attacked by any other European nation.

But when the allies began preparing for NATO's post-Cold War enlargement, they made clear to potential applicants that they must resolve differences with their neighbors in order to be seriously considered for NATO membership. The NATO countries insisted that new members leave their old baggage of bilateral and ethnic differences with their neighbors by the wayside when they join NATO. So far, not all issues related to ethnic nationals residing in neighboring central and east European states have been "resolved." However, the NATO commitment helps keep such differences within bounds and promotes peaceful resolution.

From a legal perspective, NATO does not have principal responsibility for collective security in Europe—the North Atlantic Treaty does not suggest such a role. In fact, the Conference on (now Organization for) Security and Cooperation in Europe (OSCE) was designed to promote peaceful relations among states "from the Atlantic to the Urals." The 1975 Helsinki Final Act of the OSCE established a series of agreed principles, or "rules of the road," to govern relations among states in Europe. The OSCE member states (all European states plus the United States and Canada) have adopted further agreements and principles, have given the organization some diplomatic tools for conflict prevention, and convene regular meetings under OSCE auspices to try to address problems before they develop more serious proportions.

The Future of the Transatlantic Bargain

In the fable of the blind men and the elephant, the king finally observes, "Well is it known that some Samanas and Brahmanas cling to such views, sink down into them, and attain not to Nirvana." An "ideal" NATO is probably beyond the reach of member governments today. And participants in the debate on the future of the transatlantic bargain may well continue to "fight among themselves with their fists," as in the fable, declaring that "such is an elephant, such is not an elephant." The future of the bargain most likely must be built on a foundation that accommodates all these perceptions to one degree or another.

In sum, the North Atlantic Treaty still accurately represents the values and goals articulated by the United States and its allies despite persistent differences among them concerning how best to promote those values and defend their interests. The collective defense commitment in the North Atlantic Treaty is an obligation assumed by all current and future members, even though Article 5 leaves much room for nations to decide collectively and individually what to do under any given crisis scenario. This was clearly demonstrated when NATO invoked Article 5 following the September 11, 2001, terrorist attacks on the United States. Continuing defense cooperation in NATO keeps alive the potential to mount collective responses to aggression against alliance members. Defense cooperation also creates policy options, though no obligation, for responses to crises beyond NATO's borders and serves as a tool for changing political relationships between NATO countries and other nations, most importantly Russia. NATO is not a collective security organization; it is designed primarily not to keep peace among its members but rather to protect and advance the interests of the members in dealing with the world around them. But some of NATO's activities contribute to the goal of collective security, helping maintain peaceful and cooperative relations among all states in Europe.

These attributes of NATO bear witness to the continuing relevance of the North Atlantic Treaty and the importance of continued US-European security cooperation. However, two decades have passed since the dramatic changes at the end of the Cold War. Over that time, the transatlantic allies have sought to understand and relate effectively to a fundamentally new international system. The allies have passed through another period of crisis brought on by divergent US and European views on how best to deal with Saddam Hussein's Iraq. Now the time may be approaching for the United States, Canada, and the European allies to decide whether their thoroughly intertwined interests and still-potent shared political values require a broader framework for cooperation than that provided by NATO, the US-EU dialogue, and other bilateral and multilateral Euro-Atlantic institutions. The concept of an "Atlantic Community" is not a new one. It has been brought forward many times during the history of the alliance, and on each occasion it has been judged an idea whose time has not yet come.

US unilateralist tendencies and their counterpart in some European countries have threatened commitments to the alliance on both sides of the Atlantic. But as the United States and its allies focus on the newly framed threats of terrorism and weapons of mass destruction, it may now be the hour in which a serious reconsideration is warranted to ensure that this historic transatlantic bond survives into the uncertain future. Without a strong new commitment to the indivisibility of security and well-being in the Euro-Atlantic area, the transatlantic bargain could well begin to come undone.

The way of life represented by the societies of NATO and European Union member states faces a great variety of challenges. Rising powers such as China, India, and Brazil will, over time, rebalance international power relationships. Demographic decline in traditional European populations may threaten the very fabric of those societies. In this setting, a renewed commitment to the importance of transat-lantic ties could give rise to the speculation that this alliance is indeed becoming "permanent." NATO—the organization that symbolizes and operationalizes transatlantic security ties—may not last forever. But the transatlantic community is much more than NATO, and that community may be seen by its members as increasingly relevant to their values and interests in the years to come.

Notes

1. Harlan Cleveland, *NATO: The Transatlantic Bargain* (New York: Harper & Row, 1970).
2. Lawrence S. Kaplan, *NATO 1948, The Birth of the Transatlantic Alliance*, (Lanham, Md.: Rowman & Littlefield, 2007), 223. Professor Kaplan, widely recognized as NATO's premier historian, has produced a number of books that chronicle in detail NATO's evolution from its origins through the Cold War. They include, in addition to *NATO 1948*, *The United States and NATO: The Formative Years* (Lexington: University Press of Kentucky, 1984) and *NATO and the United States: The Enduring Alliance* (New York: Twayne, 1988).
3. Examined in detail by Wallace Thies in *Why NATO Endures* (London: Cambridge University Press, 2009).
4. The Treaty of Washington was signed on April 4, 1949 by the governments of Belgium, Canada, Denmark, France, Iceland, Italy, Luxembourg, the Netherlands, Norway, Portugal, the United Kingdom and the United States.
5. Canadian priorities and diplomacy resulted in the Treaty's Article 2: "The Parties will contribute toward the further development of peaceful and friendly interna-tional relations by strengthening their free institutions, by bringing about a better understanding of the principles upon which these institutions are founded, and by promoting conditions of stability and well-being. They will seek to eliminate conflict in their international economic policies and will encourage economic collaboration between any or all of them." For discussion of the Canadian role in shaping the treaty, see Sean Kay, *NATO and the Future of European Security* (Lanham, Md.: Rowman & Littlefield, 1998), 21–31.
6. According to The Udana, or the Solemn Utterances of the Buddha, the story goes something like this:

> And the King went to where the blind men were, and drawing near said to them: "Do you now know what an elephant is like?" And those blind men who had felt the head of the elephant said: "An elephant, Sir, is like a large round jar."
> Those who had felt its ears said: "it is like a winnowing basket."
> Those who had felt its tusks said: "it is like a plough-share."

Those who had felt its trunk said: "it is like a plough."
Those who had felt its body said: "it is like a granary."
Those who had felt its feet said: "it is like a pillar."
Those who had felt its back said: "it is like a mortar."
Those who had felt its tail said: "it is like a pestle."
Those who had felt the tuft of its tail said: "it is like a broom."
And they fought amongst themselves with their fists, declaring, "such is an elephant, such is not an elephant, an elephant is not like that, it is like this."

7. The text of the Treaty of Washington of 1949 (North Atlantic Treaty) can be found at Appendix 1.
8. US Senate Committee on Foreign Relations, North Atlantic Treaty, Hearings before the Committee on Foreign Relations, 81st Cong., 1st sess., April 27–29 and May 2–3, 1949.

CHAPTER 2

Genesis of the Bargain

The transatlantic bargain finds its origins in a series of political decisions and diplomatic events in the mid- to late 1940s. As the end of World War II neared, US President Franklin D. Roosevelt was particularly sensitive to fact that President Woodrow Wilson's failure at the end of World War I to engage the United States in the League of Nations had been a contributing factor to the rise of Adolf Hitler in Germany and the events leading to World War II. Roosevelt wanted to ensure that the United States played a leading role in constructing a new international system under the auspices of a United Nations organization. Unlike Wilson, Roosevelt carefully engaged leading members of Congress in the process, including the influential and prewar isolationist Senator Arthur H. Vandenberg, to increase the chances that the United States would commit to the venture.

Meanwhile, wartime ally Great Britain, led by Prime Minister Winston Churchill, was naturally focused on how postwar Europe could be organized to protect British interests and particularly on how to keep German power contained and prevent further Soviet advances into Western Europe. Roosevelt died in 1945, just before the end of the war in Europe and the signature of the UN Charter in San Francisco. In Great Britain, the Labour Party, led by Clement R. Attlee, defeated Churchill's Conservatives, putting the postwar conclusion and reconstruction in the hands of successors in both countries.

The United States, under President Harry Truman, moved into a debate on how best to deal with the Soviet Union as it increasingly appeared that the wartime cooperation between Roosevelt and Soviet leader Joseph Stalin was turning toward a more competitive and even hostile relationship. British Foreign Secretary Ernest Bevin set out to convince the United States to lend its power and influence to a postwar system in Europe that would prevent further Soviet political and military advances. Out of office, Winston Churchill, speaking in Fulton, Missouri, warned of the expansionist tendencies of the Soviet Union, saying, "From Stettin in the Baltic to Trieste in the Adriatic an iron curtain has descended across the Continent."

Responding to the growing perception of a Soviet threat, in March 1947, President Truman promulgated what became known as the Truman Doctrine, urging the United States "to support free peoples who are resisting attempted subjugation by armed minorities or by outside pressure." A few days later, Great Britain and France, demonstrating that they worried not just about the Soviet threat but also about the possibility of a resurgent German challenge, signed the Treaty of Dunkirk, agreeing to give mutual support to each other in the event of renewed German aggression. The process of shaping the transatlantic bargain had begun in earnest.

In a June 5, 1947, speech by Secretary of State George C. Marshall, the Truman administration proposed what became known as the Marshall Plan to provide funds for economic reconstruction to war-ravaged nations in western and southern Europe. The plan was warmly welcomed by Great Britain and other European countries not only because it would provide much-needed assistance but also because it was a sign of US commitment to Europe's future. Then, speaking before the British House of Commons on January 22, 1948, Foreign Secretary Bevin proposed creation of a Western Union comprised of the United Kingdom, France, and the Benelux countries. As one author has observed, this step "launched the making of the Atlantic Alliance."[1]

Over the course of the next two years, three formative steps shaped the transatlantic bargain: the Brussels Treaty (1948), which resulted from the Bevin initiative; the Vandenberg Resolution (1948); and the North Atlantic Treaty, also known as the Washington Treaty (1949; the text of the treaty is given in Appendix 1). These events outlined the objectives of the bargain, identified the partners in the deal, and suggested some of the reciprocal obligations to be borne by the participants.

In the Brussels Treaty of Economic, Social and Cultural Collaboration and Collective Self-Defence of March 17, 1948, the governments of France, the United Kingdom, Belgium, the Netherlands, and Luxembourg provided the initial framework for postwar West European cooperation. More important, these five countries signaled to the United States their intent to structure postwar intra-European relations to encourage internal stability and defense against external threats. The treaty stated the basic European commitment to the transatlantic bargain-to-be. To make sure that the signal would be heard loudly and clearly where it needed to be heard the most—in the halls of the US Congress—President Truman, coincident with the Brussels Treaty signing, told a special joint session of Congress that he was "sure the determination of the free countries of Europe to protect themselves will be matched by an equal determination on our part to help them protect themselves." And so the first part of the bargain was in place, and the foundation had been laid for the next act of alliance construction.

The second part of the bargain was America's response to the European signal. The basic structure of the bargain was being hammered out behind the scenes primarily by officials of American and European governments. But these officials recognized that the bargain's political viability ultimately depended on its acceptance by Congress. They were keenly aware, as had been Franklin Roosevelt, that Woodrow Wilson's plan for US engagement and leadership in the League of Nations had failed because it lacked the essential support of Congress. Midcentury statesmen were determined not to ignore history only to pay the price of repeating it. On the US side, Congress had to be a partner in the deal.

Vital congressional acceptance of the bargain was given political life in the so-called Vandenberg Resolution, personalized, as are many important congressional actions, to acknowledge the role of the principal congressional architect, Senator Arthur Vandenberg, the sponsor and chairman of the Senate Committee on Foreign Relations. The Truman administration went to great lengths to encourage Vandenberg's postwar conversion from isolationism to a more "internationalist" inclination. Christopher S. Raj, in *American Military in Europe*, relates, "The Administration had skillfully placated Vandenberg by including him in US delegations, and the State Department cultivated him assiduously by consulting him often on European affairs."[2]

Following signature of the Brussels Treaty, the State Department asked Vandenberg to prepare a resolution that would express congressional support for the administration's desire to affiliate the United States with the European self-help project. Vandenberg complied and crafted a resolution that, in part, suggested that the United States should support "the progressive development of regional and other collective self-defense in accordance with the purposes, principles, and provisions of the [United Nations] charter." The resolution was approved by the Senate on June 11, 1948, with overwhelming bipartisan support, providing political sustenance, in principle, for the emerging bargain. The Soviet Union infused the project with added urgency by imposing a blockade of Berlin late in June 1948. After six more months of debate and negotiation among the founding partners in the bargain, the deal was consummated. By the spring of 1949, ten European governments, the United States, and Canada were prepared to sign the North Atlantic Treaty. The document, finally signed on April 4, 1949, reflected a compromise between the European desire for explicit US commitments to provide military assistance to prospective NATO allies and the American desire, strongly expressed in Congress, for more general, less specific assistance provisions. In this fundamental aspect of the bargain, the Europeans had to settle for a general commitment that was more consistent with the mood in Congress.

Between Congress and the Europeans, the Truman administration practiced a form of diplomatic footwork that subsequently became a standard part of the repertoire of every American administration from Truman to Obama. In the 1949 context, the Truman administration was challenged "to convince Western Europe that the American commitment through the North Atlantic Treaty was a strong one, and . . . to assure Congress that the treaty did not involve the United States in an 'entangling' military alliance."[3] Since that time, subsequent administrations have been required, under a great variety of circumstances, to continue to reassure the Europeans of the validity of the American defense commitments to Western Europe while justifying to Congress the price tag for the "entangling alliance" that NATO became.

Consequently, when the Senate approved ratification of the treaty in 1949, it did so despite some strong concerns about the potential long-term costs of a US commitment to defense of Europe—misgivings that then-opponents of the Treaty today might well believe to have been justified.[4] On the other hand, most of those senators who voted for ratification based on the strategic arguments for the alliance would

Photo 2.1: President Truman watches while Secretary of State Acheson signs the North Atlantic Treaty

Source: NATO Photos.

probably today see their action as having been legitimized by history, particularly in light of NATO's contributions to deterrence during the Cold War and the alliance's role promoting stability and cooperation in post-Cold War Europe. Some of the issues debated in the halls of Congress in recent decades over NATO enlargement, burden sharing, Bosnia, Kosovo, Afghanistan, and Iraq echo those heard in the ratification debate of 1949.

At the end of the day, as Lawrence S. Kaplan has observed, it took "an awareness of America's new weight in the world combined with the weakness of Europe and the power of Soviet Communism to win over the Senate and the nation."[5] Importantly, the Senate's close involvement in the treaty's development and its approval implied that the bargain was not a simple partnership. It was a deal struck among governments, to be sure, but with the clear implication that two branches of the American government were parties to the deal and that management of the bargain would be a shared responsibility as long as the alliance endured.

Unresolved Issues

With signature and subsequent ratification of the North Atlantic Treaty in 1949, NATO's founding fathers had shaped the basic deal: the United States had pledged its continued involvement in European security arrangements in return for a European commitment to organize itself for both external defense and internal stability.

But two central and intimately related issues were left unresolved by these formative steps. The first was how the US commitment would be implemented. The Treaty neither suggested the institutional framework for US involvement nor specified whether the US military contribution would consist primarily of strategic bombing and naval capabilities or whether it would also include substantial US ground forces in Europe—issues regularly raised throughout most of NATO's history.

The second issue was how western Germany would fit into this Euro-Atlantic framework of defense obligations. The treaty did not clarify Germany's status vis-à-vis its West European neighbors, leaving open the question of whether western Germany would be permitted to rearm and, if so, under what circumstances.

In 1949, there was no consensus among the allies or between the Truman administration and Congress concerning how best to deal with these two issues. The national security priorities of the United States, Britain, and France were sharply in contrast. These three leading powers agreed that the Euro-Atlantic partnership, in its broadest form, was designed for the dual purpose of balancing Soviet power and providing an acceptable way to integrate western Germany into the Western community of nations. But it was by no means self-evident how this would be accomplished.

The basic conflict was between French and American priorities—another underlying factor that has affected Euro-Atlantic relations through most of the alliance's history. The French government, not without good cause, was obsessed with preventing Germany from acquiring any substantial independent military capabilities and placing political constraints on Germany in both the European and the Atlantic frameworks.

In 1949, the French government, doubting the US willingness to remain involved in any European power balance, was not confident it could provide, on its own, the economic or military counterweight to a Germany already demonstrating its potential for industrial recovery and resurgence. Timothy P. Ireland has observed that "As it became apparent to the allies that (1) the defense of Europe would have to begin with the Federal Republic and that (2) West Germany's industrial strength was necessary for a successful rearmament program, traditional French apprehensions vis-à-vis Germany became more and more manifest."[6]

The United States was not unsympathetic to France's preoccupation but was fixed on its own priority: balancing the power of the Soviet Union in central Europe. From the American perspective, German industrial capabilities and manpower were assets that could not be overlooked, particularly given Germany's geographic position in the center of Europe. Furthermore, Secretary of State Dean Acheson, sensitive to the fact that the North Atlantic Treaty might not win Senate approval if it appeared to commit the United States to a large military buildup in Europe, had assured the Senate Committee on Foreign Relations that the United States would not, as a consequence of treaty ratification, be required to send large numbers of troops to Europe.[7] Thus, Congress, one of the important partners in the bargain, had signed on to the deal with the tacit understanding that the US contribution to the alliance would consist largely of strategic bombing (the nuclear guarantee) and sea control.

To complicate the problem further, the British absolutely opposed any suggestion that they maintain a substantial presence on the Continent to help balance potential German power. The reluctance of the British to play a large military role in the central European balancing act reflected London's own priorities. Even though the United Kingdom remained strongly committed to a transatlantic alliance, the British Labour government of the time viewed a major political and military commitment on the Continent as less important to British interests than its Commonwealth ties and global responsibilities. Britain's eyes were still turned away from the Continent, across the Atlantic toward the "special relationship" with the United States and around the world to its vast colonial holdings.

In retrospect, this British orientation was as unfortunate for the postwar alliance as the French paranoia concerning Germany was troublesome for the United States. More than two decades would pass before Britain even tentatively acknowledged that its future world role and internal well-being were intimately dependent on the United Kingdom's relationship with its neighbors across the English Channel. But in the meantime, the British attitude denied the postwar allies the potential for a more coherent and effective European pillar for the Atlantic partnership. It is therefore ironic, but perhaps historically appropriate, that in 1999 another Labour government under Prime Minister Tony Blair helped jump-start the process aimed at creating a defense capability for the European Union.

The contrasting French and American preoccupations, combined with the British orientation away from continental involvement, produced two distinctly different sets of preferences for the way Euro-Atlantic relations should be structured to serve the "agreed" purposes of the alliance. The American preference was to help balance Soviet power in central Europe by rearming western Germany. To ensure that Germany's rearmament took place within a stabilized framework, the United States envisioned West Germany's membership in NATO as well as its cooperation in a multilateral European framework growing out of the Brussels Treaty. From the American perspective, German, French, and other continental nations should provide the bulk of ground force manpower in central Europe, with less substantial, primarily symbolic, contributions by the United States, Great Britain, and Canada. West German membership in NATO would legitimize German participation in the military effort, and the European cooperative arrangements would provide France a means of monitoring and controlling German power.

The French preference was, first and foremost, to avoid German rearmament. France also opposed German entry into NATO, viewing such entry as validation of a rearmament program, eventually permitting Germany to escape from any control provisions established in a European framework. Second, the French hoped to convince the United States to commit substantial forces to forward defense of

Western Europe in Germany. Third, Paris wanted to weave a web of political and economic relationships within Western Europe that would reinforce German self-interest in cooperation and deter any possible future hegemonic or aggressive behavior.

In fact, the French National Assembly authorized ratification of the North Atlantic Treaty with the understanding that the pact would not lead to Germany's rearmament. Foreign Minister Robert Schuman reassured French parliamentarians prior to the Assembly's vote for the treaty, saying, "Germany has no army and should not have one. It has no arms and will not have any. . . . It is therefore unthinkable, for France and her allies, that Germany could be allowed to adhere to the Atlantic pact as a nation capable of defending itself or of aiding in the defense of other nations."[8]

The conflict between French and American priorities could not have been sharper. While the United States had refocused its policies toward confronting the threat posed by the Soviet Union, French vision remained fixed on the "German problem," which it hoped to solve once and for all by denying Germany the armed forces with which it could once again threaten France.

The Korean Catalyst

On June 25, 1950, North Korean troops attacked the Republic of South Korea. This aggression, almost halfway around the world from Western Europe, proved to be the catalyst for shaping postwar Euro-Atlantic relations and resolving the Franco-American impasse on German rearmament. The Korean War, seen as demonstrating the global threat of communist aggression, provided the political momentum required to overcome congressional resistance to a substantial deployment of US ground forces in Europe. Such an American commitment undoubtedly was essential in helping to ease French concerns about the potential of a resurgent German neighbor.

For more than a year, the State Department and the Pentagon had argued the issue of German rearmament. The Pentagon, and particularly the Joint Chiefs of Staff, contended that German armed forces would be required if the West hoped to balance Soviet power in central Europe. But the Department of State resisted any formal discussion of German rearmament with the allies, believing that the political costs of such an initiative would be greater than the military benefits. Secretary of State Acheson "feared that any plans to associate Germany with the Atlantic alliance would undermine the whole structure of western defense by running the risk of alienating France."[9]

The Pentagon was not anxious to take on what appeared to be a massive and potentially open-ended commitment in Europe without parallel development of West European defense forces. Given the British reluctance to play a major role on the Continent and the fact that France, with forces tied down in Indochina, would not provide sufficient ground forces to balance the Soviet Union in central Europe, German rearmament seemed an inescapable prerequisite for any major US commitment to continental defense. This position was considerably strengthened by the reasonable expectation that Congress too would not approve a buildup of US forces in Europe without a parallel European effort.

And so, stimulated by the Korean War, a most significant elaboration of the original bargain began to take shape. The United States would deploy substantial ground forces to Western Europe and place them within an integrated NATO command structure. This structure would serve the practical role of coordinating Western defense efforts in Europe as well as providing the crucial Atlantic framework for bringing German military forces into the Western defense against the Soviet Union.

President Truman announced his decision to send a substantial number of American troops to Europe on September 9, 1950, after difficult negotiations during the preceding summer had forged a common Defense and State Department position on the question. The decision marked a momentous change in US policy toward Europe, declaring that the United States would commit combat troops to peacetime defense forces in Western Europe. Truman's declaration linked this commitment to the efforts expected from the European allies, without specifically raising the issue of German rearmament, even though reconstituting the German military had become a principal goal of US policy:

> On the basis of recommendation of the Joint Chiefs of Staff, concurred in by the Secretaries of State and Defense, I have today approved substantial increases in the strength of the United States forces to be stationed in Western Europe in the interest of the defense of that area. The extent of these increases and the timing thereof will be worked out in close coordination with our North Atlantic Treaty partners. *A basic element in the implementation of the decision is the degree to which our friends match our action in this regard.* Firm programs for the development of their forces will be expected to keep full step with the dispatch of additional United States forces to Europe. *Our plans are based on the sincere expectation that our efforts will be met with similar action on their part.*[10] (emphasis added)

The Truman administration recognized that it would first have to get the French government to move away from its strong opposition to German rearmament in order to make the deployment of US troops to Europe acceptable to Congress. American pressure on the French government throughout the summer of 1950 intensified in September. Truman's statement of September 9 added a sense of even greater urgency, and the French understood that they would have to respond to the US action. The United States, after all, had now expressed its willingness to deploy combat troops in Europe, just as Paris had desired.

But the French acceptance of the need to act did not mean that Paris was yet prepared to contemplate German rearmament within the NATO framework. The French still hoped to win acceptance for some European organization within which future governments in Paris would be able to control German military efforts.

The French responded to their apparent dilemma by proposing the creation of a European Defense Community. The so-called Pleven Plan, proposed by economist Jean Monnet and named for French Premier René Pleven, envisioned the eventual creation of a European army within which token German units would be included. The army would not be formed until a European decision-making framework had been established, with a European defense minister and a European parliament to approve funds for the operation. The French National Assembly initially approved the plan on October 24, 1950.

The Pleven Plan did not respond fully to the American requirement for German rearmament, and American officials were skeptical concerning the motives of the French (to put off German rearmament indefinitely?). They also questioned whether it would be wise to allow the French to exercise the greatest influence of any European nation over the future role of Germany.[11] Nonetheless, the Pleven Plan moved the French one step closer to the American position and helped prepare the way for compromise at the NATO meetings of foreign and defense ministers scheduled for December.

The Compromise and Congress

As the allies prepared for the regular end-of-year meetings of NATO foreign ministers, both Secretary of State Acheson and French Foreign Minister Schuman signaled their interest in reaching a compromise on the German rearmament issue. Encouraged by signs of flexibility from Paris, US Deputy Representative to the North Atlantic Council Charles Spofford crafted a compromise proposal that suggested that the United States endorse the long-term concept of an integrated European defense force in return for French acceptance of short-term measures to start bringing German manpower into use "under strong provisional controls" until a more permanent system of European cooperation could be developed.[12] Under the Spofford Compromise, the United States would appoint a Supreme Allied Commander and begin deploying US forces to Europe without waiting for German troops to materialize.

A number of factors convinced Acheson that moving too rapidly on the rearmament issue could be destabilizing in Germany as well as in France. The opposition Social Democrats in Germany were not at all enthusiastic about the prospect of integration into a Euro-Atlantic framework, believing that it would destroy chances for eventual German reunification. In response to domestic criticism, Chancellor Konrad Adenauer felt compelled to press for equal treatment for Germany in return for Germany's willingness to join in the economic and military enterprises that were being designed mainly in Paris, London, and Washington. Adenauer had his own agenda: independent statehood for Germany. But Acheson apparently was convinced that the French government might lose a vote of confidence in the National Assembly should it be forced to move too far too fast on the rearmament issue.

Acheson communicated to Schuman his willingness to compromise in a letter sent to Paris on November 29; the American secretary of state tried to reassure

Schuman of the US intent to appoint a supreme commander and, by implication, to begin deployment of American troops to Europe. Acheson argued that the United States had already demonstrated "the depth and permanence of its interests in Europe, its support for closer European association, its willingness to cooperate with Europe." He told Schuman that cooperation between France and the United States in NATO was "an essential corollary to an orderly progression from German cooperation in defense, to European integration, and thus final solution of the problem of relations with Germany."[13]

On December 17, 1950, the North Atlantic Council—NATO's decision-making body—approved the package Spofford had designed and the French and American governments had ultimately accepted. The council approved the French plan for creating a European Defense Force on the condition that the plan not delay the availability of German manpower for Western defenses, and it authorized the establishment of a supreme headquarters with the expectation that a US officer would be appointed supreme commander. At the meeting, Secretary of State Acheson announced that President Truman had appointed General Dwight D. Eisenhower as

Photo 2.2: General Dwight D. Eisenhower, NATO's First Supreme Allied Commander (SACEUR)

Source: NATO Photos.

supreme commander and that the number of US forces in Europe would be increased in the near future.

The bottom line, according to Timothy Ireland's study of this period, was that the compromise satisfied the principal objectives of the French government and the US administration: "The United States had gained French adherence to at least the idea of German rearmament. The French gained an immediate American military commitment to the defense of Europe while delaying the rearming of Germany."[14] The deal, however, had not yet been approved by another party to the original bargain: the US Congress. While the path for approval of the original North Atlantic Treaty had been carefully prepared in the Senate, Congress had not been formally involved in the steps leading to the Franco-American compromise. As the subsequent "Great Debate" in Congress would demonstrate, Congress had no intention of relinquishing its role in helping manage the transatlantic bargain.

Congress was in recess following the midterm elections when the NATO meetings concluded, but when the legislators returned to session in January 1951, the new American commitment moved rapidly to the top of the congressional agenda. Troop deployment was most severely questioned by conservatives among the Republican majority in the Senate. They were supported by some influential conservative spokesmen outside Congress, most notably former President Herbert Hoover. On December 19, 1950, Hoover, reacting to the appointment of General Eisenhower as Supreme Allied Commander, Europe (SACEUR), had commented the next day that "the prime obligation of defense of Western continental Europe rests upon the nations of Europe. The test is whether they have the spiritual force, the will and acceptance of unity among them by their own volition. America cannot create their spiritual forces; we cannot buy them with money."[15]

The conservative Republicans focused on two principal issues: whether it was appropriate for the United States to deploy substantial ground forces to Europe as part of an integrated Atlantic defense structure and whether the president could, without congressional authorization, deploy American troops overseas—the "war powers" question that later returned to prominence with the Vietnam War and has remained a sticking point between subsequent US administrations and Congress. The war powers issue was pointedly raised by Senator Robert Taft, who argued, "The President has no power to send American troops to fight in Europe in a war between the members of the Atlantic Pact and Soviet Russia. Without authority he involved us in the Korean War. Without authority, he apparently is now adopting a similar policy in Europe."[16] The administration and its supporters in Congress argued that the president did not need specific congressional approval to make such a deployment. The argument, however, was not convincing for those senators who questioned not only the constitutional validity of the action but also the defense and foreign policy rationale underlying the troop deployment and participation in an integrated command structure in NATO.

Following Truman's January 8 State of the Union Address, in which he strongly defended American involvement in the defense of Western Europe, the debate was joined in Congress. Senator Kenneth Wherry, the Republican floor leader, introduced Senate Resolution 8, which asked the Senate to resolve "that it is the sense of the Senate that no ground forces of the United States should be assigned to duty in the European area for the purposes of the North Atlantic Treaty pending the formulation of a policy thereto by the Congress."[17] The Wherry resolution was referred to the Foreign Relations and Armed Services Committees, which then held joint hearings on the troop deployment issue. During these hearings, the Truman administration sought to avoid a direct conflict with Congress on the central war powers issue raised by Wherry's resolution. Administration strategy apparently was to defend the president's constitutional right to deploy US forces while at the same time not attacking directly the congressional prerogatives in this area. The administration carefully avoided any acceptance of the idea that it needed congressional approval to do what it had already told the allies it would do.

After extensive hearings, in which a wide range of constitutional, strategic, and economic aspects of the issue were aired, the committees submitted a joint report to the full Senate. Senator Tom Connally, chairman of the Senate Committee on Foreign Relations, then introduced Senate Resolution 99 on behalf of the committees. With Senate Resolution 99, the committees attempted to deal with concerns that had been raised by Senator Taft and others while, at the same time, supporting the appointment of General Eisenhower as SACEUR and the deployment of four US Army divisions to Europe.

Senate Resolution 99 was approved by the Senate on April 4, 1951, by a vote of 69 to 21. Senator Taft, who had so severely questioned the commitment, voted with the majority, apparently believing that his concerns were reflected in the bill.

And so the Truman administration's decision was vindicated in the Senate vote, but not without qualification. The resolution endorsed General Eisenhower's appointment and approved the four-division Army deployment. The Senate also declared, however, that the Joint Chiefs of Staff should certify that the European allies were making a realistic effort on behalf of European defense, that the European allies should make the major contribution to allied ground forces, and that provisions should be made to utilize the military resources of Italy, West Germany, and Spain.

The form of the congressional action—a "sense of the Senate" resolution—did not insist on congressional authority over the president's decision, but the Senate did not give up its claim to exercise such control in the future. Incorporated in the final version of the resolution was an amendment offered by Senator John McClellan that expressed the Senate's desire that "no ground troops in addition to such four divisions should be sent to Western Europe in implementation of Article 3 of the North Atlantic Treaty without further Congressional approval."

The Senate once again had made clear that it wanted to be regarded as an active partner in the transatlantic bargain. It remained reluctant to contemplate an extensive, open-ended US commitment to the defense of Europe, and it expected Europe to carry the bulk of responsibilities, particularly in ground forces, for the

Continent's defense. The Senate sought the rearmament of Germany as central to the success of the NATO effort, and it pointedly reminded the administration that it retained the right to involve itself more decisively in US policy toward the alliance should its wishes be overlooked.

Wrapping up the Package in Lisbon

With the requisite congressional mandate in hand, the Truman administration could move toward firming up the deal with the allies. Throughout the remainder of 1951, administration officials worked with allied counterparts on plans for NATO's future organization and force posture, developed the outline for a European Defense Community (EDC), and planned for the relationship between NATO and the defense community. The significant progress made in these discussions was confirmed at a meeting of NATO foreign, defense, and finance ministers in Lisbon, Portugal, in February 1952.

The Lisbon meeting is perhaps remembered best for the fact that it set force goals for NATO that remained elusive for the alliance until they no longer needed them at the end of the Cold War. A report adopted by the ministers set the goal of deploying 50 allied divisions, 4,000 aircraft, and listed substantial additional targets for future years. The allies never reached these so-called Lisbon Goals. The failure of the European members of NATO to build up their conventional military forces to balance those of the Warsaw Pact created the burden-sharing issue that, in one way or another, dominated congressional consideration of the US role in NATO throughout the Cold War.

The NATO ministers also reorganized the civilian management of NATO, making the North Atlantic Council a permanent body, with member governments represented by senior officials and supporting delegations at NATO headquarters in Paris. This organizational change established NATO as a permanent forum for diplomatic exchanges and foreign policy consultations among the allies.

And the allies took note of NATO's further expansion into the Mediterranean region, welcoming the accession of Greece and Turkey to the alliance. Both countries, in advance of the Lisbon meeting, had signed and ratified the North Atlantic Treaty. The addition of these two countries was seen as a critical move to block expansion of communist influence in southeastern Europe. But it also brought subsequent problems to the alliance. Greece and Turkey's bilateral disputes over the control of Cyprus and the territorial waters between them frequently disrupted internal alliance cohesion and, from time to time, verged on war between the two allies. (In the twenty-first century, Greek/Turkish issues still block much-needed cooperation between NATO and the European Union.)

In diplomatic exchanges prior to the Lisbon session, some of the most intensive negotiations among the allies had dealt with the question of West Germany's future role in the Western alliance. The Franco-American compromise formally endorsed in Lisbon had taken shape over the two previous years. A year prior to the Lisbon gathering, France had hosted the first session of the Conference for the Organization of an EDC. The early meetings of the conference were attended by representatives of West Germany, Belgium, Italy, Luxembourg, and the host government, France. The Netherlands had joined the project in October 1951. In Lisbon, these countries presented a report on their progress to the NATO ministers.

The conference report on the EDC described in detail the considerable technical progress that had been made toward establishing a defense community. The participants were, in fact, able to report that they had begun preparation of a draft treaty and associated protocols. In the conclusion of the report, they reaffirmed the purpose of their work:

> To create a European Defense Community which can fulfill the imperative requirements of military effectiveness; to give the Western World a guarantee against the rebirth of conflicts which have divided it in the past; and to give an impetus to the achievement of a closer association between the Member countries on a federal or confederate basis.[18]

When the Lisbon session adjourned on February 25, the ministers announced that they had concluded that the principles underlying the treaty to establish an EDC conformed to the interests of the parties to the North Atlantic Treaty. They also said they had agreed on the principles that would govern the relationship between the proposed community and NATO. And so, when the 35 foreign, defense, and finance ministers and their delegations completed the intensive round of meetings in Lisbon, they had seen the bargain through another significant stage of development. NATO now had an integrated military command structure with a Supreme Allied Commander. The NATO countries had agreed to make substantial ground, air, and naval commitments to the integrated command. Greece and Turkey had been welcomed into the alliance. Progress had been recorded toward the establishment of an EDC, designed to reassure France against future German power and to provide a constructive framework for the creation of a united Europe.

The stage was set for Secretary of State Acheson to travel to Bonn to negotiate and sign, on May 26, 1952, the Convention on General Relations among the Federal Republic of Germany, France, the United Kingdom, and the United States. Acheson then flew to Paris to participate in the May 27 signing of the treaty establishing an EDC and the various associated agreements specifying the intended relationship between that community and NATO. Not too long after these historic ceremonies, however, the package started to come undone.

Notes

1. Don Cook, *Forging the Alliance* (New York: Arbor House, 1989), 114.
2. Christopher S. Raj, *American Military in Europe* (New Delhi: ABC Publishing House, 1983), 8.

3. Timothy P. Ireland, *Creating the Entangling Alliance: The Origins of the North Atlantic Treaty Organization* (Westport, Conn.: Greenwood, 1981), 119.

4. For a discussion of the concerns raised by senators and administration efforts to deal with those concerns, see Phil Williams, *The Senate and U.S. Troops in Europe* (London: Macmillan, 1985), 12–27.

5. Lawrence S. Kaplan, "The United States and NATO: The Relevance of History," in *NATO after Fifty Years*, ed. S. Victor Papacosma, Sean Kay, and Mark R. Rubin (Wilmington, Del.: Scholarly Resources, 2001), 246.

6. Ireland, *Creating the Entangling Alliance*, 177.

7. US Senate Committee on Foreign Relations, *Executive Sessions of the Senate Foreign Relations Committee*, vol. 4, 82d Cong., 2d sess., 1952. Historical Series, 1976.

8. *Journal Officiale*, July 25, 1949, p. 5277, as cited in Michael M. Harrison, *The Reluctant Ally: France and Atlantic Security* (Baltimore, Md.: The Johns Hopkins University Press, 1981), 14.

9. Ireland, *Creating the Entangling Alliance*, 186. This discussion of events in 1950–1951 benefited substantially from Ireland's account, which is based largely on the US State Department's Foreign Relations of the United States series covering this period (hereafter cited as FRUS).

10. *New York Times*, September 10, 1950, as cited in Raj, *American Military in Europe*, 22.

11. Such reactions are found in detail in diplomatic exchanges recorded in FRUS, 1950, vol. 3, *Western Europe*.

12. FRUS, 1950, vol. 3, *Western Europe*, 480.

13. FRUS, 1950, vol. 3, *Western Europe*, 498.

14. Ireland, *Creating the Entangling Alliance*, 207.

15. *New York Times*, December 21, 1950, as cited in Raj, *American Military in Europe*, 26–27.

16. *New York Times*, January 6, 1951, as cited in Raj, *American Military in Europe*, 27.

17. US Senate Committee on Foreign Relations, *Executive Sessions of the Senate Foreign Relations Committee*, vol. 3, pt. 1, 82d Cong., 1st sess., 1951, Historical Series, 1976, 559.

18. FRUS, 1952–1954, vol. 5, *Western European Security*, 246.

CHAPTER 3

The Transatlantic Bargain Revised

The ink was barely dry on the European Defense Community (EDC) treaty when the Lisbon package started to come apart. The force goals so bravely adopted in Lisbon soon appeared unreasonably optimistic. Neither the British nor the French government could fit substantial troop increases into budgets already stretched thin by non-European military commitments—the French bogged down in Indochina, and the British struggling to keep a global role intact. Rumors spread around Europe that the United States was reducing its aid to the NATO countries. Press sources speculated that the entire NATO structure was on the verge of total breakdown (a prediction heard many times since).

The Long Road from Lisbon to Paris

The State Department, alarmed by the emerging trends in US as well as European public opinion, drafted a message to send to the embassies in London and Paris. The cable expressed Washington's concern with all-too-common suggestions in the press that "(1) [the] NATO force plan has already been revised unilaterally; (2) Sov[iet] tension has diminished; [and] (3) [the] entire NATO defense program is facing collapse."[1]

The secret cable noted that it apparently was becoming popular in Europe to blame cutbacks in American assistance for French and British inability to meet force goals. The cable suggested that should such misleading information continue to be so prominent in the European press, the US government would be forced to point out some facts—"US defense expenditures [are] four times [the] total [of] all other NATO countries combined; [the] US with smaller population has more men under arms than all other NATO countries combined; [the] percentage of GNP spent by [the] US is above all others and twice [the] NATO average; US per capita defense expenditures are six time[s the] NATO average." Noting the potential impact on US domestic opinion, the cable argued that placing the blame on the United States for European shortfalls would "infuriate Amer[icans] and cause them [to] recall with indignation vast US contributions to Eur[opean] recovery and defense." The message continued with the warning that such duplicity reinforces the arguments of NATO critics who assert that Europe is a "'bottomless pit' and will 'do nothing for itself.'"[2]

After making the State Department's concerns so clear, the cable instructed the embassies in London and Paris to encourage the British and French governments to "find opportunities" to clarify the situation to the public, especially making these tersely worded points:

a. There has been no revision NATO targets adopted at Lisbon; cannot be revised unilaterally. What we face is possible shortfall in meeting targets.
b. US is fulfilling aid commitments and has not reduced them.
c. There is no evidence easing of Soviet threat, and NATO defenses remain inadequate.
d. Prospective shortfall, while increasing and prolonging security risks, should not be interpreted as NATO "breakdown." Defense buildup will continue forward as rapidly as possible.[3]

The NATO ministers met in December 1952, following the elections in the United States in which NATO's first Supreme Allied Commander Europe, General Dwight David Eisenhower, had won his Republican Party campaign for the White House. Perhaps with little anticipation of how crucial events in Indochina could be for the NATO alliance, the ministers issued a communiqué proclaiming that the campaign being waged in Indochina by the forces of the French Union deserved the support of the NATO governments.[4]

When the new secretary of state, John Foster Dulles, returned from his first NATO ministerial meetings in April 1953, he reported that the allies had accepted, though with some qualms, the new administration's inclination to concentrate on the quality rather than the quantity of assistance to the NATO allies. The Eisenhower administration was working toward a "new look" at American defense policy—an approach that, 50 years later, the George W. Bush administration brought to the table during its first year in office, before more radical defense and foreign policies were instigated by the 9/11 attacks.

The Eisenhower administration, while seriously concerned about the Soviet challenge, was equally intent on rationalizing US commitments abroad as part of an overall program of economic austerity. The Truman administration had not been able to decide to what extent US strategy should depend on nuclear weapons, but the Eisenhower administration was inclined virtually from the outset to use nuclear weapons deployments to meet national security objectives while pursuing fiscal solvency. Dulles had attempted to reassure the allies that rationalization in no way suggested a US tendency toward isolationism.

At the same time, the new administration clearly hoped that closer cooperation among the NATO European allies would eventually relieve the United States of some of its European defense burdens—a theme of US policy that has persisted until today. In his 1953 New Year's message to Chancellor Konrad Adenauer, Eisenhower made a special point of saying that the development of an EDC "would contribute much to promote peace and the security of the free world."[5] At a meeting at the Pentagon a few weeks later, Eisenhower argued strongly for support of the EDC, saying,

"The real problem is that of getting German participation. Anything which does not accomplish that doesn't mean very much." The general-turned-president went on to recall, "In hearings before the Congress, I have always had to face the question as to when we were going to get German help in defending Europe. It would be difficult to justify Congressional appropriations for Europe if there were no such prospect."[6]

It is therefore no surprise that Dulles was concerned, as had been the previous administration, by the slow progress toward implementation of the EDC plan. On his return from Europe, he reported to a meeting of the National Security Council that his "one great worry in retrospect . . . was the delay and failure to ratify the EDC treaties and to secure the desired German contribution."[7] Dulles felt that the political steam had gone out of the drive toward an EDC. The post-Stalin leadership in the Soviet Union, through its first "peace campaign," had already managed to dispel some of the sense of urgency that had earlier helped motivate work toward an EDC.

As 1953 passed without any of the six EDC signatories having ratified the treaty, the dilemmas inherent in European security arrangements became increasingly apparent to US officials. At a meeting of the National Security Council on December 10, 1953, preparatory to a scheduled NATO ministerial meeting in Paris, Secretary of Defense Charles Wilson expressed his "distress" that the United States seemed "hopelessly caught between the fear of the Europeans as to the use of atomic weapons, and our own desire to bring our forces home."[8]

Responding to Wilson's concerns, President Eisenhower explained, "Our one great objective at the moment was to secure the ratification of EDC." Eisenhower said that the United States could not afford "to take any steps toward redeployment, or even to talk about redeployment [of troops in Europe to the United States], until these objectives have been reached." To buttress his point, the president added, "The French have an almost hysterical fear that we and the British will one day pull out of Western Europe and leave them to face a superior German armed force."[9]

When Secretary of State Dulles left for the Paris meetings, he apparently hoped to provoke some new movement toward realization of the EDC, which had become key to the US goal of German integration in Western defenses and eventual withdrawal of some US forces from Europe. At a press conference held during the NATO meetings on December 14, Dulles administered shock treatment in an attempt to resuscitate the defense community project when he said,

> We also understand that action [creating a united Europe to prevent future Franco-German antagonism] will be taken within the framework of the North Atlantic Treaty, which will bring into association with the European Defense Community (E.D.C.) this strength which lies around the periphery of E.D.C.
>
> It is that policy, in regard to Europe, to which the United States is committed. In essence that is the European policy which we are trying to cooperate with, and we earnestly hope that policy will be brought to a successful conclusion.
>
> If, contrary to our hopes and beliefs, it should not happen that way, it would force from the United States *an agonizing reappraisal* of its foreign policy.[10] (emphasis added)

The implication that the United States would reconsider its commitment to European defense should the EDC not be approved appeared reasonable from Washington's perspective. The US Defense Department, impatient with the slow progress toward ratification of the EDC, had already considered some contingency plans for incorporating German forces in Western defenses in the absence of an EDC. But in Paris, the Dulles statement probably looked like a strong-arm tactic, raising the hackles of the consistently nationalistic and sensitive French.

The US minister in France at the time, Theodore Achilles, observed in a memorandum to Dulles that "it is too soon to tell whether your press conference has arrested [an] unfavorable trend [in France against the EDC], but it has certainly provided food for thought and again posed clearly the issue and the urgency."[11] But Achilles also recorded the prophetic reaction of one French Foreign Ministry official who reportedly said that

> the press conference had finished EDC, that it must have been deliberate, that the problem now was to save the Atlantic Alliance, that some new way would have to be found to tie Germany to the West, perhaps through NATO, and finally that France would now have to do some painful rethinking of its own policies.[12]

In the first half of 1954, US policy struggled to shore up the transatlantic bargain with constant reassurances to France and its prospective EDC partners that the United States remained supportive of the EDC concept and committed to European defense. The United States was unable to dispel a lingering concern in France that once the EDC was in place, the United States would take its leave of Europe, exposing France to German power. There was, of course, some cause for this concern. The Eisenhower administration did see the EDC as a potential source of relief, though not an escape, from the burdens of European defense. Many in Congress, however, hoped that the EDC would in fact provide the escape route many Europeans feared the United States would take all too quickly once the EDC was set up.

Congress had demonstrated clearly its desire to see the EDC ratified. The Mutual Security Act of 1953, governing military assistance to the NATO allies, required the administration to withhold portions of the aid intended for EDC nations that had not ratified the treaty. In the spring of 1954, a modified form of the provision was incorporated in the Mutual Security Act of 1954, effectively preventing future deliveries of military equipment to the two countries that had not yet ratified the EDC: Italy and France. The Eisenhower administration had originally opposed the prohibition but supported the version incorporated in the 1954 legislation, apparently believing that it might add pressure to the campaign for EDC ratification.

At the same time, however, the administration's nuclear weapons policies may have undermined the credibility of its case for French ratification of the EDC. The administration's intent to increase substantially US and consequently NATO reliance on nuclear weapons, tactical as well as strategic, suggested the United States had given up hope of mounting a credible nonnuclear defense against the Soviet Union in central Europe, even if West German forces were incorporated in Western defenses via the EDC. Under such circumstances, why should France be willing to risk sacrificing substantial national sovereignty for the sake of participation in a European army that US nuclear weapons policy was making increasingly less relevant?

Despite the potentially counterproductive interaction between the new-look strategy, which emerged full blown in 1954, and the EDC goal, the United States moved assertively on both fronts. At the NATO ministerial meetings in April 1954 (by then the Netherlands, Belgium, Luxembourg, and the Federal Republic of Germany had ratified the EDC treaty), Secretary of State Dulles cautioned the gathered ministers:

> Without the availability for use of atomic weapons, the security of all NATO forces in Europe would be in grave jeopardy in the event of a surprise Soviet attack. The United States considers that the ability to use atomic weapons is essential for the defense of the NATO area in the face of the present threat.

Then Dulles summarized his argument with a judgment undoubtedly not accepted by all his colleagues around the table: "In short, such weapons must now be treated as in fact having become 'conventional.'"[13]

The Defeat of the EDC

As Secretary of State Dulles was preaching the gospel of nuclear dependence, the EDC story was moving toward a dramatic conclusion. The French government formed by Pierre Mendes-France in June 1954, the latest in a succession of politically vulnerable Fourth Republic regimes, was preparing a ratification vote on the EDC treaty in the French National Assembly. Mendes-France suspected that the treaty as it stood would probably not be approved by the Assembly or that it would be approved by such a slim margin that it might undermine the entire program of his government. Apparently hoping to generate a more substantial majority for the treaty, Mendes-France asked the other EDC signatories to approve a package of modifications in the treaty. The foreign ministers of the six nations met in Brussels from August 19 to 22 to consider the French proposals. The Belgian foreign minister, Paul-Henri Spaak, submitted a set of compromise proposals that was accepted by all the other countries except France. The conference adjourned without agreeing on modifications to the EDC plan, and Mendes-France prepared with little enthusiasm to move toward a vote in the National Assembly. It is still not clear whether Mendes-France, had he obtained the changes he requested, could have won ratification of the accord. In any case, with an unenthusiastic governmental advocacy of the EDC case, the treaty failed on an August 19, 1954, procedural vote by a margin of 264 deputies for and 319 against.

According to a postmortem on the ratification vote, drafted by the American embassy in Paris early in September 1954, changes in French perceptions of the threat influenced the outcome. Although the French remained concerned about the potential German threat, they had become more relaxed about the Soviet threat and somewhat more wary of American intentions. The embassy's analysis suggested that

> in 1954, the fear of Russia was less than in 1953, when it was less than in 1952 and much less than in 1951 and 1950. Correspondingly, there existed, perhaps not only in France, a greater fear of some future action or reaction on the part of the US which might lead to world war; and in the specific case of EDC a greater fear that the US might in some way back the irredentist aspirations of Germany in a manner detrimental to French security interests.[14]

French perceptions of the threat had changed, but a number of other factors also influenced the mood in Paris. The French had been freed from their Indochinese dilemma by the July 1954 Geneva accords, but only in the wake of military defeat. This defeat, combined with the prospect of a long struggle against an independence movement in France's North African Algerian colony, presumably made more than a few French deputies wary of taking on additional military commitments. Furthermore, the structure of the Fourth Republic consistently produced weak governments, and as the embassy postmortem pointed out, "No French government ever dared to challenge the opponents of EDC and carry the battle to them. Indeed, they could not have done so without breaking up the governing coalition."[15]

History has yielded no single explanation for France's defeat of a French idea that had been adopted in principle by the entire Western alliance. Some analysts have speculated that a deal had been cut between Mendes-France and Soviet Foreign Minister V. M. Molotov. According to this theory, in return for Soviet cooperation in the Geneva negotiations in July 1954 bringing an end to the war in Indochina, Mendes-France chose not to compromise at Brussels, thereby guaranteeing defeat of the treaty in the National Assembly. Moscow was strongly opposed to the EDC, and its active peace campaign of 1953–1954 bore witness to the depth of Soviet concern. But there is still no firm evidence of any deal between Moscow and Paris to receive a graceful exit from Indochina in return for defeat of the EDC.

The Soviet campaign certainly contributed to the delay and indecision that characterized the French approach to EDC ratification between 1952 and 1954, and French Communist Party deputies, closely following the Moscow line, were unalterably opposed to the treaty. The Soviet campaign's main influence, however, probably was on the large number of French Socialist deputies, many of whom could have gone either way on the treaty.

The Indochina episode had a profound effect on French attitudes toward the United States. As France was being pushed out of the region, the United States was moving in, creating the Southeast Asia Treaty Organization (SEATO) with the mission of containing Communist expansion in Asia and tasked specifically with protecting South Vietnam. According to Lawrence S. Kaplan, "The Indochina trauma poisoned Franco-American relations in the Fourth Republic and provided a major justification for Charles de Gaulle's treatment of NATO in the next decade. For France, the Indochina humiliation at the hands of the United States was replicated at Suez in 1956."[16]

In the final analysis, France's fear of a resurgent Germany remains the most prominent factor in the rejection of the EDC. Had France been in an optimistic frame of mind, perhaps the nation would have been able to suppress its sense of insecurity toward the Germans and take on the challenge. But the economic outlook was gloomy, France had lost the war in Indochina, and the French governmental system was weak and ineffective. As a result, "the whole debate took place in an atmosphere of a tremendous national inferiority feeling." And noting this mind-set, the embassy commented further, "One of the most important, though usually unspoken arguments against EDC had long been the belief that in any community including France and Germany the latter would inevitably gain the upper hand because the Germans are more capable soldiers, organizers, businessmen and politicians."[17]

More than 60 years later, concerns about Germany's potential political and economic domination of Europe still haunt many French politicians and influence French attitudes toward European integration and transatlantic relations—*plus ça change, plus c'est la même chose!* (the more things change, the more they remain the same). However, French concerns about Germany today relate more to the studied pacifism that influences Germany's contemporary approach to security challenges and Berlin's economic power, rather than any fear of German militarism.

The decision against the EDC was a tragic chapter in the history of Western post-war alliance construction. Ironically, it was France, the original author of the EDC plan, which had become uncertain about its work and had finally torn up the script. The embassy concluded, "This deep pessimism, it must be recognized, is perhaps justified," awkwardly adding the phrase "at least in part" to the end of the sentence, seemingly trying to take some of the edge off this dark assessment of the French national psyche. The phrase perhaps also reflected some acknowledgment that the policies of the Eisenhower administration had helped undermine the EDC project by intensifying French fears of being seduced into the defense community with Germany and then abandoned by the United States.

Picking up the Pieces

France's rejection of the EDC removed what had been intended as a vital link between the postwar Western alliance arrangements and the goal of a sovereign and rearmed West Germany. While the action destroyed the intended framework for Germany's integration into the Western community as a sovereign and equal participant, it by no means meant that such a link would be impossible.

The United States had quietly been considering possible alternatives to the EDC for more than a year and had discussed such options with the British early in 1954. All along, the United States had viewed the EDC principally as a means to an end: the rearming of western Germany as part of the Western alliance against the Soviet

Union. Secretary of State Dulles affirmed this priority in a statement issued just two days after the vote in the National Assembly. Expressing regret that France had turned "away from her own historic proposal," Dulles stated that the United States would now be required to "reappraise its foreign policies, particularly those in relation to Europe," as he had promised eight months earlier. At the heart of this reappraisal would be the place of the Federal Republic of Germany in the Western alliance:

> The Western nations now owe it to the Federal Republic of Germany to do quickly all that lies in their power to restore sovereignty to that Republic and to enable it to contribute to international peace and security. The existing Treaty to restore sovereignty is by its terms contingent upon the coming into force of EDC. It would be unconscionable if the failure to realize EDC through no fault of Germany's should now be used as an excuse for penalizing Germany. The Federal German Republic should take its place as a free and equal member of the society of nations. That was the purport of the resolution which the United States Senate adopted unanimously last July, and the United States will act accordingly.[18]

Officials in the United States did in fact move very quickly, as Dulles wished, to develop alternative arrangements. Interagency discussions, although revealing somewhat different (and natural) priorities among the State and Defense Department officials involved, nonetheless produced agreement on the general objectives. By mid-September, Dulles had met with Chancellor Adenauer in Bonn and British Foreign Secretary Anthony Eden in London, and a strategy had been agreed on. The goal was a four-power meeting among the United States, Great Britain, the Federal Republic of Germany, and France to obtain French agreement on three points:

(1) Further progress toward European unity by expansion of the Brussels Pact so as to admit Germany and Italy.
(2) Admission of Germany to NATO.
(3) The working out of "accompanying arrangements" by the Federal Republic and the occupying Powers, who should at the same time declare their intentions with regards to restoration of sovereignty.[19]

This agenda, based on a British initiative, stimulated a flurry of diplomatic activity in September that culminated in the Nine-Power and Four-Power Conferences at London from September 28 to October 3. The Four-Power Conference meetings involved foreign ministers from the United States, the United Kingdom, France, and West Germany, and the Nine-Power Conference added foreign ministers from Belgium, Canada, Italy, Luxembourg, and the Netherlands. Those present decided to end the occupation of Germany, to allow West Germany to join NATO, and to strengthen and expand the Brussels Treaty with the membership of West Germany and Italy.

The foreign ministers of the same countries reconvened in Paris on October 20 and were joined by those of the remaining NATO countries: Denmark, Norway, Iceland, Greece, and Turkey. The formal decisions were confirmed on October 23 at three different levels. First, the foreign ministers of the United States, the United Kingdom, France, and the Federal Republic of Germany signed the Protocol on the Termination of the Occupation Regime in the Federal Republic of Germany, the Convention on the Presence of Foreign Forces in the Federal Republic of Germany, and the Tripartite Agreement on the Exercise of Retained Rights in Germany.

Next, the foreign ministers of the United Kingdom, France, Belgium, the Netherlands, and Luxembourg signed the Declaration Inviting Italy and the Federal Republic of Germany to accede to the Brussels Treaty and its four protocols. (Italy was an original signatory of the North Atlantic Treaty but not of the Brussels Treaty.)

Photo 3.1: October 23, 1954 Signature of Paris Agreements, inviting the Federal Republic of Germany to join NATO

Source: NATO Photos.

Finally, the 14 NATO foreign ministers signed the Protocol to the North Atlantic Treaty on the Accession of the Federal Republic of Germany.

With these agreements, the three occupying powers had recognized the Federal Republic of Germany as a sovereign state and ended their occupation. In return, the Federal Republic agreed to authorize the stationing on its territory of foreign forces at least equal to the strength existing at the date the agreements came into force. West Germany and Italy joined the Brussels Treaty, and the "Western Union" became the Western European Union (WEU). West German military capabilities would be monitored within the WEU framework, but Germany would become a member of NATO. The United States and the United Kingdom agreed to station forces on the European continent for as long as necessary.

The French National Assembly voted in favor of the London/Paris agreements on December 30, 1954, and the bargain was put back together again—but not according to the original plan. West Germany became a NATO member on May 5, 1955, and nine days later the Soviet Union concluded the Warsaw Pact with the governments of Albania, Bulgaria, Czechoslovakia, East Germany, Hungary, Poland, and Romania, with whom Moscow had earlier negotiated bilateral defense pacts.

Meanwhile, the US campaign for allied approval of the new-look strategy had also moved to a conclusion. The NATO ministers, meeting in mid-December 1954, adopted a report prepared by the NATO military committee designated "MC 48," modestly titled "The Most Effective Pattern of NATO Military Strength for the Next Few Years." In a memorandum to President Eisenhower in November 1954, the presidential staff secretary, Colonel Andrew J. Goodpaster, summarized the proposed change in NATO strategy by writing, "An effective atomic capability is indispensable to a maximum deterrent and essential to defense in Western Europe." Goodpaster continued,

> [The first] element of proposed action is to secure NATO-wide approval of the concept of the capability to use A-weapons as a major element of military operations in event of hostilities. For this purpose, the US should be prepared, if required subject to constitutional limitations, to give assurances that A-weapons would be available in the hands of US forces for such operations.[20]

On his return from the NATO sessions, Secretary of State Dulles reported to the National Security Council that a number of allies were concerned that the new policy might take vital crisis decisions out of the hands of civilian leaders of allied countries. Dulles had met with British Foreign Secretary Anthony Eden and Canadian Secretary for External Affairs Lester Pearson prior to the NATO meetings, and the three worked out a formula whereby the new strategy would be adopted under the condition that "there was to be no delegation by the NATO governments of their right as the civilian leaders to give the signal for bringing the atomic defense into action."[21] With this reassurance and the belief that any crisis would allow time for allied consultation prior to the use of nuclear weapons, NATO Secretary-General

Lord Ismay formally put the proposal before the ministerial session of the North Atlantic Council. Dulles reported that the resolution occasioned "virtually no discussion or debate, and was unanimously approved by the Council."[22]

And so, apparently with little controversy, the alliance quietly mortgaged its future strategy to nuclear weapons. The mortgage came with relatively small payments in the early years, a consideration that, at the time, seemed more important than any foreseeable future costs. By the end of 1954, therefore, the alliance had assumed its basic shape, with the way cleared for the admission of the Federal Republic of Germany. Alliance strategy had evolved toward heavy dependence on nuclear weapons and a continuing US ground force presence in Europe.

But this formative period for the Western alliance had left two fundamental desires unfulfilled. First, the plan to coordinate European contributions to the alliance through an EDC had failed to materialize. This failure meant that Germany would not remain a military midget within a French-controlled EDC; it also frustrated American hopes that such a community would eventually make it possible for the United States to withdraw most of its ground forces from Europe.

Second, even at this early stage of alliance development, it became clear that the United States and its allies would not match the quantitative force levels fielded by the Soviet Union and its allies. Despite a continued substantial American troop presence and the rearming of West Germany, the Lisbon force goals had become little more than paper promises, even though the alliance was not as yet willing to backtrack formally on the commitments made at the Lisbon ministerial meetings.

As a result of these two changes in the goals agreed on at Lisbon, the military strategy of the alliance came to rest heavily on the threat of the United States to use nuclear weapons against the Soviet Union should Soviet forces attack Western Europe. At the same time, the credibility of that threat depended on a continuing and substantial American military presence in Europe. These two changes in the original bargain bequeathed a legacy that troubled the alliance throughout the Cold War. The fact that NATO's military credibility was so dependent on the US force presence in Europe ensured that burden sharing would remain an issue between the United States and Europe as well as between successive US administrations and Congress.

Notes

1. US State Department, Foreign Relations of the United States (hereafter cited as FRUS), 1953–1954, vol. 5, *Western European Security*, 313.
2. FRUS, *Western European Security*, 314.
3. FRUS, *Western European Security*, 314.
4. *NATO Facts and Figures* (Brussels: NATO Information Service, 1981), 32.
5. *New York Times*, January 7, 1953, A1.
6. FRUS, *Western European Security*, 711–12.

7. FRUS, *Western European Security*, 398.
8. FRUS, *Western European Security*, 451.
9. FRUS, *Western European Security*, 451.
10. FRUS, *Western European Security*, 468.
11. FRUS, *Western European Security*, 868.
12. FRUS, *Western European Security*, 469.
13. FRUS, *Western European Security*, 511–12.
14. FRUS, *Western European Security*, 1112.
15. FRUS, *Western European Security*, 1112.
16. Lawrence S. Kaplan, *NATO Divided, NATO United: The Evolution of an Alliance* (Westport, Conn.: Praeger 2004), 24.
17. FRUS, *Western European Security*, 1113.
18. FRUS, *Western European Security*, 1121.
19. FRUS, *Western European Security*, 1221.
20. FRUS, *Western European Security*, 534–35.
21. FRUS, *Western European Security*, 561.
22. FRUS, *Western European Security*, 561.

CHAPTER 4

The Bargain through the Cold War, 1954–1989

It is difficult to look at the roots of the original transatlantic bargain without being impressed by the persistence of some factors, and the significance of change in some others. After more than 60 years, US policy toward the alliance is debated by Congress in virtually the same terms that it was in the early 1950s, with a focus on better burden sharing and more European defense efforts, today meaning better contributions to security challenges outside Europe, particularly in Afghanistan. Presidential administrations have not always been comfortable with the bargain but, except during the first term in office of President George W. Bush, have consistently defended it in the face of congressional skepticism. The United States and France continued through much of the alliance's first 60 years to pursue different visions for the future of transatlantic relations, but at the end of the first decade of the twenty-first century new leaders in Washington (President Barack Obama) and Paris (President Nicolas Sarkozy) narrowed the gap between American and French attitudes. In Europe, France still worries about Germany, but now it is a reunited Germany's "soft" power that troubles Paris the most.

In this mix of continuity and change, the bargain has constantly evolved, even while the Cold War helped sustain NATO's basic strategy and structure. More dramatic change was to come after the Cold War ended, but even in the 35 years between 1954 and 1989, a number of things changed. The allies, acting unilaterally in some cases and in concert in others, made conscious changes in and amendments to the bargain. Some of these changes were inspired by developments over which the allies had little control (such as the Soviet Union's drive toward nuclear parity with the United States, calling into question NATO's nuclear strategy), while political and economic trends rooted primarily within the alliance spawned other changes.

Identifying certain events or developments as representing significant changes in the bargain, while leaving some others aside, is in itself a subjective exercise. With that in mind, the following alterations in the bargain before the end of the Cold War are suggested as having produced changes that were important in their time and relevant to the Atlantic Community's future:

1. France's development of an independent security policy, culminating in withdrawal from NATO's integrated military command structure;
2. NATO's adoption of the "Harmel Doctrine," giving the alliance a dual defense and détente role in East-West relations;

3. NATO's approval of the military strategy of "flexible response" and the efforts to keep the strategy viable with deployment of intermediate-range nuclear forces in Europe;
4. British acceptance of an active role in continental Europe's future through membership in the European Community (now European Union);
5. Political maturation of the Federal Republic of Germany;
6. Emergence of European Political Cooperation as a forum for shaping common European positions on foreign policy issues and as a foundation for a European "pillar" in the alliance.

All these developments represented fundamental changes in the nature of the transatlantic bargain. There were other shifts, to be sure, such as the wavering commitments of some allies (e.g., Greece) and the admission of Spain to NATO. There were attempted shifts that failed, such as Secretary of State Henry Kissinger's "Year of Europe" initiative in 1973, designed to convince the European allies that the transatlantic bargain should take into account "out of area" challenges to Western interests and redress the balance between economic costs and benefits of the transatlantic bargain for the United States.[1] Enthusiasm about and policies toward the alliance fluctuated over time in most alliance countries. But the factors discussed in this chapter are the ones that most fundamentally influenced the core of the transatlantic bargain.

The French Rebellion

When President Charles de Gaulle withdrew France from NATO's integrated military command structure in 1966, he unilaterally altered the transatlantic bargain with a flair befitting this most French of modern French leaders. The general's move, however, was not so much a break from Fourth Republic policies as it was the culmination of attitudes and frustrations that had roots in a uniquely French mixture of historical doubts about the reliability of the United States and concerns about US domination. France had never been comfortable with the way the original bargain turned out. De Gaulle's strong will and unique leadership ability, combined with the powers that he had insisted be built into the constitution of the Fifth Republic, simply provided the means for translating French displeasure into political action.

From the beginning, France had substantially different objectives for and interests in the transatlantic alliance than did the United States. The earliest French proposals for tripartite French, British, and US management of the alliance emanated from Fourth Republic governments, even though this approach may best be remembered as a "Gaullist" line. The directorate concept was an expression of the French image of itself as the leading continental European power as well as of the French desire to be acknowledged clearly as having rights and powers superior to those available to the Federal Republic of Germany. The structure of the alliance favored by the United States, granting in theory equal rights to all members, provided a framework for the American superpower to exercise a primus inter pares role within the alliance, subordinating France to a position, in this sense, no more privileged than that of West Germany.

Fourth Republic governments had already decided that France, in order to obtain the status they thought essential to French security and national independence, would be required to take unilateral measures. One route available to France but denied to Germany was to become a nuclear power. When the Fourth Republic gave way to de Gaulle and the Fifth in 1958, development of a French nuclear weapons capability was well under way. It remained only for de Gaulle to articulate a political philosophy and develop a military strategy to give the *force de frappe* a major role in projecting French independence.

Perhaps from a French perspective, de Gaulle's stunning unilateral change in the transatlantic bargain was not totally unprovoked. France had hoped, indeed expected, from the early days of the alliance that its role as a global power would be acknowledged as an asset to the Western alliance and that the rhetorical support that the NATO countries accorded the French role in Indochina in the December 1952 ministerial communiqué would be followed by more substantive assistance. Seen from Paris, however, the United States not only failed to provide that assistance but also eventually turned against French interests in the Third World. The disenchantment in this regard perhaps began with the French defeat in Indochina, when the United States was faulted by Paris for not providing crucial military assistance to besieged French forces at Dien Bien Phu. The "lesson" of Indochina for Paris was bitterly repeated with American failure to support France's struggle in Algeria and, in 1956, with active American opposition to France and Great Britain in the Suez crisis. French leaders could be forgiven for seeing the United States as having made the first unilateral change in the original bargain. Michael Harrison, in his book *The Reluctant Ally*, reaches this conclusion: "NATO's value to France never recovered from the allied failure to support her cause in Africa, from the American reaction to Suez, and from the conviction that the United States had morally and materially turned against France and violated the Alliance tie."[2]

Whether or not one is sympathetic to the French case, it remains clear that the experiences of the Fourth Republic governments had set the stage for de Gaulle's rebellion against the Western "order." This is not to say that de Gaulle was simply following through on Fourth Republic initiatives. De Gaulle's wartime experiences had galvanized his doubts that the United States could be counted on to defend French interests. This skepticism eventually was reinforced by postwar-era nuclear politics, which led him to believe that France (or any other country for that matter) could not expect the United States to risk nuclear destruction of an American city to defend that of any ally. Only if France had an autonomous nuclear deterrent could it truly be independent. And de Gaulle believed strongly that a nation, once robbed of its independence, would soon lose its spirit and eventually die. These beliefs made de Gaulle suspicious of American plans for nuclear sharing with Europe, as manifested by the US/United Kingdom Nassau Agreement of December 1962, which made modernization of British nuclear capabilities dependent on American assistance, and by the abortive multilateral nuclear force plan of the early 1960s. His concerns about French independence were heightened by what appeared to be a growing tendency toward US-Soviet condominium in the wake of the Cuban Missile Crisis and by the signature of the Test Ban Treaty in July 1963, which de Gaulle saw as symbolizing a US-Soviet collaboration to monopolize the nuclear arena and eventually squeeze France into a nonnuclear status.

Just prior to de Gaulle's ascent to the presidency of France in 1958, the Rome Treaties had taken effect, establishing the European Economic Community, precursor of the European Community (EC) and now the European Union (EU). De Gaulle, believing as strongly as he did in the nation-state as the heart of the international system, hoped to lead his European partners away from the supranational inspiration of the Rome Treaties and toward a *Europe des patries*, a European unity based on sovereignty of the nation-states and led, of course, by France. An important part of the French plan was the so-called Fouchet initiative for political cooperation among the EC members, conceived to build the foundation for an independent European coalition positioned between the American and Soviet superpowers.

When the uncompromising Gaullist approach to European unity proved unacceptable to the other five Community members, de Gaulle became convinced that only unilateral French action, within Europe as well as toward the United States and in East-West relations, could effectively promote French interests. In 1963, de Gaulle vetoed the British application to join the European Economic Community, seeing the United Kingdom as still too Atlanticist to be a committed "European" partner. De Gaulle also provoked an internal crisis within the Community in order to block a scheduled transition to qualified majority voting on certain Community policy decisions. The move had been intended to subordinate national interests in specified policy area to broader "community" interests as well as to make Community decision making more effective.

Then, in 1966, de Gaulle took his boldest step, announcing France's decision to leave NATO's integrated military command and asking NATO to remove its headquarters, forces, and facilities from French territory by April 1, 1967. De Gaulle made it clear that France would continue as a participant in the political aspects of NATO and would remain true to its treaty obligations. But from that point forward, France would declare itself independent of American leadership as symbolized and, to a certain extent, operationalized by NATO's integrated command structure.

What could have been a devastating event for NATO actually was turned into a positive stimulus for the alliance. The 14 other allies carefully avoided emotional responses to the French action and concentrated on the practical challenges that the withdrawal posed. Harlan Cleveland, US ambassador to NATO at the time, recalls, "President Johnson, whose private references to General de Gaulle stretched his considerable talent for colorful language, imposed an icy correctness on those who had reason to discuss French policy in public."[3] The allies quickly relocated NATO headquarters to Brussels, Belgium, and went on with the business of the alliance almost as if nothing had happened.

In fact, the French move appeared to have had so inconsequential an impact on the alliance that some observers questioned whether it had any importance at all other than producing domestic political points for de Gaulle. One such observer, a NATO diplomat, described the action as "a cheap anti-American gesture, which changed almost nothing militarily, certainly did no harm to French security, yet enabled the General to crow that he had 'withdrawn from NATO'—for home consumption."[4]

In retrospect, however, de Gaulle's withdrawal from the alliance did have some long-term consequences, some of them quite detrimental to the transatlantic bargain despite the admirable fashion in which the 14 other allies adjusted to the French action.

Militarily, the French move weakened NATO's lines of supply and communications. Even if the allies could in theory have counted on France to join in the battle should Warsaw Pact forces have attacked Western Europe, the infrastructure for supporting NATO's front lines and for bringing in new supplies and reinforcements would be closer to the front and more vulnerable to enemy interdiction. Some of the negative effects were mitigated by continued French participation in certain NATO infrastructure projects and by the fairly extensive but low-key military cooperation that developed between France and the other allies in subsequent years. But the benefits to allied defense plans that full access to French territory would have offered were lost.

The political costs to the alliance, however, may have been far more important than the military consequences. The French withdrawal substantially altered the political balance within the alliance. With France conferring on itself an "independent" status, the alliance became even more dependent on American leadership than it was before. This strengthening of American preeminence in the alliance ironically came at a time when Western Europe was moving toward a more powerful position in the Atlantic relationship as a result of its economic strength, the increasingly important role of West German forces in the alliance, and the growing strategic importance of French and British nuclear forces.

It was also ironic that one consequence of the French move was to enhance the importance of the German role within the alliance. The withdrawal virtually guaranteed that the Federal Republic, even without nuclear weapons of its own, would become the most influential continental European member of NATO and perhaps even more important to the alliance than the United Kingdom, given its position on the front lines opposite Warsaw Pact forces. Even though France remained a participant in all aspects of the alliance not directly associated with the integrated military command structure, its voice in alliance councils became less influential as a consequence of its decision to limit its formal military participation in the alliance.

The French withdrawal also raised serious political and structural obstacles to the chances for European defense cooperation within the alliance. In the years following the withdrawal, the allies actively tried to develop ways to expand cooperation with the French. The West Germans sought to exploit the avenue of bilateral Franco-German military cooperation, which de Gaulle saw as preferable to such cooperation within the NATO framework. The West Germans walked a fine line in such cooperation, attempting to expand the relationship in every way possible without jeopardizing in any fashion Germany's NATO obligations and its relations with the United States. But the political conditions imposed by France's qualified participation in NATO severely limited the options available for closer defense cooperation among the European allies.

It is difficult, in retrospect, to see any unequivocal gains for France as a consequence of the withdrawal. French security may not have been damaged, but it also was not appreciably enhanced by the move. Perhaps it could be said that an "independent" French position resulted in more political energy and financial resources being devoted to defense than if France had remained in the integrated military structure, but this is hard to prove. Furthermore, France did not become a more valued interlocutor with the Soviet Union because the United States and the Federal Republic of Germany held the cards of greatest interest to Moscow. An independent position might have seemed of some tactical value to the Soviet Union from time to time, but in the end Moscow sought to deal principally with the two Western countries that could most benefit or harm Soviet interests.

The alliance may, however, have benefited in one regard from the French withdrawal. The establishment of a truly independent alternative Western nuclear decision-making center produced additional complications for Soviet strategy. Whatever uncertainty French nuclear forces and strategies created for Moscow may have enhanced Western deterrence. This was in fact recognized in Washington and officially by NATO. As Pascale Boniface has written,

> Once the French force de frappe became a reality . . . the United States was obliged to accept it. Washington eventually made a virtue out of necessity—by acknowledging in the Ottawa Declaration of 1974 that France's nuclear capability was in fact useful for the defense of the West and for greater European security.[5]

On balance, however, the French rebellion was to the detriment of the long-term viability of the Western alliance. Most important, the withdrawal made it more difficult for the alliance to translate increased European strength into a more substantial European role in the alliance. This alteration in the bargain, therefore, is one of the most important factors that had to be accommodated when the allies turned to the business of building a European pillar for the alliance after the end of the Cold War.

NATO's Role in Defense and Détente

The French rebellion had shaken the foundations of the alliance. But another fundamental challenge lay at hand. The North Atlantic Treaty was approaching its twentieth anniversary, auspicious primarily because the Treaty's escape clause gave members the opportunity to leave the alliance after 20 years. As the alliance closed in on the 1969 opportunity for desertion, the greatest challenge to its political viability was not the French challenge. Rather, it was the question of whether this alliance, constructed in the chilly atmosphere of the Cold War, could survive in the warming climate of East-West détente.

In Germany, Social Democrat Willy Brandt had come into government as foreign minister in a "grand coalition" with the Christian Democrats, assuming the position on December 6, 1966. He believed that the Federal Republic's policy of nonrecognition of East Germany and of existing European borders stood in the way of improving human conditions in Europe and particularly in the German Democratic Republic. Brandt's concept of "Ostpolitik" represented a major shift from Germany's orientation under Chancellor Konrad Adenauer, and he brought this new philosophy to his first NATO foreign ministerial meeting in Paris later that month.[6] Brandt's Belgian counterpart, Foreign Minister Pierre Harmel, felt strongly that the alliance would have to respond to critics who charged that NATO had become irrelevant under the changed international conditions. On the basis of Harmel's initiative, at least partly inspired by Brandt's philosophy that NATO defense and East-West détente could be compatible, the December 1966 meeting of NATO foreign ministers commissioned a yearlong study of "The Future Tasks of the Alliance." According to Harlan Cleveland, even the title of the study took on special meaning in the context of the mid-1960s. Cleveland, who represented the United States in the North Atlantic Council in the period before, during, and after the study, recalled that "if the 'Future of the alliance' had been studied, that would have implied doubt about continuation of the Alliance beyond 1969. 'Future tasks' assumed that NATO would survive its twentieth birthday, and called only its functions and priorities into question."[7]

The critique of NATO that inspired the Harmel exercise suggested that NATO's emphasis on the military aspects of security tended to undermine prospects for political solutions to East-West problems. The alliance had, of course, focused primarily on ways to maintain and improve Western defenses. It had not, however, been totally blind to the political aspects of security. Already by the mid-1950s, the allies had recognized that a narrowly focused Western military approach to the Soviet threat would not be sufficient to serve the broad range of allied political and economic as well as security objectives. The communiqué issued by the NATO foreign ministerial meeting in Paris in December 1955 marked the first formal alliance initiative broadening its perspectives on security, taking the Soviet Union to task for Moscow's refusal to consider intrusive systems of arms control verification, such as President Eisenhower's "Open Skies" proposal.[8]

In 1956, the allies began developing the rationale and mandate for arms control consultations in the alliance. The spring ministerial of that year appointed a "Committee of Three on Nonmilitary Cooperation" to study ways in which NATO nonmilitary cooperation could be expanded. The "three wise men"—Foreign Minister Gaetano Martino of Italy, Halvard Lange of Norway, and Lester Pearson of

Canada—reaffirmed the necessity for collective defense efforts but strongly empha-sized the need for better political consultation among the members. In particular, their report, approved by the North Atlantic Council in December 1956, observed that consultation "means more than letting the NATO Council know about national decisions that have already been taken; or trying to enlist support for those decisions. It means the discussion of problems collectively, in the early stages of policy formation, and before national positions become fixed."[9]

"The habit of consultation," strongly advocated by the three wise men, became an important part of alliance rhetoric, almost approaching theological heights. Even before the report—and ever since—NATO problems, to one extent or another, have been blamed on the failure of one or more allies to consult adequately. Virtually no report or commentary on the alliance can reach its conclusion without recommend-ing "improved consultations."

The Harmel Report appropriately commended the virtues of improved consultation. The report's most important contribution, however, was its conclusion that "military security and the policy of détente are not contradictory but comple-mentary." The report, the product of a prestigious committee led by Harmel, asserted that the alliance had two main functions. The first function, and the one with which the alliance had become most closely identified, was "to maintain adequate military strength and political solidarity to deter aggression and other forms of pressure and to defend the territory of member countries if aggression should occur." The second, newly assigned function of the alliance, was "to pursue the search for progress towards a more stable relationship [with the East] in which the underlying political issues can be solved." Approved by all the allies, including de Gaulle's France, the report offered this summary perspective:

> Collective defense is a stabilizing factor in world politics. It is a necessary condition for effective policies directed towards a greater relaxation of tensions. The way to peace and stability in Europe rests in particular on the use of the Alliance constructively in the interest of détente. The participation of the USSR and the USA will be necessary to achieve a settlement of the political problems in Europe.[10]

The allies adopted the Harmel Report at their ministerial meeting in December 1967 and, in this bold stroke, fundamentally altered the objectives, image, and "future tasks" of the alliance. The report's "defense and détente" combination pro-vided an intellectual and political framework for NATO policies that accommodated the growing split in the alliance between left and right. By bridging two different views of how best to ameliorate East-West tensions, it broadened the potential base of political support for NATO in European countries and in the United States. Subsequently, instead of polarizing Western politicians, policy elites, and publics, the alliance could serve as a fulcrum for balancing divergent perspectives on the requirements for the West's security policy in Europe. Not inconsequentially, this critical addition to NATO's role provided the foundation for NATO to become an important political instrument following the end of the Cold War, when its military relevance appeared open for debate following disappearance of the Soviet threat.

Acceptance of the Harmel Report also provided a way to deal with another problem that had been brewing between the United States and the European allies. The United States had become actively involved in bilateral arms control discussions with the Soviet Union, and these discussions occasionally left the allies wondering whether their interests would be protected by their American ally. At the same time, American officials had become increasingly concerned that the European allies would become "infected" by the Soviet peace campaign, with individual allies drifting off to cut their own deals with Moscow. The Harmel Report implied that NATO consultations could serve to coordinate Western approaches to the East. This coordination function would help alleviate European concerns about US-Soviet bilateralism while providing a brake on any European tendencies toward excessive détente fever.

In a very practical sense, the Harmel exercise created a whole new set of responsibilities for NATO. A few weeks after the Harmel Report had been approved, the allies agreed to strengthen the political institutions of the alliance by establishing a "Senior Political Committee." This step could be regarded as institutional sleight of hand because the new box on the organizational chart simply referred to meetings of the NATO Political Committee, with the allies represented by the deputy permanent representatives (instead of the lower-ranking political counselors). Nonetheless, to the extent that bureaucratic structures can be manipulated to send political signals, the alliance in this way marked the increased importance of the political side of alliance activities. A further institutional signal was sent later in 1968, when a new section in the NATO international staff was created to deal with disarmament and arms control issues.

The allies wasted no time translating the Harmel mandate into alliance policy. When the North Atlantic Council met in Reykjavik, Iceland, in June 1968, the allies issued a "Declaration on Mutual and Balanced Force Reductions." The so-called Reykjavik signal announced allied agreement that "it was desirable that a process leading to mutual force reductions should be initiated." They agreed "to make all necessary preparations for discussions on this subject with the Soviet Union and other countries of Eastern Europe," and they urged the Warsaw Pact countries "to join in this search for progress toward peace."[11]

The Reykjavik signal echoed NATO's June 1967 expression of interest in mutual force reductions. However, the Reykjavik declaration was notable in that it not only expressed interest but also voiced NATO's intention to prepare for discussions that the East was invited to join. The Reykjavik signal, therefore, marked NATO's formal entry into the world of arms control initiatives, putting into action the recommendations adopted in the Harmel Report six months before.

The Harmel exercise revitalized the foundations of the alliance. It reiterated NATO's commitment to maintain a strong defense, but broadened substantially the goals of the alliance. This amendment to the original transatlantic bargain provided a political framework more relevant to the challenges posed by the East-West environment of the 1960s. It also responded to the evolving relationships between the United States and its West European allies. The Harmel formula gave the alliance a new lease on life and a renewed sense of purpose.

Perhaps the most lasting contribution of the Harmel exercise was the change in NATO's mission that would become so relevant at the end of the Cold War. For many years, NATO's search for the fruits of détente appeared unproductive and to some perhaps even counterproductive. Negotiations on Mutual and Balanced Force Reductions (MBFR)[12] opened in 1973, and some us involved in the talks were hopeful that this first serious East-West negotiation on the military confrontation in Europe could reduce the danger of war breaking out there. In spite of this hope, the talks in a sense became a victim of the East-West competition and droned on for more than a decade before being converted into negotiations on Conventional Forces in Europe in the mid-1980s. The latter negotiations finally produced a deal, largely because the fading Cold War finally made it possible. That deal not only provided the framework for dramatic cuts in military forces and equipment across Europe but also established an intensive, cooperative monitoring system that would eventually help ease the transition from Cold War confrontation to a more cooperative security system in Europe.[13]

Photo 4.1: UK and US delegations at 1973 opening of Mutual and Balanced Force Reduction negotiations in Vienna (author is seen immediately behind US Ambassador Jonathan Dean)

Source: US Delegation to MBFR.

In addition, in 1975, NATO's initiatives helped turn Moscow's propagandistic proposals for a "Conference on European Security" into the Conference on Security and Cooperation in Europe (CSCE), a meaningful East-West forum on a broad spectrum of issues.[14] The East-West dialogue in the CSCE may well have contributed to undermining the control of communist regimes in the East and to the unraveling of the East-West conflict.[15]

Despite the opening of MBFR talks and the beginning of the CSCE process, many Americans saw little in the way of demonstrable benefits for NATO's pursuit of détente. When President Gerald Ford (in 1974 Ford succeeded President Richard Nixon, who had stepped down after the Watergate scandal) suggested that the term "détente" should be removed from the West's political vocabulary, many Europeans winced but hoped that the comment would not be prophetic. Ford's declaration, inspired by some deeper trends in American thinking, in fact did project accurately the future course of American policy.

The administration of President Jimmy Carter (1977–1980) was unsure in its early years what it would do about the growing disenchantment, particularly among American conservatives, with the era of détente. The administration revealed a split personality in its approach to the Soviets. On the one hand, it wanted—and negotiated—a strategic arms control accord with Moscow. On the other hand, the administration's fixation on human rights issues produced a strong critique of the Soviet Union's treatment of its own citizens, criticism that cohabited very uncomfortably with the administration's attempts to sell a US-Soviet arms control deal to the US Congress.

While the Strategic Arms Limitation Talks (SALT II) treaty was languishing in the US Senate, the Soviet Union provided the stimulus for resolution of the dilemma in Carter administration policy. In the closing days of 1979, Moscow sent troops into neighboring Afghanistan, collapsing whatever was left of US-Soviet détente. A US Atlantic Council report in 1983 noted, "The death of détente was sounded when the Soviets invaded Afghanistan in 1979. President Carter imposed sanctions, withdrew the SALT II agreement from Senate ratification, and recommended substantial increases in US defense spending which were further enlarged under the Reagan Administration."[16]

Washington's unilateral declaration of the death of détente, however, was never fully accepted in Europe. The Soviet invasion of Afghanistan was seen as distasteful evidence of Soviet insecurity and interventionism but not as a direct threat to Europe and certainly not as a sufficient rationale for jeopardizing the fruits of détente in Europe. As Josef Joffe put it, "For the United States, détente did not 'work,' for the Europeans it did—hence their almost obsessive attempts to snatch as many pieces as possible from the jaws of the rattled giants."[17]

Even before the invasion of Afghanistan, Henry Kissinger had argued that the Harmel formula was inappropriate for the circumstances of the late 1970s. Addressing a conference on the future of NATO in Brussels in September 1979, Kissinger dismissed NATO's détente role as an intrusion on the real business of the alliance.

European (and some American) participants in the conference shook their heads in amazement that Kissinger could so lightly dismiss a political aspect of NATO that had been so important to the credibility of the alliance for more than a decade. Kissinger's approach, however, was a clear warning that the critique from the political right in the United States was increasingly affecting American perspectives on the alliance and its policies.[18]

In the late 1970s and into the 1980s, the United States and the European allies struggled with the great variety of issues raised by their differing perspectives on the importance of détente and whether détente was "divisible," applicable to Europe but not the Third World. The debate intensified with the advent in 1981 of the Reagan administration which was determined to implement a tough new American policy toward the Soviet Union, backed by a substantial defense buildup.

The allies managed to work out compromises on many of the specific issues raised by the differing American and European perspectives. But European governments never accepted the American contention that détente was dead or that the alliance should jettison its mandate for pursuing improved relations and arms control agreements with the Soviet Union.

Ironically, the Reagan administration, whose hard line toward Moscow had troubled the Europeans so much, managed to initiate the end-game negotiations on both intermediate range nuclear missile cuts and conventional force reduction negotiations in Europe. In subsequent years, supporters of President Reagan claimed that his tough policies toward the Soviet Union had helped bring about its collapse. Critics of the American president suggested that Soviet leader Mikhail Gorbachev should be given most of the credit for opening both the Soviet Union and the Warsaw Pact for change. Looking back, it would appear that both factors played a role and that, to some extent, the outcomes that unraveled the Warsaw Pact and dissolved the Soviet Union were unexpected consequences of Soviet and American policies. In any case, the relevance and importance of the Harmel doctrine appear in historical perspective to have been borne out by the end of the Cold War and the need for NATO to adapt its role further to accommodate the dramatically new international realities.

NATO's Nuclear Strategy

From Massive Retaliation to Flexible Response

NATO's reliance on the threat of a massive nuclear attack on the Soviet Union had been suspect virtually from the day MC 48 was approved in December 1954. NATO's first nuclear strategy was not quite as simple as implied by the image of "massive retaliation" most frequently used to describe the essence of MC 48. The strategy spelled out in this document did not exclude the possibility that nuclear weapons might be used only within the confines of the battlefield. Despite US deployment in the 1950s of a variety of nonstrategic nuclear weapons in Western Europe, alliance strategy remained at least implicitly reliant on the suggestion that the Soviet Union would risk a massive nuclear strike on its territory should its forces attack Western Europe.

This nuclear strategy, driven principally by the austerity program of the Eisenhower administration and the failure of the allies to meet the Lisbon conventional force goals, did not sufficiently anticipate the implications of Soviet nuclear force deployments. The Soviet Union had successfully tested an atomic device in 1949 and a hydrogen bomb in 1953, but when MC 48 was approved, the Soviet Union had only limited means for delivering its few weapons on Western targets and virtually no credible means for threatening American territory. The United States, meanwhile, had surrounded Soviet territory with a bomber force capable of devastating strikes on the Soviet Union. This situation was, for obvious reasons, intolerable for the Soviets, and even as the NATO ministers were approving MC 48, Moscow was developing its own long-range bomber force and planning to deploy medium- and intermediate-range ballistic missiles targeted on Western Europe. The launch of the Sputnik satellite in 1957 symbolized the dramatic progress the Soviet Union had made in a very few years toward developing its own strategic nuclear weapons force capable of holding both European and American cities hostage to a nuclear threat, calling into question the US policy of massive retaliation.

The NATO allies struggled from the mid-1950s with attempts to adjust NATO's strategy and force posture to the evolving strategic environment. In 1959, the Eisenhower administration deployed US medium-range ballistic missiles to Europe: 60 Thor missiles to England and 90 Jupiter missiles divided evenly between Italy and Turkey. The missile deployments were intended to help offset the Soviet deployment of SS-4 and SS-5 missiles that had begun in the late 1950s and to bolster the confidence of European governments in the ability of the United States to implement its nuclear guarantee.

The alliance was at the same time grappling with some internal political dynamics that had begun to undermine its nuclear weapons strategy. European fretting about civilian control of nuclear weapons, so much in evidence when the United States had first attempted to sell the new-look strategy to the alliance in 1954, developed into a more specific European desire to have a say in Western nuclear decision making. By the late 1950s, the British had an independent nuclear capability, and the French were on the way toward nuclear power status. The United States was by no means anxious to encourage the proliferation of nuclear weapons states and would have preferred that neither France nor Great Britain develop nuclear forces.

Between 1959 and 1963, a number of schemes emerged for some form of nuclear sharing among the NATO allies. These schemes were motivated to varying degrees by Soviet nuclear weapons advances and by the tension within the alliance about the American monopoly in nuclear decision making. Of these proposals, only the Multilateral Force (MLF) made any headway. The MLF would have been a force of 25 surface ships, each carrying eight Polaris nuclear missiles, manned by multinational crews, funded jointly by participating allies and assigned to the NATO Supreme

Allied Commander. The United States would have retained ultimate veto power over the use of the MLF weapons.

The MLF proposal, ingenious as it might have been, never had much chance of political acceptance. President de Gaulle interpreted the scheme simply as a means for the United States to retain control over Western nuclear policies while appearing to share it. He saw his suspicions confirmed when the British, seeking to modernize their nuclear forces, chose to purchase Polaris missiles from the United States. According to de Gaulle, British Prime Minister Harold Macmillan "mortgaged" Britain's future nuclear capability to the United States in the Nassau Agreement with President John F. Kennedy in December 1962, when he agreed to buy Polaris submarine-launched ballistic missiles from the United States. After further NATO discussions of various MLF variants that continued into the administration of Lyndon B. Johnson, MLF was consigned to the closet of historic curiosities.

The MLF failure left unresolved the issues it had been designed to address, in particular, the political requirement for broader allied participation in nuclear decision making. Even if France and Great Britain were determined to maintain their own nuclear forces, US officials remained convinced that West Germany would have to be given a more acceptable role in nuclear decision making given Bonn's increasingly central role in the alliance.

By the early 1960s, the United States had positioned in Western Europe a wide array of nuclear weapons, ranging from intermediate-range systems to short-range weapons intended for use on the battlefield. However, it kept either full control over the weapons or joint control by retaining one of two keys necessary to release them. This massive infusion of US nuclear weapons in NATO defenses, combined with the desire of some West European allies for a more influential role in NATO nuclear planning, led to the creation of the Nuclear Planning Group (NPG) in 1966. The NPG was designed to allow alliance members to influence planning for the potential use of nuclear weapons and to give them a role in nuclear decision making in a crisis. The United States also agreed to assign 64 Polaris submarine-launched ballistic missiles directly to NATO along with the British Polaris force, both of which would be responsive to requirements of the SACEUR.[19]

The abortive MLF project and the subsequent creation of the NPG were responses largely to developments within the alliance. During the same period, the alliance was also moving toward a substantial shift in its nuclear strategy. Although massive retaliation had died years before, it had never been formally buried; the United States started pushing for a proper interment in the early 1960s.

From an American perspective, the steady growth of Soviet nuclear capabilities clearly necessitated a more flexible set of guidelines for the use of nuclear weapons. It was no longer credible simply to threaten attacks on the Soviet heartland with nuclear weapons in response to a Warsaw Pact offensive in Western Europe— the American heartland had become vulnerable to a response in kind. The need for change had been signaled by Secretary of Defense Robert McNamara in 1962.

Such a momentous change in nuclear strategy, however, met with skepticism in Western Europe, largely from fear that the credibility of the nuclear guarantee would be destroyed by a strategy that foresaw the possibility of limited or controlled nuclear exchanges. The concepts that lay behind MC 48 had been of American origin, but they had been embraced by the European allies, and in the 1960s the threat of a massive nuclear strike still seemed a needed deterrent to Soviet aggression in Europe, as well as an affordable substitute for adequate nonnuclear forces.

In 1967, following France's departure from NATO's integrated military command structure and after several wrenching years of discussion and debate among the allies, NATO adopted the doctrine of flexible response. According to the new strategy, NATO would be prepared to meet any level of aggression with equivalent force, conventional or nuclear, and would increase the level of force, if necessary, to end the conflict. The doctrine attempted to accommodate the American desire for more flexible nuclear options and West European concerns about the nuclear umbrella. Under the doctrine, Chicago might not be put at risk in the early stages of a conflict, but the possibility of escalation supposedly "coupled" the fate of Chicago to that of Paris, Hamburg, or London.

The new strategy, substantially altering the original transatlantic bargain, compromised conflicting US and European perspectives on the requirements of deterrence. As Simon Lunn wrote, "While theoretically sound, it [flexible response] left considerable latitude for differences concerning the levels of forces necessary at each stage to insure credible deterrence. This ambiguity permitted the accommodation of conflicting American and European interests, but it did not represent their reconciliation."[20]

While the new nuclear doctrine did not reconcile American and European differences on nuclear strategy, it did provide a formula that was sufficiently ambiguous to achieve political credibility on both sides of the Atlantic—at least for a while. The strategy, combined with the advent of allied consultations on NATO's nuclear policy in the NPG, formally accorded nuclear weapons, from the smallest-yield battlefield systems to the strategic forces of the United States, their own unique places in NATO military strategy. Not only would nuclear weapons serve as a deterrent against a Warsaw Pact attack, but, under flexible response, the entire range of nuclear weapons had a potential role to play in wartime scenarios. Furthermore, the United States had acknowledged the legitimate interests of the allies in shaping NATO nuclear doctrine and sharing the responsibilities of decision making in a crisis. The United States provided no iron-clad guarantee about how extensive consultations might be in a crisis, but at least the NPG provided the ways and means for such consultations.

The decision also recalled the long-standing but unfulfilled NATO objective of mounting a credible nonnuclear defense against the Warsaw Pact. A more substantial conventional capability would fit comfortably within the flexible response framework. In this regard, the new strategy was at least superficially consistent with the original bargain, in which substantial European nonnuclear forces were to be a key support for NATO strategy. Under the circumstances of conventional insufficiency, however, the new doctrine implied greater reliance on the possible use of short-range nuclear weapons as well as the possibility that a nuclear exchange might be limited to the battlefield or to the European continent.

Flexible response, in this sense, was a double-edged sword. Reliance on a wide range of battlefield nuclear weapons implied an even more permanent US commitment to its force presence in Europe because virtually all of NATO's nuclear weapons were under exclusive US control or subject to US veto. NATO's defense options as well as its deterrent strategy had become more dependent on the US troop presence. The October 1954 American commitment to maintain troops in Europe for "as long as is necessary" therefore became longer and more necessary under the flexible response strategy.

At the same time, whether or not the US intent was to provide a greater buffer between its homeland and a possible war in Europe, the new doctrine clearly left open the possibility that the United States would place a higher value on avoiding nuclear strikes on the United States than it would on protecting West European territory. Although the first edge of the sword committed the United States even more firmly to participate in the defense of Europe, the second edge of the sword cut away some of the credibility of that commitment.

In fact, the Soviet Union's drive, first to obtain the means to threaten the United States directly and then to achieve nuclear parity, changed one of the most important conditioning factors for the original transatlantic bargain. The American homeland became dangerously exposed for the first time since the young upstart of a nation had chased the European powers from the Western Hemisphere. Technological advances had given the Soviet Union the potential to threaten all of the United States with its nuclear weapons. But the Atlantic Ocean still separated the United States from its European allies. It therefore remained possible, at least in theory, for the United States to limit its involvement in a war in Europe in order to save the American homeland, and, given the emerging Soviet nuclear capabilities, it had much more reason to do so.

Flexible Response Undermined

With the advent of flexible response and the development of limited nuclear options, the certainty implied by massive retaliation was replaced by the elusive goal of "escalation control." That NATO "advantage" was countered in the 1970s by Soviet nuclear force improvements, including deployment of the SS-20, a mobile, accurate missile system capable of carrying three independently targeted warheads on each missile.

For many West Europeans, the nuclear deterrent had remained credible throughout the perturbations in the nuclear balance and adjustments in Western nuclear policy. There was no certain guarantee that the American president would push the button for Europe, but no iron-clad commitment could be expected. The Soviet

Union had not risked an attack on Western Europe and did not seem likely to do so. A qualified guarantee, therefore, appeared sufficient for deterrence. For many nuclear strategists, however, there was no such confidence.

In the 1970s, West German Chancellor Helmut Schmidt became the single most influential European commentator on alliance strategy and force posture. By the mid-1970s, Schmidt had become convinced that Soviet conventional force advantages over NATO, combined with its superiority in theater nuclear forces, put Europe at risk. Schmidt was concerned that the codification of a US-Soviet balance of strategic weapons in the SALT process could make these weapons of "last resort," weaken extended deterrence, and leave Europe exposed to Soviet power. He highlighted such concerns in a major address to the London International Institute for Strategic Studies in October 1977. Although Schmidt's comments did not refer to theater nuclear forces, they "focused public attention on the concept that a gap was appearing in NATO's deterrent capability."[21]

In the fall of 1979, Henry Kissinger, having served earlier as national security adviser and then secretary of state under Presidents Nixon and Ford, strongly criticized European and American governments for permitting the fate of their nations to rest on such a foundation of hope rather than on adequate deterrence forces. Kissinger "confessed" to a Brussels meeting of American and European defense experts and officials that he had "sat around the NATO council table in Brussels and elsewhere and uttered the magic words [promising extended deterrence for Western Europe] which had a profoundly reassuring effect and which permitted [allied] ministers to return home with a rationale for not increasing defense expenditures." Then Kissinger stunned much of his audience with his conclusion:

> If my analysis is correct, these words cannot be true. And we must face the fact that it is absurd to base the strategy of the West on the credibility of the threat of mutual suicide. Therefore, I would say—which I might not say in office—the European allies should not keep asking us to multiply strategic assurances that we cannot possibly mean, or, if we do mean, we should not want to execute, because if we execute we risk the destruction of civilization.[22]

Kissinger urged that NATO modernize its European-based nuclear forces (an action the alliance was already preparing to take three months later) and encouraged the allies to strengthen conventional defense, an objective sought with limited enthusiasm since the alliance was founded. In other words, Kissinger argued primarily for more "credible" nuclear options combined with a stronger conventional defense to deal with NATO's nuclear dilemma. His analysis suggested that extended deterrence had been invalidated by the advent of Soviet strategic nuclear parity and that the expansion of Soviet theater nuclear forces, particularly deployment of the SS-20 missiles capable of striking targets throughout Western Europe, had checkmated NATO's adoption of the flexible response strategy and deployment of thousands of short-range nuclear weapons in Europe. Kissinger's argument, framed by a politically conservative analysis and a pessimistic perspective on trends in the East-West military balance, represented the conventional wisdom that justified NATO's December 1979 decision to deploy new long-range theater nuclear forces.

Kissinger's message, while compelling, gave short shrift to some additional requirements of Western policy. First, NATO's political viability had come to depend on a fine balance between allied defense efforts and Western attempts to reach mutually acceptable accommodations with the East. Second, any unilateral NATO efforts to improve its nuclear force posture would likely produce a countervailing response from the Soviet Union. As a consequence of the first requirement, NATO's plan for dealing with the perceived deterioration in the nuclear deterrent would have to make sense to European and American publics. In order to gain public confidence, the allies would have to make a serious arms control proposal to the East. Furthermore, the only way to reduce the threat posed by Soviet SS-20 missiles and to forestall a countervailing Soviet response would be to negotiate limits on such systems with the Soviet Union.

And so, in December 1979, led by the US administration of President Carter, the NATO allies decided to modernize its theater nuclear forces while seeking to negotiate limits on such forces with the Soviet Union.[23] The decision came despite growing public opposition in several West European countries to new missile deployments, particularly on their soil.

The debate between East and West and within the Western community that preceded the initial deployments tended to obscure rather than illuminate the rationale of the original decision. The debate between East and West became a contest for the "hearts and minds" of the Europeans. Within the West, the issue became part of a larger struggle between competing concepts of how best to deal with the Soviet Union. The 1979 decision therefore became a surrogate for the discussion of much broader aspects of East-West relations. The initial deployments, marking as they did a "victory" for one side of the debate, perhaps opened the way for a more reflective look at the fate of the 1979 decision and its implications for the future of NATO.

The 1979 "dual-track" decision was, after all, perfectly consistent with the stated objectives and strategies of the alliance. The decision attempted to deal with conflicting American and European perspectives on deterrence by providing more flexible nuclear systems—in response to the American requirement for credible nuclear options—which, nonetheless in their ability to strike Soviet territory, could be seen as strengthening the link between the European theater and the strategic nuclear standoff—in response to the European requirement for extended deterrence.

According to the decision's rationale, deterrence for Europe would be strengthened because the Soviet Union, in contemplating any attack on Western Europe, would be forced to calculate that the West might respond by striking Soviet territory with the new systems. And, in using the systems, the West would know that the Soviet Union might respond by striking American, not just European, targets. Therefore, both sides would be aware that hostilities initiated in Europe might escalate rapidly to a strategic exchange.

This logic was no foolproof guarantee of extended deterrence. The American president could, in theory, decide not to use the new systems in case of a Soviet attack and could even choose to "lose" them rather than invite strategic retaliation. That decision, however, would have to be made much earlier in the conflict than might previously have been the case. The new deployments, therefore, compressed the time in which the Soviet Union could advance through Western Europe without risking a nuclear strike on Soviet territory. The new missiles were not principally intended as a means for physically targeting the Soviet SS-20 missiles, as some observers mistakenly thought, but rather for deterring any attack from the east. Because of this linkage rationale for deploying the new weapons, there was no magic number of missiles that had to be deployed. The deployment would have to be sufficiently large to guarantee (in combination with other factors, such as mobility) survival of enough weapons to remain a serious option in a crisis. Beyond this pragmatic rationale, the final number of 572 missiles was also influenced by the desire to deploy systems in a number of allied countries to "share" the risks and responsibilities of the decision.

The arms control "track" of the dual-track decision also had a very specific purpose. It brought the decision in line with the Harmel formula, which the allies had developed in 1967 to give NATO a role in promoting détente with the East as well as sustaining defense and deterrence. It undoubtedly was clear to the allies that they might need to demonstrate their interest in arms control in order to defend the deployment decision before their publics. The arms control initiative, however, could do something that the deployment would not accomplish on its own. Only if there were an arms control agreement with the Soviet Union to limit intermediate-range nuclear systems could the West restrict the extent of the SS-20 threat to Western Europe.

Why, when the decision on intermediate-range nuclear forces seemed so well designed to serve the strategy of extended deterrence, did it ultimately provoke in Europe fear of nuclear war rather than produce increased confidence that war would be deterred? The answer lies in the fact that the viability of extended deterrence rested on three pillars: the weapons themselves, a credible strategy relating the weapons to the purpose of the alliance, and political confidence that the weapons and the strategy would make it less rather than more likely that war would occur. Historically, the United States has tended to place greater emphasis on the weapons and the strategy for their use than on the political context for their deployment. Europeans, on the other hand, have tended to place greater emphasis on the political context, believing that wars usually are "about something," the product of political disagreements rather than spontaneous unexplainable events. Critiquing the 1979 decision, one European analyst suggested,

> The historical record since the Second World War demonstrates that the faith of Europeans in Washington's ability to use its power in a measured and prompt way to defend Western interests, whether inside or outside the NATO area, is a far more important determinant of their confidence in the reliability of the US

nuclear umbrella and of their acceptance of nuclear defence than is the nuclear balance between the Superpowers.[24]

Even under the best of circumstances, it would not have been easy to negotiate an arms control agreement limiting intermediate-range nuclear systems. As it happened, the negotiations began under a dark cloud because of the general deterioration in US-Soviet relations that had begun in the years immediately prior to the NATO decision and that quickened in its wake.

The Soviet invasion of Afghanistan, only two weeks after the NATO 1979 decision, provided a rallying point for the critique of Soviet global intervention that had been building in the United States for a number of years. The critique had already been a major factor in the failure of the Senate to ratify the SALT II treaty. The invasion brought consideration of the treaty to a full stop.

Ronald Reagan, after trouncing Jimmy Carter in the 1980 elections, set American foreign policy on a new course. President Carter had already begun a defense buildup that the Reagan administration promptly accelerated. Just as important, the Reagan administration came to office infused with great skepticism about arms control based on a perception of unrelenting Soviet antagonism toward US interests. The administration put arms control on a back burner and concentrated on developing its defense program.

The Reagan administration's approach to the 1979 decision was based on its dominant philosophy that the Soviet Union—the "evil empire"—would not act seriously in arms control negotiations until Moscow saw that an expensive arms race was the alternative to arms control agreements. It took six months for the administration even to announce that it intended to open arms control negotiations on intermediate-range nuclear weapons. That decision came only after urgent pleading from the allies and a contentious decision-making process within the administration in which officials argued whether arms control negotiations would undermine deployment plans or, on the other hand, make it easier to deploy the missiles.

Almost another six months passed before the administration set its goal for the negotiations. The famous "zero-option" proposal, announced by President Reagan on November 18, 1981, called for the total elimination of all Soviet intermediate-range nuclear weapons in return for cancellation of NATO deployment plans. The plan was received with skepticism by many experts. Some suspected that the far-reaching nature of the approach was designed to produce a Soviet rejection, allowing deployment to proceed.

The initial Soviet response was negative, as was to be expected. Tough negotiations stretched out over several years, seemingly destined to become an arms control failure. Meanwhile, however, other factors were working on the Soviet Union. At home, the Soviet system was proving increasingly incapable of providing basic necessities. As a consequence, Soviet President Gorbachev judged that the Soviet Union could not afford to engage in an open-ended arms competition with the United States. He decided to cut a deal.

On December 8, 1987, the United States and the Soviet Union signed the Intermediate-Range Nuclear Forces (INF) Treaty designed to eliminate two categories of their intermediate-range nuclear missiles: long-range INF, with a range between 600 and 3,400 miles, and short-range INF, with a range between 300 and 600 miles. The treaty did not cover short-range (under 300 miles) nuclear force missiles. In this shorter-range category, NATO countries still had the aging LANCE missile system with approximately 700 warheads. The United States deployed some 36 LANCE missile launchers in Western Europe. Belgium, the Netherlands, West Germany, Italy, and the United Kingdom deployed around 60 LANCE launchers with nuclear warheads available under dual-key arrangements with the United States. These missiles could not reach Soviet targets from their launch sites in Europe and therefore were not of great concern to Moscow and did not accomplish the same strategic objectives intended in deployment of the INF missiles.

Although European as well as American public opinion strongly supported the INF Treaty, some observers judged that elimination of the missiles would undermine the credibility of flexible response and argued that the alliance would have to compensate for the loss of the INF missiles to keep its strategy intact. Others argued, however, that the United States still committed a small but strategically significant portion of its relatively invulnerable sea-launched ballistic missile force for use by NATO's Supreme Allied Commander, and that this force, plus nuclear weapons carried on FB-111 and B-52 bombers based in the United States, preserved a strategic strike potential for NATO. They also argued that a substantial US troop presence in Europe served as a "trip wire" and thus ensured linkage to US strategic nuclear forces.

In addition, British and French strategic capabilities, capable of hitting targets in the Soviet Union, which were not included in the INF negotiations or in US-Soviet strategic arms talks, were being modernized and expanded.

In the event, implementation of the INF Treaty became part of the process of winding down the Cold War, a circumstance anticipated by no one when the treaty was signed in 1987. The intensive inspection regime associated with provisions for dismantling the missiles created a vehicle for testing the possibilities for US-Russian cooperation in the post-Cold War era.

With the end of the Cold War and the dissolution of the Soviet Union, NATO's struggles with nuclear doctrine and extended deterrence promised to enter a dramatically new phase. The aspect of the transatlantic relationship that, in many ways, had been the most difficult for the allies to sustain in capabilities and public support was suddenly overtaken by welcome events.

Britain Joins Europe

The original transatlantic bargain had been seriously flawed by the British refusal to become more closely involved in postwar continental European affairs. The United Kingdom had been centrally involved in shaping the Western alliance and had promised to maintain forces on the Continent, at least as long as the troop presence in Europe did not conflict with British global commitments. But the British commitment to Europe was highly qualified and purposefully distant. The United Kingdom had wanted no role in a European Defense Community and could not see itself as any part of a European unity movement. The United Kingdom's European role in the 1950s was, in effect, an extension of its special relationship with the United States and a distraction from British global political and military involvements. Furthermore, British foreign trade with the Commonwealth was more substantial than that with continental Europe.

The United States valued the special relationship and appreciated the important role that the United Kingdom had played in the formative years of the alliance. Only in retrospect, perhaps, is it possible to see so clearly how Great Britain's distance from the Continent handicapped efforts to organize a more coherent European pillar for the alliance. Had the United Kingdom been willing to join in the European Defense Community or to make a stronger commitment to European defense, perhaps French concerns about balancing Germany on its own would have been allayed. Of course, such speculation serves very little purpose other than to suggest how much the alliance needs British involvement on the European side of the bargain. It would have been unreasonable to expect this global power to acknowledge in the early years of its decline that its future would have to be more intimately linked to that of its neighbors across the English Channel. Luigi Barzini captured the British attitude with this colorful portrait:

> Most of the men who at the beginning rejected the European idea had had responsible roles in World War II. They kept on considering their country what it had been indisputably only a few years before, one of the three great powers. . . . Such men naturally found it unthinkable to join a condominium of defeated, weak, frightened, and impecunious second-rank nations. . . . Were they not still better than any Continental in every—well, practically every—field that really counted? Didn't the ordinary inferior humans still begin at Calais? To be sure, some individual Continentals could be brilliant and sometimes admirable, but most of them were bizarre, slippery, and often incomprehensible. They ate inedible things such as octopuses, frogs, and snails. "Only foreigners waltz backward," Englishmen said contemptuously in the past, when the waltz was still fashionable.[25]

A new generation of British politicians in the 1960s decided the United Kingdom should join the European Economic Community, but the commitment to Europe remained highly qualified. When the British finally joined the Community in 1973, they did so, according to Barzini's interpretation, "reluctantly and somewhat squeamishly, though politely concealing their feelings, like decayed aristocrats obliged by adverse circumstances to eat in a soup kitchen for the needy."[26]

Britain's first tentative approach to Europe, of course, ran into General de Gaulle's veto in 1963. De Gaulle accurately perceived Great Britain's commitment to Europe as still prejudiced by its Commonwealth ties and, most important, by its special relationship with the United States. Seeing Great Britain as an "Atlanticist" Trojan horse, de Gaulle explained his action by saying that with Britain in the Community, European cohesion would not last for long, and "in the end there would appear a colossal Atlantic Community under American dependence and leadership which would completely swallow up the European Community."[27]

By the time Britain made its second attempt to join the Community, much had changed. De Gaulle had been replaced by a Gaullist but more pragmatic leader, President Georges Pompidou, whose prestige was not at issue over British membership in the European Community. More important, the United Kingdom's circumstances had substantially altered. British defense policy had become more Eurocentric with the withdrawal of its forces east of Suez. British trade with the Commonwealth had declined in the 1960s as a share of total British foreign trade, while commerce with continental Europe had steadily increased. The special relationship with the United States had become less and less of an equal partnership as symbolized by the British withdrawal from a far-flung global presence.

The English, as a people, still had not fully accepted their place as a "European" country. Even now, some still talk of "going to Europe" when they cross the Channel. But by the early 1970s, it was already more than clear to objective observers that Britain's strategic interests could be served only as a European power, "waltzing backwards," following Barzini's image, as a member of the European Community even while perhaps resisting the temptation to eat snails.

The British turn toward Europe represented a fundamental change in the transatlantic bargain. British membership in the European Community could not change the fact that the bargain might have been a far different deal had the United Kingdom joined Europe 20 years earlier. It nonetheless enhanced the potential for Europe to become a true second pillar for the alliance, and this became a crucial factor as the Europeans—not only including the United Kingdom but also with British leadership—began trying to construct a new transatlantic bargain at the end of the twentieth century.

West Germany's Ascendance

When the original transatlantic bargain was struck, it was principally a deal between the United States and France. The British actively participated as facilitators, negotiators, and mediators. The Germans were actively involved but more like lobbyists, trying to protect German interests from just outside the formal negotiating process rather than as full-fledged participants. After all, the bargain was partly about Germany's future, about how German power could be contained as well as utilized within the Western alliance.

Luigi Barzini observed, in mock-Germanic style, "The future of Europe appears largely to depend today once again, for good or evil, whether we like it or not, as it did for many centuries, on the future of Germany."[28] Germany was a central issue when the alliance was formed. Throughout the Cold War, Germany remained at the heart of Europe's future, and the Federal Republic gained in strength, stature, and influence within and outside the alliance.

By the late 1980s, Germany had become a key player in the Western alliance. Only because it was not a nuclear weapons state did Germany rank second in power to any other European country. German armed forces provided the backbone of NATO active-duty forces in central Europe as well as a large reserve component. The German economy, even as it struggled in the recession of the early 1980s, had become more vibrant than that of either France or Great Britain. The fact that the German question remained at the core of intra-Western as well as of East-West relations granted the Federal Republic substantial political influence in both Western and Eastern capitals. In the late 1960s and early 1970s, Foreign Minister and then Chancellor Willy Brandt's Ostpolitik exercised a major influence on Western alliance policy by seeking to overcome East-West divisions with contacts and cooperation rather than confrontation.

West Germany, however, remained constrained in unique ways—the residue of World War II and the postwar division of Europe. The Western powers continued to exercise certain rights with regard to Germany, and some of the constraints that were wrapped up in the 1954 London and Paris accords remained in effect. Most of the limitations on nonnuclear West German military operations and arms production had been removed or liberalized, but there still were legal constraints on the production or possession of chemical or nuclear weapons. And the Soviet Union still held effective veto power over the future of relations between the two Germanys, with Berlin's hostage status the leading symbol of Moscow's line of influence to the West German government in Bonn.

The Germans accepted the constraints placed on them by the Western postwar security framework as a price of the war and a ticket to independent statehood and renewed respectability. Over time, those constraints were woven into the fabric of West German political life. One close observer of German-American relations, Gebhard Schweigler, has observed that the outside constraints on Germany became progressively irrelevant as West German policies and political behavior were shaped according to the preferences of Bonn's Western allies. Once West Germany had "internalized" those constraints, Schweigler maintained, many policy differences with the United States grew out of the fact that West Germany was not willing to change from directions originally taken at the insistence or urging of its Western allies.[29] In the early years of the twenty-first century, Germany's "lessons learned" from the World War II victors remain a source of differences with the United States and other allies due to a united Germany's political constraints on the use of its military forces in combat roles beyond German borders.

Despite these external and internalized limitations, in the Cold War confrontation with the Soviet Union, West Germany became America's most important NATO ally. The fact that West Germany's development as an independent power included its emergence as a potent military ally, at least within the confines of Western Europe, represented a major geostrategic gain for the United States.

The progress of West German national growth can be observed in many aspects of US-German relations. One of the best examples, perhaps, is the evolution in the financial aspects of the relationship. In the early 1950s, the United States was still providing substantial financial assistance to support West German rearmament. As the US balance of payments weakened in the late 1950s and the German economy accelerated, the United States looked for ways to retrieve some of the costs of its military presence in Europe. In 1961, the United States and West Germany agreed to an offset program whereby West Germany would purchase military equipment in the United States to compensate for US military expenditures in West Germany. These agreements were renewed and expanded during the Johnson and Nixon presidencies to include German purchases of US Treasury bonds and, in the 1970s, the repair of barracks used by US forces in Germany.

By the early 1970s, however, the Germans had grown uncomfortable with the idea of paying the United States to maintain troops in Germany. Bonn did not like the idea of paying for American "mercenaries" and preferred to concentrate its resources on improving German military capabilities. The United States accepted German arguments for a more "normal" relationship between the two allies, and the offset agreement was allowed to expire in 1975. As the German "White Paper 1983" on defense recalled, "The changes that had meanwhile taken place in the international monetary structure and the extensive contribution made by the Federal Republic of Germany to common defense no longer justified these additional burdens on the Federal budget."[30]

By the mid-1980s, some Germans were arguing that US economic policy was effectively making Germany (and other countries as well) pay for the US defense buildup. The logic of the argument ran something like this: continuing deficits in the United States kept US interest rates high, attracting investment capital to the United States and artificially elevating the value of the dollar on international exchange markets; the investment capital attracted to the United States was therefore not available to help prime a German economic recovery while the elevated value of the dollar kept energy prices high in Germany (because oil is traded in dollars), also restricting German economic recovery. Although the argument certainly does not tell the whole story of Germany's economic problems, it does illustrate how substantially the defense economics of US-German relations had changed since the early 1950s.

The German assertion that the United States was making Germany pay for the American defense buildup suggested that Germany's maturation had brought with it some changes that have been difficult for the United States to accept. Over the years, a number of the factors that guaranteed the United States substantial influence over West German policies had eroded. The United States no longer served as the model of society and government it once did for many Germans. West Germans might not have been fully satisfied with their own political and social institutions, but they no longer felt burdened with a sense of systemic inferiority toward the United States. As a consequence, the West Germans no longer believed it was necessary to look to Washington to define West German security interests. The Federal Republic, with greater confidence than ever since World War II, began basing its foreign and defense policies more and more on home-grown assessments of German interests.

The process of German maturation could have been viewed as one result of the then-perceived deterioration in the US position of international leadership. Alternatively, it could be seen as a logical consequence of the Federal Republic's development into a more normal participant in the international system and in the Western alliance.

The emergence of West Germany as a more independent participant in international relations produced a fundamental change in the transatlantic bargain. In many ways, Germany filled the vacuum that France created when it abandoned NATO's integrated commands in search of a defense policy more independent of the United States.

Virtually no one expected that Germany's situation would change even more radically with the end of the Cold War. West Germany's evolution during the Cold War helped prepare German leaders and citizens to face the consequences of what they had long hoped for but dared not expect: a peaceful and sudden reunification of the two Germanys. The emergence of self-identified interests in West Germany accelerated after reunification, whose advent owed much to the support of its Washington ally, overcoming resistance in Moscow and in West European capitals as well.

Foreign and Defense Policy in the Process of European Unification

A central feature of the original transatlantic bargain had been the pledge of the European allies to work toward greater unity among their separate nations. The United States, in fact, had made Marshall Plan assistance contingent on the development of coordinated European approaches to the use of that aid. While the Europeans were unable to translate their unification efforts into a European Defense Community, they did expand economic cooperation through a community approach.

The cooperative West European efforts encouraged by the Marshall Plan were transformed into the European Coal and Steel Community in the early 1950s. The scope of West European cooperation was dramatically expanded when, on March 25, 1957, the governments of France, West Germany, Italy, Belgium, the Netherlands, and Luxembourg signed the Rome Treaties. These six original Community members agreed in Rome to establish the European Economic Community and the European Atomic Energy Community as sister organizations to the Coal and Steel Community. The treaties sought progressively to eliminate obstacles to trade among the six countries while building up common policies among them. A common agricultural policy was the original centerpiece, designed in particular to benefit French farmers. Over the years, these three communities, with their decision-making processes and civil servants, were combined under one institutional roof. By the mid-1980s, the European acronymic stew was most accurately referred to as the "European Community," capturing in one simple phrase most of the activities and institutions that formed the core of a uniting Europe, today known as the "European Union (EU)."

Even though de Gaulle's rebellion had frustrated plans for expansion of the membership and powers of the Community, Europe's healthy economic growth in the 1960s provided the economic margins for steady integration in the near term and lofty dreams of full economic union in the not-too-distant future. But the oil price-induced recessions of the 1970s, carrying into the early 1980s, combined with strong nationalistic approaches among the members, slowed the integrative process to an almost imperceptible crawl and dashed hopes for early progress toward full economic and monetary union.

Nevertheless, the "six" became "nine" in 1973 when the United Kingdom, Ireland, and Denmark became EC members and "ten" when Greece joined in 1981. The Community became "twelve" with the accession of Spain and Portugal in 1986. This expansion of the Community, however, brought with it additional economic problems, and the integration process stalled in the mid-1980s, waiting for renewed economic growth to provide the financial margins to underwrite further integration.

While the process of European unification was struggling through the bad economic weather, the European Community members moved forward on the political front. The foundations of the Community remained firmly planted in the economic integration process established in the Rome Treaties. Advocates of European unity nonetheless always recognized that the economic heart of the Community would eventually need to be guided by a political soul.

For many years, the search for greater political unity was caught up in debates over the purposes and methods of cooperation—between advocates of a suprana-tional Europe and partisans of a Europe of nation-states, between the Gaullists and the "Communitarians," and between the "Europeanists" and the "Atlanticists." Finally, in December 1969, the leaders of the original six EC members, meeting in The Hague, bypassed these traditional conflicts and instructed their foreign minis-ters "to study the best way of achieving progress in the matter of political unification, within the context of enlargement" of the Community.

When the foreign ministers reported back to the heads of state and government on October 27, 1970, they recommended that the EC members initiate a process of European Political Cooperation (EPC). The report was accepted, recording agree-ment of the six countries to ensure through regular exchanges of information and consultations a better mutual understanding on important international problems and to strengthen their solidarity by promoting the harmonization of their views and the coordination of their positions and, where it appears possible and desirable, common actions.

Over the years, the members of the EC expanded the scope and content of their consultations to the point where, by the end of the Cold War, EPC had become a regular and accepted part of the process of foreign policy formulation in the 12 EC countries. One result of this process of foreign policy coordination was a proliferation of foreign policy issues on which there was a European consensus or a record of previous joint actions. Political cooperation produced a number of results (many of which could also be called "successes"): coordinated positions in a variety of international forums, including the CSCE and the United Nations; various declarations on the Middle East; agreement on a package of sanctions in response to the declaration of martial law in Poland; and a coordinated reaction to Argentina's occupation of the Falkland Islands.

This expansion of topics and problems covered by the political consultations inevitably led the EC in the direction of "security policy." The EC members consciously stopped short of what could be considered "military policy," an area that until the late 1990s remained reserved almost exclusively for NATO cooperation. But even though the EC members were careful to steer clear of actions that would conflict with NATO's prerogatives, EC consultations by the mid-1980s regularly included issues that were on NATO's consultative agenda as well.

In 1987, the European allies took some significant steps toward European defense cooperation. France and Germany agreed to form a "European brigade," and in September of that year, the two countries conducted a major joint military exercise in Germany with combined French and German forces operating under French command.[31] Perhaps most notably, the Western European Union (WEU) countries in October 1987 issued a "Platform on European Security Interests" that constituted the most explicit and far-reaching European statement to date on common approaches to European security issues. The document emphasized the continuing importance for Western security interests of both nuclear weapons and American involvement in European defense. The West Europeans also used WEU consultative and decision-making procedures to coordinate their enhanced naval contributions to the Western presence in the Persian Gulf in 1987.[32]

The political consultations in the European Community and the revival of activity in the Western European Union remained exercises of coordination among the member states rather than a process of political integration. They nonetheless established the foundation for much more dramatic developments during the 1990s, after the end of the Cold War and the dissolution of the Soviet Union had created an entirely new set of international, transatlantic, and European circumstances.

Lessons from Cold War History

Judged by the outcome of the Cold War, the North Atlantic Alliance had served the allies well despite the failure of the European allies to deploy the nonnuclear forces they had promised at Lisbon in 1952. The hallmark of the alliance was its adaptability. The transatlantic bargain was revised and reshaped almost constantly from 1949 to 1989. Some of the internal battles were bitter and left scars. But, on balance, there was much more success than failure and much of which NATO's founding fathers would be proud. The next period of history would bring with it even more dramatic changes. The way in which the NATO allies would deal with those changes was influenced by their experiences and interactions during the Cold War. The next chapter turns to some observations about the transatlantic bargain drawn from the Cold War years.

Notes

1. Kissinger's so-called Year of Europe in US foreign policy heightened European suspicions of US intentions and laid bare a number of conflicting interests, particularly regarding how to deal with Western vulnerability to a disruption of Middle East oil supplies. The exercise yielded a "Declaration on Atlantic Relations," approved by the NATO foreign ministers in Ottawa in June 1974. The document reflected no fundamental change in the transatlantic bargain, but the difficulties encountered in producing the declaration perhaps provided a foretaste of things to come.
2. Michael M. Harrison, *The Reluctant Ally: France and Atlantic Security* (Baltimore, Md.: The Johns Hopkins University Press, 1981), 48.
3. Harlan Cleveland, *NATO: The Transatlantic Bargain* (New York: Harper & Row, 1970), 106.
4. Unnamed diplomat as cited in Cleveland, *NATO*, 104.
5. Pascale Boniface, "The Specter of Unilateralism," *Washington Quarterly* 24, no. 3 (summer 2001): 161.
6. Anthony Glees, *Reinventing Germany: German Political Development since 1945* (Oxford: Berg, 1996), 154–56.
7. Cleveland, *NATO*, 144.
8. In 1955, President Eisenhower proposed that the United States and the Soviet Union exchange maps detailing the locations of their military facilities, followed by mutual aerial inspection of the sites to confirm compliance with future arms control accords. It is unlikely that the Eisenhower administration expected Soviet agreement to the proposal, and it was predictably rejected by Soviet President Nikita Khrushchev as an "espionage plot."
9. Report of the Committee of Three, *NATO Online Library*, www.nato.int/docu/basictxt/b561213a.htm [accessed May 14, 2009].
10. *NATO Online Library*, www.nato.int/docu/basictxt/b671213a.htm [accessed May 14, 2009].
11. *NATO Online Library*, www.nato.int/docu/comm/49–95/c680624b.htm [accessed May 14, 2009].
12. MBFR was the Western term for their initiative, emphasizing the word "balanced" to imply the need for larger Warsaw Pact than NATO reductions to overcome Pact numerical advantages. Moscow, of course, objected to this term, and the agreed title of the negotiations was Mutual Reduction of Forces and Armaments in Central Europe (MURFAAMCE).
13. At a summit meeting of the Conference on Security and Cooperation in Europe in Paris on November 19, 1990, the 22 member states of NATO and the Warsaw

Treaty Organization signed a major Treaty on Conventional Armed Forces in Europe and published a joint declaration on nonaggression. The treaty included major reductions of military manpower and equipment in Europe as well as a wide array of cooperative inspection and compliance measures.

14. On August 1, 1975, the heads of state and government of 33 European states, Canada, and the United States signed the Helsinki Final Act establishing the CSCE.
15. John Fry, *The Helsinki Process: Negotiating Security and Cooperation in Europe* (Washington, D.C.: National Defense University Press, 1993), 165–73.
16. Atlantic Council of the United States, "Arms Control, East-West Relations and the Atlantic Alliance: Closing the Gaps," Washington, D.C., March 1983, 62.
17. Josef Joffe, "European-American Relations: The Enduring Crisis," *Foreign Affairs* 59 (spring 1981): 840.
18. The September 1979 gathering in Brussels received its greatest notoriety for Kissinger's warning to the European allies that they could no longer count on the American nuclear guarantee against the Soviets. Kissinger's observations were substantially edited and revised before publication, taking some of the rhetorical edge off the more dramatic statements made in the conference session (based on author's notes taken at the session). Kissinger's (revised) speech and other major statements to this conference can be found in Kenneth A. Myers, ed., *NATO—The Next Thirty Years: The Changing Political, Economic, and Military Setting* (Boulder, Colo.: Westview, 1980).
19. The Nassau agreement had included a British pledge that its Polaris force would be assigned to the alliance and withdrawn only when "supreme national interests are at stake."
20. US House of Representatives, *The Modernization of NATO's Long-Range Theater Nuclear Forces* (report prepared for the Committee on Foreign Affairs by the Congressional Research Service, Library of Congress, by Simon Lunn, Washington, D.C., 1981), 11.
21. US House of Representatives, *The Modernization of NATO's Long-Range Theater Nuclear Forces*, 16.
22. Joseph Fitchett, "Kissinger Cites Gaps in US Nuclear Role," *International Herald Tribune*, September 3, 1979, 2.
23. NATO members agreed to modernize the Europe-based US nuclear arsenal by deploying a total of 572 new ground-launched systems capable of reaching Soviet territory from West European sites. The deployment would consist of 108 Pershing II ballistic missiles and 464 ground-launched cruise missiles, all with single nuclear warheads. The missiles would be deployed in five European countries: P-IIs and cruise missiles in West Germany and cruise missiles only in the United Kingdom, Italy, the Netherlands, and Belgium. The allies also agreed to attempt to negotiate with the Soviet Union East-West limitations on theater nuclear forces in the context of SALT. For a detailed discussion of the decision, see US House of Representatives, *The Modernization of NATO's Long-Range Theater Nuclear Forces*.

24. Simon May, "On the Problems and Prerequisites of Public Support for the Defence of Western Europe" (paper presented at the annual conference of the Centre for European Policy Studies, Brussels, November 23–26, 1983), 2.

25. Luigi Barzini, *The Europeans* (New York: Simon & Schuster, 1983), 58, 59.

26. Barzini, *The Europeans*, 60–61.

27. Press conference, Ambassade de France, *Major Addresses, 1958–1964*, January 14, 1963, 214.

28. Barzini, *The Europeans*, 70.

29. Gebhard Schweigler, *West German Foreign Policy: The Domestic Setting*, Washington Papers no. 106 (New York: Praeger, 1984), 6–24.

30. Federal Republic of Germany, Federal Minister of Defence, *White Paper 1983, The Security of the Federal Republic of Germany* (Bonn, 1983), 126.

31. "Manoeuvres," *Atlantic News*, no. 1951 (September 25, 1987), 3.

32. "Allies End Week of Hesitation by Sending Ships to Gulf Region," *NATO Report* 2, no. 45 (September 21, 1987): 8.

CHAPTER 5

The United States and Europe at the End of the Cold War: Some Fundamental Factors

When, in sudden historical succession, the Berlin Wall was breached, communist regimes were swept from office throughout Eastern Europe, the Warsaw Pact was dissolved, and the Soviet Union disintegrated, the NATO allies could not believe their good fortune. These events raised concerns in Washington and in West European capitals about potential instability growing out of so much change in such a short time. But a 40-year struggle had been resolved in their favor without a shot fired in anger. The Cold War had never turned hot, deterrence had worked, and the values on which the transatlantic alliance was founded had triumphed.

The time for celebration, however, was short. The allies almost immediately found themselves dealing with the consequences of their victory and asking questions as fundamental as "Do we still need NATO if there is no more Soviet threat?"

The chapters that follow in Part II of this book discuss how the allies responded to this challenge. This chapter, however, reflects on some of the fundamental factors in transatlantic relations as seen in the Cold War experience. It is, in a sense, an assessment of the assets and liabilities that the transatlantic bargain brought to the table at the end of the Cold War. Such an assessment may seem particularly timely as the crisis in transatlantic relations over Iraq is now in the alliance's rear-view mirror and new leadership on both sides of the Atlantic looks down the road toward the futures of NATO, the European Union, and the transatlantic bargain.

NATO: More Than a Military Alliance

Had the transatlantic bargain been inspired by no more than the desire to balance Soviet power in central Europe and to control Germany, it might have survived through the Cold War and beyond, but it certainly would not have prospered. The founding of NATO reflected hopes as well as fears, and those were recorded in the North Atlantic Treaty. The treaty's preamble declared that the parties to the treaty were "determined to safeguard the freedom, common heritage and civilizations of their peoples, founded on the principles of democracy, individual liberty and the rule of law." With an economy of language that characterized most of the Treaty, the allies described the alliance as more than a traditional arrangement among nations to preserve a favorable balance of power. The treaty recorded fundamental beliefs and interests shared by the allies that might have drawn them together even in the absence of a common threat to their security.

The allies also agreed that their belief in democracy and individual liberty should be translated into some common goals in their relations with other nations. They pledged to "contribute toward the further development of peaceful and friendly international relations by strengthening their free institutions, by bringing about a better understanding of the principles upon which these institutions are founded, and by promoting conditions of stability and well-being."

After recognizing their common political heritage and ideals, the allies noted the importance of economic factors in their relationship. Fully aware that economic factors had played a major role in provoking both wars of the twentieth century, the allies pledged in Article 2 of the Treaty that they would "seek to eliminate conflict in their international economic policies" and would "encourage economic collaboration between any or all of them."

These political and economic statements of purpose have been inscribed so frequently in books about the alliance that their repetition is now regarded as an obligatory part of the NATO analyst's ritual. These phrases usually are read over quickly in order to get to the meat of the matter. Do these motherhood and apple pie declarations perhaps deserve more attention? From a cynical perspective, it would be quite easy to dismiss such exhortations as little more than treaty niceties, paid only lip service in practice. After all, the Treaty, one among believers in "the principles of democracy, individual liberty and the rule of law," was originally signed by a Portuguese regime that fell far short of democratic standards. In subsequent years, military regimes in Greece and Turkey were allowed to continue full participation in the alliance because of their geostrategic significance despite protests heard from some northern European quarters. Furthermore, the international economic policies of the allies were anything but free of conflict.

A measured dose of skepticism may indeed have been warranted by the Cold War experience. The alliance has not always lived up to its own standards. The Treaty drafters understood that the alliance would work most effectively if the policies of the member states fully reflected their shared political beliefs and intertwined economic destinies. What made the Treaty special was the allies' belief that they were defending a way of life and a means of governing that were most likely to benefit the well-being of their citizens as well as enhance the stability of the international system.

From the signing of the Treaty in 1949 until the end of the Cold War, troubles in the alliance were provoked primarily by nuclear and East-West issues, but the degree to which they threatened the solidarity of the alliance was undoubtedly influenced by the quality of relations within the West.

The alliance, like any partnership, depended on the willingness of the partners to understand and respect what is motivating the others. Each had to walk a mile in the other's shoes in order to make the arrangement work. Eventually, through compromises, the partners developed sufficient common ground to provide the basis for joint action. The beginning resided, however, in understanding.

We Are Here, and They Are There

Perhaps the most basic differences between European and American approaches to East-West relations during the Cold War could be traced to the fact that the Atlantic Ocean and many miles separate the United States from Europe, and that Western Europe occupies the same land mass as did the Soviet Union and its Warsaw Pact allies. It is less than 1,000 air miles from Moscow to Berlin, about the same distance as between Washington and New Orleans. It is approximately the same distance

Photo 5.1: This promotion for the Atlantic Community Quarterly suggested the transatlantic allies should see the Atlantic Ocean as a river, implying that shared values and interests could overcome geography

Source: Reproduced with permission of the Atlantic Council of the United States.

from Moscow to Paris or London as it is from New York to Denver. But Washington is almost 5,000 miles from Moscow.

Many Americans wondered during the Cold War why Europeans, much closer to the Soviet Union, appeared far less concerned about the "Soviet threat." The short answer, "We are here, and they are there," identified the puzzle but did not resolve it. Proximity to Soviet military power should have led to greater concern, according to the logic of the American question. But it clearly did not, suggesting that even in an age of instantaneous communications and space travel, the Atlantic Ocean divided us more than it united us.

Western Europe's proximity to Soviet power, in fact, made Europeans particularly concerned about the consequences of war and, therefore, quite determined to avoid them. For Americans, the European "theater" could be separated, at least intellectually, from their homeland; for Europeans, the homeland was the potential battlefield, whether or not nuclear weapons were used by either side. As a result, Americans and Europeans placed different emphases on deterrence versus war-fighting capabilities, on conventional versus nuclear weapons, and on arms control versus defense improvements.

These geographically based differences asserted themselves strongly in the early 1980s. One of the principal themes of the antinuclear movement in Europe was that the United States was moving toward a nuclear war-fighting posture in Europe, and the installation of new long-range theater nuclear weapons was evidence of that tendency. This charge was set against the enunciation by the Carter administration of a more flexible nuclear employment strategy (PD-59) in 1980 and the decision of the Reagan administration to construct (but not deploy) enhanced-radiation warheads—the "neutron bomb"—that would have killed people but left inanimate objects standing. The final proof for many Europeans of American willingness to contemplate "limited" nuclear war in Europe came on October 16, 1981, when President Reagan remarked that he "could see where you could have the exchange of tactical [nuclear] weapons against troops in the field without it bringing either one of the major powers to pushing the button."

When geography is married with history and related to the implications of war, the "European" perspective as opposed to the "American" view takes on special meaning. As one observer noted in the early 1980s, "Nobody in Europe, West or East, imagines that war means only fighting overseas. For all Europeans, the question of war is the question of survival, not just of superiority."[1]

But geography is a complex factor. How would you explain that Canadians, in the same relative geographic position as the United States, display some very "European" traits when it comes to defense efforts and arms control? With regard to defense spending, the Canadians have never been among NATO's big spenders by any measure. In the Canadian case, the reason (or excuse) for not doing more may have been the geographic proximity to the United States. In other words, Canada relies on the fact that the United States must regard Canada's defense as vital to its own security. (When it came to the role of the Canadian military after 9/11, however, the

Canadians joined their Anglo-Saxon allies in taking on the most dangerous assignments in Afghanistan.)

This is simply to say that the end of the Cold War did not change the geography of the Atlantic alliance, and it did not erase some of the instincts and strategic predispositions that developed on either side of the Atlantic during the Cold War. The same can be said of the profound influence of history on transatlantic attitudes.

The Different Lessons of History

It is an objective fact that the United States and Europe have passed through their own unique historical experiences and naturally have drawn somewhat different lessons from those experiences. Europe was the site of two devastating wars in the twentieth century and was the principal host to the Cold War as well. Most continental European countries, at one time or another in the past century, have been defeated and occupied by foreign forces. From a European perspective, the desire to avoid war remains an immediate and meaningful imperative. Fritz Stern, an American historian, describes the effects of these differing experiences with war:

> The Europeans cherish a different historic memory from ours. To Europeans the increase in overkill capacity is an irrational art, an absurdity: they know that we have enough to kill and be killed a hundred times over again. Their historic experience in this century—unlike America's until Vietnam—has not been the triumphant use of power but the experience of brute and futile power, blindly spent and blindly worshiped. Even an unhistorical generation in Europe remembers World War I as the epitome of the mindless worship of force; they remember the guardians of morality sanctifying violence. For the Europeans, this [20th] century has been the experience of the absurd, first as an intuition of artists, then as drama produced by history. Having lost their preeminence in repeated wars, the Europeans today seek alternatives to force.[2]

Americans also want to avoid war. But no major hostilities have been fought on American soil since the Civil War, 140 years ago. The United States emerged from both world wars "victorious," suffering neither occupation nor the ravages of war on its territory, save Pearl Harbor. The most popular American historical perspective on World Wars I and II is that the United States was forced to join the hostilities because Europe had not dealt effectively with threats to the peace. One consequence, particularly growing out of the World War II experience, is that Americans tend to view appeasement of an antagonistic power as the greatest danger for their interests.

Many Americans would say that European nations, in seeking alternatives to the use of force throughout the Cold War, opted out of responsibility to their citizens as well as to their alliance. The European starting point appeared to be the possible rather than the desirable. History, on the other hand, left Americans with an expectation of virtually unlimited possibilities—a theme that has helped to elect more than one American president.

The United States emerged from World War II wearing a "white hat." America had come to the rescue of democracy and freedom and had provided the additional force needed to defeat fascism. After the war, Americans saw themselves as the main barrier to the spread of communism. America's involvement in Vietnam called into question its moral posture and raised issues about the role that the United States should play in the world—issues that still are unresolved and perhaps were even more pointed at the opening of the twenty-first century than they were in the 1980s. But Americans still see themselves mostly as reluctant warriors who, when called into action, fight to win.

An even longer-term factor reinforces the American tendency to seek the desirable rather than to work within limits. This country matured with one frontier after another to cross and with a record of sustained accomplishment and growth. Throughout most of its history, the United States had seemingly unlimited resources to call on to support its national objectives. Some analysts and politicians have argued that the United States must begin to shape its world role in ways more compatible with finite resources. But the American psychology still inclines Americans to reach beyond their grasp and to regard limits as new frontiers to be crossed rather than as boundaries to be observed. Thus, in the Cold War competition with the Soviet Union, the United States was inclined to push beyond limits that the European allies found more judicious to accept.

Europeans are more willing to accept limits in part as a consequence of painfully bumping into each other for hundreds of years. Innumerable attempts to change national boundaries—to alter political realities by the use of force—have produced unimaginable death and destruction. The Germans, in particular, were forced to accept limits on their sovereignty as well as on their freedom of international maneuver. Economic and geostrategic factors, not legal limits, have constrained France and the United Kingdom. Most other European countries are so small and relatively weak that their ability to influence international events is effective only in the context of their participation in larger groups, such as the European Union, NATO, and the United Nations. Limits, therefore, tend to be accepted facts of life for most Europeans rather than the frustrations they are for most Americans.

In the twenty-first century, such divergent perspectives play out, for example, in attitudes toward the question of what to do about Iran possibly becoming a nuclear weapons state. No European government wants Iran to go nuclear. However, if diplomacy and other incentives fail to convince Iran not to develop nuclear weapons and their delivery systems, most European governments will regret the outcome and move on, prepared to face the new circumstances created. This choice would appear unacceptable to most Americans, who would be much more willing to use force to prevent Iran going nuclear than would most Europeans.

American scorn for the ways of the "old world" remains well engrained in US national history, and American national attitudes result in part from rejection of those ways. As Louis J. Halle wrote,

> We have to recall that the American nation had its beginnings in the seventeenth century, as a nation of refugees from the tyrannies, the persecutions and the power-politics of the Old World. . . . In our American mythology, the refugees and their children had established in their God-given land a new and entirely different kind of society in which all men were free and equal, in which all men were brothers, in which the wicked devices of the Old World . . . were happily unknown. . . . Not only had God given us a virgin continent, replete with all goods, on which to establish our society, he had given us the great oceans to protect it. Part of our American mythology, then, was that we were beyond the reach of the wicked.[3]

Europeans, including Russians, were of course never beyond the "reach of the wicked." And in another marriage of geography and history, West Europeans generally view Russian behavior as conditioned by the numerous times that marauding armies have marched across Russia's naturally exposed frontiers. Americans tended to see the Soviet Union as an expansionist power attempting to spread communism across the world. Today, as Americans watch Russia struggle to survive by calling on some instincts drawn from the Soviet period, these differing American and European perspectives on how to deal with Russia still come into play.

Debates between Americans and Europeans over East-West relations during the Cold War often turned toward what Stanley Hoffman called the "game of historical analogies." As with most historical analogies, those used in this debate could be turned to favor either side of the argument. Both Europeans and Americans hearkened back to the beginning of World War I to prove the validity of their approach to the Soviet Union. Americans likened Soviet Russia to imperial Germany, while Europeans compared the competing Cold War alliances with those of 1914. Hoffman described the scenario:

> To the Europeans, Washington's view of 1914 suggests that war is the only way to curb Moscow, just as it was the only way to cut down German expansionism. To the Americans, the Europeans' view of 1914 means that—as in the Thirties—they are in effect willing to appease Moscow's expansionism. . . . To the Americans, if the Europeans failed to react strongly to as clear-cut an aggression as the recent one [the Soviet invasion of Afghanistan in 1979], what are the chances of their standing up in cases that may well be more ambiguous. . . . To the Europeans, if Americans overreact in this instance, aren't they going to push the Soviets onto a collision course that could still be averted by a wider policy?[4]

One measure commonly applied to analysis of differing US and European attitudes toward East-West relations was the (false) dichotomy between being "red or dead." During the Cold War, Europeans appeared more willing to opt for the "red" option than did Americans. It seems clear that differing historical experiences help explain the contrast between American and European perspectives on this issue. Most European countries have, at one time or another, been occupied by foreign powers or subjugated by domestic authoritarian regimes. Their more recent political freedom and relative economic well-being tell many Europeans that a condition of occupation or subjugation is not necessarily permanent and that resistance and recovery are possible. Death is quite permanent. Since chasing British colonialists from the continent, Americans have experienced neither authoritarian subjugation nor foreign occupation and find the prospect essentially intolerable.

Importantly, US and European historical experiences have produced differences in transatlantic attitudes toward vulnerability. The United States never came to terms with its vulnerability in the nuclear age and continued to long for a return to its historic invulnerability to direct external threats. This psychological orientation lay behind the Reagan administration's search for a ballistic missile defense shield, dubbed the "Star Wars Program" by its critics. This focus of US policy moved into the background in the early years of the post-Cold War period but never left American minds. The American unwillingness to tolerate vulnerability may be just as potent a motivation for US national security policy as was the Soviet Union's deep security paranoia for its military programs and policies. It helps explain the deep shock and surprise of Americans in response to the September 11, 2001, terrorist attacks on US targets.

On the other hand, Europeans have tended to accept vulnerability as a fact of life. From an American perspective, the European allies are much too willing to tolerate vulnerability. Europeans, meanwhile, find the American search for invulnerability verging on the incomprehensible. Witness the quite different European and American reactions to the 9/11 attacks. This is not, however, a question of right or wrong but rather one of differing historical experiences and contemporary capabilities. Nevertheless, different American and European attitudes toward vulnerability create sharply differing standards for judging the requirements of a viable security policy for an ever-changing global environment.

Finally, one important exception must be noted to this discussion of historical sources of divergent transatlantic perceptions. The exception is England. The United Kingdom's experience in the two world wars of the past century created a perspective distinct from, but perhaps in fact a blend of, the American and the continental points of view. Britain suffered substantial military casualties in both wars and took heavy bombardment of its homeland in World War II. But the United Kingdom, like the United States, emerged from both wars victorious, never having been occupied.

A Mixed Ideological Heritage

Americans and Europeans are united in their desire to protect individual rights, defend their democratic political systems, and sustain equitable and strong social and economic systems. Common ideological objectives are, in fact, explicitly expressed in the North Atlantic Treaty. But despite a wide area of shared ideological commitments, there are some fundamental differences between the European and American ideological experiences and cultures—differences that were highlighted during the Cold War and that remained in the background of transatlantic relations in the post-Cold War world.

The Marxist critique of capitalism has deep historical and political roots in Europe. A number of European countries had large communist parties during the Cold War (most of which were transformed or marginalized in the post-Cold War period). Many Europeans regard Marxist ideals as a source of inspiration even if they reject the systems that were spawned by the Russian Revolution. All European countries have important Socialist or Social Democratic parties, all of which support intervention of the government in the social and economic realm to allocate more equitably the costs and benefits of life within the country. In the continental European NATO countries, such programs are so thoroughly a part of the fabric of society that even conservative parties in government embrace a much more extensive social safety net than that acceptable to American conservatives.

The Marxist critique of capitalism has virtually no roots in the United States. The Democratic Party could by no stretch of the imagination be described as having a socialist program by European standards. The very term "socialism" still attracts a visceral negative reaction in the United States, and is often used by some politicians to smear their opponents. Even though the United States has over the years developed extensive social programs, they were adopted and developed within a pragmatic rather than an ideological framework.

During the Cold War, these differing ideological perspectives contributed to divergent outlooks on East-West relations. Americans viewed the Soviet Union's communist system as more threatening than did many Europeans and saw it as the main threat to American democracy. The end of the Cold War and the dissolution of the main enemy, the Soviet Union, were seen by many Americans as a huge "victory" for the United States and its system of government.

The perspective from Europe was somewhat different. The ideology that motivated the Soviet system was unacceptable to the vast majority of West Europeans. The end of the Cold War was seen as a victory of sorts, but not one to be celebrated at the expense of the citizens of the former Soviet Union and by no means as a rejection of the more generous social services safety net deployed by European nations.

On balance, Americans at the end of the Cold War still saw most Europeans as having been too "soft" on communism, and most Europeans viewed the United States as having been too hard. The contrast in images is sharpest when the United States is being governed by a conservative Republican presidency, as it was during the

Reagan-Bush years and more recently under President George W. Bush. Socially conservative US governments usually find themselves with few soul mates among the European allies.

Roles and Capabilities

It is a simple fact that, at the end of the Cold War, the United States was a global power with global military capabilities while the European nations were, with the exception of France and to a lesser extent Great Britain, regional powers with military capabilities limited to Europe. It was not always so, and the reversal of world roles has much to do with disagreements between the United States and Europe concerning how best to deal with the Soviet challenge in the Third World in the closing years of the Cold War.

Slowly but surely, following World War II, European nations retreated from extensive Third World military involvement. The international consensus favoring the process of decolonization was the prime political factor behind Europe's withdrawal; the economic impetus was provided by Europe's need to reconstruct its devastated industrial capacity and its desire to concentrate resources on economic recovery and the process of regional economic integration. France retained a military intervention capability in Africa and an impressive naval presence in the Mediterranean and the Indian Ocean. But for the most part, Europe's ability to influence global events with military forces was steadily shrinking. The United States attempted to fill vacuums left by the European withdrawal to ensure Western interests by limiting territorial or political gains for the Soviet Union and protecting access to Third World markets and sources of vital natural resources.

The decline in Europe's ability to influence events in the Third World was accompanied by an evolution in European strategies toward Third World problems. European policies became increasingly dependent on political and economic instruments to influence events in the Third World. The American experience in Vietnam confirmed for many Europeans their skepticism regarding the utility of military force beyond Europe's borders. And the fact that the former colonial powers retained or reestablished close ties with their former colonies, based in many cases primarily on the strength of political, economic, cultural, and linguistic links, reinforced the faith of our allies in these policy tools.

As the end of the Cold War approached, the United States and the European allies carried forward fundamentally different attitudes toward the use of force in international relations. European leaders believed, for the most part, that diplomacy, development aid, and trade policies should be the weapons of first resort in dealing with Third World instability. Many Europeans feared what they saw as an American tendency to concentrate too narrowly on military responses to security challenges, believing that other approaches might be more productive and less costly in terms of Western interests. They were at least equally, if not more, interested in developing economic ties and political bonds that would both ensure cooperative relations with less developed states and discourage adventurism by the Soviet Union or potential rogue states. The 1980 British White Paper on defense, the product of a Conservative government, put the European perspective quite clearly:

> The best answer is to try to remove the sources of regional instability which create opportunities for outside intervention. In some circumstances, military measures will not be appropriate at all; in others, they may form only one component of the total response. Diplomacy, development aid and trade policies will usually have a greater contribution to make.[5]

Furthermore, Europe had gained far more in tangible benefits than the United States from the period of détente with the Soviet Union in the form of reduced tensions, increased trade opportunities, and improved human contacts. This made Europeans more inclined to see détente as "divisible," that is, to want to protect the gains of détente in Europe even if the Soviet Union misbehaved in the Third World. The United States, carrying the majority of Western global military burdens, had a much greater interest in treating détente as "indivisible," with Soviet actions outside Europe seen as providing cause for Western responses within the European framework.

The Cold War experience left several interesting questions open. Does military weakness generate faith in economic and political instruments of national purpose? To what extent did US global military capabilities permit the West European allies to concentrate on nonmilitary approaches? Does military strength generate an inclination to use force to further national objectives? These questions remain just as valid and important for the transatlantic relationship in the twenty-first century as they did at the end of the Cold War, particularly as the United States and its European allies search for the most effective ways to deal with the threats posed by terrorism and proliferation of weapons of mass destruction.

During the 1990s, while most European allies dramatically reduced spending on defense and particularly on investment in new technologies and systems, the US focus on the "revolution in military affairs" (RMA) created a growing gap between US and European military capabilities. The US RMA began revolutionizing the modern battlefield with new intelligence, communications, target identification and acquisition technologies, and "smart weapons" capabilities. After President George W. Bush declared a "war on terrorism" in September 2001, it became clear that the growing transatlantic gaps in military capabilities were reinforcing deeply rooted differences between US and European perspectives about threats and how best to deal with them.

Burden Sharing as a Perpetual Issue

Elected officials in sovereign, democratic allied states usually seek to get the best security for their populations at the most reasonable price. This means that alliances among sovereign states will always face questions concerning an equitable balance of costs and benefits among the members. This reality caused constant friction between the United States and its allies throughout the Cold War.

The burden-sharing issue was built into the transatlantic bargain, rising up in many ways from the foundation provided by contrasting US and European geographic realities, historical experiences, and military capabilities. The original concept of the alliance was that the United States and Europe would be more or less equal partners and would therefore share equitably the costs of alliance programs. The seeds for a perpetual burden-sharing problem were planted when the original transatlantic bargain was reshaped in 1954 following the failure of the European Defense Community. As described in Chapter 3, the revision of the original bargain meant that the alliance would become heavily dependent both on US nuclear weapons and on the presence of US military forces in Europe to make those weapons credible in deterrence as well as to fortify nonnuclear defense in Europe.

The US burden-sharing complaint took many forms and was translated into a great variety of policy approaches between 1954 and the end of the Cold War. In the early 1950s, the allies made arrangements for common funding of NATO infrastructure costs, such as running NATO civilian and military headquarters and building and maintaining fuel pipelines, communication systems, and so on. Each ally was allocated a share of the infrastructure costs, according to an "ability to pay" formula. As European nations recovered from World War II and experienced economic growth, the US share of infrastructure expenses was progressively reduced. However, such expenses were not the main cost of alliance efforts. The large expenses were the monies spent by nations to build, maintain and operate their military forces. In this category, the United States always outpaced its European allies.

The administration of President John F. Kennedy in the early 1960s sought a greater European contribution to Western defense. Its policy optimistically advocated an Atlantic partnership with "twin pillars" featuring shared responsibilities between the United States and an eventually united Europe. The Kennedy presidency also witnessed the beginning of the financial arrangements between the United States and West Germany designed to "offset" the costs of stationing US forces in that country. These agreements were renewed and expanded in the administrations of Lyndon B. Johnson and Richard M. Nixon to include German purchases of US Treasury bonds and, in the 1970s, the repair of barracks used by US forces in Germany.

The US experience in Vietnam, French withdrawal from NATO's integrated military structure in 1966, and US economic problems all diminished support in the US Congress for US overseas troop commitments in general and led the Johnson administration to press the Europeans to increase their defense efforts. This period saw a strong congressional movement, led by Senator Mike Mansfield, to cut US forces in Europe. Senator Mansfield introduced the first of the "Mansfield Resolutions" on August 31, 1966. The resolution judged that "the condition of our European allies, both economically and militarily, has appreciably improved since large contingents of forces were deployed"; the commitment by all members of the North Atlantic Treaty is based on the full cooperation of all treaty partners in contributing materials and men on a fair and equitable basis, but "such contributions have not been forthcoming from all other members. . . . Relations between the two parts of Europe are now characterized by an increasing two-way flow of trade, people and their peaceful exchange," and "the present policy of maintaining large contingents of United States forces and their dependents on the European Continent also contributes further to the fiscal and monetary problems of the United States." The Senate was asked to resolve that "a substantial reduction of United States forces permanently stationed in Europe can be made without adversely affecting either our resolve or ability to meet our commitment under the North Atlantic Treaty."[6]

Senator Mansfield reintroduced the resolution in 1967, 1969, and 1970, when the resolution obtained the signatures of 50 cosponsors. However, US presidents, Republican and Democrat alike, consistently opposed such efforts, and these resolutions and similar efforts through 1974 failed to win final passage. The Nixon administration, after unsuccessfully attempting to get the Europeans to increase "offset" payments, took a new tack. The Europeans objected to the prospect of American troops becoming little more than mercenaries in Europe and argued that the US troop presence was, after all, in America's as well as Europe's interests. Nixon shifted to a focus on getting allies to improve their own military capabilities rather than paying the United States to sustain its. The so-called Nixon Doctrine, applied globally, suggested that the United States would continue its efforts to support allies militarily if they made reasonable efforts to help themselves.

Despite the Nixon Doctrine, which was at least implicitly applied by all US administrations through the end of the Cold War, Congress continued to focus on offset requirements, passing legislation such as the 1974 Jackson-Nunn Amendment requiring that the European allies offset the balance-of-payments deficit incurred by the United States as a result of the 1974 costs of stationing US forces in Europe. However, a combination of events in the mid-1970s decreased congressional pressure for unilateral US troop reductions in Europe. The East-West talks on mutual force reductions that opened in Vienna, Austria, in 1973 were intended to produce negotiated troop cuts, and US administrations argued that US unilateral withdrawals would undercut the NATO negotiating position. Congress turned toward efforts to encourage the Europeans to make better use of their defense spending, and President Jimmy Carter, in 1977, proposed a new "long-term defense program" for NATO in the spirit of the Nixon Doctrine, setting the goal of increasing defense expenditures in real terms 3 percent above inflation for the life of the program.

In 1980, Congress, frustrated by allied failures to meet the 3 percent goal, required preparation of annual "allied commitments reports" to keep track of allied contributions to security requirements. Throughout the 1980s, Congress developed a number of approaches linking the continued US troop presence in Europe to improved allied defense efforts. However, the burden-sharing issue was never "resolved." In fact, the growing US concern with Soviet activities in the Third World put even more focus on the fact that the Europeans did little militarily to help the United States deal with this perceived threat to Western interests.

In sum, throughout the Cold War, the United States felt strongly that the Europeans needed to "do more." US arguments included the following:

1. By all quantitative measures, the United States spent more on defense than its allies (well documented in the annual reports on allied defense spending produced by NATO at the end of each year and published in the NATO Handbook and, in more recent years, as "Financial and Economic Data Relating to NATO Defence" on the NATO website: http://www.nato.int).
2. American global military commitments contributed to Western security; growing US military commitments in the Persian Gulf region in particular benefited European as well as US security.
3. The economic strength and political maturity of the allies required them to play a larger role on behalf of their own security interests.
4. American military efforts had allowed the Europeans to modernize their industrial plants, producing competitive advantages for European over American firms.
5. American spending on its strategic nuclear capabilities contributed directly to Europe's security.

Although some Europeans agreed that their countries should increase their relative share of the Western defense burden, the prevalent feeling was that many American criticisms of their defense efforts were unwarranted. Their responses to the US critique included a variety of arguments, including the following:

1. The United States overreacted to the threat. Particularly toward the end of the Cold War, the Soviet Union was growing weaker, and Soviet President Mikhail Gorbachev was looking for ways out of the Cold War confrontation.
2. American attitudes toward the Soviet Union swing unpredictably from great pessimism to great optimism. This produces an irregular pattern of US defense spending, with dramatic peaks and valleys, while the Europeans maintain more steady modest growth in defense efforts.
3. Through NATO, the United States protects itself and its global interests more effectively than it could if its defense perimeters were withdrawn to North America and adjacent waters.
4. Some allied contributions to Western security cannot be measured in terms of defense expenditures alone. European countries provide much more development assistance to less developed countries than does the United States, and such efforts help promote stability. Some provide important real estate for NATO bases.
5. British and French strategic nuclear capabilities enhance deterrence.

6. During the Cold War, the allies purchased far more military equipment from the United States than the United States purchased from European arms manufacturers. American industrial profits, employment, and balance of payments all benefited from this one-sided trade.

When the Cold War ended, the foundation for the burden-sharing debate was cut away. The Soviet Union's military capabilities did not disappear overnight, but its capacity to attack Western Europe vanished almost immediately with the democratic revolution in central and eastern Europe that demolished the Soviet bloc and the Warsaw Pact. Soviet nuclear forces remained a concern, but more because it was unclear whether they would remain under reliable control at a time when the Soviet Union and its empire were disintegrating.

Perhaps ironically, the biggest burden-sharing issue at the end of the Cold War was how the allies should work together to deal with non-collective defense security threats arising beyond NATO's borders, an issue that had always been a source of division among the allies. That would become one of the biggest challenges for the allies in the 1990s. However, the end of the Cold War in itself was not sufficient to produce dramatic shifts in the burden-sharing equation and did not change the fact that leaders in all NATO nations would continue to try to buy acceptable levels of security at the best price. At least in the first decade after the end of the Cold War, the United States and all its allies would look for a peace "dividend" by reducing defense expenditures, taking the opportunity to shift resources to other priorities.

The end of the Cold War totally changed the context for the tensions and debate among the allies about the best policies to pursue in the face of Soviet power and ideology. However, the underlying sources of differing perspectives that were so prominent during the Cold War did not disappear with the end of that period of history. They simply went underground for a time, waiting to reappear in other ways at other times and perhaps to be changed and modified by future circumstances.

Those circumstances came to the fore after the 9/11 terrorist attacks on the United States, and the variable US and European responses to those attacks. The US attack on Saddam Hussein's Iraq seriously split the alliance across every possible dividing line. But it was the attempt to defeat al Qaeda and the Taliban in Afghanistan, discussed in Chapter 9, which provided the new setting for transatlantic and intra-European differences about burden and risk sharing in the alliance. The burden-sharing issue would remain a permanent feature of the transatlantic bargain for as long as it should last.[7]

Notes

1. Flora Lewis, "How Europe Thinks of War," *New York Times*, June 8, 1981, A15.
2. Fritz Stern, "A Shift of Mood in Europe," *New York Times*, September 2, 1981, A27.

3. Louis J. Halle, *The Cold War as History* (New York: Harper & Row, 1967), 12–13.
4. Stanley Hoffman, "The Crisis in the West," *New York Review of Books*, July 17, 1980, 44.
5. Government of the United Kingdom, *White Paper on Defence* (London: Ministry of Defence, 1980).
6. For analysis of the resolution, see Phil Williams, *The Senate and U.S. Troops in Europe* (London: Macmillan, 1985), 139–67.
7. For an analysis of burden-sharing as an inevitable issue in the alliance, see Wallace J. Thies, *Friendly Rivals: Bargaining and Burden-shifting in NATO* (Armonk, New York: M. E. Sharpe, Inc., 2003).

PART II

Post-Cold War Alliance

CHAPTER 6

NATO Outreach and Enlargement:
The Legacy of Harmel

NATO's New Roles

NATO had been the West's indispensable institution during the Cold War. But as the Cold War era came to an end, many wondered whether NATO would or should be swept away by the breathtaking winds of change. The NATO members had already been working hard to improve security relations in Europe, largely through negotiating arms control and confidence-building measures with the Soviet Union and its Warsaw Pact allies. Now the authoritarian regimes that had held the Warsaw Pact together were crumbling, and the Warsaw Pact itself was not far behind. The West Germans and the post-communist East German authorities began negotiating reunification under the watchful eyes of the Soviet Union, the United States, France, and the United Kingdom. A new Europe was on the horizon.[1]

In this heady atmosphere many thoughtful analysts and officials in Western Europe and the United States questioned what NATO's place might be in a world in which the Warsaw Pact had been disbanded and the Soviet Union was withdrawing its forces from central Europe. On the other hand, new leaders of former Warsaw Pact nations were already focusing on the goal of joining NATO—the alliance seemed particularly relevant to them. In February 1990, Hungarian Foreign Minister Gyula Horn said that he could "imagine that, in a few years, Hungary could become a member of NATO."[2]

Early in 1990, very few Western observers were willing to talk about NATO opening its membership to former Warsaw Pact states. In fact, a variety of quite different concepts for the future organization of European security competed for official and public approval. Some experts speculated that it might be best to keep the Warsaw Pact in business to help organize future security in Europe. Others argued that NATO had outlived its usefulness because there was no longer any threat. Such advocates believed that the Conference on Security and Cooperation in Europe (CSCE), to which all European states, the United States, and Canada belonged, could take over responsibility for maintaining peace and security on the Continent. Some Europeans, including French President François Mitterrand and British Prime Minister Margaret Thatcher, tried to find alternatives to German reunification while the United States facilitated accomplishment of West Germany's long-term goal.[3]

With the world changing all around them, the leaders of NATO countries decided that they should address the question of whether NATO was needed. Instinctively, all the governments of all member states, as well as NATO Secretary General Manfred Woerner,[4] believed that NATO should be preserved—even if they were not fully agreed as to why. Some officials argued that NATO was more than a military alliance and was based, in fact, on a community of values that rose above any specific military threat. Others maintained that the Soviet Union remained an alien society that could produce new threats to its neighbors in the future. They saw NATO as an "insurance policy" against a future fire in the European house. Others pointed to new risks and uncertainties that could best be dealt with through NATO's approach, in which like-minded countries work together to handle security problems.

Meeting in London in July 1990, less than nine months after the Berlin Wall had come down, the heads of NATO governments issued the "London Declaration on a Transformed North Atlantic Alliance," announcing a "major transformation" of NATO.[5] They offered to join the Soviet Union and other Warsaw Pact states in declaring that they were no longer enemy states and offered both friendship and cooperation to the former adversaries. Importantly, the leaders also agreed that NATO should revise its military system and its nuclear and nonnuclear strategy. They set in motion a major overhaul of alliance strategy, aimed at producing a "new strategic

Photo 6.1: The fall of the Berlin Wall, November 1, 1989, with the Brandenburg Gate in the background

Source: NATO Photos.

concept" for the alliance in the course of 1991. With this decision, the NATO members began the process of defining NATO's place in the post-Cold War world.

NATO's evolution throughout the 1990s responded to the changing international environment that the allies encountered at the end of the Cold War. The process of change did not come quickly enough to prevent the conflict in the former Yugoslavia from becoming a bloody civil war. A multinational institution with no supranational powers and an established bureaucracy moves slowly in reaction to change. But the NATO allies worked their way through the inertia of past success and political resistance to new approaches in order to adapt their alliance to the new security environment.[6] And, ultimately, the changes written down in the early 1990s provided the foundation for NATO's critical role enforcing peace in the former Yugoslavia later in the decade.

The process of challenge and change that has faced the Atlantic Community nations since the end of the Cold War is addressed in the next six chapters. During the 1990s, the alliance concentrated on spreading peace, stability and the opportunity for democracy throughout Europe. This mission was performed using military capabilities in the Balkans and, more widely, with political initiatives that included partnership programs and enlargement of NATO's membership. In the 2000s, this mission continued, but the new mission of protecting alliance interests from threats originating beyond Europe, particularly those with roots in Afghanistan, joined the European stability mission.

This chapter focuses on the process of reaching out to other countries by creating the Partnership for Peace program, offering membership to qualified candidates, and cooperating with non-NATO countries in the Mediterranean and Middle Eastern region. NATO's important relationship with Russia is discussed in Chapter 7. Chapter 8 examines the evolution of NATO's military tasks and strategy through the 1990s, the influence of NATO's role in the Balkans on that evolution, and the development of NATO nuclear policies and forces since the end of the Cold War. Chapter 9 looks specifically at the new and demanding mission that NATO took on in Afghanistan, and its possible implications for the alliance. Chapter 10 explores the movement toward a new transatlantic bargain, first through the creation of a "European Security and Defense Identity" and then through the establishment of an autonomous "European Security and Defense Policy"[7] among the members of the European Union. The traumatic developments in Euro-Atlantic relations after George W. Bush's election as American president, the 9/11 attacks on the United States and the US invasion of Iraq are analyzed in Chapter 11. This final chapter of Part II concludes by examining the question: how and why did the Euro-Atlantic alliance survive this difficult period?

The Legacy of Harmel

Particularly after NATO adopted the Harmel Report in 1967, NATO governments actively sought to promote dialogue and cooperation with the Soviet Union and its Warsaw Pact allies. The goal was to try to overcome the East-West division in Europe and prevent the war for which NATO nonetheless continued to prepare. This commitment to détente (discussed in Chapter 4) led the allies to join with the Warsaw Pact and other European countries in 1972 to begin preparations for the CSCE and to open East-West talks on Mutual and Balanced Force Reductions (MBFR) in 1973. It provided the underlying political rationale for negotiations with Moscow on Intermediate Range Nuclear Forces (INF), which opened in 1985. The CSCE, originally proposed by the Soviet Union primarily to win recognition of the European status quo, was used by the West to promote human rights and other fundamental principles that should govern the behavior of governments—in relations with their own peoples as well as with other states.

The Helsinki Process, as the CSCE forum was called, was widely credited with legitimizing human rights groups in Eastern Europe and weakening the hold of communist regimes on those countries. The CSCE process also included negotiations on confidence-building and stabilizing measures. In 1986, these talks resulted in an agreement signed in Stockholm, Sweden, on Confidence and Security Building Measures and Disarmament. The MBFR talks, after many years of stalemate, were converted into negotiations on Conventional Forces in Europe, which yielded an agreement limiting nonnuclear and their armaments deployed in Europe just as the Cold War was ending in 1990. In 1987, the INF negotiations resulted in an agreement to eliminate Intermediate Range Nuclear Forces from Europe.

NATO's active pursuit of détente through arms control negotiations and security cooperation initiatives in the 1970s and 1980s demonstrated that the allies were prepared to take diplomatic steps to reduce the chance of war even if Warsaw Pact military strength required NATO to maintain a credible defense and deterrence posture. Some political conservatives in the United States doubted the relevance or utility of NATO's détente role, seeing it mainly as a palliative for the left in Europe. Meanwhile, some on the European left regarded NATO's détente role as a political sham, designed for show but not likely to help overcome Europe's division.

Seen at some distance two decades after the end of the Cold War, it appears that a combination of allied détente, deterrence, and defense policies contributed to the events that culminated in the end of the Cold War, the dissolution of the Warsaw Pact, and the disintegration of the Soviet Union. Meanwhile, the Harmel formula provided a sufficiently broad rationale for NATO to sustain public support for the alliance in Europe and in the United States, even if the formula was not highly valued by those on the political extremes on either side of the Atlantic.

It therefore was not a desperate or illogical step for the NATO allies in the first years of the post-Cold War period to adopt a new version of the Harmel concept to adapt to the radically new circumstances that had emerged in just a matter of months. In so doing, the NATO allies began the process of engineering another fundamental adjustment to the transatlantic bargain, extending the bargain's reach to include potentially all of democratic Europe.

From the CSCE to the OSCE

One of the first necessities was to adapt the CSCE, shaped as it was by Cold War conditions, to the new circumstances in Europe. The CSCE had played an important role in the Cold War, helping regulate relations among European states and also keeping up a human rights critique of Soviet and East European communist regimes. The Helsinki Final Act, signed by all these states in 1975, was not legally binding on the participants. But the Final Act provided the "rules of the road" for interstate relations in Europe and constructive guidelines for the development of democracy in all European countries.

At a summit meeting in London in July 1990, NATO leaders had agreed that the CSCE should be strengthened as one of the critical supports for European peace and stability. NATO reasserted this approach at its summit in Rome in November 1991. In an important token of NATO's intentions, a NATO summit meeting in Oslo, Norway, in June 1992 agreed that, on a case-by-case basis, NATO would support peacekeeping operations initiated by the CSCE. Subsequently, NATO called for strengthening the CSCE's ability to prevent conflicts, manage crises, and settle disputes peacefully.

The key to the CSCE's ability to take on an expanded operational mandate was resources. As a "process," the CSCE had only an ad hoc structure that was not capable of supporting a more ambitious role. In December 1994, a CSCE summit meeting agreed to turn the process into an organization—hence the name change to the Organization for Security and Cooperation in Europe (OSCE) and the decision to provide staff and financial resources so that the OSCE could send missions into European nations to mediate disputes, monitor elections, and conduct other activities designed to prevent conflict.

By the end of the 1990s, NATO and the OSCE were working hand in hand to deal with potential threats to peace. In Bosnia, the OSCE played a critical role in helping establish a process of free elections and respect for human rights. NATO provided the military backing required to give such efforts a chance to succeed. OSCE monitors and mediators played important roles in helping to resolve conflicts and build democracy from Abkhazia and Tajikistan to South Ossetia and Ukraine. The relationship between NATO and the OSCE became one of the key ingredients in an evolving cooperative European security system.

Today's OSCE has its headquarters in Vienna, Austria and employs an international staff of some 450 in its various institutions as well as some 3,000 in its field operations. The OSCE is governed by a council which meets in permanent session as well as at the summit and ministerial level. Its activities are supported by a rotating chairmanship, a secretary general with an international secretariat, and other institutions including an advisory parliamentary assembly.

Recent OSCE projects have included such diverse activities as promoting border management cooperation among member states, facilitating participation of minority populations in public life, promoting military reform, including the human rights of uniformed military personnel, helping train police forces in Serbia and Kosovo, helping dispose of excess small arms and ammunition in Tajikistan and obsolete munitions in Georgia, supporting the development of small businesses in Serbia, working against human traffickers in Kosovo and elsewhere, providing monitors to ensure fair and free elections in Albania and in many other OSCE member states, and promoting a free press throughout the OSCE area.

Even though the OSCE has no enforcement powers and can be kept from acting by just one dissenting state, it has played an important role in filling gaps between missions of other European security actors, most notably NATO and the European Union. The OSCE has been helpful in promoting the development of peaceful and cooperative relations among its members, particularly when they seek such an outcome. Its election monitoring missions have become an important source of credibility for democratic processes in member states with fledgling democratic systems. The main question about its future is the fact that Russia is increasingly skeptical about the organization, and can use the consensus rule to prevent the OSCE from intervening whenever that suits its purposes.

Wrapping up Cold War Conventional Arms Negotiations

In 1990, negotiations aimed at cutting nonnuclear forces in Europe, which had begun in 1973 as MBFR talks, concluded with the Treaty on Conventional Armed Forces in Europe (CFE). This landmark agreement produced reductions and controls on nonnuclear military forces from the Atlantic Ocean in the west to the Ural Mountains in the Soviet Union.

The CFE Treaty of November 19, 1990, is the most comprehensive, legally binding agreement on conventional arms control ever produced. Its goal, now largely accomplished, was to reduce imbalances in the numbers of major conventional weapon systems in Europe to eliminate the potential for surprise attack or large-scale offensive operations. Since the treaty entered into force on November 9, 1992, some 60,000 battle tanks, armored combat vehicles, artillery pieces, attack helicopters, and combat aircraft have been removed from the area and destroyed.

Perhaps the CFE Treaty's biggest accomplishment has been its contribution to transparency—making all military establishments and forces more visible to all other states. The treaty's required declarations of information and inspection procedures help reduce concern about intentions and capabilities of neighboring states. It would be very difficult to hide any significant military capabilities in today's system of military relations in Europe, in part because of the provisions of the treaty.

Throughout the 1990s, the countries that signed the CFE Treaty worked to adapt the treaty to the new security conditions in Europe. The adaptation process had to take into account special concerns of states located on the southern and northern flanks of Europe. An adapted version of the treaty was negotiated in 1999, but final ratification has remained a contentious issue between Russia and the alliance.

The treaty was negotiated on a "non-bloc-to-bloc" basis, but nonetheless reflected the reality of two opposing alliances that still existed when the treaty was originally signed in 1990. Over the years, the foundations for the CFE treaty have crumbled with the demise of the Warsaw Pact, disintegration of the Soviet Union, deterioration of Russian military forces, and the membership of former Warsaw Pact and Soviet republics in NATO. Russia ratified the adapted treaty in July 2004, but NATO countries refused to complete their ratification processes "until Russia fulfills commitments it made to Georgia and Moldova. . . . Specifically, the Kremlin pledged to finish negotiations by the end of 2000 to close Russian military bases on Georgian soil and to remove all of its troops and weaponry from Moldova by the end of 2002. Neither objective has been met."[8] Russia suspended compliance with the treaty in 2007 claiming that the NATO countries' rationale for not ratifying were illegitimate and that NATO's enlargement steps had increased NATO's equipment totals above treaty limits.

Dialogue and Cooperation as a New Mission

As democratic governments emerged from the shadow of communism in Eastern and central Europe at the end of the Cold War, many of the new democracies sought membership in NATO as one of their main national goals. The NATO countries approached these desires carefully, offering the new democracies friendship and cooperation but not initially membership.

Photo 6.2: Secretary General Manfred Woerner played key role in NATO's transformation to post-Cold War institution

Source: NATO Photos.

In July 1991, the Warsaw Pact was dissolved, leaving NATO standing but still in need of greater clarity concerning its future relationship with former members of the Pact. NATO took the first formal step in the November 1991 Rome Declaration, inviting former Warsaw Pact members to join in a more structured relationship of "consultation and cooperation on political and security issues." They created the North Atlantic Cooperation Council (NACC) and invited the foreign ministers of the former Pact countries to the first meeting of the new council in December 1991. When the Soviet Union was dissolved in the same month, the NATO countries immediately invited Russia to join the NACC, and Russia became one of the founding members (for more detailed discussion of NATO's relationship with Russia, see Chapter 7). The main goal of the NACC was to serve as a forum for dialogue among NATO members and nonmember states on a wide range of security topics.[9] Sixteen NATO members and 22 former Warsaw Pact members and former Soviet republics participated in the new body.

The NACC represented a major statement of intent by the allies. They said, in effect, that NATO was not going to remain an exclusive club. Although the allies at that point were reluctant to envision offering NATO membership to former Warsaw Pact members, the creation of the NACC opened the door to that prospect down the road. The East European leaders who wanted their countries to join NATO saw the NACC as totally inadequate for their needs, but they accepted this initial offer and immediately began working for more.[10]

The NACC was essentially the brainchild of US President George H. W. Bush's administration. President Bush and his foreign policy team had played a major role in the process of negotiating German reunification and ensuring that a united Germany would remain a member of NATO. German reunification in effect represented the first expansion of NATO in the post-Cold War era and the first since Spain had been admitted in 1982.

In addition, President Bush made a major contribution to the process of winding down the Cold War by declaring substantial unilateral US reductions in its short-range nuclear forces (discussed in Chapter 8). At the same time, Bush developed and maintained a sympathetic working relationship with Soviet President Mikhail Gorbachev, helping support the transition to a post-communist political system in Russia after the Soviet Union was dissolved.

In 1990, neither the Bush administration nor any of the European allies were prepared to signal publicly their acceptance of the possibility that countries that had just left the Warsaw Pact might in the near future become members of NATO. After all, in 1990 the question was whether NATO remained necessary, not whether its membership should be expanded. Moreover, most European governments, as well as President Bush, were focused primarily on how to ensure that the transition in the Soviet Union and then in Russia would confirm the end of the Cold War and not lead to a new one.

Nevertheless, toward the end of the Bush presidency, senior administration officials began acknowledging that the desires of East European governments to join

NATO were indeed legitimate. Late in 1992, after Bill Clinton had beaten George Bush in the presidential elections, both Secretary of Defense Richard Cheney and Secretary of State Lawrence Eagleburger suggested that the process of opening up NATO that had begun with the NACC could lead toward NATO membership for some NACC partners.[11]

The advent of the Clinton administration was to bring new and dramatic developments to the process of NATO outreach. The George H. W. Bush administration had put the process on track but had not had time to move beyond the relatively limited and "easy" NACC initiative.

From Partnership to Membership

When President Bill Clinton came to office in January 1993, the administration took over without a clear line on the issue of NATO enlargement. Its top priority was the economy, following the political rhetoric ("it's the economy stupid") that had helped pave Clinton's way to the presidency. In the administration's first year, Europe was seen mainly as a problem: the source of economic competition for the United States and the locale for a bloody conflict in Bosnia that would not go away. However, one of the important rituals for any new US president is the first NATO summit. Officials in charge of preparations for President Clinton's inaugural NATO summit, scheduled for January 1994, were not of one mind on NATO's future in general and on enlargement in particular. One high-level National Security Council staffer, Jenonne Walker, had written in 1990 that the United States should pull all its troops out of Europe as an incentive for the Soviet Union to withdraw from Eastern Europe.[12] This official was skeptical that the Clinton administration should promote NATO enlargement and had the task of chairing the initial interdepartmental review of the issue. Strobe Talbot, a close personal friend of the president and leading Russian expert at the Department of State, was concerned that moving too quickly on enlargement would sour prospects for reform in Russia. At the Pentagon, Secretary of Defense Les Aspin and his top officials, including Deputy Assistant Secretary of Defense Joseph Kruzel, were skeptical that the United States and NATO should take on the potential burdens of preparing countries for NATO membership that were so far from meeting NATO military standards.

However, as James M. Goldgeier has documented, two key officials leaned in favor of enlargement: National Security Adviser Tony Lake and President Clinton himself.[13] Clinton had not spent much time or energy on foreign policy issues in the campaign, but one of his campaign themes had emphasized that US foreign policy should be focused on "enlarging" the democratic and free-market area in the post-Cold War world. Both he and Lake apparently came to believe that NATO enlargement would directly serve this end. This approach made Clinton ripe for the message from the new democracies in central Europe, a message that he heard loud and clear when he met with several central European leaders, including Poland's Lech Walesa and the Czech Republic's Vaclav Havel, at the opening of the US Holocaust Memorial

Museum in Washington, D.C., on April 21, 1993. Clinton subsequently reflected on the meeting, saying, "When they came here a few weeks ago for the Holocaust dedication, every one of those presidents said that their number one priority was to get into NATO. They know it will provide a security umbrella for the people who are members." From the Holocaust meetings on, Clinton had an emotional as well as philosophical predisposition toward enlarging NATO.[14] And even if other administration officials favoring enlargement had geostrategic rationales for the move, such as hedging against future Russian power and ensuring continued US prominence in European security affairs, it was the value-based rationale that would tip the balance in convincing the public and members of the US Congress that NATO enlargement was in the US interest.

Even as official policy largely favored deferring a decision on enlargement at the January 1994 summit, some administration officials and others outside the administration were putting together a case for moving ahead. In an assessment for Congress at the end of 1992, I noted the logic of the case for enlargement, writing,

> How can the existing members of Western institutions, who have throughout the Cold War touted the western system, now deny participation in the system to countries that choose democracy, to convert to free market economic systems, respect human rights, and pursue peaceful relations with their neighbors? This suggests the need for creative and flexible attitudes toward countries making credible efforts to meet the criteria for membership.[15]

And in a statement to a special committee of the North Atlantic Assembly in January 1993, I added that "Poland, Hungary and the Czech Republic deserve serious consideration for NATO membership in the near future."[16]

In Europe, German Minister of Defense Volker Rühe became the most outspoken official European proponent of enlargement.[17] Early in 1993, he organized a small conference of US and European experts designed to provide ammunition for his position on Europe's future (at the time, Rühe was considered not only a leading official expert on defense but also a potential candidate for the chancellorship). The conference outside Bonn, Germany, provided some of the initial foundations for Rühe's enlargement position.[18] To augment his resources, Rühe contracted the services of a team from the well-respected US think tank Rand. The Rand analysts— Ronald Asmus, F. Stephen Larrabee, and Richard Kugler—had been developing an advocacy of enlargement based on work they were doing under a contract with the US Army and Air Force. In June 1993, Rühe and the Rand analysts were joined by Republican Senator Richard Lugar (R-Ind.), who became the most forceful of US official proponents of enlargement, arguing for early consideration of the membership desires of Poland, Hungary, and the Czech Republic. The Rand team published a major statement of the case for enlargement in the fall of 1993, providing a key reference point for the coming enlargement debate.[19] Senator Lugar remained a strong supporter of NATO and of enlargement, even though his cool relationship with

Senate Foreign Relations Committee Chairman Jesse Helms prevented Lugar from playing a formal role in the process.

These proponents of enlargement were in a minority in Europe as well as in the United States, but they were not alone. While most of the US foreign policy bureaucracy was working on finessing the enlargement issue at the January 1994 summit, others, including Lynn Davis, undersecretary for arms control and international security affairs, and two key staffers on the Department of State policy planning staff—Stephen Flanagan and Hans Binnendijk—were developing the case for moving enlargement ahead. Both Flanagan and Binnendijk had leaned forward on enlargement in the early 1990s; Davis had close ties to the work of the Rand team.

However, the ship of state changes directions slowly, and the weight of thinking in the bureaucracy and even among the majority of policy-level officials leaned toward deferring the difficult and demanding enlargement issue while continuing to develop ties to the new democracies. As the administration prepared for President Clinton's first NATO summit meeting, the more cautious approach dominated. Secretary of State Warren Christopher observed that NATO enlargement, while possible down the road, was currently "not on the agenda." Deputy Secretary of State Strobe Talbot, with his focus on facilitating Russia's transition to democracy and free markets, reinforced the secretary's cautious inclination.

Meanwhile, US civilian and military officials were searching for a concept to serve as the centerpiece for NATO outreach activities. The concept that developed in collaboration between General John Shalikashvili (the Supreme Allied Commander, Europe), his staff, and senior Pentagon officials, particularly Deputy Secretary of Defense Joseph Kruzel,[20] was premised on the need for aspiring members to meet certain political and military criteria before being considered for membership. The second assumption was that NATO should help such countries become producers, not just consumers, of security. The end result of this thinking was the proposal for the Partnership for Peace (PFP).

The PFP concept was a policymaker's dream. It signaled to those who aspired to NATO membership that they had been heard. Yet it made no commitment concerning the future. Perhaps most crucial, it bought time. It avoided destabilizing relations with Russia at a perilous moment in that country's post-Soviet development. It (temporarily) bridged differences between those in the US administration who favored enlargement and those who were skeptical.

The PFP initiative also served some practical needs. Countries that wanted to join NATO could not expect to do so until they had begun to exchange old Warsaw Pact military systems and habits for those of NATO. Partnership would provide a channel for US and other NATO assistance to aspiring members. And the PFP would serve as a vehicle for aspirants to make contributions to NATO's new role as a regional peacekeeping instrument, potentially spreading burdens among NATO and non-NATO countries.

On the negative side, PFP clearly would not be the end of the story. The central European democracies recognized that, although active engagement in PFP was essential to their longer-term goal of NATO membership, it could also serve as a long-term excuse for NATO to postpone serious consideration of their membership objective (hence the occasionally heard derogatory references to PFP as a "Policy for Postponement"). In addition, as experience would come to show, under PFP scrutiny of their defense reform and modernization, shortcomings could not easily be hidden from their publics or from NATO members.

The Cooperation Track

In any case, at the NATO summit meeting in Brussels in January 1994, allied leaders endorsed the PFP program to give countries that wished to develop a detailed cooperative relationship with NATO the opportunity to do so. The program would provide the possibility for nonmember military leaders and forces to interact with and learn from NATO militaries. This created a formal framework for the development of NATO military outreach activities and, incidentally, began to shape a new mission for NATO military forces. The PFP was destined to become a successful program in its own right, helping reform regimes in central and Eastern Europe accelerate the process of democratization as well as to become NATO compatible.

Because these countries were at a variety of stages of political, economic, and military evolution, US and allied officials knew that a program of association with NATO would have to be sufficiently flexible to accommodate such diversity. The NACC already had provided a forum in which such countries could discuss military security issues with NATO allies. The PFP added a way for individual countries to tailor their relationship with NATO to meet their national needs and circumstances. The PFP sought initially to promote greater transparency in national defense planning and budgeting as a way of building confidence in the peaceful intentions of all participants. It also aimed to encourage effective democratic control of defense forces; to help develop each partner as a potential contributor to NATO-led peacekeeping, search-and-rescue, or humanitarian missions; and to enhance the ability of partners' military forces to operate with NATO units. Each partner was invited to identify the extent and intensity of cooperation it wished to develop within the broad agenda of the program.

Since 1994, some 29 countries have become PFP partners—three graduated to the status of NATO membership in 1999, seven more in 2004, and two in 2009. Most partners have seen their participation as a road to NATO membership. The Czech Republic, Hungary, and Poland used their PFP involvement constructively as a way to strengthen their bid for membership. Albania, Bulgaria, Croatia, Estonia, Latvia, Lithuania, Romania, Slovakia and Slovenia, have followed their example.

In mid-1997, the allies decided to add some new and important elements to the PFP agenda to "enhance" the program. When the Clinton administration proposed the PFP, it could not decide what to do with the NACC, even though it could logically have served as a communal consultative forum to complement the more individualized partnership program. (NATO officials observed that the Clinton administration, perhaps in a "not invented here" mode, wanted to ensure that the focus was on the PFP, not on the NACC, which Clinton officials saw as a Bush administration initiative.[21]) The PFP and the NACC existed in parallel but mostly-separate worlds until the Clinton administration proposed replacing NACC with the Euro-Atlantic Partnership Council (EAPC). The EAPC was formally established by the foreign ministers of NATO and partner nations when they met in Sintra, Portugal, in May 1997.

Also at Sintra, the allies gave partners a much stronger role in developing and deciding on PFP programs. They created the concept of partnership "cells," or units made up of partner military and civilian officials working hand in hand with NATO international and member-state officials. A special Partnership Coordination Cell was established in Mons, Belgium, collocated with NATO's top European command, to coordinate activities directly with the Supreme Allied Commander, Europe, and his staff. Through the new Planning and Review Process (PARP), partner countries that were making contributions to NATO operations, such as those in Kosovo and Bosnia-Herzegovina, could participate more actively in planning and overseeing conduct of such operations. As a result of these changes, the PFP became an important part of the evolving cooperative European security system, even if it was seen as a transitional device by many of its participants.

The EAPC continued as a forum that brought together all NATO allies with all partner countries. The EAPC had 46 members in 2004. The purpose of the EAPC was to serve as the overarching framework for political and security-related consultations and enhanced cooperation under the PFP program. This framework was designed to provide partners the opportunity to develop a direct political relationship with the alliance. It also gave partner governments the chance to participate in decisions related to activities involving NATO and partner nations.

The EAPC meets twice a year at both foreign and defense minister levels and on a more routine basis at the ambassadorial level monthly in Brussels. The EAPC originally adopted the NACC Work Plan for Dialogue, Partnership and Cooperation, which included regular consultations on political and security-related matters, and then enlarged and adapted that agenda. Consultations have come to include a wide range of topics, such as crisis management issues; regional matters; arms control issues; nuclear, biological, and chemical weapons proliferation; international terrorism; defense planning and budgets; defense policy and strategy; and security implications of economic developments. In addition, the agenda covered consultations and cooperation on emergency and disaster preparedness, armaments cooperation, nuclear safety, defense-related environmental issues, civil-military coordination of air traffic management and control, scientific cooperation, and issues related to peace support operations.

The EAPC has been used as a forum for discussions among the allies and partner countries about the situation in the former Yugoslavia, including developments in Bosnia and Herzegovina and the crises in Kosovo and Macedonia, terrorism, and developments in Afghanistan. Under the auspices of the EAPC, a Euro-Atlantic Disaster Response Coordination Center was created in the spring of 1998.

Both allies and partners alike regard the EAPC as an important token of NATO's commitment to openness, cooperation, and extending the benefits of peace and stability to all European nations. However, given the large EAPC membership, formal meetings have consisted largely of set-piece statements by participating governments. This has provided an opportunity for participants to put their national positions on the record but hardly a chance for discussion and dialogue. As with many other international organizations, those opportunities come as part of the "corridor" conversations and informal meetings on the margins of the routine EAPC sessions. The EAPC as an institution, therefore, has played an important informal role but has not become an important factor in NATO's decision-making process.

The Enlargement Track

NATO has expended considerable time and energy developing or supporting a variety of cooperative security arrangements in its relations with nonmembers. But the membership track of NATO's outreach program generated the greatest controversy. The January 1994 Brussels summit deferred decisions on enlargement and put the PFP forward as NATO's premier outreach vehicle, but the allies did agree to keep the membership door open.

The drafters of the North Atlantic Treaty in 1949 anticipated that other European states might subsequently wish to join the alliance. The Treaty's Article 10 said that the allies may, "by unanimous agreement, invite any other European state in a position to further the principles of this Treaty and to contribute to the security of the North Atlantic area to accede to this Treaty." The 12 original members were, over the years, joined by Greece and Turkey (1951), Germany (1955), and then Spain (1982). At the NATO summit meeting in Brussels in January 1994, allied leaders said that the commitment in Article 10 would be honored and that NATO's door would be opened to qualified candidates. The allies began a study in December 1994 of the "why and how" of NATO enlargement.

More important, President Clinton left the Brussels summit apparently ready to move on to the next step, even as those who favored a go-slow approach were reassured that the PFP would buy time and defer tough decisions on enlargement. On a visit to Warsaw in July 1994, interviewed on Polish television, Clinton pushed the issue further down the road, saying,

> I want to make it clear that, in my view, NATO will be expanded, that it should be expanded, and that it should be expanded as a way of strengthening security and not conditioned on events in any other country or some new threat arising to NATO. . . . I think that a timetable should be developed, but I can't do that alone.[22]

Clinton's comments affirmed that NATO should be enlarged because it was the right thing to do. The Warsaw remarks were taken by pro-enlargement officials in Washington as a green light to move ahead.

According to Goldgeier, a number of factors combined to get enlargement on track inside the US administration. These included the appointment as assistant secretary of state for European and Canadian affairs of Richard Holbrooke, who had become an enlargement believer during his time as US ambassador to Germany; the shift of Strobe Talbot from enlargement skeptic to enlargement supporter; and the appointment of several enlargement enthusiasts to key positions on the National Security Council staff, including Alexander (Sandy) Vershbow to direct European affairs and Daniel Fried covering central and Eastern European policy. While the Pentagon remained largely skeptical, administration policy began moving slowly but surely toward an activist enlargement approach.[23]

Meanwhile, the opposition Republicans took control of the US House of Representatives in the fall 1994 midterm elections. The new leaders of the House brought with them a "Contract with America," listing their policy priorities. Perhaps the only priority on which Clinton and the Republicans could agree was the Contract's advocacy of NATO enlargement. The Contract's enlargement position suggested that despite disparate motivations, NATO enlargement might enjoy a fairly wide bipartisan base of support in Congress.

In Brussels, necessary NATO work on enlargement moved ahead. In September 1995, the allies released the "Study on NATO Enlargement," which explained why enlargement was warranted.[24] It also drew out a road map for countries seeking membership to follow on their way to the open door. The report said that enlargement would support NATO's broader goal of enhancing security and extending stability throughout the Euro-Atlantic area. It would support the process of democratization and the establishment of market economic systems in candidate countries. They said that enlargement would threaten no one because NATO would remain a defensive alliance whose fundamental purpose is to preserve peace and provide security to its members.

With regard to the "how" of enlargement, the allies established a framework of principles to follow, including that new members should assume all the rights and responsibilities of current members and accept the policies and procedures in effect at the time of their entry; no country should enter with the goal of closing the door behind it, using its vote as a member to block other candidates; countries should resolve ethnic disputes or external territorial disputes before joining NATO; candidates should be able to contribute to the missions of the alliance; and no country outside the alliance (e.g., Russia) would have the right to interfere with the process. In this area, the report drew on a set of principles, articulated earlier in 1995 by Secretary of Defense William Perry, which had become known as the "Perry Principles," and on further enlargement analyses by the Asmus, Kugler, and Larrabee Rand team under their contract with the German Ministry of Defense.[25]

The NATO allies made clear that one of the key factors influencing readiness for membership would be the applicant country's ability to work within NATO's Integrated Command Structure. NATO military leaders were expected to help applicant countries help themselves prepare for becoming effective military contributors to the alliance, adding another important task to NATO's military mission profile.

During 1996–1997, NATO officials conducted intensified dialogues with 12 countries that had expressed an active interest in NATO membership. The candidacies of all countries were thoroughly examined from a wide range of perspectives. It was clear, however, that the United States would play the decisive role in the question of whom to invite for the first round of enlargement.

Bringing new members into the alliance constitutes an "amendment" to the North Atlantic Treaty and, as such, has to be ratified by all NATO members. On balance, NATO enlargement had not been a hot issue in Congress, but to the extent that there was interest, there was sustained bipartisan support for NATO and for bringing in new members.[26] This support included passage of the NATO Participation Act of 1994 (Title II of P.L. 103–447), which backed NATO enlargement as a way of encouraging development of democratic institutions and free-market structures in the new democracies. The low-intensity but fairly consistent support was a good foundation for the collaboration between the White House and the Senate that would be critical to eventual ratification of any enlargement decision. Meanwhile, the private, nonprofit Committee to Expand NATO was established in 1996 to support the enlargement cause. This group, which involved an impressive collection of corporate leaders, former civilian officials, and retired senior military officers, largely from the ranks of the Republican Party, actively courted congressional support for enlargement and played a major role in the lobbying effort on behalf of the initiative over the next two years.

The United States entered a presidential election year in 1996. Once again, foreign policy was not a big issue in the campaign. On the issue of NATO enlargement, President Clinton and his Republican opponent, Senator Robert Dole, competed mainly to see who could stand closer to the enlargement flagpole. Dole criticized the president for being too attentive to Russia's views—Clinton had worked hard to reassure Russian President Boris Yeltsin that legitimate Russian interests would not be threatened while keeping enlargement moving ahead. But Dole's criticism had virtually no political impact, and most observers saw very little difference between the Republican and Democratic positions on the issue. It was yet another sign of the bipartisan nature of support for bringing new members into NATO, although it certainly did not guarantee that the approach to be taken by the president and the alliance would win the necessary two-thirds majority in the Senate.

The election campaign provided the opportunity for the administration to move ahead decisively. President Yeltsin had survived his reelection campaign in July 1996 and was no longer in imminent danger of being undercut by the US position on enlargement. In September 1996, Clinton called for a NATO summit in 1997 to name the first post-Cold War candidates for NATO membership. In October 1996, Clinton told an audience in Detroit that "by 1999, NATO's 50th anniversary and 10 years after the fall of the Berlin Wall, the first group of countries we invite to join should be full-fledged members of NATO."[27]

The prominent use of the enlargement issue during Clinton's campaign visits to the Midwest—home to many central European immigrant communities—was subsequently cited by opponents of enlargement in the United States and by skeptics in Europe as evidence that the US position was driven primarily by domestic politics. The history of administration policy, as documented by Goldgeier and observed personally by me, suggests a different conclusion. The president's commitment to enlargement grew much more fundamentally out of his acceptance of and belief in fairly basic Wilsonian principles of international relations, promoting peace and stability through inclusive and cooperative relations among democratic states. Ethnic communities in the United States provided important support for both the president and the issue. But had enlargement not made sense in terms of basic US values and interests, it would have withered on the vine despite the enthusiasm of Polish and other central European lobby groups.

By the end of 1996 and Clinton's successful reelection effort, collaboration between the White House and Congress was becoming more serious. The White House was fully aware that if the Senate felt it had not participated directly in the enlargement process, the issue could fail to gain the required two-thirds majority even if two-thirds of the Senate leaned toward enlargement, as appeared to be the case. The administration was sensitive to the fact that President Woodrow Wilson had failed to win US involvement in the League of Nations because he had not made the effort to get the Senate on board. It therefore followed President Harry Truman's strategy for Senate consideration of the North Atlantic Treaty in 1948–1949, a strategy that brought key senators into the process early enough to win their commitment but not too early to complicate the policymaking process prematurely.[28]

As the White House began developing working relationships with critical Capitol Hill staff, a related but more immediate question was which countries should be invited when the NATO "enlargement" summit convened in Madrid, Spain, in July 1997. There was virtually unanimous agreement in the administration and among the European allies that the Czech Republic, Hungary, and Poland were a lock. Only Poland would add significantly to the military strength of the alliance. But these three probably could be sold to the Senate as strategically important and politically acceptable. From Germany's point of view, these three satisfied its desire to move off the "front lines" in central Europe. Being surrounded by NATO members would give Germany a political and military buffer between it and Russia. The United Kingdom preferred to keep the package as small as possible, not being a big fan of the process of enlargement in any case, concerned that too rapid or large an increase in membership would weaken the alliance. However, France, Italy, and some other allies wanted to give enlargement a southern focus as well and favored including Slovenia and Romania in the first tranche. Several members of the Senate, led by Senator Joseph Biden (D-Del.), ranking minority member of the Senate Foreign Relations Committee, and Senator William V. Roth Jr. (R-Del.) favored the inclusion of Slovenia—a small former Yugoslav republic that would add a land bridge between existing NATO territory (Italy) and Hungary.

The Clinton administration decided, despite these senatorial sentiments for Slovenia, that the core package of three candidates would be a sufficient challenge for the process of ratification in the United States as well as for absorption by the alliance. Romania, with an important geostrategic position in southeastern Europe and with substantial military forces, lagged far behind the three core candidates in political and economic development. Slovenia could be kept as a given for the next round. The administration came to an internal consensus on putting just three candidates forward.

Even though intensive discussions had been held at NATO and among NATO allies in preparation for the Madrid meeting, the US choice of three and only three was publicly revealed in a Pentagon press briefing by Secretary of Defense William Cohen in mid-June. Cohen suggested that, as far as the US government was concerned, the case was closed. His assertion was confirmed by the White House, which claimed that a NATO decision had been made, but in fact NATO consultations had not been completed. The way the United States appeared to close the door to further discussion stunned the allies and was instantly interpreted by the French and others as just one more sign of hegemonic US behavior. The United States had always been "first among equals" in NATO, where decisions are taken by consensus but where US preferences almost always carried the day. Nonetheless, the allies resented what seemed to them a cavalier US approach to the consultation process.

The challenge for the Clinton administration and for US administrations before and after was to be a hegemon without acting like one. The administration had made the mistake of acting like one. The Madrid meeting endorsed the US preference, but not without significant grumbling by French President Jacques Chirac and others. The allies found much to complain about, including the fact that the United States wanted seats in the session for US senators who had been brought along with the US summit delegation to help ensure a favorable ratification process.

At Madrid, to help smooth the many feathers ruffled by US actions, other candidate states were encouraged to continue to work toward eventual membership by following the guidelines laid out in the "Study on NATO Enlargement" and developing bilateral cooperation with NATO through the PFP program. The allies reaffirmed their commitment to the open-door policy in which all European countries meeting the conditions of Article 10 and the guidelines of the study could be considered for eventual membership.

The next task for NATO was to negotiate the terms of entry with the candidate states. The Clinton administration, however, had its own challenging task: to convince at least two-thirds of the members of the Senate that NATO enlargement was in the US interest. The administration had already begun preparing the ground. A respected former Clinton White House aide and expert on congressional-executive relations, Jeremy Rosner, was brought back to serve as coordinator of the ratification process with both a State Department position and staff and the status of special adviser to the president. The administration had been wise to include senators in the Madrid delegation, but now the serious lobbying work would begin.

In the Senate, the Committee on Foreign Relations, chaired by arch-conservative Jesse Helms, would have primary jurisdiction over the legislation, with the Senate

Committee on Armed Services playing an important advisory role. Senate Majority Leader Trent Lott (R-Miss.) had already created the Senate NATO Observer Group, chaired by Senators Biden and Roth, designed to help manage the process in support of the Senate's advice and consent role.

In the summer of 1997, even though it appeared that Rosner and his administration team were starting with a good core of support in the Senate, they would need a strong lobbying effort to ensure final victory. In the course of a luncheon meeting in August hosted by a Scandinavian embassy officer, Rosner and I had a few moments to discuss his challenge. I said that I presumed that President Clinton would be personally involved in the lobbying effort. Rosner assured me that, in the coming months, the president would invite senators to the White House for dinners and private meetings focused on lining up the required votes. However, despite the fact that Clinton had played an important part in getting NATO enlargement on the US and NATO agenda, the fall of 1997 and spring of 1998 found him increasingly captured by impeachment proceedings against him in Congress. He never conducted the lobbying dinners and meetings Rosner had expected. At the numerous official events marking various stages of the ratification process, the president was present and involved, but one had to wonder whether his mind was not on other problems.[29]

Opponents of enlargement in the United States, right up until the Senate vote on April 30, 1998, complained that the issue had not been given the kind of serious attention that was warranted by such an important national commitment. It is true that the issue did not set the public on fire. Public opinion polls showed broad but somewhat shallow support for enlargement. The positive numbers seemed to reflect the public's positive image of NATO and of the idea that the US approach to international cooperation should be inclusive. However, a large percentage of those queried in polls showed a lack of basic knowledge about what was going on. For example, a large number of respondents in some polls believed that Russia was already a NATO member.[30]

The debate that did rage on editorial and op-ed pages of major American newspapers was largely among the academic and policy elite and was not of great interest to the American public. On the other hand, most foreign policy issues, such as NATO enlargement, are debated and decided largely by the elite public. The public at large is moved to action and involvement only by more headline-making events, particularly those with imminent life-or-death consequences.

In the deliberative body that had to debate and decide the issue, however, there was a thorough and serious process of consideration[31] in keeping with the Senate's role as a "partner" to the transatlantic bargain. Despite the president's "absence" from the process,[32] the work of the NATO Observer Group moved into high gear in close collaboration with the administration. The process relied heavily on teamwork between Rosner and key Senate staffers, particularly Senate Foreign Relations Committee staffer Steve Biegen, Ian Brzezinski, who worked for Senator Roth, and Michael Haltzel from Senator Biden's staff. Other staffers, including Ken Myers of Senator Lugar's staff and David Stevens, who worked for Senator Jon Kyl (R-Ariz.), played key roles in the period leading up to the Senate debate.

The Senate NATO Observer Group, almost completely out of public view, organized a steady stream of classified and unclassified briefings and meetings in the course of 1997–1998. Some of these sessions were intended largely for administration officials to communicate information to Senate staff. Others provided the opportunity for members to meet with senior NATO-nation military officials. One critical session of the NATO Observer Group brought senators together with the foreign ministers of the candidate countries. The meeting appeared to be a turning point for at least one senator who had been skeptical about enlargement. Senator Kay Bailey Hutchison (R-Tex.) had profound concerns about the plan and engaged deeply in the issue, asking her staff, with the help of the Congressional Research Service, to research a number of enlargement issues. At the session with the candidate country foreign ministers, however, it became clear to this observer that Senator Hutchison's feeling of respect and admiration for the accomplishments of the three new democracies would likely bring her into the "yea" column. It did. The Senate Committee on Foreign Relations held a series of public hearings in October and November 1997 in which both supporters and opponents of enlargement were invited to address the committee.[33] Proponents and critics of enlargement in the Senate engaged their staffs in investigation of major issues, calling in a wide range of outside experts to brief senators and staff and engaging hundreds of hours of support from Congressional Research Service analysts.

One of the most sensitive challenges for Jeremy Rosner and other administration officials was to hold together a coalition of Senate supporters and potential supporters who were motivated by substantially different assumptions and objectives. Supporters ranged from conservative Republicans to liberal Democrats. Senator Helms and a few other conservative Republican senators saw NATO enlargement first and foremost as an insurance policy against a resurgent Russia laying claim once again to the sovereignty of central and East European states. Helms was particularly interested in how the administration saw the future of NATO-Russia relations. In the process of introducing Secretary of State Madeleine Albright at the committee's opening enlargement hearing, Helms cautioned, "NATO's relations with Russia must be restrained by the reality that Russia's future commitment to peace and democracy, as of this date, is far from certain. In fact, I confess a fear that the United States' overture toward Russia may have already gone a bit far."[34]

In addition, many senators had not signed off on the "new NATO" (in which members cooperated to deal with new security challenges, including peace operations in the Balkans) and still believed that the "old NATO" (focused primarily on Article 5, the commitment to assist a fellow member that has come under attack) was what was still needed. On the other hand, some senators found the old NATO to be of decreasing relevance and were more interested in the idea of expanding the number of democratic states that could help deal with new security challenges in and beyond Europe. Others (e.g., Senator Barbara Mikulski, D-Md.) were motivated most strongly by the fact that Poland, the Czech Republic, and Hungary had thrown off communism and committed themselves to a democratic path. How, such proponents asked, could they be denied membership in the Western system, of which NATO was a core part?

The Senate opponents of enlargement were also all over the map politically and philosophically. Senator John Warner (R-Va.) became one of the most severe critics of enlargement. He believed that too many members would make the alliance impossible to manage and would doom it to future irrelevance because it would be unable to make timely consensual decisions with 19-plus members. Senator Warner's attempt to impose a formal pause on the enlargement process was rejected, but a number of senators who voted for enlargement voted with Warner in favor of a pause. Some 41 senators voted for the Warner amendment, enough to block a two-thirds majority of the Senate for the next candidate(s) if they were all to vote against. The most strongly committed enlargement opponent, Senator John Ashcroft (R-Mo.), simply believed that the United States was already overburdened and that NATO enlargement would perpetuate a responsibility that had long ago outlived its utility. Among the opponents, Ashcroft's position came closest to representing a neo-isolationist stance. His perspective related in part to concerns about the potential cost of NATO enlargement. The cost question promised at one point to be the most difficult of issues in the Senate debate. However, conflicting and confusing estimates of the cost blurred the issue and made it a virtual nonfactor in the final debate. Ashcroft's attempt to amend the resolution of ratification to mandate a narrow interpretation of NATO's future mission was defeated through deft parliamentary procedures on the Senate floor. Instead, the Senate passed an amendment offered by Senator Jon Kyl (R-Ariz.) that affirmed the continuing importance of NATO's collective defense role while allowing that NATO now had utility in non-Article 5 missions as well.

The other main school of thought motivating opponents of enlargement was concern about the impact on relations with Russia. George Kennan, the highly respected Russia expert who played a major role in developing the US containment strategy toward the Soviet Union, had opined[35] that NATO enlargement would be a disaster for US-Russian relations, and some members, including Senators Paul Wellstone (D-Minn.) and Patrick Leahy (D-Vt.), cast their votes against enlargement largely on the basis of Kennan's warning.[36] Another opponent, Senator Daniel Patrick Moynihan (D-N.Y.), argued that the European Union, not NATO, should take the lead in including the new democracies in Western institutions. After several abortive attempts to organize a debate and final vote in the Senate, Senator Lott devoted the entire day of April 30 to the enlargement issue. The opponents, led by Senators Warner, Robert Smith (R-N.H.), Moynihan, Ashcroft, and Wellstone, put on a strong show of their concerns. Because Senator Helms was not well, Senator Biden managed the bill for the Senate Foreign Relations Committee with single-minded energy and enthusiasm that left some of his democratic colleagues standing impatiently waiting to be given the floor. Several senators made impressive contributions to the advocate's side, including Mikulski, Joseph Lieberman (D-Conn.), and Gordon Smith (R-Ore.).

The decisive vote was taken late that evening. At the suggestion of Senator Robert Byrd (D-W.Va.) in his role as the unofficial guardian of the procedures and practices of the Senate, all senators took their seats and then rose when called to deliver their "yea" or "nay" vote. Byrd suggested that "the Senate would make a much better impression . . . [if senators would] learn to sit in their seats to answer the roll-call . . . [rather than] what we have been accustomed to seeing down here in the well, which looks like the floor of a stock market."[37] The Senate, with 99 of its 100 members seated with the decorum requested by Senator Byrd, voted 80 to 19 to give the Senate's advice and consent to ratification of the membership of Poland, the Czech Republic, and Hungary in NATO.

The missing vote was that of Senator Kyl, an enlargement supporter who left Washington on an official overseas trip a few hours before the vote was taken, reassured that his side would win by a clear margin. After observing the daylong drama from the floor of the Senate, I walked out of the Capitol into a pleasant Washington night feeling that I had witnessed an historic event. That impression had been enhanced by the sight of the entire Senate seated in the chamber, thanks to Senator Byrd. Although enlargement supporters managed to beat back all potential "killer" amendments, the number of votes attracted by Senator Warner's proposed "pause" in the enlargement process reflected an important sentiment. Few enlargement advocates were anxious to take on a new round in the near future. Even Jeremy Rosner, who had dedicated so much time and energy to NATO enlargement, judged that the system would not be able to support another round until the first candidates had demonstrated their successful entry into the NATO system.[38]

Some enlargement proponents, however, thought it was important to keep the process moving ahead. The first package had left aside Slovenia, a small but relatively attractive candidate. Senator William V. Roth Jr., one of the leading forces behind the enlargement process, argued that the process should "be carefully paced, not paused." In a special report for the North Atlantic Assembly (now the NATO Parliamentary Assembly) in September 1998, for which the author was rapporteur, Roth proposed that when the allies met in Washington in 1999 to celebrate NATO's fiftieth anniversary, "Slovenia should be invited to begin negotiations aimed at accession to the North Atlantic Treaty. In addition to reflecting Slovenia's preparedness for membership, the invitation would demonstrate that the enlargement door remains open without overloading the enlargement process."[39] Senator Roth's advocacy was considered by, and had some supporters in, the Clinton administration. But the administration ultimately decided that it was too early to move ahead with new candidates. That step was left for the next US administration to handle.

Seen more than a decade later, the US debate on the first round of post-Cold War NATO enlargement was, in effect, a legislative referendum on the future of the alliance. The decision, contested though it was, nonetheless constituted a vote by the United States for NATO's continuing importance. It affirmed and strengthened the transatlantic bargain's important new role of helping emerging European democracies find their way in the world free from control by their large neighbor to the East.

The European allies were relieved that the United States did not want to push ahead immediately with another round of enlargement. The strongest European proponent of enlargement, Germany, accomplished its main objectives with the accession of the first three candidates. It no longer stood on NATO's front lines looking east, and it no longer manifested such great enthusiasm for the enlargement process. Most of the other allies did not look forward to negotiating the next round, in which the potential candidates would likely include one or more of the three Baltic states—former Soviet republics whose NATO membership Moscow strongly opposed.

At the fiftieth-anniversary NATO summit in Washington on April 23–25, 1999, all aspiring candidates for NATO membership were given some cause for hope, even though Slovenia was left standing outside the door. The leaders pledged that "NATO will continue to welcome new members in a position to further the principles of the Treaty and contribute to peace and security in the Euro-Atlantic area." The allies created the Membership Action Plan (MAP), which promised cooperation beyond possibilities in the PFP and, perhaps more important, feedback from NATO concerning their progress toward membership. Nine aspirants—Albania, Bulgaria, Estonia, Latvia, Lithuania, Romania, Slovakia, Slovenia, and the Former Yugoslav Republic of Macedonia—initially signed up for the program. These nine were promised that NATO would formally review the enlargement process again no later than 2002.

According to NATO, "The MAP gives substance to NATO's commitment to keep its door open. However, participation in the MAP does not guarantee future membership, nor does the Plan consist simply of a checklist for aspiring countries to fulfill." What MAP did do, however, was to provide "concrete feedback and advice from NATO to aspiring countries on their own preparations directed at achieving future membership." The MAP did not substitute for full participation in NATO's PFP Planning and Review Process, which, in NATO's view, "is essential because it allows aspirant countries to develop interoperability with NATO forces and to prepare their force structures and capabilities for possible future membership."[40]

In 2000, with the United States preparing to elect its next president—the man who would make the next critical decisions on enlargement—the nine candidate states joined together in support of a "big bang" approach to enlargement. Meeting in Vilnius, Lithuania, the nine foreign ministers pledged that their countries would work for entry in NATO as a group rather than compete against each other for a favored position in 2002. Both major presidential candidates in the United States, Vice President Al Gore and Texas Governor George W. Bush, sent letters of support to the session.[41]

With his close victory in the November 2000 election, it was Bush who would take on the challenge of leading the alliance toward its enlargement decision, as promised, in Prague in November 2002.

Moving toward the Second Enlargement Round

The Bush administration and the NATO allies faced a number of issues as they confronted the next enlargement decision. They included several questions that played into the first enlargement debate and some others that were created by specific circumstances surrounding the next batch of candidates. The issues included the following:

1. Had the first round of enlargement (with the Czech Republic, Hungary, and Poland) proceeded successfully enough to warrant a second round? Did short-comings in military reform and defense improvements of the three new mem-bers suggest that leverage on candidate states disappears when they become members?
2. Did the increase to 19 members have any discernible effect on NATO's decision-making ability? Is there a magic number beyond which NATO's consensus-based deliberative process will become unworkable?
3. If countries that do not fully meet the military guidelines for membership laid out in the NATO enlargement study[42] are nonetheless invited to join, does this imply that NATO is becoming "more political," making military capabilities of potential members less relevant?
4. What are the likely consequences for relations with Russia of various possible enlargement scenarios?
5. How would further enlargement interact with other policy initiatives, for exam-ple, the Bush administration's attempt to develop a collaborative approach with Moscow on nuclear missile reductions and ballistic missile defenses?
6. Can the financial costs of the next enlargement be kept reasonable and shared effectively?
7. Would senators be more wary of extending defense commitments to additional, less familiar countries than they were for the first three candidates?[43]
8. How should further NATO enlargement be linked to the process of EU enlarge-ment, given that several leading candidates for NATO enlargement were headed for EU membership?
9. Should enlargement be linked in any way to the process of further reforming NATO to make it more relevant to the war on terrorism?[44]
10. Will membership of the Baltic states in NATO and a closer NATO-Russia rela-tionship lead Finland and Sweden to seek membership? If they do, will Austria and Ireland, the other two of four formerly neutral EU members, follow?

In a speech in Warsaw on June 15, 2001, President George W. Bush outlined his vision of a Europe" whole, free, and at peace "and said that all new European democ-racies, "from the Baltic to the Black Sea and all that lie between," should be able to join European institutions, especially NATO. Bush's declaration opened the way for a second enlargement round—one that might have been expected to be controversial but which turned out to be far less contentious than the first one.

Before the September 11, 2001, terrorist attacks, political interest in and support for NATO's second enlargement round could not be compared to that for the first round. President Bush said that his administration was a strong supporter of NATO enlargement. But the administration had no eager European partner on this issue. Germany, the key European architect of the first round, had less of a strategic stake in the next stages and, until late in 2001, had been reluctant to upset Moscow.

In the wake of the terrorist attacks on the United States, some observers questioned the wisdom of moving ahead with NATO enlargement. However, within a few months of the attacks it appeared that a consensus was growing in favor of a major enlargement initiative when allied leaders met in Prague, the Czech Republic, in November 2002.

According to a study by the Brookings Institution released late in 2001,

> ... the case for enlargement ... is stronger than before. Enlargement will contribute to the process of integration that has helped stabilize Europe over the past fifty years and promote the development of strong new allies in the war on terrorism. ... Far from backing away from NATO enlargement, the Bush administration should welcome all those European democracies whose political stability, military contributions, and commitment to NATO solidarity would be assets to the Alliance. Now more than ever, Alliance leaders can and should pursue a wider, integrated NATO and a strong and cooperative relationship with Russia at the same time.[45]

As it turned out, the track record of the three countries in the first round, while not perfect, did not hurt prospects for the second. Predictions of opponents that enlargement would be expensive for the United States, other NATO states, and the candidates never materialized. The military performance of the new members was mixed: Poland was seen as having done quite well in modernizing its forces, and Hungary and the Czech Republic less so. But all three were generally judged to have made contributions to stability in Europe and to the war on terror and other security challenges.[46]

The credentials of the nine candidates (countries participating in the Membership Assistance Plan: Albania, Bulgaria, Estonia, Former Yugoslav Republic of Macedonia, Latvia, Lithuania, Romania, Slovakia, and Slovenia) were uneven, measured against the standards set in the 1995 NATO Enlargement Study.[47] In the end, neither Albania nor Macedonia was deemed ready for membership. Slovenia, a small country that almost made it into the first round, was judged to be the strongest candidate, at least in terms of how far its democracy and reform of its military establishment had progressed. Slovakia had removed a potential question mark about the development of its democracy when elections in September 2002 supported continued democratic reform in the country. Romania and Bulgaria had large military establishments that had a long way to go to meet NATO standards, but southern NATO allies (Italy, Greece, and Turkey) supported their accession. NATO's northern European members advocated membership for the three Baltic states: Estonia, Latvia, and Lithuania. Russia's potential reaction remained the main concern about membership for these candidates.

Because the Bush administration had offered US support for a "big bang" enlargement, the path became relatively clear for the seven leading candidates. The Republican-controlled Congress fell in behind the president. In October 2002, the House of Representatives passed by an overwhelming margin of 358–9 H. Res. 468 strongly supporting NATO membership for the group of seven.[48] When the NATO leaders met at Prague in November 2002, membership invitations were issued to these leading candidates. The enlargement process had originally been expected to be the main focus of the meeting. For the seven countries it undoubtedly was. For the alliance overall, however, the process of adapting the alliance to the new challenges posed by terrorism and NATO's emerging role beyond Europe (see discussion in Chapter 8) became the big news out of Prague. The ratification process went smoothly, with virtually no controversy or debate in the US Senate or in other NATO countries. By March 29, 2004, all 19 current and the seven prospective members of the alliance had deposited their instruments of ratification with the United States government, and the alliance had grown to 26 members.

This process left five potential candidates in the alliance waiting room. Albania, Croatia and the Former Yugoslav Republic of Macedonia appeared likely to qualify for membership in the not-too-distant future. Albania and Croatia joined in 2009, and Macedonia was on track to join except for the fact that it had not been able to resolve the issue of its formal name. Greece, which must approve Macedonia's membership along with all other allies, objected to the use of "Macedonia" because it believes its neighbor's use of the name would imply claims on the adjoining Greek province by the same name.

Two former Soviet republics stood out as issues, inside their countries, in relations with Moscow, and among the NATO allies. The Government of Georgia, under President Mikheil Saakhashvili, had for several years lobbied and worked hard for an invitation to join NATO, and had found supporters in the Bush administration and among Members of Congress. The situation in Ukraine was less clear, as public support for joining NATO remained very weak, in spite of the fact that President Viktor Yushchenko, who had come to power following the pro-western 2004 "orange revolution," strongly supported joining. President Bush, visiting Kiev on April 1, 2008, on his way to a NATO summit meeting in Bucharest, Romania, unconditionally advocated offering both Georgia and Ukraine membership action plans (MAP) to put them on the path to NATO membership. Bush told reporters "I strongly believe that Ukraine and Georgia should be given MAP, and there are no tradeoffs – period."[49] Both countries had contributed troops to the war in Iraq and Bush's support for their NATO membership goal was widely seen as a reward for their contributions.

Russia, for its part, had made it clear for some time that it strongly objected to either of these countries joining NATO (see more on this in Chapter 7). Moscow's strong stance had support within NATO going into the Bucharest summit, as both France and Germany opposed pushing these two countries ahead at that point. As a result, there was no consensus at Bucharest to offer MAP status to Georgia and Ukraine, but the reluctant European allies conceded a point of principle to the Bush administration: in their final communiqué the Euro-Atlantic leaders declared

"NATO welcomes Ukraine's and Georgia's Euro-Atlantic aspirations for membership in NATO. We agreed today that these countries will become members of NATO."[50] This somewhat-surprising declaration that NATO membership for Ukraine and Georgia was inevitable was the last major contribution by the Bush administration to the process of NATO enlargement, and one that may come back to haunt the alliance in the future.

Table 6.1: Participation in Euro-Atlantic Security Institutions (2009)

NATO: North Atlantic Treaty Organization
EAPC: [NATO] Euro-Atlantic Partnership Council
PFP: [NATO] Partnership for Peace
EU: European Union
OSCE: Organization for Security and Cooperation in Europe

	NATO	EAPC	PFP	EU	OSCE		NATO	EAPC	PFP	EU	OSCE
Albania	*	*	*		*	United Kingdom	*	*	*	*	*
Belgium	*	*	*	*	*	United States	*	*	*		*
Bulgaria	*	*	*	*	*	Austria		*	*	*	*
Canada	*	*	*		*	Cyprus				*	*
Croatia	*	*	*		*	Finland		*	*	*	*
Czech Republic	*	*	*	*	*	Ireland		*	*	*	*
Denmark	*	*	*	*	*	Malta		*	*	*	*
Estonia	*	*	*	*	*	Sweden		*	*		*
France	*	*	*	*	*	Switzerland		*	*		*
Germany	*	*	*	*	*	Armenia		*	*		*
Greece	*	*	*	*	*	Azerbaijan		*	*		*
Hungary	*	*	*	*	*	Belarus		*	*		*
Iceland	*	*	*		*	Bosnia-Herzegovina		*	*		*
Italy	*	*	*	*	*	F.Y.R. Macedonia		*	*		*
Latvia	*	*	*	*	*	Georgia		*	*		*
Lithuania	*	*	*	*	*	Kazakhstan		*	*		*
Luxembourg	*	*	*	*	*	Kyrgyz Republic		*	*		*
Netherlands	*	*	*	*	*	Moldova		*	*		*
Norway	*	*	*		*	Montenegro		*	*		*
Poland	*	*	*	*	*	Russian Federation		*	*		*
Portugal	*	*	*	*	*	Serbia		*	*		*
Romania	*	*	*	*	*	Tajikistan		*	*		*
Slovak Republic	*	*	*	*	*	Turkmenistan		*	*		*
Slovenia	*	*	*	*	*	Ukraine		*	*		*
Spain	*	*	*	*	*	Uzbekistan		*	*		*
Turkey	*	*	*		*	Others**					*

* = Member
** = Andorra, the Holy See, Liechtenstein, Monaco and San Marino.

In sum, NATO has remained true to the pledge its members made in the mid-1990s to continue to expand its membership to qualified European states and develop cooperation with other European and Mediterranean countries. The 2009 addition of Albania and Croatia will not be the end of the enlargement process, and the former Yugoslav Republic of Macedonia will join as soon as the name issue can be resolved with Greece. At least a few other European countries probably will join in the years ahead. The continued process of stabilizing the Balkans could lead eventually to membership for Montenegro and, at some point, even former-adversary Serbia. As for EU members Austria, Finland, Sweden and Ireland, the US-European and internal European divisions over Iraq provided additional reasons for these countries not to apply for NATO membership, but those attitudes will likely fade with time. More threatening Russian behavior could bring the issue to the fore particularly in Finland and Sweden. In the meantime, partnerships with NATO provide a way for countries to participate in NATO programs at a time when membership might not be an option as well as helping those who seek membership to get prepared to apply.

NATO's Outreach to Mediterranean and Middle Eastern Countries

The North Atlantic Treaty Organization has always had a Mediterranean face, but since the end of the Cold War the members have tried to reach out more actively to non-NATO members in the region. NATO's efforts paralleled similar efforts by the European Union (the so-called "Barcelona Process") and the Organization for Security and Cooperation in Europe's Mediterranean Initiative to develop cooperation with the increasingly important states in the Mediterranean region. NATO opened a "dialogue" with five Mediterranean countries— Egypt, Israel, Mauritania, Morocco, and Tunisia—in 1994. Jordan joined the dialogue in 1995 and Algeria in 2000, bringing the membership to seven. The original goal was to make NATO more transparent to Mediterranean countries and to promote understanding and cooperation. Most activities have been relatively low-key and noncontroversial, but have built up a fairly impressive record of programs and activities over the years.[51] Going beyond meetings and training activities, Mediterranean Dialogue countries contributed military forces to NATO's peacekeeping operations in Bosnia and Herzegovina and Kosovo. At their summit meeting in Istanbul in June 2004, NATO leaders agreed to develop a more ambitious agenda aimed at elevating the Mediterranean Dialogue to a "genuine partnership" with the goals of: enhancing the existing political dialogue; achieving interoperability [of defense systems]; developing defense reform; contributing to the fight against terrorism.[52]

The explicit inclusion of the goal of fighting terrorism carried the Mediterranean Dialogue well beyond its modest beginnings and into the midst of NATO's current security concerns. Going beyond the initiative, the NATO leaders at Istanbul approved the "Istanbul Cooperation Initiative" aimed at the broader Middle East region. According to the NATO official responsible for the public diplomacy aspects of the initiative and the Mediterranean Dialogue, the program is aimed at cooperative activities where NATO can provide "value added," including defense reform, budgeting and planning, military-to-military cooperation and training, and steps to deal with terrorist threats and proliferation of weapons of mass destruction. The initial focus of the program was on members of the Gulf Cooperation Council: Bahrain, Kuwait, Oman, Qatar, Saudi Arabia, and the United Arab Emirates. Of this group, only Saudi Arabia has not joined the initiative. According to NATO, the initiative is "open to all interested countries in the broader Middle East who subscribe to its aims and content, including combating terrorism and the proliferation of weapons of mass destruction. Indeed, to be successful, it requires their engagement."[53]

NATO's initiatives in this region will not solve the problems in the Middle East that pose threats to US and European security. It is another sign, however, that the purposes of the transatlantic bargain now stretch well beyond Europe's borders. Already, military officers from Mediterranean Dialogue and Istanbul Initiative states join in classes at the NATO College in Rome, helping increase their familiarity with the nature and missions of the alliance, gradually providing a foundation for further cooperation down the road.

Relations with Non-European Democracies

With NATO in the midst of a difficult and demanding mission in Afghanistan, pressures developed for expanding the partnership concept well beyond any geographic limits to include any and all democratic nations. In 2005–2006 the Bush administration promoted the global partnership concept and some American analysts suggested that this process should go beyond partnership to include possible membership for countries like Australia, Brazil, Japan, India, New Zealand, South Africa, and South Korea.[54] Advocates included Ivo Daalder, who became the Obama administration's first designated Permanent Representative to NATO. The argument was that such states were making important contributions to NATO missions, particularly in Afghanistan, and deserved a seat at the decision-making table. Most European allies have doubts about the wisdom of this proposal, and it remains unclear whether or not the Obama administration will place a high priority on it. The idea was vigorously promoted by the Bush administration, as one aspect of the administration's desire to promote democracy around the globe, and that fact probably still prejudices consideration of the issues raised by the concept.[55]

However, the question of whether and how to link up with democratic states that contribute to international security missions will not likely go away, and has been a contentious issue in the shaping of NATO's new strategic concept. The split in the alliance on this question suggests that such states could, at least in the near term, be offered meaningful "global partnerships" rather than full membership. This could involve, as some have recommended, creating a "Global Partnership Council" bringing together representatives of NATO countries and "like-minded" states beyond the North American, European, and Mediterranean regions to discuss operations in which those countries participate as well as future security objectives and concerns.

This issue is part of the larger question discussed in Chapter 12 of whether today's NATO remains necessary but is becoming insufficient for the security requirements of its members.

Net Assessment

The 20-year process of opening NATO membership to former Warsaw Pact states, former Soviet republics, and other European states that sought such membership and met the conditions for joining has made a major contribution to the stability, well-being, and democratization of Europe. The requirement in the 1995 NATO Enlargement Study for aspiring members to establish democratic civilian control over the military, and NATO's assistance to partners in this area, has been a significant factor in the democratization process for many of Europe's new democracies. For many countries, the process has operated hand-in-hand with that of enlarging the membership of the European Union, another major contributor to the goal of making Europe "whole and free." EU membership stood at 27 in 2009 following the accession of Romania and Bulgaria in 2007 (see Table 6.1).

During the Bush administration, countries were moved toward NATO membership in many cases to reward their governments for support for controversial US policies, most notably the war in Iraq. During the Iraq war debate, the new NATO states and those aspiring to membership generally lined up behind the United States. Two of the original new members – Poland and the Czech Republic – controversially agreed to host key components of a missile defense system that the administration planned to counter future threats from Iranian missiles.

A few of the candidates admitted in the past decade have been reasonably well-prepared to join, although several would not have measured up to strict adherence to the terms of the NATO Enlargement Study. The Bush administration had no difficulty selling enlargement to the Congress, as it controlled both the Senate and House during the key enlargement decisions. It ran into trouble only when it attempted to move Georgia and Ukraine toward membership, and that trouble was mainly with the allies, not the Congress.

So far, enlargement has not brought NATO decision-making to a standstill, although the consensus-building process requires more complex and time-consuming diplomacy. Enlargement has not cost the United States or other "old" members large sums of money, and the new states have been willing, albeit small, contributors to NATO operations.

The major challenge, however, remains dealing with Russian reactions to NATO and its enlargement process. There is no new "cold war" between Russia and the NATO nations, in spite of many points of difference. However, there also is only limited common ground between Moscow and the NATO countries regarding how to manage future European security issues. The next chapter discusses in more detail this particular challenge for the allies.

Notes

1. Elizabeth Pond, *The Rebirth of Europe* (Washington, D.C.: Brookings Institution Press, 1999), 56, 57.
2. Speech by Guyla Horn, Hungarian foreign minister, at the meeting of the Hungarian Society of Political Sciences, Budapest, February 20, 1990.
3. For a variety of perspectives on the process by which Germany's was reunified, particularly the role of the United States, see Stephen F. Szabo, *The Diplomacy of German Unification* (New York: St. Martin's, 1992); Philip Zelikow and Condoleezza Rice, *Germany Unified and Europe Transformed: A Study in Statecraft* (Cambridge, Mass.: Harvard University Press, 1995); James A. Baker, *The Politics of Diplomacy: Revolution, War and Peace, 1989–1992* (New York: G. P. Putnam's, 1995); George Bush and Brent Scowcroft, *A World Transformed* (New York: Knopf, 1998); Hans-Dietrich Genscher, *Rebuilding a House Divided* (New York: Broadway Books, 1998); and Alexander Moens, "American Diplomacy and German Unification," *Survival* 33 (November–December 1991): 531–45.
4. Woerner, a German Christian Democrat and former West German defense minister, played an important creative role in the process of adapting NATO to the new international circumstances.
5. North Atlantic Council, London Declaration on a Transformed North Atlantic Alliance, July 6, 1990.
6. For an excellent, thoroughly documented account of NATO's transformation in the 1990s, see David S. Yost, *NATO Transformed: The Alliance's New Roles in International Security* (Washington, D.C.: United States Institute of Peace Press, 1998).
7. Originally referred to as a "Common European Security and Defense Policy (CESDP)." The EU members dropped the "Common" in 2001.
8. Wade Boese, "Dispute over Russian Withdrawals from Georgia, Moldova Stall CFE Treaty," *Arms Control Today*, September 2004.
9. David Yost has documented the fact that France was the only NATO ally to have serious reservations about the NACC. According to Yost, "The French had two preoccupations in this regard: resisting the tendency to give more substantial content to NACC activities, which might increasingly compete with those of the CSCE and maintaining coherence with the Alliance participation policy they had pursued since 1966." It is also evident that France's Socialist President François Mitterrand did not want to strengthen NATO's position in post-Cold War Europe at a time when other options might better suit French preferences. See David S. Yost, *NATO Transformed: The Alliance's New Roles in International Security* (Washington, D.C.: United States Institute of Peace Press, 1998), 95–96.
10. In the fall of 1990, on one my lectures at the NATO College in Rome, I served on a panel with a West European security expert and a Polish professor to discuss the future of NATO. The Polish panelist urged that the NATO countries take

Polish pleas seriously, while the West European judged that the question of membership in NATO was many years away from serious consideration. Sympathetic to the Polish case, the best I could do was to suggest that Poland be patient and that the logic of their case would bring them through.

11. James M. Goldgeier, *Not Whether but When: The U.S. Decision to Enlarge NATO* (Washington, D.C.: Brookings Institution Press, 1999). Goldgeier's account of the enlargement decision-making process in the Clinton administration is an insightful look at the US decision-making process that led to the entry of the Czech Republic, Hungary, and Poland into the alliance.

12. Jenonne Walker, "U.S., Soviet Troops: Pull Them All Out," *New York Times*, March 18, 1990, E19.

13. Goldgeier, *Not Whether but When*, 23–24. Goldgeier reports that at the first meeting of the interagency working group formed to prepare for Clinton's first NATO summit in January 1994, "Walker announced that there were two people in the White House who thought NATO expansion was a good idea—Bill Clinton and Tony Lake."

14. Goldgeier, *Not Whether but When*, 20.

15. Late in 1992, within constraints imposed by the Congressional Research Service mandate to produce "objective and non-partisan" analyses, I anticipated the issue facing the new administration:

> The goals of supporting democracy, the development of free market economies, and the observance of human rights probably will be served best by an inclusive rather than an exclusive approach to participation in components of a new European security system. In spite of the complications involved, inclusion may have to be the rule; exclusion the exception. How can the existing members of Western institutions, who have throughout the Cold War touted the western system, now deny participation in the system to countries that choose democracy, attempt to convert to free market economic systems, respect human rights, and pursue peaceful relations with their neighbors? This suggests the need for creative and flexible attitudes toward countries making credible efforts to meet the criteria for membership. Stanley R. Sloan, "The Future of U.S.-European Security Cooperation" (Congressional Research Service Report for Congress 92–907, Washington, D.C., December 4, 1992), 2–3.

16. In a statement to the North Atlantic Assembly Presidential Task Force on America and Europe, on January 21, 1993, I carried the point to its logical conclusion, arguing at that early date for an approach that eventually became US policy:

> Full membership in specific institutions, such as NATO, should be based on the desire and demonstrated ability of countries to adopt the norms and obligations of membership. Not all former members of the Warsaw Pact may be

able to meet such standards in the near future. But can the allies in good conscience deny participation in their security system to countries that have overthrown communist dictatorships and committed themselves to a democratic future?

This suggests, in practical terms, that Poland, Hungary, and the Czech Republic deserve serious consideration for NATO membership in the near future. Clearly, taking such a step would require that the NATO countries reassure Russia and other non-NATO European states that growing membership in the alliance will help create conditions of stability and peace that will support their own attempts to become constructive participants in the international community. Stanley R. Sloan, "Trends and Transitions in U.S.-European Security Cooperation" (statement before the North Atlantic Assembly Presidential Task Force on America and Europe, Washington, D.C., January 21, 1993).

17. Gebhard Schweigler, "A Wider Atlantic?" *Foreign Policy*, September/October 2001, 88.
18. The invitation to me and others suggested that the session was designed as an off-the-record opportunity to think and talk prospectively about transatlantic security issues.
19. Ronald D. Asmus, Richard L. Kugler, and F. Stephen Larrabee, "Building a New NATO," *Foreign Affairs*, September–October 1993, 28–40.
20. Kruzel, a central and creative participant in NATO policy formulation in the early Clinton years; Col. Nelson Drew, the main architect of the Combined Joint Task Force concept; and respected career diplomat Robert Frasure, who played a key role in the process leading to the peace accord in Bosnia, all lost their lives when the vehicle in which they were riding plunged off a dirt road outside Sarajevo. Just days before the tragic accident, my wife and I were guests along with Kruzel and his wife at an informal dinner in Washington hosted by then-Danish Minister of Defense Hans Haekerrup. In the course of our conversation over dinner, I asked Joe if he did not sometimes regret the price he had to pay in lost time with his family given his demanding job. He acknowledged that this cost was the most difficult part of the job. In the end, he and his family paid a much larger price than either of us could have contemplated that enjoyable evening.
21. Off-the-record interviews with the author.
22. Goldgeier, *Not Whether but When*, 68.
23. Goldgeier, *Not Whether but When*, 69–70.
24. NATO, "Study on NATO Enlargement" (Brussels: NATO, September 1995).
25. Goldgeier, *Not Whether but When*, 94–95.
26. At the time, I was the lead Congressional Research Service NATO expert and a source for Congress of objective and nonpartisan analysis on NATO issues. When the NATO Observer Group was established in the Senate to manage the

process of NATO enlargement, I was asked to serve as adviser to the group and as the Congressional Research Service liaison with both the Senate Observer Group and the Senate Foreign Relations Committee on NATO enlargement issues.

27. White House, "Remarks by the President to the People of Detroit," October 22, 1996.

28. For a thorough, well-documented history of this process, see Lawrence S. Kaplan, *NATO 1948, The Birth of the Transatlantic Alliance* (Lanham, Md.: Rowman and Littlefield, 2007).

29. As a participant in several such ceremonies, I was impressed by the distant look in the president's eyes, suggesting, even as he artfully presented prepared remarks, that his thoughts and priorities were elsewhere.

30. See, for example, results of polls conducted by the Pew Research Center for the People and the Press, Washington, D.C., in *America's Place in the World, Part II*. The data, released on October 7, 1997, found that support for enlargement ran more than three to one in favor (63 percent for, 18 percent opposed); however, only 10 percent of the public could identify even one of the potential new members.

31. A partial record of Senate activities related to NATO enlargement, along with the Foreign Relations Committee's Resolution of Ratification and separate views of the Senate Committee on Armed Services and the Senate Select Committee on Intelligence can be found in US Senate Committee on Foreign Relations, *Protocols to the North Atlantic Treaty of 1949 on Accession of Poland, Hungary and the Czech Republic*, 105th Cong., 2d sess., Exec. Rept. 105–14, March 6, 1998.

32. This aspect of the ratification process went completely unnoted in Goldgeier's otherwise excellent account of NATO enlargement decision making.

33. US Senate Committee on Foreign Relations, *The Debate on NATO Enlargement*, 105th Cong., 1st sess., October 7, 9, 22, 28, and 30 and November 5, 1997, S. Hrg. 105–285.

34. US Senate Committee on Foreign Relations, *The Debate on NATO Enlargement*, 2.

35. George F. Kennan, "A Fateful Error," *New York Times*, February 5, 1887, A23.

36. Following one Senate NATO Observer Group session in the weeks before the Senate vote, Wellstone engaged me in a discussion of the Russia issue. I attempted to provide a balanced perspective but suggested that Kennan's prediction was probably exaggerated. It was clear from that discussion, however, that Wellstone's vote probably would be with the enlargement opponents.

37. Even though the Standing Order of the Senate says that "votes shall be cast from assigned desk," roll-call votes are routinely taken with senators walking into the chamber and milling about the clerk's desk until their names are called. Byrd's comments can be found in *Congressional Record*, 105th Cong., 2d sess., April 30, 1998: S3906.

38. Discussion with author in 1998.

39. William V. Roth Jr., *NATO in the 21st Century* (Brussels: North Atlantic Assembly, September 1998), 53.
40. NATO, "NATO's Membership Action Plan," *NATO on-line-library fact sheet* (Brussels: NATO, April 20, 2000).
41. William Drozdiak, "9 NATO Candidates Pledge to Join in a 'Big Bang' Bid," *International Herald Tribune*, May 20–21, 2000, 1.
42. In 2001, a Rand Corporation study evaluated the qualifications of potential candidates and produced the following conclusions:

> Of the MAP states, Slovenia and Slovakia largely meet the criteria outlined by NATO [in the 1995 "Study on NATO Enlargement"] and their accession poses no major strategic problems for NATO. Estonia, Lithuania, and Latvia are advanced in terms of meeting NATO's preconditions, but the strategic ramifications of their accession [vis-à-vis Russia] loom large. Bulgaria and Romania have the opposite problem of being unable to meet NATO's preconditions, even though the strategic implications of their accession are not problematic. Macedonia and Albania are least advanced in meeting NATO's preconditions and their prospects for membership are distinctly long term. Of the European Union members currently not in NATO, Austria is in a good position to join if it chooses to do so. To a lesser extent, so is Sweden. Finnish membership, however, would entail some difficulties because of the strategic cost it would impose on NATO [also with regard to relations with Russia]. Thomas S. Szayna, "NATO Enlargement 2000–2015: Implications for Defense Planning," Rand Research Brief 62 (Santa Monica, Calif.: Rand Corporation, 2001).
>
> The brief summarizes the analysis completed by Szayna in *NATO Enlargement 2000–2015: Determinants and Implications for Defense Planning and Shaping* (MR-1243-AF) (Santa Monica, Calif.: Rand Corporation, 2001). See also Jeffrey Simon, *Roadmap to NATO Accession: Preparing for Membership*, (Washington, D.C.: Institute for National Strategic Studies, National Defense University, October 2001).

43. For a discussion of this issue by Professor Lawrence S. Kaplan, a distinguished NATO historian and enlargement skeptic, see Lawrence S. Kaplan, "NATO Enlargement: The Article 5 Angle," *Bulletin of the Atlantic Council of the United States* 12, no. 2 (February 2001), entire issue.
44. Sean Kay, "Use NATO to Fight Terror," *Wall Street Journal Europe*, November 16, 2001.
45. Phillip H. Gordon and James B. Steinberg, "NATO Enlargement: Moving Forward," Policy Brief (Washington, D.C.: The Brookings Institution, December 2001), 1.
46. Paul E. Gallis, "NATO Enlargement," Congressional Research Service Report for Congress RS21055 (Washington, D.C.: Congressional Research Service), May 5, 2003, 2.

47. A particularly thorough study by the Rand Corporation released in 2001 judged Slovenia to be the strongest candidate for membership, with Slovakia next in line. Estonia, Latvia, and Lithuania were judged to be "mid-term (or longer) candidates" because of the "strategic ramifications" of their accession—meaning the potential costs of contemporary and future Russian reactions. Bulgaria and Romania were rated next, their "relative strategic attractiveness . . . offset by their inability to meet NATO's criteria." Macedonia and Albania were judged to be least advanced in this group. The report also examined the standing of European Union members that had not applied for NATO membership, concluding that Austria and Sweden were reasonably well-prepared for membership. Finland was rated below these two because of the "strategic costs it would impose on NATO," with reference to Finland's long border with Russia and Russia's potential reaction to Finland's joining NATO. Thomas S. Szayna, "NATO Enlargement, 2000–2015," The Rand Corporation, 2001, 100–03.

48. Gallis, "NATO Enlargement," 6.

49. Luke Harding, "Bush backs Ukraine and Georgia for NATO membership," *The Guardian*, April 1, 2008.

50. North Atlantic Treaty Organization, "Bucharest Summit Declaration," para. 23, April 3, 2008.

51. NATO's website (www.nato.int/) includes comprehensive information on the Mediterranean Dialogue's activities.

52. "A More Ambitious and Expanded Framework for the Mediterranean Dialogue," NATO policy document, July 9, 2004.

53. Nicola de Santis, "Opening to the Mediterranean and Broader Middle East," *NATO Review*, Autumn 2004.

54. Ivo Daalder and James Goldgeier, "Global NATO," *Foreign Affairs*, September/October 2006, p.109.

55. For an excellent summary assessment of the 2006 debate see: Karl-Heinz Kamp, "'Global Partnership:' A New Conflict within NATO?" Analysen und Argumente aus der Konrad-Adenauer-Stiftung, No. 29, May 2006.

CHAPTER 7

NATO and Russia: Partnership or New Cold War?

As a result of NATO's post-Cold War enlargement and the evolving transformation of the missions and methods of the alliance, NATO's focus coming into the twenty-first century could be said to have moved beyond Russia. Russia was no longer the primary security concern for the alliance, even though Russia's evolution remained a critical variable in Europe's future. This process of change began in the early 1990s as the NATO allies reacted to the emerging reality that the Soviet Union and the Warsaw Pact no longer existed as threats to their security. The debate on the first phase of NATO enlargement in the mid-1990s foreshadowed some of the challenges facing the alliance today as controversy continues about how a new NATO strategic concept should shape future alliance goals and activities, particularly in light of the alliance's mission in Afghanistan.

In spite of NATO's efforts to create special partnership status for Russia, Moscow has from the beginning resented the fact that former Warsaw Pact allies and even former Soviet republics were becoming members of what had been the opposing Cold War alliance. After four decades of tension and competition between NATO and the Warsaw Pact, Russian leaders and the public had been well-conditioned to view the United States and its Western allies through an enemy-image prism. In addition, the Russian leadership still views what it calls Russia's "near abroad" as legitimately within its sphere of interest, even if Moscow no longer dominates that region. Russians believe they should defend the interests of ethnic Russians in Ukraine and in the Baltic states, even if those populations are now represented by governments in sovereign independent states. The NATO enlargement process directly threatened these perceptions of Russian security interests, even if, from the point of view of its former allies and neighboring republics, it was fully within their right and even in their vital interests to join NATO and the European Union.

In the meantime, Russia has moved into a period of increased repression and authoritarian approach to governance. This process has translated, once again, into Russian efforts to look for external threats that can be used to justify internal repression. And, the NATO members who escaped from Russian domination in the Soviet Union – led by Poland and the Baltic states – now are increasingly concerned that the new missions NATO has taken on could undermine the collective defense commitment in the North Atlantic Treaty. That commitment, after all, was the decisive factor in their strong desire to join the alliance in the first place.

Reaching Out to Moscow

The military and ideological threat posed by the Soviet Union, with Russia at its core, along with European concerns about a resurgent Germany, provided the original stimulus for the transatlantic bargain. These two factors also provided motivation for the steps taken in the 1940s and 1950s to initiate the process of European unification. The German "threat" was dissipated by decades of liberal German democracy, loyalty to the Western alliance, and the process of European integration. When the Soviet Union imploded at the end of the Cold War, the United States and its European allies discovered that even though this founding threat was also disappearing, the cooperation that had developed over the years was not only based on solid common values and interests, but also had continuing utility in a post-Soviet world.

Nevertheless, Russia remained a major factor in allied calculations. In spite of Russia's devastated economy and military forces so weakened as to be incapable of putting down rebellion in the former Soviet Republic of Chechnya, Russia remained a world-class nuclear power with a natural resource base that could serve as the foundation for future economic growth and renewed strategic significance. The development of a liberal democratic system in Russia would constitute a dramatic gain for international peace and stability. An autocratic, deprived and dissatisfied Russia could constitute a major source of instability for the indefinite future. As a consequence, the transatlantic allies moved carefully throughout the 1990s trying to assess how steps that they were taking to adapt their alliance would affect and be affected by Russia. They opened the cooperation path to all former Warsaw Pact members and Soviet republics, including Russia.

Despite the generally positive development of cooperation, the issue of NATO enlargement troubled the relationship. Russia's negative attitude toward NATO enlargement reflected feelings about the alliance that had been reinforced by decades of Soviet propaganda. Even the Russian elite found it difficult to understand the fundamental differences between NATO, a voluntary alliance among independent countries, and the Warsaw Pact, where membership was imposed by the Soviet Union. Expansion of NATO's role and membership meant that US power and influence would stretch ever closer to Russia's borders, displacing what had been Soviet/Russian zones of influence in central and eastern Europe. Some Russian officials believed that when Moscow agreed to facilitate German reunification, the Soviet Union had been promised that NATO would not expand up to its borders—a claim rejected by US officials who represented the United States in the negotiations.[1] The Russian perception may help explain Moscow's strong reaction to NATO's enlargement plans. The bottom line, of course, was that even if the negotiations led the Russians to such a conclusion, no such commitment was ever made formal.

In the mid-1990s the NATO allies decided that it was important to respond to the enthusiastic desire of the new democracies to join NATO while at the same time trying to overcome Russian opposition with a cooperative embrace. NATO's attempt to reassure the Russians took several forms. The NATO allies pledged that they had "no intention, no plan, and no reason" to deploy nuclear weapons on the territory of new members. They also said that they planned no permanent, substantial deployments of NATO soldiers in any new member states. Perhaps most important, the allies authorized NATO Secretary-General Javier Solana, acting on behalf of the member states, to negotiate a more permanent cooperative relationship with Russia. Those negotiations, guided by Strobe Talbott and other US officials, resulted in the Founding Act on Mutual Relations, Cooperation and Security between NATO and the Russia Federation, signed in Paris in May 1997 just before NATO announced its decision to invite three former Warsaw Pact nations to join NATO.

The Founding Act set a large agenda of topics on which NATO and Russia would attempt to collaborate. It created a Permanent Joint Council (NATO nations plus Russia) as a framework for continuing consultations. Creating this channel for communications was an important step, but there were limits on its effectiveness. From the beginning, there was a tension between the Russian desire to use the forum to "participate in" NATO decision-making while the NATO allies sought to ensure that the Permanent Joint Council remained a place for consultations and not cooperative decision-making. Russia's acceptance of the PJC was always grudging. Russian leaders wanted something more—something that would more directly acknowledge Russia's importance in European security. The NATO countries, on the other hand, did not want to give Russia a direct say in NATO deliberations and certainly not a veto over NATO actions—a concern directly expressed by American conservatives during the 1990s debate on NATO enlargement.

The NATO-Russia relationship was at least superficially enhanced in January 1996 when Russian forces joined NATO troops in the Implementation Force, organized to enforce the military aspects of the Peace Agreement in Bosnia-Herzegovina. Russian forces also joined NATO troops to keep the peace in Kosovo after hostilities had ended in 1999, but were withdrawn from both Bosnia and Kosovo in the summer of 2003. Moscow's participation may have had as much to do with Russia's paternal feeling toward their Serbian cousins, whom they perceived as under attack by the United States and its NATO allies, as it did with wanting to cooperate with NATO.

Vladimir Putin, in the early stages of his presidency (which ran from December 31, 1999 until May 7, 2008), led Russia toward a pragmatic and even constructive relationship with NATO, while trying to restore a degree of internal order following the tumultuous presidency of Boris Yeltsin. The most important stimulus was provided by the September 11 terrorist attacks, which prompted Putin to offer assistance in the US-declared war against terrorism. Putin's position clearly helped strengthen his relationship with President George W. Bush, and facilitated work toward agreements on dramatic cuts in strategic nuclear weapons arsenals and possible agreements on missile defenses. Putin also hinted at new Russian perspectives regarding its relationship to NATO and Russia's attitude toward NATO enlargement.

Photo 7.1: Secretary General George Robertson and Russian President Putin meeting in Brussels after Putin's reaction to the 9/11 attacks had led to one of the few high points in Russia/NATO relations

Source: NATO Photos.

In November 2001, Bush's political ally, British Prime Minister Tony Blair, initiated discussion of a new Russia-NATO relationship by proposing creation of an updated forum for Russia-NATO cooperation. Blair, in a letter to NATO Secretary General George Robertson, suggested creation of a "Russia/North Atlantic Council" which would take decisions by consensus on certain issues affecting both NATO and Russia including, for example, terrorism, arms proliferation and peacekeeping. According to press reports, British officials suggested privately that post-9/11 events could lead to a new world order, ending old enmities and building new bridges. "The prime minister believes the fact that the world is such a different place since September 11 does give us opportunities as well as threats," one official said.[2]

Apparently with the blessing of the Bush administration, Secretary General Robertson put the idea forward during an official visit to Moscow. Headlines shouted "Russia Could Get Veto Power in New NATO."[3] Russian conservatives worried that Putin was about to give away the farm, while other Russian analysts speculated that the move would give Russia associate membership in the alliance. American conservatives remained concerned that the move might end NATO's useful existence. Polish observers fretted that this might be the first step toward Russian membership in NATO. French observers wondered if events were moving too fast for rational consideration of their consequences.

Two former officials responsible for the Clinton administration's NATO enlargement policy, Jeremy D. Rosner and Ronald D. Asmus, argued for simply revitalizing current NATO-Russia relations: "Mr. Putin has complained that the existing

NATO-Russia relationship is moribund. He is right. But the reason why it is moribund is that Russia walked away from the table in protest over NATO's air campaign in Kosovo and has since pursued an obstructionist policy. That fact alone should give us pause. There is nothing wrong with the NATO-Russia Permanent Joint Council that a dose of good will and hard work could not fix."[4]

On December 6, 2001, in spite of such arguments, the allies agreed to establish a new Russia-NATO council to identify and pursue opportunities for joint action between Russia and the NATO allies. The ministers made it clear that the new council would not give Russia a veto over NATO decisions.

Agreement on the new arrangements was confirmed at a NATO-Russia summit outside Rome, Italy on May 28, 2002. The Permanent Joint Council was replaced by a new Russia-NATO Council. The new council was intended to meet more regularly, and to make decisions on some subjects. However, the regular agenda of the North Atlantic Council would not be shifted to the new framework. The NAC would decide when issues should be submitted to decision by the NATO-Russia Council and when they should be kept within usual NATO decision-making channels. Unlike the PJC, however, the allies would not bring "pre-cooked" NATO positions to the table with Russia. If the new council became deadlocked on an issue because of Russian disagreement, this would not block the NATO members from acting in the NAC without Russian agreement or participation. Lord Robertson argued that the real differences between the former arrangement and the new forum were a matter of "chemistry rather than arithmetic, as even the best format and seating arrangements can be no substitute for genuine political will and open minds on both sides."[5] In other words, the change was largely cosmetic, intended as a political statement rather than a structural change.

In spite of the new consultative arrangements, resentment of NATO's enlargement to include the three former Soviet republics of Estonia, Latvia and Lithuania persisted in some Russian quarters. In March 2004, Russia's lower house of parliament adopted a resolution denouncing NATO enlargement and the deployment of four Belgian F-16 fighter jets to a Lithuanian air base to patrol the air space of the new Baltic members of NATO. This, however, did not stop President Putin just one week later from signing agreements with NATO Secretary General Jaap de Hoop Scheffer establishing Russian military liaison offices at NATO's top military headquarters.

Even as Putin took such practical steps in relations with NATO, he increasingly adopted an autocratic approach to governance in Moscow, which carried over into the term of his hand-picked successor, Dmitry Medvedev. Initially using the struggle against Chechen separatists as his rationale, Putin began re-centralizing power. In 2004, he involved himself actively in the presidential election campaign in Ukraine, supporting the pro-Moscow candidate Viktor Yanukovych against the more Western-oriented opposition.

In July 2006, as Putin continued consolidating power, Russia hosted the G-8 economic summit – the annual gathering of the leaders of the world's industrial powers.

Russia had become a full participant in the G-8 in 1998, having been invited partly to encourage and facilitate Russia's democratization and modernization process as well as to acknowledge Russia's natural resource base and nuclear weapons capabilities (at the time, Russia was just the 17th leading industrial power). Meeting in Moscow, the G-8 leaders successfully sought a non-controversial meeting, generally regarded as a success for the host government.[6] Many observers hoped that Russia might be on its way to becoming a respected and influential member of the international community.

Ukraine and Georgia as Issues between NATO and Moscow

In the early years of the twenty-first century, Russia's economic fortunes brightened considerably with its international sales of oil and gas, apparently encouraging Russian leaders to begin flexing their foreign policy muscles again. Russia first began deploying its new-found sense of confidence and bravado in relations with former Soviet republics Ukraine and Georgia. The accession of the Baltic States to NATO had been viewed in the 1990s as a step that could lead back to a new "Cold War" environment. But there was little that Russia could do when NATO's "big bang" expansion took place in 2004. The crunch did not come until both Ukraine and Georgia began moving closer to membership at a time when Russia was feeling more confident about throwing its weight around once again. Moscow used various forms of hard and soft power to pressure the Ukrainians against joining NATO, including restricting access to gas supplies that flowed to and through Ukraine. In the unstable Caucasus, the Kremlin vocally supported the separatism of two Georgian regions and then invaded Georgia to enforce the regions' independence.

Ukraine's Case

NATO's relationship with the next most significant independent country formed by a former Soviet republic, Ukraine, has been of an entirely different character than that with Russia. As part of the unwinding of the Cold War, Ukraine gave up the Soviet-era nuclear weapons that had been deployed on its territory in return for Western financial assistance and the tacit promise of acceptance into the Western community of nations. By the mid-1990s, many in the Ukraine elite quietly aspired to eventual membership in both NATO and the European Union (EU). However, domestic political divisions called for a cautious approach. Ukraine did not ask to be considered for NATO membership but strongly supported the process of NATO enlargement. The NATO allies responded to Ukraine's aspirations at their summit meeting in Madrid in July 1997, agreeing to establish a Ukraine-NATO Charter on Distinctive Partnership, creating an intensified consultative and cooperative relationship between NATO and Ukraine.[7]

In May 2002, President Leonid Kuchma announced Ukraine's goal of eventually joining NATO. Following this pronouncement, and building on the cooperative relationship established with Ukraine in the 1990s, NATO-Ukraine cooperation was deepened and broadened with the adoption of the NATO-Ukraine Action Plan in November 2002. In subsequent years, Russia worked hard to ensure its future political and economic influence in Ukraine, leaving Ukraine's future orientation and role in Europe open to question.

Ukraine sent forces to join in NATO's military operations in Bosnia and Herzegovina and Kosovo and contributed over 1,600 troops to the Polish-led multinational division in Iraq. NATO-member Poland, in fact, committed itself to helping Ukraine sustain its independence and become a full member of the Euro-Atlantic security system. Illustrating Poland's concern about Ukraine's future, Janusz Onyszkiewicz, a Polish member of the European Parliament and former Polish defense minister, noted that "Poland is extremely worried about the future of Ukraine and Russia's policies in that country. If Russia establishes a dominance over Ukraine, it could give rise to new, imperialistic tendencies. If Russia can manage to do that with Ukraine, why not Belarus, Moldova, and other countries in the Caucasus?"[8]

Entering the twenty-first century, Ukraine remained torn between its past and its future. The eastern cities of Ukraine are traditionally more russified—both linguistically and politically, while the more rural western regions of the country preserve their ethnically Ukrainian character and have been a hotbed for nationalistic sentiments. The United States, NATO, and the European Union have sought to encourage Ukraine to work toward becoming part of the Euro-Atlantic community of democracies. This goal is supported by significant elements in the political elite and among the public. But another powerful contingent in Ukraine— largely living in Ukraine's eastern half—favors close links to Moscow, if not reintegration with Russia. This constituency has been actively lobbied and encouraged by Russia, which views Ukraine as its missing half. Russia is an important country on its own, but it would be much more powerful if reunited with Ukraine. As Zbigniew Brzezinski wrote in the mid-1990s, "Without Ukraine, Russia ceases to be a Eurasian empire. . . . if Moscow regains control over Ukraine, with its 52 million people and major resources, as well as access to the Black Sea, Russia automatically again regains the wherewithal to become a powerful imperial state, spanning Europe and Asia."[9]

The electoral crisis in Ukraine at the end of 2004 illustrated how divided Ukraine is between the pro-Western and pro-Russian tendencies. The conflicting interests translated into international discord at the December 2004 ministerial meeting of the Organization for Security and Cooperation in Europe. Russia, led by President Putin's overt support for the pro-Moscow presidential candidate, had actively intervened in the election campaign, and the results of the first round were marred by serious charges of voting fraud. OSCE foreign ministers were unable to reach agreement on a statement including language on the Ukrainian Supreme Court's ruling that the "victory" of the pro-Moscow candidate in the November 2004 presidential polling should be invalidated and new elections held. Agreement was reportedly blocked by Moscow's refusal to include the references.[10]

The "Orange Revolution" in Ukraine following the disputed presidential elections not only brought a pro-Western leader, President Viktor Yushchenko, to power in internationally-monitored run-off elections, but also resulted in Ukraine's changing from a NATO partner to a country actively seeking membership in the alliance. Yushchenko's ambitions for his country were received enthusiastically in Washington, where the Bush administration supported the membership aspirations of both Ukraine and Georgia, while Russia kept up its active opposition.

In addition to overt political pressure and, presumably, clandestine assistance to Yushchenko's pro-Moscow opponents, Moscow turned to its most powerful non-military weapons to influence Ukrainian behavior. Already in 2006, Russia threatened to cut supplies of natural gas that flows via pipelines to Ukraine and onward to Western Europe. A more serious disruption came early in 2009, when the Russian gas supply monopoly Gazprom suspended gas shipments to Ukraine, accusing Ukraine of stealing gas that should be going through the system and not paying an adequate price for the gas it consumed. Regardless of whether the Russian claims reflected reality or not, the move by Gazprom was widely seen as a blatant attempt to demonstrate Ukraine's, and the rest of Europe's, dependence on Russian gas supplies.

Another sensitive issue is the Ukrainian port of Sevastopol, which has been home to Russia's Black Sea Fleet for 225 years and remains an important symbol of Russian power and influence in southeastern Europe. Russia currently pays rent to Ukraine for use of its territory, a lease arrangement that is scheduled to expire in 2017, at which time Ukraine says that the fleet can no longer be based on Ukrainian territory. Russia's potential loss of this facility and its embodiment of Russian power has been a source of consternation for Russian leaders. Russia is building a new naval base on Russian territory at Novorossiysk, but the head of Moscow's general staff has expressed the hope that the new base will be in addition to, and not instead of, continued Russian use of the Sevastopol base.[11] The future of Sevastopol and the naval base there apparently remains open, at least as far as Moscow is concerned.

As discussed in Chapter 6, the Bush administration wanted the alliance to grant both Ukraine and Georgia entry to NATO's Membership Action Plan (MAP) at the NATO summit scheduled for April 2008 in Bucharest, Romania. President Bush's advocacy of giving the two aspirants MAP status was not convincing for many European governments, led by France and Germany, who thought such a decision would be premature. The summit, instead, issued a statement that surprisingly promised that Georgia and Ukraine would one day become NATO members. Russia had won a tactical victory, but presumably was surprised and disturbed by the long-term NATO commitment to the membership of Ukraine and Georgia—a victory for the lame-duck American president.

In 2009, the new US administration led by President Barack Obama supported the "open door" for NATO enlargement but did not put a high priority on pushing the matter ahead with any urgency. This suggested that the alliance would work with Ukraine and Georgia to help them move toward meeting the requirements for NATO membership without specifically putting them on the track toward membership. This also meant that Russia would continue to lobby against the eventuality and would likely use sources of influence available to it to support the outcomes it prefers.

The Georgia Case

When the Cold War ended and the Soviet Union began to break apart, the Georgian province of South Ossetia sought to break away, leading to serious fighting between the separatists and Georgian forces. (South Ossetia had pursued independence in the 1920s until forcibly incorporated in the Soviet Union as an autonomous region in Georgia.) A peace agreement was brokered by Russia, and "peacekeepers" from Russia, South Ossetia and Georgia were authorized for the region. Tensions continued, however, over the next two decades, while Russia worked to support South Ossetia's goal of secession from Georgia, including issuing Russian passports to South Ossetians who wanted them. Georgia never accepted the South Ossetian claims to independence and resented Moscow's active efforts to support that goal.[12]

Following the 2003 pro-democracy "Rose Revolution" in Georgia, the new Western-leaning Georgian government led by Mikheil Saakashvili pledged to re-establish Georgian authority over South Ossetia and Georgia's other separatist region of Abkhazia. Both the pro-Western nature of Saakashvili's government and its goal of regaining central government control of the separatist regions ran counter to Moscow's perceived interests.

After a number of failed attempts to negotiate a settlement between Georgia and the two regions, tensions began to build in July 2008, leading to skirmishes between Georgian and South Ossetian units in the province, followed by Russian intervention and attacks on Georgian forces and targets in the two regions and in Georgia itself. Russia took the opportunity not only to "punish" Georgian forces involved but also to push into Georgia, destroy Georgian military and civilian infrastructure, and seal off Georgia from its two break-away republics. Russian officials claimed they would never again be part of Georgia.

The last thing the NATO nations wanted was a new cold war with Russia, but Russian actions in Georgia chilled the atmosphere across Europe as well as between Russia and the United States. As one expert observed, NATO and the European Union need to work together on this difficult relationship and "Russia must be reminded that cooperation with NATO, as an alliance of democratic states, requires compliance with democratic rules."[13]

The longer-term consequences of this affair remain to be seen, but, at the very least, many European states see Russia's actions as a sign that they will be safer in the future with a NATO security blanket than without. The impression of a more threatening Russia was enhanced by Russian behavior in other areas. In 2007, a number of Estonian government web sites suffered "denial of service" attacks at a time of tension between Estonia and Russia over Tallinn's decision to move a Soviet-era war memorial to a less prominent spot in the capitol. The source of the attacks has not been publically confirmed, but the likelihood that the attacks originated in Russia raised questions about how such attacks in the future could pose serious security threats to NATO allies.[14]

The Russian Alternative for European Security

From the beginning of the end of the Soviet Union and the Warsaw Pact, Russian leaders have struggled to create or propose alternatives to a European security system dominated by NATO and the United States. The Russian-led Commonwealth of Independent States, founded in December 1991, was Moscow's first attempt to reassert a degree of Russian leadership of former Soviet republics. However, Russian weakness in the early 1990s gave their leaders no real possibility of having decisive influence over the unfolding developments that were leading former Warsaw Pact allies and key Soviet Republics into alliance, or at least partnership, with NATO. This weakness inevitably led to resentment of the fact that the United States and its NATO allies were largely dictating the terms of the new European security system, even if the Western powers made serious attempts to develop a special partnership with Russia.

With the advent of the new century, Russia was beginning to realize some of the financial and political benefits from demand for its natural resources, particularly natural gas, on international markets. Even though the Russian military was still in disastrous condition, the improved financial situation gave rise to a belief in Moscow that it could take certain initiatives to counter what appeared to be increasing Western dominance all around Russia's borders. In 2002, Russia led a group of former Soviet republics to establish the Collective Security Treaty Organization (CSTO). Armenia, Belarus, Kazakhstan, Kyrgyzstan, and Tajikistan joined Russia as members. Uzbekistan joined the organization in 2006. The members pledged to come to the defense of a member that had been attacked, and have agreed to create a peace-keeping force that could be deployed at the request of the United Nations. Most objective observers see the CSTO mainly as a way for Moscow to attempt to maintain its influence in former Soviet republics that were not yet seeking close relations with NATO. The extent to which Russia has been successful in pursuing its interests through the CSTO was called into question by the fact that no CSTO member immediately followed Russia's lead in recognizing the governments of the breakaway Georgian regions of South Ossetia and Abkhazia.

In June 2008, Russian President Medvedev proposed creating a new all-European security organization, suggesting that the OSCE as well as NATO were increasingly irrelevant to the new circumstances in Europe. Perhaps more importantly, Russia has been willing to use its veto to limit the OSCE's role in issues important to Russian interests, particularly in the aftermath of Russia's August 2008 invasion of Georgia. In the spring of 2009, Russia blocked extension of the mandate for both United

Nations and OSCE monitors in Abkhazia and South Ossetia.[15] As one expert has noted, "Russia's relations with the Euro-Atlantic community in its institutional formats are characterized by a sense of strategic dissonance."[16]

The initial Medvedev proposal seemed to suggest that the new framework should be constructed by Europeans, implying no role for the United States or NATO. However, when the European response raised many questions about Russian intentions and motivations, Medvedev softened the approach to suggest that all existing security organizations as well as all key players in European security should be involved in shaping the new system.[17] By early 2010, the European security initiative had not been formally presented in full detail, but it remained part of a larger Russian package of initiatives apparently designed to begin restructuring European and international security, energy and political relations along lines more favorable to Russian influence and interests.[18]

None of the Russian initiatives achieved much traction in Europe, and were viewed with great skepticism by the former Soviet republics and Warsaw Pact countries that had achieved or aspired to NATO membership. With international condemnation of Russian behavior in Georgia and with Russian economic fortunes hard hit by the global recession in 2009, Moscow adopted what appeared to be a more modest approach. The focus of Russian policy turned slowly toward developing a new and more constructive policy with the American government led by Barack Obama, which seemed perhaps to offer more promise than suspect schemes for reorganizing the European security system.

Military Issues, Nuclear Weapons, and Missile Defense

One of the most difficult policy issues confronting the process of enlarging NATO, particularly to the Baltic states of Latvia, Lithuania, and Estonia, was the question of how to reassure Russia that a growing NATO would not diminish Russian security. The allies faced the challenging task of keeping their commitment to enlarge while avoiding a new confrontational relationship with Moscow. The issue was a very broad one that included important political, psychological, security, and economic dimensions.

Russian officials expressed particular concern that NATO enlargement could lead to the deployment of nuclear weapons on Russia's borders. This complaint could be dismissed as, at best, a bargaining strategy to the extent that Russian defense officials and experts knew that NATO had no nuclear-armed missiles or other nuclear weapons systems that it would want to deploy forward on European territory. As is discussed in Chapter 8, there are even questions about the continued need for the United States to deploy the several hundred free-fall bombs on west European territory. However, this information may be well understood only among Russian defense specialists and not by average citizens or even many political leaders.

As it happened, the nuclear issue did not create a serious crisis with Russia in the first enlargement (when the Czech Republic, Hungary, and Poland were admitted to NATO) or even in the potentially more sensitive second enlargement (when Estonia, Latvia, and Lithuania as well as the Slovak Republic, Slovenia, Bulgaria, and Romania were admitted). Russian President Vladimir Putin decided not to make a major issue out of the nuclear aspects of enlargement, and the NATO countries were not required to make any apparent concessions to win Putin's relatively grudging acceptance of the new reality. Some Russian politicians and defense officials still grumble about the fact that NATO membership for the three Baltic States has brought NATO forces close to the Russian heartland. But, for the most part, nuclear weapons in the context of NATO enlargement never became as difficult an issue as had been feared when the enlargement process began in the 1990s.

The question of missile defenses sparked the big differences, however, between Russia and NATO. One of the first actions of the Bush administration after taking office in 2001 was to withdraw from the 1972 Anti-Ballistic Missile Defense Treaty with the Soviet Union, freeing the United States from any treaty obligation not to deploy such systems. The administration argued that looming missile threats from nuclear weapons state North Korea and nuclear weapons aspirant Iran warranted US movement toward deployment of systems that could protect the United States and its allies from such future threats. The ABM treaty stood in the way, and the United States did not plan to deploy a system that would neutralize Russian nuclear missile capabilities in any case.

In 2001, the Bush administration argued, with some logic, that continuing to base relations with a post-Cold War Russia on premises and agreements that governed relations with a Cold War Soviet Union would not lead to new, constructive ties. They saw the ABM Treaty as a relic of the Cold War. Moreover, the treaty blocked the testing the United States deemed necessary to develop critical missile defense capabilities. European allies accepted that relations with Russia needed to be set on new ground but generally believed that treaties such as the ABM accord still help shape a framework of stability that should not be thrown away lightly. These differing approaches began the process of splitting the transatlantic allies in the first month of the Bush administration.

The September 11, 2001, attacks on the United States added new elements to the missile defense debate. On the one hand, those who had been skeptical about Bush missile defense plans could interpret the September 11 attacks as demonstrating that building defenses against strategic missiles was pointless. Terrorists and rogue states clearly could find ways around US defenses to attack and destroy select US targets, create fear, and disrupt the US economy and way of life. On the other hand, those who supported a robust missile defense program could see the September 11 events as fully justifying their position. The demonstrated willingness of the al Qaeda network to attack US targets using hijacked aircraft made it even more likely that such groups or rogue states in the future might acquire ballistic missiles to deliver weapons of mass destruction on US or allied targets.

While the United States was tied down fighting in Iraq, new concerns arose about the potential for neighboring Iran, led by a radical Islamic regime that no longer was pre-occupied with Saddam Hussein's Iraq, to develop both nuclear weapons and the missile systems to deliver them on European and American targets. In 2007, this concern led the administration to decide to negotiate deployment of missile interceptors in Poland and a radar facility in the Czech Republic as key components of a defense against long-range Iranian missiles. The administration decided to move ahead with preparatory steps even though the missile intercept system had not proven itself ready for deployment.[19]

The strong Russian reaction against this decision had many components. Russian officials knew that the number (10) and location of the planned deployments posed no threat to their intercontinental ballistic missile capabilities. They also knew that the proposed systems had not yet proven their viability. They nonetheless chose to characterize the decision as a threat to their security. Even though their arguments were in part disingenuous, designed largely for domestic consumption, they did reveal continued Russian sensitivity to the fact that NATO and US power were moving even closer to their borders. And, Russian officials argued that the missile deployments could, in the future, be used as the basis for expansion to pose a threat to Russian missiles.[20] In November 2008, Russian President Medvedev, presumably attempting to raise the stakes on the issue, suggested that the deployment of the US anti-missile systems could lead Russia to deploy the conventionally armed tactical ballistic Iskander-M missile system in the Russian enclave of Kaliningrad.[21]

The US decision created political divisions among the allies and within the deployment countries. One particularly serious issue was the fact that the interceptors might be able to protect some NATO allies from attack, but would not be capable of stopping attacks against others, particularly to the south of the locations of the interceptors. The Polish and Czech governments in 2008 nonetheless confirmed their participation in the program.

In 2009, one of the early decisions of the new Obama administration in Washington was to slow the pace of progress toward deploying missile defense systems in Europe, largely due to questions about whether the system would work or not, but also consistent with its attempt to "reset" US relations with Russia.[22] Following President Obama's discussions with Russian President Medvedev in July 2009, the Pentagon announced that the European missile plans were "not set in concrete," and that, in consultation with the Polish and Czech governments, the deployments could be adjusted depending on future developments.[23] In September 2009, following the advice of his senior military advisors, including Secretary of Defense Robert Gates, Obama announced that the scheduled deployments in Europe would be canceled. The United States would instead deploy a new missile defense land- and sea-based system focused on the Iranian short- and medium-range missile threat.[24]

The Russian reaction to Obama's Moscow visit confirmed that a renewed dialogue and nuclear arms control negotiations with the United States may be more important to the Russian leadership than persistent opposition to NATO plans and policies. Russia has always valued the bilateral US-Russian relationship because it is seen in Moscow as implying Russia's continued status as a major power. However, internal political developments in Russia continue to give rise to concern, and could in the longer term create demands on Russian policy that make progress in arms control and missile defense relations with the United States and NATO more difficult.

On the less prominent issue of conventional arms control in Europe, the Obama administration has not put a high priority on rescuing it from the current impasse between Russia and NATO. As noted in Chapter 6, the terms of the treaty have in many ways been overtaken by events, and its adaptation has been held up by a number of issues. Russia has suspended compliance with the treaty's terms, and has refused requests from NATO states for inspections provided for under the treaty.[25] Final approval of the treaty might still be important from a confidence-building perspective, but is largely irrelevant to contemporary security relations in Europe. Moscow's broader intentions regarding Georgia, in particular to ensure that the breakaway Georgian provinces of Abkhazia and South Ossetia gain their independence within a Russian sphere of influence, pose the greatest obstacles to progress.

Looking Ahead

The dark cloud on the horizon is the apparent drift of Russia back toward an authoritarian regime with the trappings of democracy. The authoritarian tendencies have included severe constraints on freedom of the press, suppression of political dissent with assassinations of prominent journalists that some suspect were ordered by Moscow, and renationalization of businesses.

Such tendencies are most alarming to NATO countries around Russia's borders. The Poles, for example, remain particularly concerned that Russia will use its role as a key energy supplier to Europe as a way of holding Poland, Ukraine and other states hostage to Russian interests. Estonia and Latvia, Baltic states with large ethnic Russian minority populations, still worry about their physical security, particularly in light of Russia's actions against Georgia. Many West European states are concerned about how Russia intends to use the leverage gained from its position as an energy supplier but have been reluctant to criticize Russia too strongly or publicly, perhaps judging that quiet diplomacy will work best with President Medvedev and Prime Minister Putin. Seen less generously, it could be suggested that European leaders wanted to avoid offending an important energy supplier at a time when other sources were potentially in jeopardy.

Determining the legitimacy of Moscow's concerns about NATO enlargement and other issues, of course, is a subjective task. However, the influence of Russian domestic politics needs to be weighed in the equation. It seems likely that the resurgent authoritarian tendencies in Moscow are intended to ensure that Russia does not itself fall apart, as did the Soviet Union. The goal of preserving Russia's integrity by reasserting central societal, economic and political control from Moscow is understandable, but the consequences of re-centralization and limits on basic freedoms are inconsistent with the values that are required for Russia to be a trusted partner of NATO countries.

In addition, it is well-established that governments, and authoritarian regimes in particular, frequently use real or imagined foreign threats to help control domestic opposition. In Moscow's case, NATO and the United States make convenient whipping boys to help quell complaints about restrictions on free speech, freedom of the press, and other basic civil rights.

Taking all these considerations together, NATO faces a true dilemma: cooperation with Russia is a key element of future European and international peace; but NATO's integrity requires that the values for which the alliance stands—democracy, individual liberty and the rule of law—and the interests of the allies in defending their security remain at the heart of the alliance's purpose.

At a time when most of the threats to allied security emanate well beyond Europe, the United States and the European allies cannot lose track of important processes of transition still underway in Europe that could affect their future security. First and foremost, the NATO countries will be required to manage their relationship with Russia in ways that encourage the development of a democratic country that one day could be considered for NATO membership. In the meantime, the cooperation NATO has developed with Russia can be expanded in every way consistent with NATO's value base and current missions. The NATO countries in fact have many security interests in common with Russia, including combating international terrorism and the proliferation of weapons of mass destruction.

One expert on Russian foreign policy, Dmitri Trenin, has suggested that the West will most likely have to rely on economic forces rather than lectures about democracy to bend Russia back in more positive directions. Trenin advises caution and patience: "Today's Russia may not be pro-Western, but neither is it anti-Western . . . the West needs to calm down and take Russia for what it is: a major outside player that is neither an eternal foe nor an automatic friend."[26]

The fact that the allies have promised that "one day" Ukraine and Georgia will become NATO members limits the alliance's room for maneuver. However, it is a commitment that, depending on the decisions made by those countries and their preparedness for membership, will have to be sustained in alliance proclamations. Neither country today meets the requirements for membership as laid down in the 1995 NATO Enlargement Study. In order finally to qualify for membership, both Ukraine and Georgia will have to work hard to establish conditions in which their application for membership would be approved.

In retrospect, NATO enlargement has troubled but not destroyed the possibilities for a cooperative relationship between the alliance and Russia—it has not led to a "new cold war." Political developments in Russia and their reflection in Moscow's foreign and defense policies—with no connection to NATO's enlargement process—have turned out to be far more important to the relationship than the addition of former Warsaw Pact allies and the Baltic Republics to the alliance.

Russia's future nonetheless remains critically important to the NATO allies. Neither the United States nor any European ally wishes to see Russia re-emerge as a challenge to Europe's peace and stability. NATO policies therefore have for the most part been designed to invite Russia's constructive involvement in European and global security affairs while at the same time critiquing Moscow's recent tendencies to reverse the process of democratization and liberalization that began after the Soviet Union was dissolved.

At the end of the first decade of the twenty-first century, Russia remains an enigma for the NATO nations. They know that European security cannot be confidently secured without Moscow's constructive participation. Yet they also know that European security on Russian terms would be unacceptable. At the end of the day, the evolution of Russia's internal politics is arguably the most important variable. The recent authoritarian tendencies have produced accompanying inclinations to create or enhance foreign "threats" as a way of justifying domestic repression. As long as these factors influence Russian domestic politics and foreign policy, Russia's behavior will be unpredictable and its relationship with the members of NATO and the European Union will remain troubled.

The relationship with Russia will also influence the next stages of development of NATO's military strategy. The evolution of that strategy since the end of the Cold War is the topic of the next chapter.

Notes

1. David Yost, *NATO Transformed: The Alliance's New Roles in International Security* (Washington, D.C.: United States Institute of Peace Press, 1998), 133–34.
2. Mike Peacock, "Blair Pushes for a New NATO/Russia Relationship," *Reuters*, November 16, 2001.
3. Michael Wines, "Russia Could Get Veto Power in New NATO," *International Herald Tribune*, November 23, 2001, 1.
4. Ronald D. Asmus and Jeremy D. Rosner, "Don't Give Russia a Veto," *Washington Times*, December 5, 2001, A19.
5. Lord Robertson, "NATO in the 21st Century," Speech at Charles University, Prague, March 21, 2002 (full text on NATO web site at www.nato.int/).
6. Claire Bigg, "Russia: Putin 'Satisfied' as G-8 Summit Winds to a Close," RFE/RL Report, July 17, 2006.
7. For an excellent collection of analyses of Ukraine's early post-Cold War role in European security, see David E. Albright and Semyen J. Appatov, *Ukraine and European Security* (New York: St. Martin's, 1999).
8. Judy Dempsey, "Neighbors See Need for Kiev Incentives," *International Herald Tribune*, November 23, 2004.
9. Zbigniew Brzezinski, *The Grand Chessboard: American Primacy and its Geostrategic Imperatives* (New York: Basic Books, 1997), 46.

10. Joel Brinkley, "Powell Trades Tough Talk with Russian Leaders over Ukraine," *The New York Times*, December 8, 2004.
11. Denis Dyomkin, "Russia hopes to keep naval base in Ukraine," *Reuters India*, July 14, 2009.
12. For an excellent unbiased account of the Russia/Georgia conflict see: Jim Nichol, "Russia-Georgia Conflict in August 2008: Context and Implications for U.S. Interests," Congressional Research Service Report for Congress RL34618, March 3, 2009.
13. Karl-Heinz Kamp, "Frozen Conflict," *Internationale Politik*, German Council on Foreign Relations, Berlin, Summer 2008: http://www.ip-global.org/archiv/2008/summer2008/frozen-conflict.html [accessed July 15, 2009].
14. In 2009 a Russian State Duma Deputy claimed that his assistant had initiated the attacks. This claim was not accepted by Estonian authorities who judge that such an attack was too intense and complex to have been mounted by one individual. See Robert Coalson, "Behind the Estonian Cyberattacks," Radio Free Europe, Radio Liberty Transmission, March 6, 2009: http://www.rferl.org/content/Behind_The_Estonia_Cyberattacks/1505613.html [accessed July 14, 2009].
15. At the time, Greek Foreign Minister and OSCE chair Dora Bakoyanni regretted the Russian move, observing that "As a result, one of the largest on-the-ground missions of the OSCE in the region was led to an end— despite the clear need, recognized by many states taking part in it, for the organization to be present in order to contribute toward security and stability in the region." Matt Robinson, "U.N. monitors leave Georgia, OSCE mission shut," boston.com, June 30, 2009.
16. Andrew Monaghan, "At the table or on the menu? Moscow's proposals for strategic reform," NATO Defense College Research Division Research Report, June 2009, 1.
17. Bobo Lo, "Medvedev and the new European security architecture," Centre for European Reform Policy Brief, July 2009, 3–5.
18. Monaghan, "At the table . . . ," 2–3.
19. Sean Kay, "Missile Defenses and the European Security Dilemma," Paper Prepared for Presentation at the Annual Meeting of the International Studies Association, New York, February 2009, 5–6.
20. An excellent analysis of Russia's attitudes can be found in John P. Caves, Jr. and M. Elaine Bunn, "Russia's Cold War Perspective on Missile Defense in Europe," *Foundation pour la Recherche Stratégique*, May 3, 2007: http://www.frstrategie.org/barreFRS/publications/pv/defenseAntimissile/pv_20070503_eng.pdf [accessed July 16, 2009].
21. Global Security.org, " 9K720 Iskander-M (SS-26 Stone) http://www.globalsecurity.org/wmd/world/russia/ss-26.htm [accessed July 24, 2009].
22. Tomas Valasek, "Obama, Russia and Europe," Centre for European Reform Policy Brief, London, June 2009, 1–2.
23. Gordon Lubold, "European missile shield not set in stone, Pentagon says," *Christian Science Monitor*, July 14, 2009.

24. Barack Obama, "President Obama Delivers Remarks on Missile Defense," Transcript, *washingtonpost.com*, September 17, 2009: http://www.washingtonpost.com/wp-dyn/content/article/2009/09/17/AR2009091701818.html?sid= ST2009091701841 [accessed September 17, 2009].
25. Wade Boese, "Russia Unflinching on CFE Treaty Suspension," *Arms Control Today*, June 2008.
26. Dmitri Trenin, "Russia Leaves the West," *Foreign Affairs*, July/August 2006, p. 95.

CHAPTER 8

NATO's Post-Cold War Military Missions in Theory and Practice

NATO has survived for more than sixty years in large part because the allies have constantly adapted a fundamentally sound, principled relationship to changing international circumstances. This continuing process of adaptation began with the military buildup and elaboration of an integrated command structure in the early 1950s after North Korea invaded South Korea—measures not anticipated when the North Atlantic Treaty was signed. The alliance was adjusted again following the failure of the European Defense Community in 1954. In the mid-1960s, NATO was forced to adapt to France's departure from the integrated command structure. In 1967, the allies revamped NATO's strategy with the doctrine of "flexible response" to a possible Warsaw Pact attack, broadening NATO's military options. In the same year, they approved the Harmel Report, which gave the alliance the mission of promoting détente as well as sustaining deterrence and defense. The process continued in the 1970s and 1980s as NATO allies adapted their alliance to the emerging period of détente in relations with the Soviet Union and sought arms control accords with Moscow to reduce the dangers of an East-West confrontation.

NATO's 1991 Strategic Concept

Since 1949, NATO has always had a strategic concept to guide its policies and force structures. All previous concepts, however, had been classified and were available only in summary form for public consumption. The London Declaration of July 1990 authorized preparation of a new strategic concept. The allies decided that new times required new approaches. In November 1991 in Rome, NATO leaders approved the new concept and released it for all to see.[1]

In Rome, the allies established three areas of particular emphasis for future NATO policies. First, they said that, as part of a "broader" approach to security, they would actively seek cooperation and dialogue among all European states and particularly with the former Warsaw Pact adversaries—a process discussed in Chapter 6. Second, they declared that NATO's nuclear and nonnuclear military forces would be reduced and that remaining forces would be restructured to take into account the need for militaries that could handle crisis management tasks (such as the one that soon emerged in Bosnia) as well as collective defense. Third, the allies agreed that the

European members of NATO would assume greater responsibility for their own security—the topic of Chapter 10.

In the 1991 concept, the allies acknowledged the radical changes that had recently occurred in the world and in Europe in particular. When the concept was released, the Soviet Union still existed and still deployed powerful nuclear and nonnuclear military forces. But virtually everything else had changed. Democratic governments were getting organized across central and Eastern Europe, the terms on which Germany would be reunified had been negotiated, the Treaty on Conventional Armed Forces in Europe had been signed, the Warsaw Pact had been disbanded, an antidemocratic coup against Soviet leader Mikhail Gorbachev had been defeated, and governments in Poland, Hungary, and Czechoslovakia had expressed their wish to be included in NATO activities.

The 1991 concept said that NATO's policies and force posture should be adapted to those remarkable changes. But the allies also reaffirmed some elements of continuity. NATO's core function, they declared, was to defend its members against attack, and NATO's integrated command structure and coalition approach to defense remained essential to the interests of the members. The transatlantic link between Europe and North America continued to be vital to NATO's future relevance. Defense of democracy, human rights, and the rule of law still constituted the heart and soul of the alliance. Allied leaders noted that, even with all the positive changes, the world remained a dangerous place and that NATO cooperation would be essential to help them deal with the remaining risks and uncertainties. They agreed that the North Atlantic Treaty, in addition to providing for collective defense, included a mandate to work together to deal with threats to the security interests of the members, not just an attack on one of them.

This concept provided a new foundation for NATO initiatives throughout the 1990s and for substantial changes in NATO's military priorities. The allies dramatically reduced and streamlined military forces and NATO's command structure. In 1993, the allies agreed that peacetime strength of their forces could be reduced approximately 25 percent below 1990 levels. In subsequent years, additional cuts were taken. NATO's command structure was reduced from 65 headquarters down to 20 in the new system.

The force structure implications of the post-Cold War security environment were recognized early in the 1990s, even if most NATO governments were not prepared to act on the implications. The new challenges to allied security arose almost entirely well beyond the borders of NATO countries. Most allies, however, had forces designed largely to defend their own territory or that of a neighbor. They had little capacity to project and sustain forces in operations beyond their borders. The 1991 strategic concept assumed that allies would be reducing military spending and forces in view of the reduced threat. The concept also envisioned, however, that allies would restructure remaining military forces to give them greater force projection capabilities. The Balkan conflicts of the 1990s brought home the importance of these words in the 1991 concept.

The allies addressed directly the reality that the end of the Cold War did not resolve all sources of conflict and tension in the world, even though it certainly improved the prospects for a more peaceful future. Unfortunately, there remained countries and subnational groups, including terrorists, who did not accept the post-Cold War distribution of territory, resources, political influence, or generally accepted norms of international behavior. In some cases, these countries and groups saw the threat or use of force as a way to change the status quo—Saddam Hussein's attack on Kuwait in 1990 was a good example, as have been the terrorist acts instigated by the radical Islamic militant Osama bin Laden. Some of these activities rely on conventional weapons and terrorist tactics. But there was reason to be particularly concerned about access of such countries and groups to nuclear, chemical, and biological weapons of mass destruction (WMD) and modern means to deliver such weapons.

At the time, only the United States and a few other allied governments were prepared to move ahead with new military programs designed to respond to the terrorist/WMD problem. Thus, the allies focused initially on the politics of the issue, examining the underlying causes of dissatisfaction with the status quo that gave rise to WMD threats and terrorist activities. They also sought to identify the political, economic, and security tools available to the international community to eliminate the sources of proliferation or to prevent it in some way, including active support for existing arms control regimes. The NATO allies pledged to support political and diplomatic efforts aimed at preventing proliferation without duplicating the work of other organizations. However, the allies never made a serious commitment to coordinate their approaches to terrorist threats or their possible responses to terrorist attacks. This failure was due in part to underlying disagreements about the sources of and appropriate responses to terrorist threats. In addition, the terrorist activities of greatest concern to date had been the responsibility of internal, not external, groups (e.g., bombings of British targets to protest the United Kingdom's involvement in Northern Ireland and attacks by Basque separatists in Spain) and were regarded by the target states as domestic affairs.

At the same time, weapons of mass destruction and terrorism raised specific security problems for NATO. A terrorist's missile carrying a weapon of mass destruction fired at any NATO country would become a collective defense issue for all the allies. And political efforts to prevent proliferation or deter the use of weapons of mass destruction might not always be successful on their own. The NATO members therefore decided that NATO's military posture must make it clear to any potential aggressor that the alliance cannot be coerced by the threat or use of weapons of mass destruction and that it could respond effectively to threats to its security as they develop.

NATO's 1991 strategy called for maintaining military capabilities that would be sufficient to signal how seriously NATO took the proliferation threat. Under post-Cold War conditions, the allies decided that they could best communicate their intentions by maintaining a mix of nuclear and nonnuclear response weapons, passive and active defenses, and effective intelligence and surveillance means. NATO forces, they determined, should be capable of anticipating (through high-quality intelligence information and analysis), deterring (through maintenance of credible forces), defending (by protecting against a variety of delivery systems and the effects of biological and chemical agents on troops), and, if necessary, defeating (using whatever force may be required) any threat from weapons of mass destruction that might emerge from any source in the future.

NATO's approach to the new challenges of weapons of mass destruction and terrorism was a contemporary application of the commitment the allies made in the North Atlantic Treaty to cooperate in preserving the peace and dealing with threats to the security of the alliance. Such threats were likely to remain politically complex, they might arise from several different possible directions, and they could be difficult to predict and assess. NATO, however, could help coordinate allied diplomatic efforts to prevent such challenges from arising and, if necessary, develop appropriate responses to more imminent and dangerous military threats that do emerge. Unfortunately, the alliance did little in real terms to respond to the terrorist challenge prior to the September 11, 2001, attacks on the United States.

The allies did, however, make an active commitment to military cooperation with their former adversaries. Even before the 1991 new strategic concept was issued, the allies began engaging their military forces in cooperative programs with former Warsaw Pact and other European nations. In support of the dialogues with Russia and Ukraine, NATO military forces tried to reach out to the militaries that had formed the core of the Soviet Union's defense establishment. Thus, while the NATO force structure was being reduced, new roles and missions were being added to the plate of allied military forces. This expansion of functions and responsibilities preceded the burdens that were subsequently imposed by the peace operations in Bosnia and Kosovo.

An important reform of the NATO integrated command structure began at the January 1994 NATO summit meeting in Brussels when the allies approved the US-proposed idea of establishing Combined Joint Task Force (CJTF) headquarters as part of NATO's integrated command structure.[2]

The intent of the CJTF initiative was to provide flexible command arrangements within which allied forces could be organized on a task-specific basis to take on a wide variety of missions beyond the borders of alliance countries. Specifically, the concept sought the following:

1. Giving NATO's force and command structure sufficient flexibility to respond to alliance security requirements and new missions other than responses to an attack on a NATO country.
2. Facilitating the dual use of NATO forces and command structures for alliance and/or operations run by the Western European Union, the defense organization whose membership included only European countries and that had been chosen as the framework for constructing a "European pillar" in NATO; the purpose

would be to encourage European nations to undertake missions with forces that are "separable but not separate" from NATO in the context of an emerging European Security and Defense Identity.

3. Permitting non-NATO partners to join NATO countries in operations, exercises, and training as envisioned in the Partnership for Peace program of cooperation open to all non-NATO European states.[3]

All these new directions had direct implications for the NATO command structure and, in April 1994, the Chiefs of the Defense Staffs of NATO countries initiated the "Long-Term Study" intended to form the basis for a new command structure. For starters, it was decided to reduce major NATO commands from three to two—Allied Command Europe and Allied Command Atlantic—with the elimination of the Allied Command Channel. But more difficult issues lay immediately ahead.

NATO's Bosnia Experience: From Theory to Practice

While the NATO nations were trying to calculate how the alliance would relate to and operate in the new international environment of the post-Cold War world, that world was already posing new and difficult challenges. With very little concern for allied preferences and priorities, the real world reminded the United States and its European allies that "life is what's happening while you are busy doing other things."

By 1991, life in the Balkans had already become increasingly conflicted. Yugoslavia was a multiethnic communist state that remained relatively independent of the Soviet Union during the Cold War. Following the death of the communist dictator Josip Broz Tito in 1980, the country had been tenuously held together with a power-sharing approach that more or less continued to balance the interests of the country's main ethnic groups (Serbian, Croatian, Muslim, and Albanian). But attempts to modernize Yugoslavia's economic and political system were failing just as the world celebrated the end of the Cold War. The failure became a new Balkan tragedy when the process of disintegration turned violent. The Slovene Republic, a part of the former Yugoslavia that was blessed with a relatively homogeneous population and no substantial minority concentrations, managed to break away with limited fighting. But the Republic of Croatia's breakaway was strongly resisted by the Serbian-controlled military, producing approximately 20,000 dead and more than 350,000 displaced persons.[4]

The conflict quickly spread to Bosnia-Herzegovina, where Serbian, Croatian, and Muslim populations were interspersed around the republic and where the conflict became a brutal and bloody internecine battle among the ethnic populations. When the Bosnian War began in March 1992, the NATO countries had just issued their new strategic concept, which, in principle, suggested that they should prepare to deal with such circumstances. But they were nowhere near being ready to do so. In fact, NATO leaders in Rome had made clear their desire to keep NATO at arm's length from the conflict, proclaiming their concern but suggesting that the parties to the Balkan conflicts "cooperate fully with the European Community in its efforts under the mandate given it by the CSCE [Conference on Security and Cooperation in Europe], both in the implementation of cease-fire and monitoring agreements and in the negotiating process within the Conference on Yugoslavia."[5]

A key reason for NATO's reticence was the reluctance of the United States to get involved. President George H. W. Bush was facing a reelection contest in which it was clear that the Democratic opposition would charge him with spending too much time on foreign policy at the expense of domestic issues. Bush may have been additionally motivated by Soviet President Gorbachev's warning in the spring of 1991 that the West should not intervene in Yugoslavia, obviously not wanting a precedent for Western intervention to be set that subsequently could be applied to a crumbling Soviet Union.[6]

If the Bush administration needed additional cover for a reticent US approach, a way out had been provided earlier by the European allies. On June 28, 1991, Jacques Poos, the foreign minister of Luxembourg, speaking for the members of the European Community, bravely claimed that the problems in the Balkans presented an opportunity for the Europeans to take charge of their own security affairs, pronouncing that it was "the hour of Europe." According to Poos, "If one problem can be solved by the Europeans, it's the Yugoslav problem. This is a European country and it's not up to the Americans and not up to anybody else."[7] Under these circumstances, the Bush administration was satisfied to leave it at this. NATO's role was restricted to helping enforce the UN embargo against weapons deliveries to any of the warring parties in Yugoslavia. The operation was conducted in parallel with a seaborne monitoring operation organized through the Western European Union.[8]

With the United States unwilling to get involved, NATO's role clearly would remain limited. However, the brutality of the conflict and the suffering of noncombatants, broadcast up close and personal for the world to see, could not be ignored.

The international community responded to the immediate consequences of the conflict by mounting a humanitarian relief operation backed up by a UN protection force (UNPROFOR), manned largely by lightly armed French, British, and other European troops whose mission was effectively limited to ensuring the safety of the relief efforts. Despite the care that President Bush took not to get involved in the Balkan conflicts, the criticism that he had spent too much time and energy on foreign policy and not enough on the US economy apparently hit home with the American people. In November 1992, George Bush lost the presidency to Democrat Bill Clinton, who came to office in 1993.

During the US presidential election campaign, Clinton had criticized Bush's hands-off Bosnia policy but, after taking office, he followed much the same approach. In April 1993, the UN Security Council agreed to impose an embargo of all land, sea, and air traffic attempting to enter Serbia and Montenegro. The Clinton administration and the European allies agreed that NATO would help enforce the enhanced embargo, but the new administration remained reluctant to get too deeply involved, fearing that the presidency could in its early months be drawn into what Secretary of State Warren Christopher called "the problem from hell."[9]

Transatlantic relations over Bosnia policy were also troubled by the fact that the United States saw and understood the conflict largely as one involving an aggressor—the Bosnian Serbs, supported by Serbia—against the much weaker Bosnian Muslims. The Europeans, for the most part, believed the conflict should be seen as a civil war in which all parties were to blame. These two different interpretations of the conflict produced divergent policy preferences. The approach to the conflict favored by many members of the US Congress was to lift the embargo against military assistance to Bosnia in order to equip and train Bosnian forces to produce a balance of power in Bosnia that would provide the necessary incentives for peace. This approach was based on the model of Serbia as the aggressor and the assumption that the United States should provide only air power and no ground forces to help resolve the conflict. The European allies strongly objected to any such "lift-and-strike" approach, particularly because the forces they had deployed in UNPROFOR depended on being seen as "neutral" in the conflict and were there only to help mitigate the humanitarian tragedy. The Europeans at that point had put troops in harm's way and the United States had not. This led to the growing perception in the 1990s that the United States would involve itself in overseas conflicts only if risks to American forces could be minimized.

The United States really did not want to touch the Bosnian tar baby. But when it became clear that international relief efforts and UNPROFOR were dealing with some of the consequences but none of the causes of the conflict, the United States, and therefore NATO, were slowly drawn toward deeper involvement. The Clinton administration still hoped to avoid placing US troops on the ground in Bosnia unless they were sent to help enforce a negotiated peace accord. Clinton sent Secretary of State Christopher on a mission to Europe to try to convince the allies to accept the lift-and-strike approach. Christopher made what has been described as a halfhearted pitch to the allies, reportedly conveying the message that he had come in a "listening mode."[10] The Europeans perceived accurately the lack of the administration's commitment to the initiative.

However, by the summer of 1993, Bosnian Serb forces were winning military victory after victory. They had encircled virtually all the "safe areas" that UNPROFOR had established to help protect civilian populations, including the major center of Sarajevo. In response, the NATO members agreed to draw up plans for air strikes by NATO forces against those threatening the viability of UNPROFOR's mission, mainly the Bosnian Serbs. The option was created with a "dual-key" arrangement in which both NATO and the United Nations would have to agree on striking any particular target.

The UN-NATO collaboration was necessitated by the fact that international involvement in the Balkans was largely under the mandate provided by UN Security Council resolutions.[11] Most countries wanted it that way, but the arrangement made for difficult relations between the United States, which provided most of the military capabilities necessary for the NATO air strikes, and the European allies, led by the British and French, whose troops were on the ground and exposed to retaliation by Bosnian Serb forces.

The Bosnian Serbs fully recognized the advantages to their cause of the split between the United States and its allies. They responded to NATO air strikes by backing off when necessary, taking UNPROFOR soldiers hostage when advantageous, and playing for time to complete their military victory.

During 1995, it became increasingly clear that the UNPROFOR approach, even backed up by NATO air strikes, could not be sustained much longer. The European allies suggested that UNPROFOR would have to be withdrawn, and this would require that the United States fulfill its pledge to protect allied forces as they were being pulled out. But such a withdrawal also would mean a victory for those seen by the United States as the aggressors, and such an outcome would have been a serious setback for US foreign policy. Trying to escape from its policy dilemma, the Clinton administration was impelled forward by the Bosnian Serb attack on the UN safe area of Srebrenica early in July 1995. The United Nations rejected the request from Dutch UNPROFOR troops for air strikes to deter the Serb attack. When it came, the Bosnian Serbs conducted a brutal campaign of blatant war crimes in the wake of their military victory. Serbian forces executed some 8,000 Bosnian boys and men and tortured and sexually abused thousands of women and children. The shocking story emerging in the aftermath of Srebrenica began to galvanize an international view that something more had to be done. The commander of the Bosnian Serb forces bragged that Srebrenica was simply the beginning of the end of the conflict. As one observer has written, "This challenge confronted the United Nations, NATO and especially the leading member states with a fundamental choice. They could act to oppose what was unfolding before them by force of arms or they could declare defeat."[12]

At a meeting in London following the Srebrenica disaster, the United States and its key European allies agreed that Serbian preparations for an attack on the safe area of Gorazde would be met with a strong air campaign, hitting Bosnian Serb targets throughout Bosnia. The United States also produced a plan for negotiations that the allies readily accepted as a way out of the crisis. Operation Deliberate Force began on August 30 after it was determined that a deadly artillery attack on a marketplace in Sarajevo had been conducted by Bosnian Serb forces. The bombing campaign, combined with a successful Croatian offensive against Serbian forces that had begun in early August, brought the Serbs and the other combatants to the bargaining table.

The United States, represented by the bright, ambitious, and controversial Richard Holbrooke and a very capable interagency team of officials, provided much of the energy behind the talks.[13] Following complex and difficult negotiations, a peace accord was completed in Dayton, Ohio, and then signed in Paris on December 14, 1995. The United Nations gave NATO a mandate to help implement the accord, and on December 16, the allies decided to launch what was at the time the largest military operation ever undertaken by NATO. NATO sent to Bosnia an Implementation

Force (IFOR) of more than 60,000 troops from NATO, partner, and other nations to maintain the peace, keep the warring factions separated, oversee the transfer of territory between the parties as specified in the peace accord, and supervise the storage of heavy weapons of the parties in approved sites. IFOR had been given one year to accomplish its tasks—a time frame recognized by most observers as inadequate for the purpose of establishing peace but perhaps necessary to appease domestic politics in the United States. At the end of that year, in December 1996, it was decided that peace would not yet be self-sustaining without continued external encouragement. NATO, with a UN mandate, replaced IFOR with a Stabilization Force (SFOR), which remained in Bosnia until replaced by a force under European Union command in December 2004.

Over the years, NATO helped establish relative peace in Bosnia-Herzegovina, but questions remained about whether the goal of producing a self-sustaining peace in the multiethnic state cobbled together at Dayton would be achieved. According to most observers, international civilian assistance had not achieved a level of effectiveness to stimulate progress toward a more stable society. In addition to a less-than-effective international response to Bosnia-Herzegovina's civilian needs, the three ethnic communities—Bosnian, Croatian, and Serbian—had made insufficient efforts to start a serious process of reconciliation that would be needed for a multiethnic state to function in the long run.

In 2002, although NATO had reduced the size of SFOR in recognition of the less imminent chance of open conflict, it was still not clear whether the Dayton approach to peace in Bosnia-Herzegovina would succeed or fail. In 2004, however, the decision to turn the mission over to the European Union suggested that the challenges had become less military and more political, economic, and social. One of the main tasks of the new European Union command would be to fight crime and corruption, which threatened to undermine Bosnia's democracy. NATO nonetheless decided to keep a small headquarters in Bosnia and Herzegovina, partly as a symbol of its continuing support for stability there.

The Bosnia experience demonstrated that the 1991 new strategic concept had been on target when it suggested that NATO needed to prepare for non-Article 5 military contingencies. Even though Article 5—the pledge to respond to an attack on another ally—remained the most profound commitment made by each NATO ally, a major attack on a NATO country had become the least likely near-term challenge to the security of the NATO members.

The conflicts in the Balkans did not directly threaten the security of most NATO allies, particularly the United States. This assessment produced the reluctance of the United States and its allies to respond effectively when the Balkan wars broke out. However, the lofty goals of making Europe whole, free, and at peace were challenged directly, as were the moral standards embraced by the United States and its allies. The danger that the conflict would spread to the borders of NATO allies, and perhaps lead to political and even military conflicts between NATO allies, did pose a threat to allied security. And if NATO was not going to be used to deal with this crisis in Europe, would it simply become an insurance policy, ceasing to be an important vehicle for the future management of Euro-Atlantic relations?

NATO's role in helping promote and then enforce a peace in Bosnia-Herzegovina answered, at least temporarily, some of these questions. NATO's continued value as an instrument for transatlantic consultation and a vehicle for political and military action became more obvious. The original European preference to handle the crisis through the United Nations and the US preference to avoid putting troops on the ground caused a costly delay in bringing an end to the brutal conflict. The fact that NATO's "habits of cooperation" facilitated putting together collaborative responses to contemporary security challenges was demonstrated, as was the utility of NATO's integrated command structure.

Some questions, however, were not answered. Could the allies in the future respond to an emerging crisis more quickly and therefore minimize the civilian casualties and dislocations that characterized the Balkan conflicts? How could rapid responses be produced by an organization in which one ally, the United States, had a wide range of military options available to it—and therefore might be more inclined to use them—while the rest of the allies had more limited military options and therefore might be more reluctant to resort to the use of force? Would responses to future crises be handicapped because the United States had grown suspicious and mistrustful of the United Nations while the European allies still believed in the necessity of obtaining a UN mandate for military operations? Would the fact that France, one of two European allies with meaningful intervention forces, still did not participate fully in NATO's integrated military structure hamper the construction of future NATO coalition operations? Would the United States be a reluctant partici-pant—and therefore an ineffective leader—in future NATO peace operations, par-ticularly given the attitude of many US conservatives that US military forces should be held in reserve for the "big" contingencies and not wasted on the more menial labor of "doing the windows" in peace operations?

Back to the NATO Adaptation Process

These and other questions remained very much open in 1996 when, with the Bosnia experience in hand and the difficult process of implementing the Dayton peace accord under way, the allies prepared to take the next steps needed to adapt the alliance to the new security environment. In many respects, the allies found it almost as difficult and time consuming to agree on the principles to guide new arrange-ments as they did arriving at a common approach to the conflict in Bosnia.[14]

The allies still faced the challenge of implementing agreements that they had made in principle in 1994 designed to give NATO a more flexible structure that would facilitate responses to new security problems. In June 1996, following months of difficult negotiations which on many occasions found the United States and France at loggerheads, the allies neared a breakthrough concerning how to organize responses to future non-Article 5 security challenges. The French had interpreted the Clinton administration's initiatives at the January 1994 Brussels summit as a sign that the United States was prepared for "Europeanization" of the alliance. The administration, on the other hand, was thinking more in terms of an evolutionary development toward greater European responsibility.[15]

At a critical meeting in Berlin, NATO foreign ministers agreed on significant new steps that, when implemented, would constitute a major transformation of NATO's missions and methods of operation. In Berlin, the allies agreed to move ahead with implementation of the CJTF concept that had been agreed on in principle at Brussels in 1994. In addition, they agreed that a European Security and Defense Identity would be created within the alliance by making NATO "assets and capabilities" available for future military operations commanded by the Western European Union (WEU), the defense organization whose membership included only European countries based on the 1948 Brussels Treaty. Such decisions would be made by consensus on a case-by-case basis. To facilitate such operations, European officers in the NATO structure would, when appropriate, shift from their NATO responsibilities to WEU command positions.[16]

The allies determined that adaptation of the alliance should be guided by three fundamental objectives: to ensure the alliance's military effectiveness and ability to perform its traditional mission of collective defense while undertaking new military roles, to preserve the transatlantic link by strengthening NATO as a forum for political consultation and military cooperation, and to support development of a European Security and Defense Identity by creating the possibility for NATO-supported task forces to perform missions under the direction of the WEU nations.

NATO forces in Europe have always been commanded by an American officer who occupies the position of Supreme Allied Commander, Europe (SACEUR), and the allies unanimously agreed that the United States should retain this top command. But the allies decided that the Deputy Supreme Allied Commander, Europe (D-SACEUR), a senior European officer, and other European officers in the NATO command structure would in the future wear WEU command hats as well as their NATO command hats.[17] This multiple-hatting procedure would, without duplicating resources and personnel, permit the WEU countries to use the NATO command structure to organize and conduct a military operation largely under European auspices.[18]

The Berlin Accord was designed to help transform NATO's role for the post-Cold War world, respond to calls from Congress for more effective sharing of international security burdens, and accommodate a more cohesive European role in the alliance. The government of France facilitated the outcome by deciding to move toward much closer military cooperation with its NATO allies to help deal with new challenges to security in Europe. The United States and other allies made major contributions to the outcome by agreeing to fundamental changes in the way that NATO had traditionally organized and run its military forces.

Agreement did not come easily. SACEUR General George Joulwan and the US Joint Chiefs of Staff had objected to the plan for strengthening the Deputy SACEUR's role and for making NATO (US) military assets available for some European-led military operations. The resistance was overcome only hours before the Berlin meeting was set to convene. President Clinton overruled Joulwan and the Joint Chiefs, giving the green light for the reform to proceed.[19]

The Berlin Accord suggested the importance the allies attached to the need for a flexible and dynamic alliance. It demonstrated the commitment of the United States, Canada, and the European allies to ensure that NATO could respond to contemporary security needs. It revealed transatlantic consensus on the need to accommodate development of greater European defense cohesion and military capabilities.

It was hoped that the agreement, giving the Europeans the potential for a more prominent role in NATO's military affairs, would also lead France to return to NATO's integrated military command. French President Jacques Chirac had implied that such a move might be possible. In the wake of the Berlin Accord, however, a series of events prevented the deal from being consummated. First, in the summer of 1996, Chirac sent a letter to President Clinton suggesting that the reform of NATO should include transfer of the position of Supreme Allied Commander Allied Forces South from the United States to a European country. The French saw such a potential shift in commands as a necessary token of the US willingness to let Europe take more responsibility in the alliance. Given the importance of the Mediterranean region to US interests and the fact that Clinton had just overruled the Joint Chiefs in order to agree to the Berlin Accord, Clinton was not going to "give away" such an important position. Following the small crisis that this request and its rejection caused in US-French relations, the door to a French return apparently was firmly closed early in 1997, when Chirac called early legislative elections (which his party lost, ceding control to the left) and did not want to be accused of abandoning an important Gaullist policy of independence from NATO's integrated command. Only in 2009 did French President Nicolas Sarkozy open the door and walk France back into the Integrated Command Structure (ICS).

Meanwhile, implementation of the Berlin Accord moved ahead slowly, complicated by divergent US and French interpretations of what the agreement actually meant. Even though NATO had already constructed a combined joint task force (IFOR) to conduct the peace enforcement operation in Bosnia and a second one (SFOR) to help keep that peace, the alliance could not declare the CJTF concept operational until the allies had worked through all the details and conducted the requisite tests and exercises. This highly deliberate process gave rise to circulation of a number of anecdotes. Most quoted is the one about a NATO discussion of the CJTF approach in which, after the US representative had described the great virtues of the concept, the French representative supposedly replied, "It looks as though it will work in practice, but will it work in theory?"

The Kosovo Campaign

Even as NATO conducted a relatively successful peace enforcement operation in Bosnia, the story of conflict in the Balkans was far from over, and the allies were to get yet another chance to test the CJTF theory in practice. As noted earlier, the disintegration of the former Yugoslavia unleashed several power struggles among ethnic and religious groups whose animosities toward one another had been suppressed for decades. Kosovo, a region in southern Serbia (more formally known as the Federal Republic of Yugoslavia), was populated mainly by ethnic Albanians. In 1989, Serbian leader Slobodan Milosevic removed the region's former autonomy. Kosovo became an explosion waiting to happen.

During 1998, open conflict between Serbian military and police forces and ethnic Albanian forces in Kosovo resulted in more than 1,500 ethnic Albanian deaths and displaced 400,000 from their homes. The NATO allies became gravely concerned about the escalating conflict, its humanitarian consequences, and Milosevic's disregard for diplomatic efforts aimed at peaceful resolution. In October 1998, NATO decided to begin a phased air campaign against Yugoslavia if the Milosevic regime did not withdraw part of its forces from Kosovo, cooperate in bringing an end to the violence there, and facilitate the return of refugees to their homes. A UN resolution had called for these and other measures. At the last moment, Milosevic agreed to comply with the resolution, and the air strikes were called off. In addition, it was agreed that the Organization for Security and Cooperation in Europe (OSCE) would establish a verification mission in Kosovo to observe compliance with UN resolutions.

NATO assumed two special responsibilities in support of the OSCE mission. First, it established an aerial surveillance mission, Operation Eagle Eye, to observe compliance with the agreement. Several partner nations agreed to participate in the operation. Second, NATO established a special military task force, led by France, to be deployed in the Former Yugoslav Republic of Macedonia (FYROM). Under the overall direction of NATO's SACEUR, this force was designed to rescue members of the OSCE Kosovo verification mission if renewed conflict should put them at risk.

The deteriorating situation in Kosovo in late 1998 led the international Contact Group (the United States, Britain, France, Germany, Italy, and Russia)[20] to produce a draft peace plan on January 29, 1999, that they then proposed to the Serbian authorities and representatives of the Kosovo Serbian population. On January 30, the North Atlantic Council agreed to authorize NATO Secretary-General Javier Solana to initiate NATO air attacks against Serbian targets if Milosevic did not accept the terms of the plan. The Kosovo Albanian authorities accepted the plan on March 18, but the Serbians rejected it. NATO initiated air strikes against Serbian targets in both Serbia and Kosovo on March 24. In response, Serbian forces began driving Kosovo ethnic Albanians from their homes, killing some 10,000 ethnic Albanians and torturing and raping many others.

The NATO air campaign, conducted largely by US forces with high-tech capabilities, lasted for 78 days, targeting Yugoslav military forces and important civilian and military infrastructure.[21] The campaign was conducted without a mandate from the UN Security Council, where it could have been vetoed by the Russian and Chinese permanent members. The European allies would have much preferred having such a mandate but accepted the US argument that it was more important in this case to send a forceful message to Milosevic and stop the ethnic cleansing than to stick to international niceties. The allies pledged in the North Atlantic Treaty to "refrain in their international relations from the threat or use of force in any manner inconsistent with the purposes of the United Nations." In this case, the allies judged that use of force against Serbia was consistent with the purposes of the United Nations, even if they could not get a UN mandate.

Serbian President Milosevic agreed to a peace plan based on NATO conditions on June 3. It required the removal of all Yugoslav forces from Kosovo and provided for the deployment of a NATO-led force (KFOR) to keep the peace while Kosovo was put under international administration until autonomous, elected institutions and officials could be established. Kosovo's final status was left unsettled.

The Kosovo operation ultimately succeeded in driving out Serbian forces and allowing the Albanian population to return, in many cases to homes, neighborhoods, and entire towns that had been destroyed by the Serbs. But the victory was not without a price. Even during the operation, critics complained that NATO's military campaign had provoked the final and most brutal phase of Serbia's ethnic cleansing operation. As the air campaign dragged on with no sign of a Milosevic concession, differences arose among allies and in domestic political debates about an air campaign that was conducted under rules intended to minimize the risks to allied forces and that denied strategically important targets to NATO forces. Some argued strongly that ground forces would have to go in to drive Yugoslav forces out. The debate produced partially accurate images of a United States that thought all wars could be fought without risk to friendly forces versus Europeans who better appreciated the facts on the ground. Perhaps the most dramatic impact, however, was on the perception of a growing gap in deployed technology between the United States and its allies and, from the European side, a realization that Europe could influence the conduct of future military operations only if it could bring more capable forces to the table.

Thus, the end of the war over Kosovo and the beginning of peacekeeping and reconstruction was a victory for NATO albeit a qualified one. The successful outcome of the air campaign meant that the allies avoided the potential casualties, intra-allied divisions, and domestic unrest that a ground force campaign could have produced. However, the interaction between political objectives and military strategy had a lasting effect on US and European attitudes toward NATO management of military operations.

The ultimate success of NATO's strategy surprised the vast majority of military experts and pundits. Most of them had blamed President Clinton, his advisers, and

Supreme Allied Commander General Wesley Clark for concocting an air-only campaign designed to avoid NATO casualties but, in their judgment, unlikely to bring Milosevic to heel. In retirement, General Clark answered his critics in a book that argued that a successful end to the campaign had been delayed by constraints imposed on his operations by Washington and interference from other NATO allies, particularly France.[22] Meanwhile, a US General Accounting (now "Accountability") Office report released in July 2001 added to the critique. The report found that the need to maintain alliance cohesion during the conflict led to important departures from standard US military doctrine and resulted in a limited mission with unclear objectives. Many American military officers and civilian officials who participated in this campaign felt that these departures resulted in a longer conflict, more extensive damage to Yugoslavia, and significant risks to alliance forces.[23]

Such critics appear to have been half right and half wrong. They were right that the air campaign allowed Milosevic to continue his ethnic cleansing policies. They were right that Milosevic would have been more convinced of Western resolve if ground forces had been on the table from the beginning. In fact, the buildup of Western forces around Kosovo prior to the end of the conflict did begin to bring ground forces into the military equation, particularly as seen from Belgrade. Moreover, the military revival of the Kosovo Liberation Army, the main Kosovo Albanian fighting force, played a crucial role in forcing Serbian units out of concealment, making them more vulnerable to Western air strikes. NATO did, in the end, have a ground force component to its strategy, even if it developed tacitly and half-heartedly.

Given Milosevic's calculating but stubborn behavior, such critics did not believe that a tacit ground force threat would be sufficient. In addition, the general anti-Clinton perspective of many such experts and, in Europe, the prevailing belief that the United States was no longer willing to take casualties in conflicts not directly linked to "vital" US interests tended to block an objective evaluation of the other important factors at work.[24]

Clinton may have been reluctant to envision US casualties, but he also faced other serious constraints. Only one NATO ally, the United Kingdom, avidly supported the threat of a ground campaign. Some allies were actively opposed, and Clinton supported the air campaign as the only approach that could keep the alliance united and at the same time avoid substantial US casualties. The second important constraint was the absence of good invasion routes, created by a combination of difficult terrain, limited infrastructure in neighboring countries, and the reluctance of some states in the region to be used as launching points for a ground campaign.

At the beginning of the air campaign, and even toward its end, there was no NATO consensus on behalf of even threatening a ground force invasion of Kosovo. The most important missing links were Germany and Greece. If the United States had tried to impose such a strategy on the alliance, divisions among NATO members, never too far beneath the surface, would have burst into the open. The German government might have fallen, and the Greek government, by denying NATO access to its port and road facilities, could have severely hampered ground operations. Even though it was popular in Europe to see NATO as following US policy in lockstep, the fact is that neither the Clinton administration nor its predecessors led the alliance successfully by dictating NATO policy.

The big plus for NATO, in addition to achieving its main declared objectives, was that, not without some difficulty, NATO unity was preserved throughout the conflict. In addition, the fact that the air campaign was conducted with such efficiency left a strong impression concerning the readiness and condition of NATO air forces. The loss of only two aircraft and no NATO military casualties in action was both objectively and statistically convincing of US and NATO military effectiveness.

There may never be another contingency that replicates the Kosovo experience. This likelihood, however, suggested the importance of flexible contingency planning, the training and equipping of NATO forces to deal with a wide range of geographic and climatic conditions, and the availability of excellent tactical and strategic intelligence resources. These directions, however, would require political commitment and resources to implement.

The reality that political factors inhibited NATO's ability to show a stronger hand to Milosevic from the beginning threatened to leave a lasting mark on alliance decision making. The NATO allies, in the future, might again face a choice between two options: keeping allied unity but compromising its military strategy or abandoning NATO unity, operating with an ad hoc coalition but deploying a more robust military strategy.

NATO theology, followed to a capital "T" by President Clinton, holds that it is almost always better to maintain a unified alliance than to abandon attempts to produce alliance consensus. However, the Kosovo experience suggested that it would not be a surprise if, in some future non-collective defense military contingency, ad hoc approaches were to appear more attractive to NATO's main military players (the United States, the United Kingdom, and France). The United States obviously chose this course when planning its campaign against Taliban and al Qaeda forces in Afghanistan, partly as a result of the "lessons learned" from the allied management of the Kosovo conflict.

Some European and even American critics of the Kosovo air campaign portrayed it as another example of the United States imposing its hegemonic solutions on a hapless Europe. Such critics echoed themes that came with a vengeance from Chinese and Russian commentaries on the war. The facts of the matter, when fully assessed, suggest the opposite. The role of the United States in this affair was to provide the critical military components for a strategy that was handicapped by political realities in Europe as well as in the United States.

The heavy European reliance on US military capabilities, once again, added urgency to the initiatives of British Prime Minister Tony Blair and other key leaders in the European Union to develop military capabilities more in keeping with Europe's economic and financial resources. There was good cause for Europeans to be concerned about their military capabilities because a healthy US-European security relationship in the future would most likely demand that both burdens and responsibilities be shared equitably. It was no accident that the first peacekeeping forces entering Kosovo were, and remained, mainly European, not American. General Clark and NATO's political leadership were sensitive to the need to balance the perception of the US-dominated air operation with the equally accurate perception of a peacekeeping operation that would rely heavily on European troops. The implications of these aspects for a developing Common European Security and Defense Policy are discussed in Chapter 10.

The question left over from the Kosovo campaign, with its heady mix of positive and negative features, was whether the alliance would in the future use the experience to improve its military preparedness and command arrangements for such conflicts. The fact that the United States and Europe learned different lessons made it difficult to translate the experience into constructive changes for the alliance. The United States learned that it did not like to run military operations largely with US forces but with substantial allied political interference; the Europeans learned that they would prefer to have more influence on the course of a conflict whose outcome directly affected their interests.

The Washington Summit and NATO's Evolving Mission Profile

In April 1999, the NATO allies met at the summit in Washington with the intent of celebrating NATO's fiftieth anniversary and approving guidance to carry the alliance into the twenty-first century. However, before the allies could issue the revised strategic concept on which they had been working for some two years, they were forced by developments in the Balkans to move from debates on principles to decisions in practice. Despite claims by some US officials that the 1999 strategic concept would guide NATO for a decade or longer,[25] the summit produced what was largely an incremental step down the road toward twenty-first-century security requirements.

The summit was held under a Kosovo cloud that the summit leaders were unable to dispel. At the time of the summit, it was unclear whether the Kosovo air campaign would ultimately have the desired result. The Clinton administration decided that the main goal of the summit should be to demonstrate allied unity. Most other allied leaders apparently agreed. British Prime Minister Tony Blair clearly had hoped to move allied governments toward a commitment to bring ground forces to bear in Kosovo. But the desire for at least a facade of unity won out. Compromise formulations were fashioned that papered over allied differences about the relationship of NATO to the United Nations and the limits on application of NATO's crisis management operations.

The Washington summit was the first for NATO's three new members, the Czech Republic, Hungary, and Poland (for a discussion of NATO's enlargement process, see Chapter 6). All additional aspiring candidates for NATO membership were given some cause for hope. The allies created a Membership Action Plan (MAP) process

Photo 8.1: Opening of the 1999 Washington 50th Anniversary Summit

Source: NATO Photos.

that promised cooperation beyond possibilities in the Partnership for Peace and, perhaps more important, feedback from NATO concerning their progress toward membership. MAP participants were promised that NATO would formally review the enlargement process again no later than 2002.[26]

The allies repeated support for the development of a more coherent European role in the alliance. But the goal of giving new impetus to the European Security and Defense Identity largely fell by the wayside, left for the European allies to develop further in subsequent European Union gatherings.

One of the problems addressed by allied defense ministers prior to the summit had been the challenge of preserving the ability of NATO militaries to fight as coalition forces in the future. The greatest concern was the growing technology gap between US armed forces and those of most European nations. European allies had been feasting on the post-Cold War "peace dividend," using reductions in military spending to help meet the requirements for European monetary union. Meanwhile, the United States had continued developing new technologies for its military forces. The consequence, a large capabilities gap between the United States and its allies, was evident in the air campaign against Serbia.

At the summit, the allies agreed on a "Defense Capabilities Initiative (DCI)"[27] designed to try to preserve the ability of allied forces to operate effectively with one another in future decades. The initiative put new political focus on the issue, which surely was needed. But the real problem was money. NATO agreement on what capabilities were needed at a time when threat perceptions were so low throughout Europe would not necessarily open up European treasuries to provide the required funding. In 2001, a NATO Parliamentary Assembly report observed that "the continuing decline in most European defence budgets may jeopardise the success of DCI, and with it the ability of the Alliance to carry out the roles and missions that it set out for itself in the 1999 Strategic Concept."[28]

NATO's 1999 Strategic Concept

One of the most anticipated products of the summit was the preparation of an updated strategic concept. The negotiations leading up to approval of the 1999 concept faced some key differences about NATO's future role and mandate. Perhaps the most important one was the question of how far NATO's mandate should extend beyond collective defense. The United States, with support from the United Kingdom, lobbied for increased alliance focus on new risks posed by the proliferation of nuclear, chemical, and biological weapons of mass destruction and by terrorism.

The North Atlantic Treaty invites the allies to cooperate on "threats" to allied interests, and these emerging risks certainly qualified. The Treaty imposes no formal constraints on the ability of the allies to decide to use their cooperative framework to deal with challenges that do not qualify as Article 5 (collective defense) missions. The United States preferred that the 1999 strategic concept impose no formal geographic limits on the relevance of NATO cooperation. Most European allies, however, did not want NATO to be seen as a "global alliance" and preferred that decisions on NATO's future operations be made on a case-by-case basis.

In the early months of 1998, as the allies began work on the strategic concept that was to be agreed in April 1999, a major issue developed between the United States and several European allies concerning the relationship between NATO non-Article 5 operations and the United Nations. In preparing the new concept, the United States wanted to keep open the possibility that NATO would from time to time be required to act in the absence of a mandate from the United Nations. France and some other European governments did not disagree with the logic of the US assessment but strongly opposed turning possible exceptions into a new rule. From the French perspective, the rule should be to seek a UN mandate and then decide what to do should such a mandate appear blocked by Russia or China.

This debate, conducted in the corridors at NATO, turned into a real and imminent policy issue over Kosovo. By the autumn of 1998, Russia and China had made it clear that they would not support a UN Security Council resolution authorizing the use of force against Serbia for its activities in Kosovo. Despite this opposition, all NATO allies accepted that Slobodan Milosevic's policies of repression against the ethnic Albanian majority in Kosovo posed a threat not only to internationally accepted values but also to peace in the Balkans and therefore to stability in Europe.

By late 1998, France and most other allies had accepted that Kosovo could constitute the kind of exception that they still opposed making into a new rule. When in March 1999 the allies saw no choice but to conduct air strikes against Serbia after the breakdown of the Rambouillet negotiations, they went ahead without the blessing of the Security Council.

Nevertheless, French and American differences over how to treat the mandate issue in the new strategic concept persisted, requiring carefully crafted compromises in the document issued by allied leaders in Washington. The strategic concept agreed to in Washington[29] acknowledged that the UN Security Council "has the primary responsibility for the maintenance of international peace and security and, as such, plays a crucial role in contributing to security and stability in the Euro-Atlantic area." The concept also noted that the OSCE "plays an essential role in promoting peace and stability, enhancing cooperative security and advancing democracy and human rights in Europe." The concept pledged that NATO "will seek, in cooperation with other organizations, to prevent conflict, or, should a crisis arise, to contribute to its effective management, consistent with international law, including through the possibility of conducting non-Article 5 crisis response operations." This language essentially met the French requirement for UN Security Council primacy regarding international security but left the door open for the allies, on a case-by-case basis, to act again in the future without a UN mandate if necessary.

The European preference for an international mandate was motivated partly by the need to demonstrate to public opinion that force is being used for the right purposes. Moreover, Europeans have a general preference for basing their foreign and security policies on international law. This is particularly important in Germany for solid historical reasons that have been embedded in both Germany's constitution and its political consciousness. Both the United Kingdom and France prefer to act on the basis of a Security Council mandate, given their positions as permanent (and veto-holding) members of the Council. France felt this need rather more strongly than the United Kingdom, which believed that it derived influence over US actions through its close ties to Washington. Other European countries, unable to take the law into their own hands, believed that their interests were best served by an international system that runs on a set of predictable rules and regulations to the maximum extent possible. In addition, most Europeans would far prefer to have the Russians on board in support of any military operation in Europe. From their perspective, Russia remained an important European influence even if, at that time, it was weak in virtually all respects (except in its possession of superpower inventories of both strategic and theater nuclear weapons—another good reason for wanting to bring Moscow along).

All the European allies accepted that the new threats identified by the United States were serious and merited their attention. They agreed with the United States when it appeared that NATO might have to use force against Serbia without a specific UN mandate to do so. But most were reluctant to make cooperation more or less automatic in any given peace enforcement or counter-proliferation operation. They saw their willingness to act against Serbia without a UN mandate as an exception.

In the end, such decisions were left to be made on a case-by-case basis, with Kosovo seen neither as a new rule nor as the last time NATO might act without a UN mandate. Nonetheless, the allies agreed to establish a new NATO center to monitor these threats and help plan NATO responses.

The new concept, however, did not settle the question of whether a UN mandate should always be required. By the same token, the concept placed no formal geographic limitations on NATO's activities, nor did it identify a specific area of operations for those activities. This somewhat "fuzzy" outcome in the new concept on such issues accurately reflected the fact that NATO is an alliance of sovereign nation-states that prefer to reserve decisions on future NATO operations that do not involve an attack on a member.

The Washington summit did not, as some US officials had hoped, lay out the course for NATO's next decade. It made a start down that road but left many crucial questions unanswered. This was not necessarily a failure of allied governments but rather a reflection of the extent to which the Kosovo experience could affect NATO's future development and the more traditional fact that no one meeting in NATO's history has ever resolved all outstanding issues.

Another issue not resolved by the 1999 concept was the question of how to distinguish between Article 5 and non-Article 5 missions, neither of which has ever been differentiated by the scope of the operations. Rather, the distinction is determined by the reason for the operation.

Article 5 is frequently seen as an "automatic" commitment, requiring all allies to come to the defense of one or more under attack. The language in the Treaty, however, is more qualified. Allies are committed to regard an attack on one as an attack on all, but then each may "take such action as it deems necessary, including the use of armed force." The virtual automaticity of the guarantee actually was a product not of the language in the Treaty but in the way the allies deployed military forces on the front lines in Europe. Multinational layer-cake deployments assured that an attack on front-line ally Germany would at the very outset engage the military forces of the United States and other allies, ensuring that they would have very little choice but to respond with military force sufficient to end hostilities on terms favorable to the allies.

There is no such automaticity either in the Treaty or in practice regarding non-Article 5 operations. The response of the alliance in such cases must be determined by individual, independent national judgments, all of which must be at least permissive of the proposed action, if not actively supportive. The strength of the Treaty's non-Article 5 provisions is that Article 5 does not provide a mandate to act in the case of threats to interests of the allies, only to deal with circumstances created by an attack on one of them. Article 4, on the other hand, specifically takes into account the possible need to consult concerning threats and to consider joint actions to deal with those threats.

That said, from a military planning perspective, the operations in Bosnia and Kosovo were of impressive size and scope. They were politically complex and militarily demanding. But they differed from traditional Article 5 planning in a number of ways. Most important, NATO planners had a fairly clear idea of what forces would be available in the case of a Warsaw Pact attack on NATO. In both the Bosnia and the Kosovo operations, there was no way to know far in advance what forces member states would send to the operation. This meant that NATO planners were forced to develop a variety of theoretical options to present to their political leaders and then hope that forces would be made available to implement the option selected by NATO national officials. In addition, while a hard core of NATO forces was deployed forward during the Cold War to form the first echelons of a defense against a Warsaw Pact attack, NATO's response to non-Article 5 contingencies must be based on forces that are capable of being moved, establishing themselves in the theater of conflict, and then conducting military operations. The logistics for such deployed operations are much more complicated than those required to support frontline forces engaging in border defense.

Lessons from the Balkans

NATO's initial involvement in the Balkans developed with reluctance and considerable political difficulty during the 1990s, but became seen as the first example of NATO's continued relevance to twenty-first-century security requirements. Only NATO could have organized and conducted the peacekeeping mission in Bosnia and Herzegovina and the air war against Serbia over Kosovo. That remained true a decade into the twenty-first century. NATO's continuing involvement in the Balkans helps sustain a degree of security and stability that provide the opportunity for development of liberal institutions in the states that are emerging from the former Yugoslavia in a more peaceful regional environment.

NATO's experiences in the Balkans have made it clear that running a war with multiple centers of political direction can be a demanding, frustrating task. On the other hand, if NATO had not existed, it is unlikely that the many NATO and non-NATO military forces that have played important roles in the Balkan operations could have worked together as effectively as they did. The NATO focus on interoperability and development of habits of cooperation in both political and military relations makes operations among the forces of NATO member states possible. It also created a framework that can accommodate contributions by other countries. It is no coincidence that the European Union is developing the forces for its European Security and Defense Policy under "NATO standards." The bottom line is that the day-to-day collaboration that takes place under the NATO banner has positive practical consequences whose potential benefits stretch well beyond collective defense requirements and well beyond Europe's borders. Even when NATO's integrated command structure is not used to run military operations, the fact that participants in ad hoc coalitions led by the United States or European Union members start out with a degree of interoperability will make such operations more effective.

In addition, the NATO role in Balkan operations created a framework in which all the NATO allies share responsibility for the security challenges there, even as they divide up tasks required to fulfill the missions. In the early 1990s, some Europeans were tempted to see the Balkan challenge as one that could and should be handled by Europeans, not the Americans. Throughout the 1990s, many Americans felt that the United States should not be required to play such a major military role in the Balkans, given that the Europeans were closer to and had a greater stake in the region. For some, this had meant that the European Union should take over responsibility for Balkan security, allowing the United States to move on to other military tasks. The George W. Bush administration came to office having made such an argument during the 2000 presidential election campaign. Once in office, however, wiser heads in the administration, notably Secretary of State Colin Powell, decided that a unilateral US withdrawal from the Balkans at that point could undermine prospects for continued development of liberal institutions and regional stability. Even though the main responsibilities for Bosnia-Herzegovina were turned over to the European Union, NATO has continued to provide a security presence in Kosovo pending a more settled situation there. In 2009, that time still did not appear near.

NATO Responds to Post-9/11 Requirements

Even though NATO was not immediately given a role to play following the September 11, 2001, terrorist attacks, it was clear to most observers that NATO would have to contribute to the struggle against international terrorism to remain relevant to the security needs of its member states. But NATO did not yet have the mandate from the member states to operate beyond Europe where many of the military operations against terrorist organizations were being conducted. The alliance was neither organized nor equipped to play a meaningful role.

Ironically, at a time when the allies were becoming seriously divided over what to do about Iraq, they nonetheless were able to move forward on a number of NATO initiatives designed to overcome barriers to a more central NATO role in the fight against terrorism. The work produced a package of measures approved at the summit meeting in Prague, the Czech Republic, in November 2002.

Perhaps the most important development came without particular notice. Discussions at NATO during the year had with little controversy moved beyond the problems encountered in Washington in 1999 concerning NATO's area of operation. NATO foreign ministers, meeting as the North Atlantic Council in May 2002 in Reykjavik, Iceland, declared that the allies must be capable of carrying out "the full range of . . . missions . . . to field forces wherever they are needed."[30] By the time of the Prague Summit, the allies were agreed that NATO had to be ready to intervene militarily anywhere the interests of NATO countries were threatened. The old "out of area" debate had ended, with no major fanfare.

NATO's Transformation

Given the nature of the challenges NATO has faced since the end of the Cold War, it is not surprising that the topic of how to "transform" the alliance has come front and center in recent years. The concept was developed originally with the thought that NATO militaries needed to transform the contingency plans, capabilities, equipment, and training to move away from border defense and toward force projection. The NATO nations even dedicated a major command to the transformation task when, in 2002, they converted the Allied Command Atlantic in Norfolk, Virginia to the Allied Command Transformation (ACT). The new command was given no operational responsibilities, but instead was intended to promote transformation of alliance military capabilities. Allied Command Transformation's goal was to ensure that NATO military forces, concepts, doctrines, and training are focused on the new security challenges faced by alliance forces. At the same time, Allied Command Europe, NATO's other strategic command, was renamed "Allied Command Operations (ACO)."

In an attempt to plant the transformation goal more firmly in the decision-making processes of the member states, the leaders formulated a "Prague Capabilities Commitment (PCC)" saying they did so as part of the continuing Alliance effort to improve and develop new military capabilities for modern warfare in a high threat environment. The Prague communiqué declared that "Individual allies have made firm and specific political commitments to improve their capabilities in the areas of chemical, biological, radiological, and nuclear defence; intelligence, surveillance, and target acquisition; air-to-ground surveillance; command, control, and communications; combat effectiveness, including precision guided munitions and suppression of enemy air defences; strategic air and sea lift; air-to-air refueling; and deployable combat support and combat service support units."[31]

The Defense Capabilities Initiative (DCI) approved at the 1999 Washington Summit had ambitiously covered about every imaginable shortcoming of NATO forces. The allies tried to give the PCC a more narrow focus on capabilities that would be required by the NATO Response Force in the hope that it also would be more successful than the DCI. The underlying problem in most European countries remained a shortage of funds devoted to defense, but the new capabilities commitment at least identified areas where available funds should be concentrated. One area of particular concern was the challenge of dealing with potential chemical, biological, and nuclear attacks. At Prague, the allies agreed to create a Multinational Chemical, Biological, Radiological and Nuclear Defense (CBRN) battalion, which was brought to operational status by December 2003. The battalion, led by the Czech Republic, helped provide security for the summer 2004 Athens Olympics.

The ACT describes itself as "NATO's leading agent for change; enabling, facilitating and advocating continuous improvement of military capabilities to enhance the military interoperability, relevance and effectiveness of the Alliance." In a vacuum, this might have been a spectacular undertaking to occupy NATO and member state militaries for many years. In the real world, NATO military interventions in the Balkans and then in Afghanistan demonstrated the need for transformation and, at the same time, made it more difficult.

It is possible to suggest that the requirement for NATO to run operations in the Balkans and Afghanistan has killed transformation. The suggestion is that the real world had intruded on NATO's classroom exercise to make it almost academic.

Perhaps the response to this judgment is that NATO must use its real world experiences as the main drivers for transformation, rather than looking at them as getting in the way. The fact is that the experience in Iraq, as troubled as it was, has been a transformational experience for the United States military. US forces encountered serious asymmetric responses from Iraqi and al Qaeda fighters, particularly the use of Improvised Explosive Devices (IEDs) against allied troops and armored vehicles. The threat forced changes not only in tactics but also in equipment, leading to a new generation of armored vehicles that are more resistant to IED attacks.

Much of the discussion of the failures and successes of transformation revolve around the story of the NATO Response Force (NRF). The concept of such a force was developed in think tank studies, and originally was supposed to bring together highly-capable American forces with forces from European allied militaries. The goal was to produce a force that was highly capable and able to respond quickly to contingencies before other forces could be mustered. In addition, it was thought that such an integrated NATO force would help spread American know-how and technological sophistication to allied militaries.

The NRF concept called for development of a combined (multiple nations participating), joint (army, air, and naval units) force some 21,000 strong. The force was designed to have modern, highly capable fighter aircraft, ships, army vehicles, combat service support, logistics, communications, intelligence, and all other attributes required to make it an agile, effective force.

When the allies approved the NRF concept in 2002, it more or less followed the plan that had been developed by experts, but did not include extensive contributions to the force, in part because Afghanistan and Iraq were already American preoccupations. From the perspective of the George W. Bush administration, the NRF became a challenge to the European allies to transform their forces to make them more relevant to contemporary security threats and responses.[32]

It could be argued that the NRF has become more of a distraction than a help to the alliance's ability to perform its missions by holding back for NRF purposes forces that were desperately needed in Afghanistan. But the forces assigned are not "locked up in a drawer," and can be used as necessary by the states from which they originated. There is no doubt that NATO's military forces still require substantial transformation at all levels. The main obstacle is the lack of political will in national capitals to devote the priority and resources to the necessary upgrading and reorientation of military forces.

Over the past 20 years, a number of factors produced this lack of will, including the desire to realize the post-Cold War peace dividend, the constraints imposed on discretionary spending, notably including defense, by the deficit spending limits imposed by European Union monetary union, and differences with the United States over the best mix of hard and soft power to deal with international security challenges. Today, even though the allies no longer have the "Bush alibi" for limiting their defense efforts, one can add the global economic downturn to the list of factors that will make political leaders unwilling and, in some cases, unable to support even current levels of defense spending. Only a handful of NATO's European members currently achieve the informal alliance goal of spending at least two percent of gross domestic product (GDP) on defense. The estimated average for NATO Europe in 2008 was 1.7 percent of GDP, while the United States came in at 4.0.[33]

This suggests that, in order to maintain capable and relevant military forces, NATO nations will have to be particularly creative and efficient. Perhaps the most important requirement will be for nations to establish clear spending priorities, and to make those priorities consistent with transformation requirements.

Another obvious conclusion is one that has been around for at least three decades: small and mid-size NATO allies need to look more closely at developing cooperative military programs and units with other allies. The 2002 Prague Capabilities Commitment pointed in the right direction, and the NATO-EU Capability Group helps put the necessary focus on the fact that NATO and EU programs should move along the same axis. Some progress has been made in this area, but stronger political will is required to make more serious headway.

There is still strong resistance in most NATO nations to giving up elements of force structure that may no longer make strategic sense. This is somewhat inconsistent with the fact that countries already depend to varying degrees on their EU and NATO partners for ultimate assurance of their well-being, but traditions die hard. The PCC walked tenderly around the question of task specialization and multinational programs, but difficult economic conditions suggest that new efforts may have to be considered in this area. Most importantly, when countries face financial circumstances in which they may be forced to abandon defense programs, units or missions, they should do so as part of a plan developed in cooperation with allies rather than unilaterally.

It would not be long before the Allied Command Operations (formerly Allied Command Europe) would have an important mission to run. Following the United States military operations that removed the Taliban from power in Afghanistan, an International Security Assistance Force (ISAF) was created under mandate from the United Nations Security Council to help secure the area around the capital of Kabul. Beginning early in 2002, the force was commanded by the United Kingdom and then in six-month rotations by Turkey and then jointly by Germany and the Netherlands with support from NATO. NATO took over command in August 2003, moving beyond the rotational leadership of the force among NATO countries.

ISAF is the first NATO operation beyond Europe. As such, and because it is an important mission in the fight against international terrorism, the success or failure of ISAF could be critically important to NATO's future. NATO's role in Afghanistan is considered in Chapter 9.

NATO Nuclear Weapons in a New Strategic Environment

From the very beginning, nuclear weapons questions played a central role in the transatlantic bargain. Ensuring that Germany would not become a nuclear weapons power was part and parcel of the transatlantic bargain. In the early 1950s, domestic financial considerations led the Eisenhower administration to make NATO's strategy heavily reliant on the threat of massive retaliation against the Soviet Union should it attack Western Europe. After Soviet advances in long-range missilery and nuclear weapons undermined massive retaliation, the allies shifted to a flexible response strategy based on deploying a spectrum of nuclear and nonnuclear forces to deter a Soviet-led Warsaw Pact attack. Soviet deployment of SS-20 missiles that could target all of NATO European territory provided the rationale for NATO's decision to deploy ground-launched cruise and Pershing II missiles that could hit Russian targets from bases in Western Europe.

When the Cold War ended, the allies faced many decisions concerning whether NATO strategy still required a nuclear component and what should be done about new threats from terrorists and rogue states for which traditional deterrence might not work. Beginning in 1989, the allies focused particularly on countering nuclear proliferation. They reaffirmed that nuclear weapons remained central to NATO's deterrence strategy. In the early glow of the post-Cold War era, the allies called them weapons of last resort, although they subsequently backed away from this description and put more emphasis on the constructive uncertainty that NATO's nuclear capabilities would raise in any potential adversary's mind.

Throughout the 1990s, the allies dramatically reduced NATO nuclear weapons beyond the cuts called for in arms control agreements with the Soviet Union. However, in terms of the transatlantic bargain, nuclear weapons policy was "the dog that didn't bark." The allies chose to move carefully and quietly on nuclear weapons policy, perhaps reflecting the concern that dramatic changes could begin to unravel the transatlantic bargain in which nuclear weapons had played such an important role.[34]

Changes to NATO Nuclear Strategy and Forces

NATO's nuclear strategy and forces were key to the alliance's ability to deter Soviet aggression during the Cold War. In the new political and strategic environment of the 1990s, NATO had to take a long, hard look at the nuclear component of its strategy. Considering that nuclear weapons and strategy had been a prominent and controversial aspect of the transatlantic bargain from the beginning, nuclear issues assumed a relatively low-key role in the 1990s. However, without formal negotiations and with no treaty to bind the two sides, the United States took the initiative to reduce short-range nuclear weapons in its arsenal, many of which were deployed in Europe, and the Soviet Union responded in kind.

On May 3, 1990, President George H. W. Bush told a Washington press conference that the United States would not modernize the obsolescent LANCE tactical nuclear missile system or US nuclear artillery shells deployed in Europe. The president's move came in response to the dramatic changes in Europe and resulting opposition in the US Congress to costly programs that made little sense in terms of the new political and military situation there. He called for a NATO summit conference to agree, among other things, on "broad objectives for future negotiations between the United States and the Soviet Union on the current short-range nuclear missile forces in Europe, which should begin shortly after a CFE [Conventional Forces in Europe] treaty has been signed."

The London Declaration, issued by NATO leaders at their summit meeting in London on July 5–6, 1990, concluded that with eventual withdrawal of Soviet forces from their deployments in Eastern Europe and implementation of an agreement reducing conventional armed forces in Europe, the alliance would be able "to adopt a new NATO strategy making nuclear forces truly weapons of last resort."[35] This shift in approach would alter NATO's long-standing flexible response doctrine in which the use of nuclear weapons could conceivably have been authorized early in a military conflict. The summit declaration did not, however, forgo the allied option of using nuclear weapons first in a conflict if necessary, and it left open the possibility that nuclear forces will be "kept up to date where necessary." The leaders nonetheless decided that NATO no longer would require all its existing inventory of short-range nuclear weapons consisting largely of nuclear artillery shells, bombs on dual-capable attack aircraft, and the LANCE missile system.

On September 27, 1991, following the failed attempt of hard-line communists to seize control in Moscow, President Bush announced a set of wide-ranging changes in US nuclear policy and deployments. He decided to remove and destroy all US land-based nuclear missiles from Europe and withdraw all US sea-based tactical nuclear weapons while inviting the Soviet Union to take reciprocal actions. The president said that the United States should keep a nuclear capability for NATO, but at the same time he discontinued the program to develop the SRAM-II missile, intended for deployment on strategic bombers. A tactical version of this system, the SRAM-T, intended for deployment in Europe, also was discontinued. This left the US nuclear deployment in Europe limited to free-fall nuclear bombs on dual-capable ground attack aircraft.

The president's decisions were positively received throughout Europe and in the Soviet Union. On October 5, 1991, Soviet President Mikhail Gorbachev announced his reciprocal intent to eliminate short-range ground-launched nuclear weapons and proposed US-Soviet limitations on air-delivered tactical nuclear weapons as well. On October 17, 1991, the process of reducing such weapons was taken a step further when NATO ministers of defense, meeting as the Nuclear Planning Group, announced a 50 percent reduction in the inventory of some 1,400 free-fall nuclear bombs deployed primarily by the United States (the United Kingdom also deployed some free-fall nuclear bombs) in Europe.

Nuclear Policy in the Post-Cold War World

The new NATO strategic concept approved by NATO leaders on November 7, 1991, in Rome declared that "the fundamental purpose of the nuclear forces of the allies is political: to preserve peace and prevent coercion and any kind of war." The allies, at US urging, rejected a no-first-use posture. Some allied governments would have favored a pledge not to be the first to use nuclear weapons. But the United States and some other allies believed that future aggression might be deterred by a potential aggressor's lingering concern that it might face a nuclear counterattack.

The new concept placed principal reliance on the strategic nuclear capabilities of the United States, France, and the United Kingdom. But it also asserted that peace-time basing of nuclear forces on European territory (meaning the residual US free-fall bombs) "provides an essential political and military link between the European and the North American members of the Alliance."[36] Even as the leaders met to approve the new concept, however, the Soviet Union itself was breaking apart, raising new issues that allied officials had not been able to take into account in drafting the new approach.

A main focus of NATO and US concern from 1992 forward was to ensure that the tactical and strategic nuclear forces of the former Soviet Union remained under reliable control. The United States and its allies sought to diminish the chances that the dissolution of the Soviet Union would result in nuclear proliferation, either from a number of former republics retaining nuclear weapons or from the transfer of nuclear weapons-making technology and know-how to other nations. By June 1992, all tactical nuclear weapons of the former Soviet Union had been consolidated within Russia, where many of the warheads were scheduled for elimination. By June 1996, Ukraine and Kazakhstan had returned all their strategic warheads to Russia. Belarus did so by the end of 1996.

Early in 1992, with regard to another issue (one much less serious than issues raised by the breakup of the Soviet Union), various French officials suggested that French nuclear forces might one day be placed in the service of a unified European political and defense entity. French President François Mitterrand raised the issue by asking, "Is it possible to develop a European [nuclear] doctrine? That question will rapidly become one of the major considerations in the building of a common European defense."[37] French officials and politicians subsequently answered Mitterrand's rhetorical question in a variety of ways, many of them supporting the idea of eventually dedicating French nuclear capabilities to the European Union. But France's European partners were skeptical about French willingness to make any real sacrifice of national sovereignty on behalf of European integration, and French nuclear strategy remained based on French national deterrence requirements.

In other respects, NATO nuclear issues stayed largely out of sight during 1993 and 1994. In 1995, they began to resurface in the context of the debate on NATO enlargement and as a consequence of French President Jacques Chirac's renewed offer of French nuclear capabilities on behalf of the European Union's defense.[38]

When the NATO defense ministers met in Brussels on June 13, 1996, they reiterated the fundamental purposes of NATO nuclear policy outlined in the new strategic concept. The communiqué also observed that NATO's nuclear forces had been "substantially reduced," and in a direct message to Moscow, the ministers declared that

NATO's nuclear forces "are no longer targeted against anyone." The ministers appeared to reinforce the point by noting that the readiness of NATO's dual-capable aircraft "has been recently adapted," presumably to a lower level of readiness for nuclear missions.[39]

The ministers concluded the very brief statement on nuclear policy by expressing satisfaction that NATO's nuclear posture would "for the foreseeable future, continue to meet the requirements of the Alliance." They then reaffirmed the strategic concept's conclusion that "nuclear forces continue to fulfill an indispensable and unique role in Alliance strategy" and emphasized that the remaining US free-fall nuclear bombs for delivery by dual-capable aircraft were still essential to link the interests of the European and North American members of NATO.

In the 1999 strategic concept, the allies essentially reiterated their view that "the fundamental purpose of the nuclear forces of the allies is political: to preserve peace and prevent coercion and any kind of war." They maintained that deploying nuclear weapons on the soil of several allied nations was an important demonstration of alliance solidarity. Finally, following another line taken consistently since the 1991 concept, the 1999 concept declared that sub-strategic forces based in Europe "provide an essential link with strategic nuclear forces, reinforcing the transatlantic link."[40] Since 1999, NATO has made no significant changes in its nuclear strategy. No link has been made between allied nuclear weapons capabilities and deterrence of threats of potential weapons of mass destruction from terrorist groups or rogue states.

Reductions in the early 1990s brought US nuclear deployments in Europe to very low levels. By the mid-1990s, all US nuclear weapons had been removed from Europe except for several hundred free-fall bombs. Neither the United States, NATO, nor those NATO nations hosting US nuclear weapons declare how many weapons are located in Europe, or where they are. However, private researchers with a good track record of following US nuclear weapons deployments judge that in 2009 the United States deployed just 350 nuclear free fall bombs at seven sites in six countries: Belgium, Germany, Italy, the Netherlands, Turkey, and the United Kingdom. The sites hosting US nuclear weapons in Greece apparently were closed in 2001, and the number of sites in the other countries has in recent years been reduced through consolidation.[41] A portion of the US submarine-launched intercontinental ballistic missile force remains committed to NATO.

Nuclear Policy Challenges

Notwithstanding consistent allied declarations concerning NATO strategy and the continued importance of US sub-strategic weapons deployed in Europe, a number of questions were left unanswered as NATO entered the twenty-first century. The most basic question was whether a US nuclear guarantee for European security remained essential and, if so, why and how to implement that guarantee.[42]

Preparation of a new strategic concept that was mandated by NATO leaders at the 60th anniversary NATO summit in Strasbourg, France and Kehl, Germany on April 3–4, 2009, will require that difficult nuclear policy issues be addressed. In particular, questions could arise regarding the continued role of the alliance as a deterrent against Russia—an aspect of the alliance that is of primary importance to the more recent members of the alliance who not long ago escaped Russian domination in the Soviet Union and who feel potentially threatened by a more ambitious Russian foreign policy.

It is possible to argue that for the foreseeable future Russia will deploy strategic nuclear forces far superior to the French and British nuclear capabilities. Given continued uncertainties about the future of democracy in Russia, it is only prudent, according to this perspective, to sustain a US nuclear guarantee for Europe and to deploy the nuclear and conventional forces that will make that guarantee credible. Others have argued that, in addition to uncertainties about Russia, potential security threats from North Africa and the Middle East warrant a continued US nuclear contribution to NATO.[43]

On the other hand, it can be argued that even an implicit US nuclear threat against Russia is inconsistent with US and Western attempts to support Russian reform and democracy or that the French and British nuclear systems should be sufficient to deter any credible threats from a weakened Russia or from others. In addition, even if it is deemed in the US interest to extend deterrence to Europe against potential non-Russian military threats, there are questions about whether the United States needs to deploy nuclear weapons in Europe itself to do so. And it remains unclear whether nuclear weapons have a significant deterrent effect on the behavior of nonnuclear rogue states or terrorist groups in any case.

Even though the Soviet threat vanished in the early 1990s, some Europeans still worried about residual Russian nuclear forces and the potential for Germany at some point to become a nuclear power. The US nuclear presence in Germany and the nuclear umbrella for the Germans have been seen as eliminating the motivation for Germany to become a nuclear power. This raises several questions. Do other European allies still value the US nuclear commitment for this purpose? Do the Germans still want some form of US nuclear guarantee? Will France offer nuclear guarantees to its European partners, including Germany, as part of its commitment to the goal of European political union on terms that would be acceptable and as a new alternative to a German nuclear option? If so, would the Germans see a French guarantee as preferable to the US commitment?

What Role for Residual US Nuclear Weapons in Europe?

Questions still remain about whether a US nuclear guarantee for Europe is warranted by prevailing political and military conditions. The NATO countries continue to emphasize that collective defense, in which nuclear strategy played a key role, remains the core function of the alliance. But the activities of US forces stationed in Europe and of NATO forces more generally were already at the end of the 1990s concentrated on NATO's new "crisis management" missions. NATO was still in the process of "adaptation," reorganizing itself to accommodate new missions and challenges, and the role of nuclear weapons and NATO nuclear planning could logically have been seen as part of that reassessment.

Before the Warsaw Pact was disbanded and the Soviet Union dissolved, it was argued that the mere presence of some US nuclear weapons in Europe played a role in deterring threats to the security of European NATO members. By the end of the 1990s, however, NATO could not say specifically who or what was being deterred. The rest of NATO strategy had been reoriented largely toward non-Article 5 challenges, but NATO's nuclear posture and strategy became strategic orphans. Even when there was a Soviet threat, many analysts believed that the US commitment to extend nuclear deterrence to its European allies was made credible simply by the presence of US military forces in Europe, now dramatically reduced, much more than by the deployment of US nuclear weapons there. Other analysts for many years have questioned whether the United States would be willing to use nuclear weapons to defend its European allies if it meant risking nuclear strikes on the American homeland. This logic, of course, provided ammunition for the George W. Bush administration's argument that the ability of the United States to defend itself against missile attacks makes its extension of deterrence to its allies more credible.

Another question still unanswered after the first decade of the twenty-first century was the military role that free-fall bombs deployed in Europe should play in NATO or US strategy. NATO projects no imminent military threat against the territorial integrity or security of its members within the unrefueled range of the fighter bombers that would carry the free-fall bombs. Even in the extreme case of a newly antagonistic Russia, the free-fall bombs would likely be the least credible component of any Western response to a Russian military threat. The fighter bombers available in Europe to deliver the bombs could not reach targets in Russia and return without air refueling arrangements, and other nuclear systems (such as US submarine-launched ballistic missiles) have longer range and are more likely to survive defenses and arrive on target. And, in a time of constrained resources, maintenance of the bombs, which in coming years will include modernizing the aircraft intended to deliver them as well as maintaining the security of the warheads, may be a questionable use of limited defense funds.

The apparent conclusion is that, from a purely military perspective, the bombs were intended largely as placeholders, designed to keep open the option of developing a new air-delivered standoff system or deploying some existing air-launched cruise missiles from the US strategic nuclear triad in support of NATO strategy. This rationale presumably is based on the assumption that withdrawal of the bombs could foreclose, or at least make politically more difficult, future US deployment of any nuclear weapons in Europe. In addition, the presence of US nuclear weapons on European soil both ensured continued nuclear risk sharing and affords European governments a consultative relationship with the United States concerning nuclear weapons strategy and doctrines.

Perhaps the most important rationale for a continuing US nuclear presence in Europe was that virtually all European governments apparently still believed that the American military presence in Europe makes a significant contribution to European stability and peace. This is particularly true for many of NATO's new members who remain concerned about Russia's intentions toward them and value highly any link to the US nuclear guarantee. NATO's 1999 strategic concept asserted that the basing of US nuclear weapons in Europe provided "an essential political and military link between the European and the North American members of the Alliance." The allies have continued to use this language in NATO communiqués, but unless there is some credible military or deterrence role for these weapons, their "linking" power may be quite limited.

The commitment by President Obama and some influential experts and former officials[44] to set the goal of a "global zero"—no nuclear weapons at all anywhere, places some pressure on removing those that make no actual contribution to deterrence and may in fact help provide additional excuses for proliferation, by Iran for example. On the other hand, there has been little significant government or public opposition to this residual nuclear presence, and it is possible that withdrawal would, over time, invite fundamental questions about the US commitment. A survey by the Atlantic Council of the United States in the mid-1990s observed that "the overwhelming consensus among political leaders and strategic thinkers in Europe is that it is premature to address major changes in future nuclear force postures." The survey noted that "Europe has long depended on the American nuclear umbrella, and few European leaders want that to change."[45] Nevertheless, the question of whether the deployment of free-fall nuclear bombs on European soil is essential to sustain extended deterrence remained open at the end of the 1990s and has not been answered in the first decade of the new century.

NATO's Future Military Role

After the first decade of the twenty-first century, NATO's military forces are expected to be able to perform many diverse missions, compared to one major mission during the Cold War. These missions include the following:

1. Maintaining collective defense preparedness for possible future major challenges and more limited collective defense contingencies that might develop in the nearer term;
2. organizing and preparing military forces as part of the fight against international terror as well as to respond to international crisis situations; forces may be required to engage in a broad range of missions including humanitarian assistance, peacekeeping, peace enforcement, anti-piracy, and preventive interventions;

3. helping control the spread of weapons of mass destruction and preparing to defend against and deal with the consequences of a chemical, biological, or nuclear weapons attack;
4. supporting participation of allied forces in ad hoc coalitions and European Union-led operations when the alliance itself is not formally conducting the operation;
5. using military-to-military cooperation to help the defense establishments of new member and partner states modernize their force structures and align with NATO standards;
6. using military-to-military cooperation to build mutual confidence and transparency with nonmember states, particularly Russia, Ukraine, and non-NATO countries in the Mediterranean region.

These missions are more complex militarily and much more diverse politically than the old Cold War collective defense mission, even though the potential costs of failure during the Cold War were much higher than they are today. NATO's military leaders and forces must accomplish these missions with significantly reduced resources than those available during the Cold War. These missions require forces that are much more flexible and agile. Forces must be adaptable to many different circumstances. No longer can forces from European states plan to operate only in their native climate and on familiar terrain. To be relevant, they have to be designed, equipped, and trained to work effectively in a much broader variety of topographic and climatic conditions.

In addition, military leaders, down to the unit level, have to be much more politically aware and sophisticated, particularly when dealing with the unstable environments found in crisis response operations and the politically sensitive setting for cooperation with Russia and other non-applicant states.

It is not beyond the capacity of NATO's militaries to deal with this broad mission profile. The question is whether political leaders in NATO countries will provide the resources to prepare forces for such diverse operations and then supply the political will required to make the most effective use of those forces.

Balancing New Mission Priorities

A difficult issue faced by the NATO allies since the end of the Cold War has been how to strike a balance between the requirements of NATO's traditional Article 5 collective defense mission and the now-proliferating crisis management missions that occupy most of NATO's attention and resources. At the end of the Cold War, the NATO countries began asking whether NATO could be sustained entirely under the umbrella of its collective defense mission. The answer in the early 1990s was mixed. In the 1991 strategic concept, the allies concluded that NATO could and should be utilized to deal with new threats to security, but they also agreed that collective defense should remain the heart and soul of the NATO commitment.

When the Soviet Union was dissolved and as Russian military capabilities deteriorated progressively throughout the 1990s, it became clear that collective defense might be at the heart of the NATO commitment but would not necessarily dominate the alliance's day-to-day activities. Rather, conflict management and preparations for a variety of peace operations would likely become the bread and butter of NATO military cooperation.

During the mid-to-late 1990s, NATO's day-to-day activities became almost entirely dominated by new roles and missions. This began with a shift in planning and exercising following the mandate of the 1991 strategic concept and then took a real and demanding form with the military missions in Bosnia (IFOR and SFOR), in Kosovo (the air war against Serbia and KFOR's peace implementation role), and in Macedonia beginning in 2001. The profile of NATO's military focus and activities changed even more dramatically following the 9/11 attacks, particularly when the allies decided the alliance would lead the International Security Assistance Force in Afghanistan.

There are nonetheless some strong substantial reasons for keeping collective defense at the heart of the alliance. First, something can be said for the role of the collective defense commitment as an insurance policy against a new Russian threat emerging in the future. Even though the allies hope that the hand of cooperation NATO has extended to Moscow will eventually be firmly grasped by the Russians, it appears that many in the Russian elite still consider NATO, the United States, and the West as inevitable antagonists toward Russia. They are inclined to resist the development of extensive NATO-Russia cooperation. These Russians include a significant number who still think like Soviet rather than Russian leaders. They aspire to restoration of the Soviet Union's superpower role under a revitalized and recentralized Russia.

Under current circumstances, it cannot be excluded that, regardless of the goodwill of NATO countries, future Russian leaders will choose some form of confrontational relationship with NATO rather than cooperation. Russia's intervention in Georgia in 2008 and its refusal to follow the terms of a negotiated cease-fire certainly suggests the need for watching Russian behavior carefully. Keeping NATO's collective defense commitment alive reassures those allies that would be most exposed to a more aggressive Russia and also could serve as a disincentive for a Russian choice of confrontation over cooperation.

Second, Russia is increasingly the least likely near-term threat to NATO allies. Turmoil to the south and east of Europe, in North Africa, and in the Middle East— fed by various forms of extremism antagonistic toward the NATO countries and their values, combined with modern weapons of mass destruction and their delivery systems—could produce direct threats to the security of NATO countries. This point was brought home all too sharply with the September 11, 2001, terrorist attacks on the United States and the military campaign against the terrorist organizations in Afghanistan that followed. The NATO collective defense commitment provides reassurance and potential deterrence and also a rationale for allied cooperation in trying to mitigate or eliminate such threats through diplomacy and other means.

Third, and perhaps most important from a practical perspective, NATO's collective defense commitment helps sustain a core of war-fighting military capabilities around which conflict management capabilities can be built and without which conflict management policies would appear much less credible. It also provides a continuing rationale for the integrated command structure, without which critical day-to-day cooperation among allied militaries would dissipate, eventually undermining the ability of NATO countries to operate in coalition formations. Former head of the NATO Military Committee, retired German General Klaus Naumann, has argued that NATO's collective defense mission and military capabilities remain essential to NATO's future. If all NATO countries developed forces capable of no more than peacekeeping operations, the alliance would become largely irrelevant to contingencies such as those already seen in Bosnia, Kosovo and Afghanistan. The high-intensity air campaign against Serbia over the Kosovo crisis demonstrated how important collective defense instruments, such as high-tech air capabilities, can be to non-Article 5 operations.

One way of looking at the relationship between collective defense and NATO's new tasks is to see them as "inner" and "outer" core missions.[46] Collective defense and the military forces and command structure associated with it provide a solid core for NATO's mission profile. Such capabilities both hedge against an uncertain future and provide a solid foundation for NATO's new, non-Article 5 missions.

In the years ahead, the allies will have to ensure that there is a seamless continuum between all political and military aspects of NATO's inner- and outer-core missions and capabilities. In this regard, NATO military authorities will be called on to develop training, exercising, deployment, and rotation concepts that enable regular forces to maintain combat capabilities while being employed in non-Article 5 operations. In addition, NATO nations will have to focus increased political attention and defense resources on emerging outer-core, non-Article 5 missions, including promoting stability in Europe, dealing with the proliferation of weapons of mass destruction, responding to the terrorist challenge, and providing options to deal with threats to security that can arise beyond NATO borders. From this perspective, NATO's outer-core missions will have to be designed and executed with the goal of diminishing the chance that NATO's inner-core mission of collective defense will need to be invoked.

Finally, NATO's collective defense commitment carries with it a degree of serious intent and political will that would not be demonstrated by a less demanding form of cooperation. Article 5, in effect, constitutes a statement by all the allies that they consider their security to be indivisible. It serves as a clear demonstration that the political values and goals articulated in the North Atlantic Treaty's preamble remain as valid for allied governments today as they were in 1949. The continuing rationale for a collective defense mission is therefore closely related to the ability of the alliance to serve as an instrument for conflict management and defense cooperation. Conceptually, the conventional wisdom among NATO governments appears logical and relevant to the likely challenges of the coming years. Some critics in the United States and Europe will continue to question the legitimacy of this conventional wisdom.

However, the main weakness of the approach may be in its execution, not its conceptualization.

Will sufficient resources be made available by allied governments to implement a multiple-mission approach? Will the emerging gap in deployed military technologies between the United States and Europe increasingly impede coalition operations, creating a dual or three-tier alliance? Will future US administrations, starting with the Obama presidency, rely on NATO cooperation or fall back, frustrated by weak European responses, into unilateralist tendencies that characterized the first administration of George W. Bush? What role will nuclear weapons and missile defenses play in future transatlantic security cooperation?

Part of the answer to these questions may lie in whether the European allies will be able to turn their aspirations for a full-fledged European Security and Defense Policy into substantial and effective military capabilities—which does not seem likely in the near term. Another part of the answer will depend on what happens to NATO's most ambitious mission in Afghanistan, to which this analysis now turns.

Notes

1. North Atlantic Council, Strategic Concept, November 8, 1991.
2. North Atlantic Council declaration, January 11, 1994.
3. The origins and purposes of the Partnership for Peace as a key element of NATO's post-Cold War outreach program is discussed in more detail in Chapter 6.
4. Susan Woodward, *Balkan Tragedy, Chaos and Dissolution after the Cold War* (Washington, D.C.: Brookings Institution Press, 1995).
5. "The Situation in Yugoslavia" (statement issued by the heads of state and government participating in the meeting of the North Atlantic Council in Rome, November 7–8, 1991), paras. 1, 4.
6. Stanley R. Sloan, "NATO beyond Bosnia" (CRS Report for Congress 94–977 S, December 7, 1994), 3.
7. As cited by James Gow, *Triumph of the Lack of Will: International Diplomacy and the Yugoslav War* (New York: Columbia University Press, 1997), 48, 50.
8. For an insider's perspective on the role of the Western European Union, see the account by the Union's secretary-general of the time, Willem van Eeckelen, Debating European Security, 1948–1998 (The Hague: Sdu Publishers, 1998), 140–83.
9. For an excellent, concise account of Clinton administration decision making concerning "the problem from hell," see Ivo H. Daalder, *Getting to Dayton: The Making of America's Bosnia Policy* (Washington, D.C.: Brookings Institution Press, 2000).
10. Daalder, *Getting to Dayton*, 16.
11. For a discussion of the UN-NATO relationship during the early stages of the Balkan conflicts, see Dick A. Leurdijk, *The United Nations and NATO in Former*

Yugoslavia, Partners in International Cooperation (The Hague: Netherlands Atlantic Commission, 1994).

12. Daalder, *Getting to Dayton*, 68.

13. For Holbrooke's perspective on the Bosnia peace process and his role in it, see Richard Holbrooke, *To End a War* (New York: Random House, 1998).

14. For an excellent insider's perspective on the political and bureaucratic struggles within NATO during the adaptation process through 1996, see Rob de Wijk, *NATO on the Brink of the New Millennium: The Battle for Consensus* (London: Brassey's, 1997).

15. Subsequent discussions with US and French officials.

16. North Atlantic Council, Berlin Accord, June 3, 1996.

17. For background on the development of NATO's missions in addition to Article 5 contingencies, see Stanley R. Sloan, *NATO's Future: Beyond Collective Defense* (Washington, D.C.: National Defense University Press McNair Papers, 1996). This study was originally issued as a Congressional Research Service Report for Congress in 1995, advancing the idea of strengthening the Deputy SACEUR's role, a concept that became one of the key reforms in the June 1996 Berlin Accord.

18. For discussion of the development of Europe's defense profile, see Chapter 10.

19. From the author's discussions with participants in the US decision-making process for the Berlin meeting.

20. The Contact Group had been formed in April 1994 among the United States, Russia, Great Britain, France, and Germany as a way of coordinating Bosnia policy in a small group of major powers. Italy was very unhappy about its original exclusion from the group, engineered by its European partners, not the United States. Italy joined the group in 1996 during its six-month term as president of the European Union's Council of Ministers and remained in the group thereafter. The tradition of smaller groups of allies forming a special committee is well established in the alliance, even if not always appreciated by allies excluded from the group. For example, during the Cold War, the Berlin Group, consisting of the United States, France, the United Kingdom, and Germany, used to meet prior to NATO ministerial meetings to discuss issues related to Berlin and Germany.

21. For a dispassionate assessment of NATO's operations in the Kosovo conflict, see John E. Peters, Stuart Johnson, Nora Bensahel, Timothy Liston, and Traci Williams, *European Contributions to Operation Allied Force: Implications for Transatlantic Cooperation* (Washington, D.C.: Rand, 2001).

22. Wesley K. Clark, *Waging Modern War: Bosnia, Kosovo, and the Future of Combat* (New York: Public Affairs, 2001).

23. US General Accounting Office, "Kosovo Air Operations: Need to Maintain Alliance Cohesion Led to Doctrinal Departures" (GAO-01–784), Washington, D.C., July 27, 2001, 2.

24. For a US perspective on the Kosovo campaign, see Ivo H. Daalder and Michael E. O'Hanlon, *Winning Ugly: NATO's War to Save Kosovo* (Washington, D.C.: Brookings Institution Press, 2000).

25. This claim was made in off-the-record administration briefings to the Senate NATO Observer Group, in which the author participated. In fact, the 1999 concept was not replaced for more than a decade, but mainly because the allies were reluctant to set a new path for the alliance in partnership with the Bush administration in Washington whose judgment they mistrusted. The decision of the allies that NATO would take command of the International Security Assistance Force in Afghanistan (discussed in Chapter 9) constituted a dramatic change from the caution of the 1999 concept concerning NATO and military operations beyond Europe. With that decision, NATO's strategy changed much more radically in practice than it had in theory.

26. North Atlantic Council, Washington Summit Communiqué, April 24, 1999, para. 7.

27. North Atlantic Council, Defense Capabilities Initiative, April 25, 1999.

28. NATO Parliamentary Assembly, Defense and Security Subcommittee on Future Security and Defense Capabilities, "Interim Report on NATO's Role in Defence Reform" (Brussels: NATO Parliamentary Assembly, October 2001), para. 90.

29. North Atlantic Council, The Alliance's Strategic Concept, April 24, 1999.

30. Final Communiqué, Ministerial Meeting of the North Atlantic Council held in Reykjavik on May 14, 2002, para. 5.

31. Prague Summit Declaration, Issued by the Heads of State and Government participating in the meeting of the North Atlantic Council in Prague on November 21, 2002.

32. The Rumsfeld initiative owes much to the research completed at National Defense University by Hans Binnendijk and Richard Kugler. The two experts developed the basic concept for the Response Force. See Hans Binnendijk and Richard Kugler, "Transforming European Forces," *Survival*, Autumn 2002, 117–32.

33. North Atlantic Treaty Organization, Public Diplomacy Division, "Financial and Economic Data Relating to NATO Defence," 19 February 2009. See: http://www.nato.int/docu/pr/2009/p09–009.pdf [accessed June 29, 2009].

34. This discussion is based on my chapter in *Controlling Non-Strategic Nuclear Weapons: Obstacles and Opportunities*, ed. Jeffrey A. Larsen and Kurt J. Klingenberger (Colorado Springs, Colo.: USAF Institute for National Security Studies, 2001).

35. North Atlantic Treaty Organization, "London Declaration on a Transformed North Atlantic Alliance, Issued by the Heads of State and Government Participating in the meeting of the North Atlantic Council in London on 5–6 July 1990," (printed in *NATO Review* 38, no. 4 [August 1990]: 32–33).

36. North Atlantic Treaty Organization, "The Alliance's New Strategic Concept, Agreed by the Heads of State and Government Participating in the Meeting of the North Atlantic Council in Rome on 7–8 November 1991" (printed in *NATO Review* 39, no. 6 [December 1991]: 25–32).

37. Mitterrand was speaking at a meeting in Paris on January 10, 1992, as reported by *Atlantic News*, no. 2387, January 14, 1992, 4.

38. Many Europeans looked skeptically on the French offer as an effort to deflect criticism of France's nuclear testing program.

39. M-DPC/NPG 1(96)88, Meeting of the Defense Planning Committee in Ministerial Session, Brussels, June 13, 1996.

40. "The Alliance's Strategic Concept, Approved by the Heads of State and Government Participating in the Meeting of the North Atlantic Council in Washington D.C. on 23rd and 24th April 1999" (NATO press release NAC-S [99]65).

41. Hans M. Kristensen, "United States Removes Nuclear Weapons from German Base, Documents Indicate," Federation of American Scientists Security Blog, http://www.fas.org/blog/ssp/2007/07/united_states_removes_nuclear.php [accessed June 15, 2009].

42. For an analysis of the role of nuclear weapons in US military strategy and foreign policy in the post-Cold War era, see Jan Lodal, *The Price of Dominance: The New Weapons of Mass Destruction and Their Challenge to American Leadership* (New York: Council on Foreign Relations Press, 2001), and the review of Lodal's book by Robert Jervis, "Weapons without Purpose? Nuclear Strategy in the Post-Cold War Era," *Foreign Affairs*, July/August 2001, 143–48.

43. The argument has been made, for example, by Thomas-Durell Young, who proposed that the United States, France, and the United Kingdom cooperate to develop a tactical air-to-surface missile (a "tripartite TASM") to provide a "state-of-the-art" air-delivered nuclear capability for NATO countries. Thomas-Durell Young, "NATO's Substrategic Nuclear Forces and Strategy: Where Do We Go from Here?" Strategic Studies Institute, US Army War College, Carlisle Barracks, Pennsylvania, January 13, 1992.

44. The Global Zero declaration was signed in Paris by a large group of former and current officials from around the globe, was delivered to US President Obama and Russian President Medvedev, and remains open for signature by additional parties. Information about the initiative can be found on the Global Zero web site: http://www.globalzero.org/ [accessed June 15, 2009].

45. "Nuclear Weapons and European Security" (policy paper, Atlantic Council of the United States, April 1996), 3.

46. The author originally developed this concept in *NATO in the 21st Century*, a special publication of the North Atlantic Assembly (now the NATO Parliamentary Assembly), for which he was rapporteur. See Senator William V. Roth Jr., president, North Atlantic Assembly, *NATO in the 21st Century* (Brussels: North Atlantic Assembly, September 1998).

CHAPTER 9

NATO in Afghanistan

NATO's invocation of Article 5 and allied offers of assistance immediately following the al Qaeda attacks on the United States met a lukewarm response in the Bush administration, where skepticism about NATO and allies was rampant in the new administration's Pentagon. When Secretary of Defense Donald Rumsfeld proclaimed in September 2001, "The mission determines the coalition. And the coalition must not be permitted to determine the mission," the message to the NATO allies was loud and clear: thanks, but no thanks.

NATO did provide some early assistance to the United States, such as sending NATO Airborne Warning and Control (AWACS) aircraft to patrol US airspace while similar American systems were supporting operations against the Taliban and al Qaeda in Afghanistan. Despite inviting a select group of individual allies to contribute forces to operations in Afghanistan, NATO as an organization was largely left aside, owing to the Bush administration's belief that alliance involvement would only complicate decision-making and slow the pace of operations.

It was not long before the United States, recognizing the scope of the task of pacifying Afghanistan, sought additional help from the international community. The Bush administration did not initially call on NATO, but asked the United Nations to authorize NATO allies to help man and manage the operation.

Within two months of initiating military operations, the United States and its allies, including Afghan anti-Taliban elements known as the "United Front" or Northern Alliance, had broken the Taliban's control over most of the country. On December 5, the "Bonn Agreement Pending the Re-establishment of Permanent Government Institutions," brokered by the United Nations, established the central role of the United Nations and the US-led coalition in the reconstruction of the country (alongside Hamid Karzai's interim Afghan government). The Bonn meeting of various Afghan factions had designated Karzai, from the ethnic Pashtun majority, to take on the interim role. This agreement was confirmed by United Nations Security Council Resolution (UNSCR) 1386 on December 20, which also called for the establishment of an International Security Assistance Force (ISAF) to "assist the Afghan Interim Authority in the maintenance of security in Kabul and its surrounding areas, so that the Afghan Interim Authority as well as the personnel of the United Nations can operate in a secure environment." The UK accepted initial responsibility for command of the operation, which was originally intended to rotate among troop-contributing nations.

When the ISAF was established, US and allied military operations against residual Taliban and al Qaeda elements continued as a coalition of the willing under the auspices of Operation Enduring Freedom (OEF), which had been created by the United States in October 2001 following the 9/11 attacks as the umbrella under which Afghanistan operations and other aspects of the Global War on Terror (GWOT) were conducted. Thus, the OEF coalition in Afghanistan and ISAF forces initially operated under parallel but separate command structures.

After a six-month period, the United Kingdom handed over command of the ISAF to Turkey and, at the end of 2002, it was commanded jointly by Germany and the Netherlands with support from NATO. During 2002, the Karzai government advocated an expanded role for the ISAF, which it hoped would help extend the authority of the fledgling central government to the provinces. This proposal was opposed by some domestic Afghan elements and the United States. The United Front feared the erosion of Afghanistan's sovereignty and the marginalization of its own forces, while the US was concerned that the move might constrain its own combat operations.[1] Furthermore, European allies were reluctant to engage more fully in the struggle.

Map 9.1: Afghanistan

Source: CIA, *The World Factbook.*

In 2003, however, as the United States began military operations intended to remove Saddam Hussein from power in Iraq, the Bush administration began to see a larger NATO role in Afghanistan as potentially relieving some pressure on US forces, which were increasingly occupied with the new and demanding operation in Iraq. Moreover, Germany and Canada saw a more prominent NATO role as politically facilitating their participation in Afghan operations, and alliance officials in Brussels leaned toward NATO taking on more responsibility.

NATO Assumes Command of the ISAF

Despite determined French and German opposition to US Iraq policy and related divisions cutting across the entire alliance, consensus was reached at NATO to take command of the ISAF; the decision to do so was confirmed in Brussels on April 16, 2003.[2] In historical perspective, this was a stunning event. Not only were the allies divided over Iraq, but, just four years earlier, the Europeans had resisted any suggestion in NATO's 1999 strategic concept that the alliance could be used to mount military operations beyond Europe. With very little debate or dissent, the allies agreed to take on a demanding military mission on soil far from Europe, for which the military forces of many allied countries were ill-prepared. The mission would become a litmus test for the ability of the alliance to be an effective contributor to contemporary security challenges.

NATO formally assumed command of the ISAF in August 2003. UNSCR 1510 (October 13, 2003) subsequently confirmed the ISAF mandate to operate outside of Kabul, using joint military-civilian Provincial Reconstruction Teams (PRTs) to bring both security and reconstruction projects to other parts of the country. As Afghanistan moved toward presidential elections scheduled for October 2004, the need to broaden NATO's operations to help ensure security for the vote became more evident. NATO allies pledged in June 2004 to increase the NATO presence from 6,500 to around 10,000 by the time of the election. When the allies met at the summit in Istanbul in June 2004, it seemed an open question whether or not the forces would be provided. In the end, allies made up the shortfall and helped ensure a relatively peaceful election process. In December 2004, NATO ministers meeting in Brussels agreed to continue the process of expanding NATO's role in Afghanistan by deploying PRTs to the country's western provinces, yet no allies pledged additional troops for the effort.

Based on the UN mandate, the allies developed a plan to work through progressive stages in Afghanistan with the goal of ultimately providing security and reconstruction programs across the entire country. The first stage, carried out in 2003–2004 by French and German troops, was to secure the more stable northern regions. Stage two began in May 2005, when Spanish and Italian forces moved into western Afghanistan. Establishment of ISAF command in the more volatile Southern and Eastern regions began on July 31, 2006 with the initiation of stage 3 and continued with the final stage 4 on October 5 of the same year. Some forces from the separate,

US-led OEF remained for counter-terror operations but, by the end of 2006, the ISAF was responsible for providing security for all of Afghanistan. As of June 2009, there were 61,130 ISAF troops in the country from 42 contributing nations and 89,500 soldiers in the Afghan National Army.

The operation was organized around five conceptual phases, the first two of which have been completed with the enactment of stage four. They are (I) assessment and preparation (in Kabul), (II) geographic expansion through Afghanistan, (III) stabilization, (IV) transition to domestically provided security, and (V) redeployment of ISAF troops.

Provincial Reconstruction Teams (PRTs)

Provincial Reconstruction Teams have been the main organizational instrument for the ISAF's contributions to the stabilization and development of Afghanistan. The alliance's comprehensive approach to the ISAF mission has brought together "civilian-military units of varying sizes, designed to extend the authority of the central government into the countryside, provide security, and undertake projects to boost the Afghan economy."[3] As of July 2009, there were 26 PRTs under ISAF jurisdiction with various lead countries, some taking over from teams formerly controlled by the United States, including those in Kandahar (Canada), Lashkar Gah (Britain), and Tarin Kowt (The Netherlands).

As late as 2009, there was still no established model for PRTs, some were civilian controlled, others military-run, but all were attempting to fulfill the goals of the UN mandate. Most US PRTs were composed of 50–100 military personnel, civilian government officials (both American and Afghan), and many had staff to train Afghan security forces. The Turkish-run PRT in Wardak province provided health care, education, police training and agricultural development. According to the 2009 NATO/ISAF Afghanistan report, PRTs had engaged in such activities as coordinating agricultural development in the poppy reliant Helmand province (Britain), renovating the Kahla Dam irrigation system near Kandahar (Canada), and strengthening government institutions providing rule of law (judiciary, police, local administration) across the country.[4]

Despite some successes, the PRT program has come under criticism for a variety of reasons, many stemming from the disconnected and non-standardized nature of the operations. One expert observed that PRTs seemed to be largely a localized form of support, leaving large swathes of territory unprotected and unaided.[5] Germany has been criticized for its operation of PRTs due to the politically imposed caveats that prevent both civilians and military PRT elements from operating beyond the borders of their PRTs. Some Nongovernmental Organizations (NGOs) have complained that PRTs tread on their feet, bringing heavy firepower and inexperienced operatives to bear on situations in which they (the NGOs) have specific experience and skills.[6] Their claims suggested that the civilian-military nature of PRTs had blurred the lines between combatants and aid workers, and thus endangered independent NGO staff, whose supposed neutrality was thus compromised, consequently exposing them to increased risk of kidnap and death.[7]

In spite of these criticisms, the PRT concept responded to the accurate perception that the war in Afghanistan could not be won without the kind of reconstruction and development that the PRTs were intended to produce. The provision of stability in Afghanistan requires a "comprehensive approach,"[8] one that provides a degree of security for the development of Afghan infrastructure, economy, educational opportunities, public health programs and a modern legal system. The main shortcomings seem to have been the low number of teams and lack of security, both of which have prevented the program from achieving its goals on a national scale. In addition, the fact that the PRTs were designed and operated on a nation-by-nation basis stood in the way of any consistent NATO or ISAF design for the country-wide operation.

Operation Enduring Freedom and the ISAF

From its inception with UNSCR 1386, the ISAF existed in parallel with but separate from the US-led Operation Enduring Freedom (OEF) that had successfully ousted the Taliban from power and continued to pursue al Qaeda and Taliban elements. In 2009, the OEF continued as a counter-insurgency combat operation with approximately 38,500 troops under US command, while the ISAF was expressly mandated by the United Nations to provide security and development for Afghanistan. With completion of stage four of ISAF, in which NATO assumed responsibility for providing security for the entire country, the line separating the objectives of the two operations became increasingly blurred, as the necessity of combating a growing Taliban/al Qaeda insurgency forced ISAF troops into more combat roles.

Some way of consolidating the commands seemed logical from early on. However, the idea met with mixed emotions on both sides of the Atlantic. Some experts claimed that initial US rejection of proposals to integrate the operations was based on its desire to retain autonomous control over its forces in the region.[9] One of these experts, Amin Saikal, has claimed it was an extension of American aversion to UN supervision that kept the ISAF and OEF separate. European resistance, Saikal said, resulted from some NATO contributors not wanting to see their troops redirected into harm's way in the unstable south of the country.[10] In addition, Markus Kaim reported that the public perception in Germany was ". . . that Enduring Freedom is the 'bad' American part of the Afghanistan mission, bombing villages and killing innocent civilians, whereas the ISAF is the 'good' one, focusing on state building and reconstruction . . ."[11]

Nevertheless, ISAF stage four requirements and the intensification of the Afghan insurgency finally forced a partial consolidation of the OEF and ISAF commands. The separate commands led to differences in both strategy and tactics, compromising attempts to produce an Afghanistan-wide approach to dealing with the insurgents and the accompanying need for development of governmental and civilian systems and infrastructure. When ISAF operations were expanded to include all of Afghanistan, 10,000 American troops were rebadged and transferred to NATO command. Additionally, all American troops, regardless of their mission affiliation, began to operate under the command of US Forces Afghanistan, which was double-hatted with command of ISAF—as of August 2009 occupied by General Stanley A. McChrystal. General McChrystal reported both to NATO's SACEUR (ISAF chain of command) in Brussels and the US Central Command (US national chain of command) in Tampa, Florida. In August 2009, the North Atlantic Council approved creation of a subordinate ISAF command, also led by an American general, in charge of day-to-day combat operations.

While the ISAF was making the transition to a more active combat capacity, the OEF continued to conduct its own, separate operations against high value targets and other militant concentrations. NATO and US planning began to reflect the realization that withdrawing from areas after completion of combat operations was resulting in the reestablishment of Taliban influence. As a result, the operational strategy for NATO forces was changed to "clear, hold and build."[12] Instead of clearing territory of Taliban and promptly leaving, NATO troops began to hold newly won territory and develop indigenous security forces and services in the hopes of fostering a more persistent stability. However, there still were insufficient forces and inadequate (corrupt, compromised or incompetent) government infrastructure to implement the concept successfully on a wide-scale basis.

The Pakistan Complication

Beginning in 2007, violence caused by the Taliban and al Qaeda insurgencies escalated with significant increases in ISAF and US casualties. The expansion of Taliban capabilities was in no small measure due to the fact that the insurgents had established their base of operations and support facilities across the border in Pakistan. The insurgent leadership, having been dislodged from Afghanistan by persistent NATO and coalition action, began operating from safe havens nearby, in Pakistan's Federally Administered Tribal Areas (FATA) and Baluchi region. The traditional Taliban under Mullah Muhammad Omar, along with two other Taliban groups with links to Al-Qaeda operated from these territories. In addition, Pakistani Jihadist elements under the separate leaderships of Gulbuddin Hekmatyar and Jalaluddin Haqqani operated from the FATA. The latter established the so-called "Islamic Emirate of Waziristan" with several thousand fighters, and claimed responsibility for a number of suicide bombings in Afghanistan.[13]

Dealing with this challenge was complicated by the fact that the government of Pakistan, for a wide variety of reasons, until the second half of 2009, was unwilling or unable to take on the Taliban and other extremist elements that had solidified their base along Pakistan's border with Afghanistan. In addition, reports suggested that elements of the Pakistani government (especially the Inter-Services Intelligence organization) were complicit in the operation of cross-border insurgent groups.

The border, demarcated by the British mandated Durban line of 1893 is effectively nonexistent for those living nearby. From a security standpoint, this makes it very difficult for NATO soldiers to keep track of who is coming in and out of the country. General David Richards, former commander of ISAF Afghanistan, describes the porous nature of the border in stark terms, "Up to 200,000 people cross that border on any given day, dressed all the same. It's not easy to distinguish the Taliban from perfectly law-abiding people."[14]

Despite their reluctance until 2009 to pursue the Taliban presence in their border frontiers, the Pakistani military did engage in combat in the FATA against foreign fighters and took part in dialogues both with the ISAF and the Afghan National Army through the Tripartite Joint Intelligence Operations Center (T-JIOC), which aims to coordinate military action on the border between the three forces. Further cooperation included opening of the Khyber Pass Border Coordination Center and the construction of two more coordination centers in Lawara and Nawa passes. Control of these passes is particularly vital to NATO efforts in the country because a vast majority of their supplies come from or over Pakistani territory. As much as 60 percent of NATO's supplies come through the Khyber Pass, where violence shot up 45 percent from 2007 to 2008.[15]

There is now widespread agreement that stability can never be secured in Afghanistan until Pakistan controls its border and resolves its own problems with the Taliban/Al-Qaeda insurgency. The resignation of President Pervez Musharraf in 2008 and the restoration of civilian rule to the country were followed by rapid deterioration of the economy, and despite the new government's pledge to combat growing insurgency and terrorism in the country, pro-Taliban militancy grew bolder, notably in the north-western city of Peshawar. But the departure of Musharraf led to improved relations between Afghanistan and Pakistan, and the program of "peace jirga" meetings between prominent tribal elders from both countries began anew.

The Obama Administration made it clear in its early months that it would deal with Afghanistan and Pakistan as key parts of the same problem. In 2009, the Government of Pakistan took a more active and effective approach to dealing with Taliban and extremist elements in the regions adjacent to Afghanistan. The Pakistan military mounted a major operation in the fall of 2009 seeking to take control of Taliban and al Qaeda strongholds in Waziristan from which the insurgent leaders mounted operations and sought refuge from US and ISAF forces on the other side of the border. The operation, for which Pakistan authorities claimed major successes, led almost immediately to an upsurge in attacks against Pakistani civilian and governmental targets. It remains clear that close cooperation among all players—the United States, NATO ISAF, Afghan authorities and Pakistani officials—will be required to reduce the threat of radical extremists in both countries, and that sustaining domestic support in Pakistan for its role in the conflict will be a challenge to the government in Karachi.

The Mission: A Self-Governing, Secure Afghanistan

The NATO allies agree that "NATO's main role in Afghanistan is to assist the Afghan Government in exercising and extending its authority and influence across the country, paving the way for reconstruction and effective governance."[16] When the NATO leaders celebrated the alliance's 60th anniversary at Strasbourg (France) and Kehl (Germany) in April 2009, they issued a Summit Declaration on Afghanistan elaborating on the mission and its rationale, declaring:

> In Afghanistan we are helping build security for the Afghan people, protecting our citizens and defending the values of freedom, democracy and human rights. Our common security is closely tied to the stability and security of Afghanistan and the region: an area of the world from where extremists planned attacks against civilian populations and democratic governments and continue to plot today. Through our UN-mandated mission, supported by our International Security Assistance Force (ISAF) partners, and working closely with the Afghan government, we remain committed for the long-run to supporting a democratic Afghanistan that does not become, once more, a base for terror attacks or a haven for violent extremism that destabilises the region and threatens the entire International Community.[17]

The task of establishing a legitimate, competent, centralized government presents a unique challenge to the international community, because Afghanistan has a long history of decentralized rule and has frequently looked much like a failed state, in which no one power possessed a monopoly on the legitimate use of force. Rule of law and provision of security was administered informally on an ad-hoc basis across the country, with little or no standardization, training, or even literate officials. The Bonn Agreement of 2001 set the goal of establishing governmental legitimacy and consolidating central control following the defeat of the Taliban, but widespread corruption and the perception of weakness in the face of the Taliban's continued insurgency cast doubts about the ability of the government to sustain itself. In fact, the Bonn Agreement itself, while seeking to strengthen the government in Kabul, led to an international approach that may have worked against the stated objective. Pursuant to the accord, NATO nations and international organizations focused many of their efforts locally and regionally without a clear national strategy and also without necessarily strengthening the influence of the central government over distant and historically autonomous regions and population centers.

A new Afghan constitution was ratified in January of 2004, establishing a strong presidency counterbalanced by a legislature, confirming equal rights for men and women, and laying a framework of Sunni Islamic law for the judiciary.[18] The head of the interim administration, Hamid Karzai, was subsequently elected with 55 percent of the popular vote and was then free to appoint a 27-member cabinet. The international community recognized that the fledgling government would require significant financial and organizational support. At the national level, the United Nations Development Program (UNDP) focused its efforts on increasing the government's ruling capacity through developing structures such as an independent election commission, support mechanisms for the newly elected Afghan Parliament, training for civil servants, financial and logistical support for police forces, and other measures.

At the provincial level, NATO-ISAF supported various efforts to extend governance by providing security, PRT operations, and support of various initiatives such as the Afghan Social Outreach Program (ASOP), which increases dialogue between provincial authority figures and their populations. In the 2009 provincial and presidential elections, the ISAF provided logistical support to domestic security forces that were taking more significant roles in maintaining stability. Consistently positive changes in indicators such as school enrollment and economic growth were presented as encouraging signs that a sense of order was returning to many parts of the country.[19]

The August 2009 elections came off without major terrorist attacks, although it appeared that the relatively light turnout had been induced by Taliban threats and attacks prior to the elections, particularly in the southern and eastern parts of the country. President Karzai won a decisive victory over his one major opponent, former Foreign Minister Dr. Abdullah Abdullah, but evidence of widespread voter fraud led to demands and plans for a runoff election. However, Abdullah withdrew from the election arguing that the runoff election would not be conducted fairly. As a consequence, President Karzai was returned to power, but with a large black cloud over his head. The outcome posed serious problems for the Obama Administration, which had hoped for a more legitimate and less corrupt government in Kabul in return for an increase in US forces there.

Despite some areas of success, the establishment of a self-sufficient, legitimate government is proving in many ways to be fraught with difficulty. It is widely acknowledged that President Karzai has tolerated corruption and appeased faction leaders with appointments to facilitate stability,[20] but endemic corruption consistently stood out as a crippling factor in the extension of effective governance, and reports indicated that the government consistently failed to provide basic services to the population. Various international efforts to provide local delivery of aid through PRTs, NGOs, Special Forces and other programs often conflicted both with one another and with domestic government processes that remained unregulated and disconnected from one another. Inefficient, highly centralized ministries in Kabul were often responsible for delivery of services across the country, and while efforts were made to delegate authority to lower levels (such as Karzai's new initiative *The Directorate for Local Governance*),[21] results were limited.

Provision of essential services is critical for establishing the legitimacy of a central Afghan Government, but as of 2009 the government lacked even the means to collect taxes. Indeed, bookkeeping, even at the national level, is so underdeveloped that the government could not keep track of aid flows. Instead it left the task of accountancy up to individual donors, who had varying recordkeeping methods that further complicated information sharing.[22] There was little subnational governmental organization in the provinces and lower level courts had not been established. According to a US RAND think-tank study, the coalition's support of the Northern Alliance in the overthrow of the Taliban ultimately led to a weakening of central authority in favor of traditional, regional warlords[23] and the sort of decentralized rule that has been a recurring theme throughout the country's history.

According to the former Interior Minister of Afghanistan Ali A. Jalali, writing in 2007, "The structural legitimacy of the current Afghan government suffers from a lack of capacity, particularly at the subnational level, where the vacuum is filled by insurgents, militia commanders, [and] local gangs, all of whom undermine human security, local governance, democratic values and the delivery of basic services."[24] The weakness of the government, he claimed, has caused a crisis of confidence and the erosion of its legitimacy. Apparently the fundamentals had not changed by 2009 when the Congressional Research Service observed that "The Karzai government's own problems are apparent: discontented warlords, endemic corruption, a vigorous drug trade, the Taliban, and a rudimentary economy and infrastructure. In the view of former NATO General and now Ambassador to Afghanistan, Carl Eikenberry, 'The enemy we face is not particularly strong, but the institutions of the Afghan state remain relatively weak.' "[25] This loss of confidence translated into a tangible hemorrhage of territory, and in recent years, the Taliban has regained "influence and control in what now amounts to nearly half of Afghanistan."[26]

Rule of law and an operational justice system, often considered keystones to the establishment of a legitimate regime, were still woefully underdeveloped and, according to a World Bank assessment, the Afghan system was still one of the worst in the world.[27] Reports indicated that warlord control over regions had dramatically disrupted attempts by the central government to appoint judges and establish authority, and allegations of serious corruption were lodged against both the attorney general's office and the Supreme Court in Kabul. In 2006, an Asia Foundation report concluded that only 16 percent of Afghan legal disputes were being brought to official courts and the vast majority was decided in traditional settings outside the authority of the state.[28] Furthermore, reports from early 2007 claimed that Taliban courts had returned in some provincial areas, where they were viewed as more efficacious than the corrupt, official ones.[29]

Corruption and incompetence in the newly reconstituted police force proved disastrous for its credibility. An International Institute for Strategic Studies report asserted in 2007 that "The Afghan National Police (ANP) has been a source of insecurity for communities across the country, rather than a solution to it."[30] The report charged that informal bribe earnings for police in the country ranged between $200 and $30,000 per month, and that besides failing to prosecute in instances of murder and torture, the police themselves engaged in crimes, such as bank robberies and kidnappings for ransom.[31] Reforms were slow moving and, despite efforts by EUPOL and the United States to raise standards, it was concluded in July 2007 that only 40 percent of the ANP was adequately equipped.[32] The bulk of police salaries were paid out of the internationally funded Law and Order Trust Fund for Afghanistan, which as of 2008 was still severely underfunded.

These problems continued virtually unabated into 2009. NATO's annual assessment reported that "The capacity of the Afghan Government at the national, provincial and district levels remains limited and suffers from corruption. Continuing insecurity, criminality and, in places, the influence of the narcotics trade further impede efforts to improve good governance."[33]

In the United States, the new Obama Administration immediately placed a high priority on improving training of the Afghan police and sent an additional 4,000 troops to Afghanistan to strengthen the training program. The United States hoped that the injection of additional trainers would make a difference in combating corruption. The unscrupulous nature of the current force was pervasive: ranking positions on police forces and judiciary frequently went to the highest bidder and, as one provincial police official observed, "This is the reason no one accepts the rule of law . . . , because the government is not going by the rule of law."[34] According to interviews with American and Afghan sources, "The list of schemes that undermine law enforcement is long and bewildering . . . : police officials who steal truckloads of gasoline; judges and prosecutors who make decisions based on bribes; high-ranking government officials who reap payoffs from hashish and chromite smuggling; and midlevel security and political jobs that are sold, sometimes for more than $50,000, money the buyers then recoup through still more bribes and theft."[35]

The irony in all this is that the Taliban reportedly are reaping large financial benefits from the illicit narcotics trade—a line of business they suppressed when in power. For many Afghans, growing poppy for that trade has become their main way of life as well as the main source of revenue for the Taliban. NATO has summarized the issue in the following terms:

There is a recognised nexus between the narcotics trade and the insurgency. Each year, the insurgency benefits from an estimated 100 million–200 million USD from the narcotics trade. Experience on the ground demonstrates that opium production and insurgent violence are correlated geographically and opium remains a major source of revenue for both the insurgency and organized crime. The drugs trade also fuels corruption and undermines the rule of law. It jeopardises the prospects of long-term economic growth and impacts on the nation's health, as drug addiction is an ever-increasing problem in Afghanistan.[36]

Since the Taliban was removed from power, opium poppy cultivation in Afghanistan has increased to supply 93 percent of the world's opium. Part of the answer to the drug problem has been destroying poppy fields and disrupting production and transportation of opium to the international market. US, ISAF and

Afghan forces cooperate in such destruction and interdiction activities. However, these approaches do not present a long-term solution to the problem, in part because so much of the Afghan economy depends on the revenue from the trade. The Executive Director of the United Nations Office on Drugs and Crime, in his 2009 assessment of the situation, suggested that "Progress depends on more than reducing the amount of opium hectarage: it depends on improving security, integrity, economic growth, and governance." He continued, "We must concentrate on winning long-term campaigns, not just short-term battles."[37] If US, NATO and Afghan government forces simply destroy crops without providing alternative sources of income for the farmers support for the Taliban will grow and the long-term battle will be lost.

Until the judicial and police systems move away from the culture of corruption, central government control in Afghanistan will be difficult to establish and maintain, and the Taliban will be seen by some Afghans as providing a more reliable form of justice and security. Given the fact that the legal and governmental system has traditionally depended on this illicit lubrication, establishing effective rule of law in Afghanistan could therefore be a decades-long process.

The Afghanistan National Security Forces (ANSF)

A critical key to the security component of Afghanistan's future is the development of domestic security forces capable of defending the political system from its enemies. This also has proven to be a daunting task, even though slow progress apparently is being made. According to NATO, in 2008 "The ANSF grew in strength and capability and Afghan forces assumed responsibility for security in the Kabul area for the first time."[38]

In its *Counterinsurgency Study*, the US RAND think tank underscores the fundamental necessity of developing an indigenous security force to combat the Taliban and other fighters. It focuses in particular on the so-called "Fallacy of External Actors" that pervades popular thinking regarding counter-insurgency strategy, which overemphasizes the role of foreign, direct military power while downplaying the importance of local forces. This ignores many realities, such as the long time frame of many insurgencies (averaging greater than ten years), the intimate knowledge domestic forces have of their cultures and geography, and frequently negative public opinion held towards foreign troops on the ground.[39] The study assesses the essential characteristics of an effective indigenous security force (which is committed to a long term counter-insurgency struggle) as high initiative, good intelligence, high integration, good leadership, competent, loyal soldiers, and adaptability.[40] Most of these characteristics are still sorely lacking in the Afghan National Security Forces.

Responsibility for training the Afghan National Army (ANA) has been primarily taken on by the United States, but includes the cooperation of French, British, Turkish and other nations' trainers in establishing an officer corps. In the Summit Declaration on Afghanistan in April 2009 NATO leaders announced the establishment of a NATO Training Mission-Afghanistan to provide higher level training for the ANA and additionally confirmed the target for army expansion to be 134,000 troops.[41] Newly trained units have encouragingly experienced early successes in combat operations alongside foreign forces and, in 2008, 62 percent were led by the ANA.[42] ISAF and coalition troops are deployed with ANA units through the Embedded Training Team (ETT) and Operational Mentoring and Liaison Team (OMLT) programs, monitoring and supporting the development of the force. By mid-March 2009, the ISAF was operating 52 OMLTs with at least 30 additional teams planned to enter service by the end of 2010.[43]

NATO has also provided support for the ANA through its Equipment Support Program and the ANA Trust Fund, which the North Atlantic Council set up in 2008. Various NATO nations have donated equipment with the intention of modernizing the Soviet-era armaments of the ANA, but internal complaints persisted regarding the dismal state of the army's weaponry and, as of early 2009, contributions to the trust fund were still limited, totaling approximately 18.5 million Euros.[44]

The driving rationale for General McChrystal's request for 40,000 additional troops was to provide both more trainers and a better security environment in which Afghan national forces could be trained up more rapidly. Speaking at the International Institute for Strategic Studies, after his report and recommendations had been leaked to the press, McChrystal summarized his assessment of what need to be done, including training Afghan security forces to take over responsibility for their country's safety:

- Gain the initiative by reversing the perceived momentum possessed by the insurgents.
- Seek rapid growth of Afghan national security forces – the army and the police.
- Improve their effectiveness and ours through closer partnering, which involves planning, living and operating together and taking advantage of each other's strengths as we go forward. Within ISAF, we will put more emphasis on every part of that, by integrating our headquarters, physically co-locating our units, and sharing ownership of the problem.
- Address shortfalls in the capacity of governance and the ability of the Afghan government to provide rule of law.
- Tackle the issue of predatory corruption by some officials or by warlords who are not in an official position but who seem to have the ability, sometimes sanctioned by existing conditions, to do that.
- Focus our resources and prioritize in those areas where the population is most threatened. We do not have enough forces to do everything everywhere at once, so this has to be prioritized and phased over time.[45]

Despite some successes, the ANA has been criticized for its crippling dependence on foreign military assistance, in the form of embedded NATO/Coalition troops, air-support and funding,[46] and for its high attrition rate.[47] That said, developments, such as the creation of the Afghan National Army Air Corps (ANAAC), spearheaded by the United States, gave the ANA greater independence. In 2008, they flew 90 percent of ANA air support missions.[48]

The development of self-sufficient Afghan military forces is a long-term project, but is one that perhaps has made more progress than the development of the judicial and legal system. This is not surprising, given the fact that the US and ISAF military forces in Afghanistan have been able to provide the resources to help mold an Afghan military with its own standards and internal relationships that perhaps will rise above those seen in Afghan civilian society. The development of Afghan security forces could, in this sense, provide part of the foundation around which a modern civil society can grow, as well as strengthen the country's ability to provide for its own security.

Implications for NATO

The ISAF mission has become NATO's most ambitious and demanding task in its history. The Cold War required large armies and defense budgets, but never brought alliance forces into a combat environment. Afghanistan has become a groundbreaking experience for the alliance, both because it requires "kinetic" active combat and counter-insurgency operations and because it is so far from the alliance's base in Europe. Questions remain as to whether the mission will transform the alliance into a global intervention instrument or, on the other hand, will threaten the future viability of the institution.

At least initially, assumption of the ISAF mission appeared to be a vote of confidence in unity and cooperation on both sides of the Atlantic. The Bush administration had been forced to acknowledge that it needed help from allies and the alliance to deal with the demands of two conflicts: one in Iraq, which was given highest priority, and the other in Afghanistan, which had begun as the immediate reaction to the 9/11 attacks. The fact that the allies fell in behind the ISAF mission at a time when the alliance was so profoundly divided over Iraq suggested that the alliance could survive its most heated disagreements.

The Issue of US Priorities

By 2008, it was clear that the combination of ISAF and OEF operations had not been sufficient to turn the tide against the Taliban or to capture Osama bin Laden. Subsequent paragraphs examine the shortcomings of ISAF that are deeply rooted in Europe. However, it seems appropriate to start with a brief acknowledgment that the US decision to invade Iraq and remove Saddam Hussein from power led to such a demanding commitment there that the goals in Afghanistan became a secondary priority. In 2007, Chairman of the US Joint Chiefs of Staff, Admiral Mike Mullen, said pointedly: "In Afghanistan, we do what we can. In Iraq, we do what we must." In May 2009, Mullen reversed field, and declared that Afghanistan was the

US military's "main effort" – a priority that would guide troop assignments, equipment purchases and deployments, and allocation of other resources.[49]

The United States did not dedicate the military manpower needed to establish and maintain control against the Taliban. It did not devote sufficient civilian capabilities and financial resources to help the government in Kabul establish itself around the country. However, the specific problems and history associated with Afghanistan suggest that even with a devoted and persistent effort, the United States might not have been able to achieve its objectives there. Regardless, it is clear that US objectives in Afghanistan would have been better served by a more serious commitment.

None of the European allies portrayed the deficient US commitment as a rationale for the shortcomings of their own contributions. And, it could be further argued that the more the United States does, the less the Europeans will feel their efforts to be essential. Nevertheless, if leadership by example has any value, the fact is that the United States constructed a very poor model for the Europeans to emulate.

Weak Allied Public Support

European involvement in ISAF combat operations has never enjoyed widespread support among the domestic populations of the contributing nations. According to the German Marshal Fund's 2008 Transatlantic Trends public opinion survey, support for deploying their troops in combat operations gains majority support only in the United Kingdom (64 percent favor) and France (52 percent favor). In Germany, 62 percent oppose using their troops to conduct operations against the Taliban. The overall results in the 12 European countries polled found an average of only 43 percent in support of troops being used for combat operations. When asked if they favored deploying troops to provide security for reconstruction, train Afghan soldiers and police, or combat narcotics production, all European countries polled produced strong majorities in support. Respondents in the United States showed strong majority support for the use of American troops in combat and non-combat operations.[50] In Canada, a country that has been on the front lines in combat operations, support for its role in ISAF eroded in 2008–2009, with its mission set to expire in 2011.[51]

The aversion to combat in Afghanistan did not necessarily reflect public loss of confidence in NATO. In spite of strong European disapproval of the Bush administration and its policies, public opinion of NATO's importance to their country's security remarkably remained relatively strong in 2008. An average of around 60 percent of European respondents in the 2008 Transatlantic Trends polling agreed that NATO was "still essential" to their country's security, a number almost identical to the percentage of Americans who thought the alliance still essential to US security. However, there certainly was the chance that Afghanistan could undermine this support in the long run. As one Norwegian defense official, Espen Barth-Eide, observed "NATO appears to our publics to be an organization that takes our sons to send them to Afghanistan."[52]

The reluctance of NATO members to provide forces to the ISAF underlines the limited enthusiasm for its mission. Despite touting the achievement that all NATO members and several partners provide forces to the ISAF, many give only token contributions, and some are withdrawing. The difficulty that European members of NATO had in 2006 finding 2,200 troops to replace departing soldiers demonstrated the failure of the allies to shoulder the burden that NATO accepted in taking command of the ISAF. Despite the UN's authorization "to take all necessary measures to fulfill its mandate," many NATO European allies have been either unable or unwilling to commit forces to the Afghanistan conflict. With the advent of the Obama Administration in Washington, hopes were raised that Obama's popularity in Europe would increase European support for ISAF. That phenomenon, however, was not immediately apparent.

Secretary of Defense Robert Gates, preparing to leave for meetings with his counterparts in June 2009, nonetheless took an upbeat approach, telling a US Senate committee that the United States was not alone in Afghanistan and that more than forty allies deploy a total of 32,000 troops there. Gates avoided criticizing those that avoid combat missions, but specifically commended Canada, Denmark, the UK and Australia, all of which have put their troops in harm's way and have taken heavy casualties.[53] In the past, Gates had taken the allies to task for the limits on their contributions, but apparently the United States decided that public praise for allied efforts would be more effective than public criticism of their shortcomings.

Public opinion against sending forces to participate in combat operations in Afghanistan certainly posed serious challenges for most European governments. However, the bottom line is that some responded by trying to lead their publics toward a rationale for participation while others simply accepted that they did not have the public or parliamentary support to make serious sacrifices. The future success or failure of ISAF will likely depend on the will and ability of European governments to sustain public and parliamentary tolerance, if not support, of the effort.

National Caveats, Casualty Differentials and Burden-sharing

Ambiguity in the UN mandate for the ISAF and the level of decision-making discretion given to NATO allies has led to a wide variety of approaches to how individual nations deploy and use PRTs and other programs and what limits govern the troops they commit to the ISAF. National caveats, placed by many nations on their forces in Afghanistan, have exacerbated tensions within the alliance. They also have reduced the flexibility of commanders to allocate forces in the country, while nationwide reconstruction programs, undertaken by various allies, have met with mixed effectiveness and occasional charges of inefficiency and redundancy. One NATO general is quoted as saying "Opponents and national caveats have polluted ISAF's command-and-control system . . . If politicians don't trust their military commanders, they should kick them out, but they should not try to run local battles from faraway capitals. It is wrong and it can kill people."[54]

In mid-2009, nearly half of all troops under ISAF command had some sort of restrictions on their operational capacities, relating to geographic deployment, mission profiles, and the use of force. According to the Congressional Research Service,

> While caveats in themselves do not generally prohibit the kinds of operations NATO forces can engage in, caveats do pose difficult problems for commanders who seek maximum flexibility in utilizing troops under their command. Some governments' troops lack the appropriate equipment to function with other NATO forces. Some nations will not permit their troops to deploy to other parts of Afghanistan. Still others prohibit their troops from participating in combat operations unless in self-defense. NATO commanders have willingly accepted troops from some 42 governments but have had to shape the conduct of the mission to fit the capabilities of and caveats on those troops.[55]

These limitations, while often a reflection of the domestic political realities of the allies, have been widely criticized outside the countries with the most constraining caveats. In 2006, SACEUR James Jones, who in 2009 became President Barack Obama's National Security Advisor, argued that "It's not enough to simply provide forces if those forces have restrictions on them that limit them from being effective."[56] At the 2008 Munich Security Conference, Secretary of Defense Gates issued an unequivocal condemnation of national caveats, saying "in NATO, some allies ought not to have the luxury of opting only for stability and civilian operations, thus forcing other allies to bear a disproportionate share of the fighting and the dying."[57]

The nationally imposed limitations on Germany's ISAF contribution have been the focus of greatest controversy. Germany's troops, largely confined to the relatively stable northern regional command, have been required to go to great lengths to avoid confrontations with militants and are prohibited from initiating combat operations, authorized by the German government to fire only in self-defense. Demilitarization and the legacy of World War II in the German collective conscious has, according to German foreign policy expert Markus Kaim, led to what military sociologists call "post-heroic society" which is "casualty-shy and risk averse," needing to rationalize military involvement as a noble, humanitarian mission of state-building.[58] Politically, taking an anti-Afghanistan war stance became tremendously profitable in Germany, and left wing parties gained serious traction by advocating immediate withdrawal and painting entanglement in Afghanistan as an outgrowth of following the Bush doctrine.[59] Chancellor Merkel's coalition government was forced to walk a fine line between placating an increasingly impatient public and destabilizing the entire NATO operation by heeding their demands. The disaffection of the German populace is not unique, and similar trends exist in other contributing nations as well, including France and the Netherlands, and even staunch US ally Great Britain.[60]

One aptly titled assessment ("Don't Shoot, We're German") has made note of the fact that the debate in Germany on the role of the Bundeswehr in Afghanistan is carried on in an unreal vocabulary:

> According to the government, the situation in Afghanistan has little to do with a violent struggle or an armed conflict. In fact, the German government appears to have blacklisted the word "war." Anybody who suggests that something like war is happening in Afghanistan risks being rebuked, especially if he or she suggests that the Bundeswehr is participating in this war as part of the NATO-led ISAF. German soldiers "are not waging war there," says Green politician Jürgen Trittin. "They are only securing the reconstruction effort. That's a fact."
> . . . The political debate on the Afghanistan mission is based on the following military policy rationale: We Germans do not fight wars. And even if we do, they are someone else's wars, or at least wars for a very good cause.[61]

The German situation in some ways illustrates the success of Western policy after World War II. Every possible political, legal, social and educational attempt was made to ensure that Germany would never again be a threat to European or international peace. The campaign was embraced by West Germany's leaders and its educational system. Furthermore, German reunification at the end of the Cold War brought in a population that had been trained to be suspicious of the West, the United States, and NATO. For some German politicians, the limits on Germany's role in Afghanistan may be largely a way of avoiding difficult decisions and commitments. But, for others, it is a matter of strong political beliefs concerning Germany's role in the world.

In spite of public pressures on European governments, and increased intensity of the conflict in Afghanistan, some have taken steps to reduce the number and severity of restrictions on their ISAF forces. In 2009, the French contingent was authorized to offer emergency assistance to other NATO forces and the Italian and Spanish commanders were granted discretionary authority concerning the use of the troops under them in urgent situations.[62] With German national elections approaching in the second half of 2009, it was clear that any loosening of constraints on the role of German forces in Afghanistan would have to await their outcome which, in any case, might not change the political dynamics limiting Germany's contribution.

Perhaps the greatest danger to success in Afghanistan and to the future utility of NATO is the development of a multi-tiered alliance, in which some countries assume much greater risks than others on behalf of a shared mission. In the relationship between the United States and the European allies, this concern takes the form of the traditional burden-sharing issue, in which the United States appears to carry most of the weight and becomes resentful of the less-robust European contributions. With the Obama Administration's shift in US priorities and resources from Iraq to Afghanistan, the gap between the North American and European contributions has grown, and the grounds for a new burden-sharing debate have expanded as well.

Photo: 9.1: NATO Secretary General Anders Fogh Rasmussen meets with Afghan President Karzai in Kabul in early August 2009, just days after assuming his post and two weeks before Afghan national elections

Source: NATO Photos.

Moreover, there are serious differentials in the casualties suffered by alliance members as a result of their contributions. Grim reality dictates that the countries that deploy their forces on the front lines of combat with the Taliban and al Qaeda will suffer the greatest casualties. The forces of United States, Great Britain, Canada, Denmark and the Netherlands consequently have faced the greatest risks and take the heaviest casualties. Countries like Germany, deployed in the more stable north, take fewer risks and sustain lighter casualties. This is a form of the burden-sharing debate that cuts across the alliance at a very personal level. It is not a matter of money, but rather concerns the lives of soldiers. Should the life of a soldier from one allied country be more valuable than that of another? Of course not. But the consequences of political decisions taken by various allies have produced the appearance of such a difference, and this casualty differential could leave long-term scars on the alliance.

A Continuing Story . . .

The story of NATO in Afghanistan is far from over. In some ways, the European allies only now are realizing the full consequences of offering to help their American allies in their hour of need. Mistakes were made. The United States made the first one by invading Afghanistan without devoting the time, attention and resources to the task of stabilizing the defeated and failed state. Yet the European allies have also contributed to the problem by severely limiting the manpower and resources they were willing to commit to the conflict. The constraints many allies placed on the forces they did deploy made if difficult if not impossible for NATO to construct a coherent effort on the ground. The European Union, which has access to many of the non-military assets not commanded by NATO, was slow and tentative in contributing, some say because EU officials were reluctant to play second fiddle to NATO and the United States in Afghanistan.[63]

Ultimately, among all the external actors in Afghanistan, the United States will have the decisive influence on success or failure. The Afghan and Pakistani people and governments will also play critical roles, frequently beyond the influence of all external actors. Yet the persistence and effectiveness of the American effort will ultimately determine whether the Western nations remain in Afghanistan long enough to help the country achieve self-sufficiency without overstaying their welcome and subsequently appearing as an enemy occupation force.

In the second half of 2009, a challenge to such an outcome emerged in the United States itself. The Obama administration's attempt to refocus American military priorities on Afghanistan, based on a calculated assessment of US interests, was challenged by shifting American public opinion. As the increased number of US troops in Afghanistan and much higher tempo of operations against Taliban targets produced growing numbers of American casualties, public opinion in the United States began to turn against continuing the war.[64] The polling results raised questions about whether the Obama administration could sustain the American presence in Afghanistan without resorting to the kind of fear-mongering that so successfully produced initial public support for the Bush administration's war against Iraq. It is obvious that, if the United States cannot sustain its role in Afghanistan, that of NATO will fail as well.

The administration was put in a particularly difficult bind by the fact that as public opinion was running away from support for the war, his military advisors were recommending a large increase in US forces devoted to the effort. The recommendation by the commander of US and ISAF forces in Afghanistan, General Stanley A. McChrystal, that as many as 40,000 additional American troops would be required to avoid mission failure, presented the administration with a difficult set of choices: go against the President's political base or against the advice of his top military commanders.

In November 2009, Obama announced he had decided to order substantial increases in the US military forces in Afghanistan. In so doing, he largely followed the advice of his military commanders. In response to concerns, expressed strongly in his own party, about escalation of the conflict, Obama declared that his strategy placed a high priority on training up the Afghan National Army to be able progressively to take over responsibilities for security to allow the United States to begin withdrawing forces by the middle of 2011. He also called for NATO allies to increase their own commitments during the same time period. He still faced criticism from the right for setting a deadline by which time to begin withdrawing forces and from the left for sending more troops in the near term and not receiving sufficient support from the international community.

It is, of course, possible that the Obama administration will be able to stay the course in Afghanistan in spite of growing public opposition. This could eventually yield a successful mission in which US efforts are sustained to the point of producing a self-reliant Afghan regime but in which NATO is perceived as having played a less-than-satisfactory role. This would not necessarily result in the end of the alliance, but certainly could translate into dramatic changes in the role that the organization plays in dealing with future international security challenges. The consequences of the burden sharing and casualty differential issues could trouble transatlantic relations for decades. The fact that NATO survived the Iraq crisis nonetheless suggests a degree of permanence that many observers would not have expected.

While NATO, the European allies and the European Union can all be faulted for either ineffective or insufficient contributions to the effort in Afghanistan, the United States carries part of the blame for not making Afghanistan a higher priority. There is plenty of blame to go around, and the "failures" in this effort may unite the allies as much as dividing them.

For its part, the United States does not want the Afghan problem to be "Americanized," and the formal involvement of NATO and NATO allies in helping shape an acceptable outcome helps ensure that the conflict remains internationalized. NATO's involvement, even as flawed as it may be, provides a critical link to international legitimacy for US policy objectives. That link runs through NATO directly to the United Nations, hopefully (from the US point of view) ensuring that the broader international community will share responsibility for guaranteeing that Afghanistan does not return to a failed state that offers a welcoming habitat for future terrorist operations.

As far as the European allies are concerned, most if not all governments appear to recognize that the future of Afghanistan does hold the key to the level of threat likely to be posed by international terrorism in the coming years. They also recognize that bailing out of responsibility for the outcome in Afghanistan would call into question the vitality of the security links among them and to the United States. They too want the broader international community to remain committed to a positive outcome in Afghanistan, and the NATO role provides an important link to international legitimacy and assistance for the European allies as well.

The bottom line, however, is that it is not just NATO's future that is at risk in Afghanistan. The entire international community has an important stake in trying to keep Afghanistan from being transformed once again into a launching pad for international terrorism and that the nuclear armed Government of Pakistan is not destabilized or taken over by radical extremists who share al Qaeda's terrorist goals.

Notes

1. Amin Saikal. "Afghanistan's transition: ISAF's stabilization role?" *Third World Quarterly* 27.3 (June 2006), 528.

2. For an excellent examination on a constantly-updated basis of NATO's involvement in Afghanistan, refer to Vincent Morelli and Paul Belkin. "NATO in Afghanistan: A Test of the Transatlantic Alliance," Congressional Research Service Report RL33627, July 2009. Updated versions of this and other CRS reports can be found online at http://www.fas.org/sgp/crs/index.html or http://opencrs.com/.

3. Morelli and Belkin. "NATO in Afghanistan," 7–8.

4. North Atlantic Treaty Organization. *Afghanistan Report 2009*. Brussels: NATO Public Diplomacy Division, 2009. Pages 18, 35, 36.

5. Anthony Cordesman. "Sanctum FATA." *The National Interest* 101 (May–June 2009): 28(11), 31.

6. Saikal. "Afghanistan's transition," 532.

7. Michael J. Dziedic and Colonel Michael K. Seidl. "Provincial Reconstruction Teams and Military Relations with International and Nongovernmental Organizations in Afghanistan." United States Institute of Peace Special Report 147, September 2005, 2.

8. The lessons of NATO operations in the Balkans and then in Afghanistan have led the alliance to recognize formally that military interventions on their own are insufficient to "win the peace." NATO has also acknowledged that, as an organization, it does not have the mandate or the in-house resources to provide everything that is required to deal with a defeated or failed state. At the April 4, 2009 Strasbourg/Kehl Summit, allied leaders in their "Declaration on Alliance Security," noted: "We aim to strengthen our cooperation with other international actors, including the United Nations, European Union, Organization for Security and Cooperation in Europe and African Union, in order to improve our ability to deliver a comprehensive approach to meeting these new challenges, combining civilian and military capabilities more effectively. In our operations today in Afghanistan and the Western Balkans, our armed forces are working alongside many other nations and organisations." PRTs and cooperation with other international organizations form the core of NATO's comprehensive approach to the ISAF mission in Afghanistan.

9. See, for example, James Sperling and Mark Webber. "NATO: from Kosovo to Kabul." *International Affairs* 85.3 (May 2009), 509, and Saikal, "Afghanistan's transition," 532.

10. Saikal, "Afghanistan's transition," 532.

11. Markus Kaim. "Germany, Afghanistan, and the future of NATO." *International Journal* 63.3 (Summer 2008), 613.

12. Michael O'Hanlon. "Toward Reconciliation in Afghanistan." *The Washington Quarterly* (April 2008), 142.

13. Cordesman, "Sanctum FATA," 31.

14. Sam Kiley and Lt. General David Richards. "Interview: Lieut. General David Richards," *From Afghanistan: The Other War*, Frontline World. PBS. Aired 10 April, 2007.

15. Cordesman, "Sanctum FATA, 32.
16. The goal is found in numerous locations on the NATO website. See, for example, http://www.nato.int/cps/en/natolive/topics_8189.htm [accessed November 12, 2009].
17. North Atlantic Treaty Organization, "Summit Declaration on Afghanistan, Issued by the Heads of State and Government participating in the meeting of the North Atlantic Council in Strasbourg / Kehl on 4 April 2009."
18. Kenneth Katzman, "Afghanistan: Government Formation and Performance," CRS Report for Congress, RL30508, June 2009 (updated regularly), 15.
19. North Atlantic Treaty Organization, *Afghanistan Report* includes updated assessments of all aspects of international assistance to Afghanistan.
20. Katzman, "Afghanistan: Government," 16.
21. Daniel Korski,. *Afghanistan: Europe's Forgotten War.* European Council on Foreign Relations, 2008, 24.
22. Korski, 10.
23. Seth G. Jones, *Counterinsurgency in Afghanistan: RAND Counterinsurgency Study–Volume 4 (2008) (RAND Counterinsurgency Study,* Arlington: RAND Corporation, 2008, 80.
24. Ali A. Jalali, "Afghanistan: regaining momentum." *Parameters* 37.4 (Winter 2007), 8.
25. Morelli and Belkin, "NATO in Afghanistan," 31.
26. Cordesman, "Sanctum FATA," 28.
27. Jones, *Counterinsurgency in Afghanistan,* 84.
28. Cyrus Hodes and Mark Sedra. *The Search for Security in Post-Taliban Afghanistan.* Abingdon: Routledge for the International Institute for Strategic Studies, 2007, 79.
29. Barnett R. Rubin, "Saving Afghanistan," *International Affairs* 86.1 (January/ February 2007), 60.
30. Hodes and Sedra, "*The Search for Security,*" 2.
31. Hodes and Sedra, "*The Search for Security,*" 62.
32. Hodes and Sedra, "*The Search for Security,*" 64.
33. North Atlantic Treaty Organization, *Afghanistan Report 2009,* 5.
34. Richard A. Oppel, Jr., "Corruption Undercuts Hopes for Afghan Police," *The New York Times,* April 8, 2009 http://www.nytimes.com/2009/04/09/world/asia/09ghazni.html [accessed November 12, 2009].
35. Oppel, "Corruption Undercuts."
36. North Atlantic Treaty Organization, *Afghanistan Report 2009,* 28.
37. Antonio Maria Costa, "Afghanistan Opium Winter Assessment Report," United Nations Office on Drugs and Crime (UNODC), January 2009, as reported in North Atlantic Treaty Organization, *Afghanistan Report 2009,* 28.
38. North Atlantic Treaty Organization, *Afghanistan Report 2009,* 5.
39. Jones, *Counterinsurgency in Afghanistan,* 11.
40. Jones, *Counterinsurgency in Afghanistan,* 15.

41. North Atlantic Treaty Organization, "Summit Declaration on Afghanistan."
42. North Atlantic Treaty Organization, *Afghanistan Report 2009*, 13.
43. North Atlantic Treaty Organization, 13.
44. North Atlantic Treaty Organization, 14.
45. Stanley A. McChrystal, "Special Address - General Stanley McChrystal, Commander, International Security Assistance Force (ISAF) and Commander, US Forces Afghanistan," speech to the International Institute of Strategic Studies, London, October 1, 2009. http://www.iiss.org/recent-key-addresses/general-stanley-mcchrystal-address [accessed November 12, 2009].
46. Jones, *Counterinsurgency in Afghanistan*, 75.
47. Hodes and Sedra, *The Search for Security*, 57.
48. North Atlantic Treaty Organization, *Afghanistan Report 2009*, 15.
49. Ann Scott Tyson, "Afghan Effort is Mullen's Top Focus," *The Washington Post*, May 5, 2009. 1.
50. German Marshal Fund of the United States, et al. "Transatlantic Trends 2008 Topline Data," October 2008. http://www.transatlantictrends.org/trends/doc/2008_English_Top.pdf [accessed November 12, 2009].
51. Morelli and Belkin, "NATO in Afghanistan," 23.
52. "Have combat experience, will travel." *The Economist*, March 26, 2009 http://www.economist.com/opinion/displaystory.cfm?story_id=13376058 [accessed November 12, 2009].
53. Al Pessin, "Gates to Meet with Allies on Afghanistan, Wants Progress Within a Year," VOANews.com, June 9, 2009, http://www.voanews.com/english/archive/2009-06/2009-06-09-voa62.cfm?CFID=264832194&CFTOKEN=30150613&jsessionid=00307cc5cba8a4a9a39e4b28425775234242 [accessed November 12, 2009].
54. Joris Janssen Lok. "Defining Objectives: Taliban and European Politics Challenge NATO mission in Afghanistan," *Defense Technology International* 1.6 (August 2007), 16.
55. Morelli and Belkin, "NATO in Afghanistan," 10.
56. "NATO Commander Asks Member Nations to Drop Troop Limits," *Mideast Stars and Stripes*, October 25, 2006.
57. Thomas Omestad, "NATO Struggles Over Who Will Send Additional Troops to Fight in Afghanistan," USNews.com, February 13, 2008, http://www.usnews.com/articles/news/world/2008/02/13/nato-struggles-over-who-will-send-additional-troops-to-fight-in-afghanistan.html [accessed November 12, 2009].
58. Kaim, "Germany, Afghanistan," 614.
59. Kaim, "Germany, Afghanistan," 613.
60. Josh Visser, "Deaths in Afghanistan Testing Britain's Resolve," CTV News, July 19, 2009. http://www.ctv.ca/servlet/ArticleNews/story/CTVNews/20090716/afghan_britain_090719/20090719?hub=TopStories [accessed November 12, 2009].
61. Eric Chauvistré, "Don't Shoot, We're German! Obstacles to a debate on the bundeswehr's international missions," *Internationale Politik*, Summer 2009, 69, 77.

62. Morelli and Belkin, "NATO in Afghanistan," 11.
63. While not officially documented, the author has heard this rationale widely rumored among European officials.
64. Jennifer Agiesta and Jon Cohen, "Public Opinion in U.S. turns Against Afghan War," *The Washington Post*, August 20, 2009, http://www.washingtonpost. com/wp-dyn/content/article/2009/08/19/AR2009081903066_pf.html [accessed November 12, 2009].

CHAPTER 10

European Security and Defense Policy and the Transatlantic Bargain

Post-Cold War adaptations in NATO's outreach and membership, relations with Russia, military missions and nuclear deployments responded to the new international realities that emerged in the early 1990s, importantly reshaping the ways and means of the transatlantic alliance. Neither these changes nor the NATO mission in Afghanistan altered the basic relationship between the United States and Europe in the alliance. At the same time, however, developments in European integration were shifting some of the terms of the transatlantic bargain.

Transatlantic discomfort with that bargain was on display as the end of the Cold War neared, with members of the US Congress complaining loudly about inadequate defense burden sharing and European officials grumbling about excessive European reliance on US leadership. As the American political scientist Michael Brenner reflected on transatlantic relations in the 1980s, "Strategic dependency did not cause European governments to suspend their critical judgment in assessing the wisdom of U.S. policy."[1]

Questions about the sustainability of a relationship that depended so heavily on the United States had been around for a long time. In the mid-1980s this author observed, "The only way to maximize the benefits of alliance will be to encourage a process of gradual evolutionary change in US-European relations toward a new transatlantic bargain." That bargain "must bring greater European responsibility and leadership to the deal; it must ensure continued American involvement in European defense while at the same time constructing a new European 'pillar' inside, not outside, the broad framework of the Western alliance." I then raised questions that are still open after one decade in a new millennium: "Will the European allies find the vision and courage to take on added responsibilities? Will the United States be wise enough to accept a more independent European partner?"[2]

In the 1990s, with the main threat to European security gone, that evolutionary process of change accelerated, suggesting that it might be leading toward the new bargain that I wrote about in 1985. That process of change, however, unfolded in fits and starts—not a surprise, given the magnitude of the task. And just as the potential for a new bargain held potential benefits for both US and European interests, it also contained risks that have weighed heavily on US officials over the last two decades. Success in this endeavor nonetheless remains critical to the future of transatlantic relations. Sean Kay, an American international relations expert, has judged that

"Balancing the transatlantic relationship is critical to keeping the US-European security partnership vibrant in the future. Indeed, it is a founding task of NATO that remains unfulfilled."[3]

As with the rest of the story of the alliance, the emergence of a more coherent Europe in the area of foreign policy and defense is part of a continuum. In Chapter 4, I discussed the development of European-level foreign and defense policy coordination as one of the significant elements of change in the transatlantic bargain. In this chapter, I look at how this process developed following the end of the Cold War, first as an attempt to build a European Security and Defense Identity in NATO and then as a major new initiative to develop an autonomous European Security and Defense Policy within the framework of the European Union (EU). Demonstrating the many challenges posed by the process, it reached a plateau one decade into the twenty-first century, and questions remained concerning whether or not the European allies would have the political will or material resources to take on the levels of responsibility in the alliance to create a "new bargain."

The European Security and Defense Identity

The first response of European governments to the end of the Cold War was to begin cutting defense expenditures to realize a "peace dividend." The United States also hoped for a peace dividend. But the higher priority for President George H. W. Bush and his top officials was ensuring continuity in US international leadership, including leadership of NATO. At a time when some were questioning whether NATO had any future, administration officials were suspicious of the moves within the European Union to give the Union a defense dimension.

American public opinion remained very favorable toward Europe and, in particular, toward EU members, reflecting deep European roots in American society, perceptions of shared values, and alliance relationships, among other factors. But the United States had always been schizophrenic about Europe's role in the world. Throughout the Cold War period, the United States supported the goal of enhanced European economic, political, and defense cooperation. However, the United States had not been forced to confront directly the prospect of European defense cooperation that could actually substitute for what in the past had been done in or through NATO and could supplant traditional US-European roles in the alliance. Even though the United States has always welcomed the potential for a stronger "European pillar" in the transatlantic alliance, it has been wary of approaches that would divide the alliance politically, take resources away from NATO military cooperation, and not yield additional military capabilities to produce more equitable burden sharing. The US approach could accurately be called a "yes, but" policy, supporting the European effort but warning of the potential negative consequences.[4]

In the early 1990s, traditional support for European integration still dominated the rhetoric of US policy, but the tendency to look somewhat skeptically at US support for European integration became more influential in the absence of the strong geostrategic requirement to support the process during the Cold War. In a "yes, but" policy environment, the "but" therefore received more emphasis.

In 1990, Bush administration National Security Adviser Brent Scowcroft was known to be skeptical about French motivations, and his relationship with officials in Paris was strained. In addition, there may have been a justifiable concern that bringing defense issues within the purview of the European Commission would open the way for anti-American sentiment present in the Commission to influence the evolution of transatlantic defense ties. The administration was also concerned that too much European rhetoric and declarations about taking on responsibility for defense would provide ammunition for traditional US critics of the US commitment to NATO.

As the United States perceived the increased momentum toward European agreement on a defense identity early in 1991, a number of alarm bells were rung by US officials. The US ambassador to NATO, William Taft IV, in speeches delivered in February and March, supported a stronger European pillar in the alliance based on a revival of the Western European Union but cautioned that the European pillar should not relax the central transatlantic bond, should not duplicate current cooperation in NATO, and should not leave out countries that are not members of the European Community. (These themes foreshadowed the Clinton administration's 1998 admonition that the European Union should avoid the dreaded "three Ds" of duplication, decoupling, and discrimination.)

The message was put more bluntly in a closely held memorandum sent to European governments by Undersecretary of State for International Security Affairs Reginald Bartholomew in February. According to published reports, the memorandum expressed concern that the United States might be "marginalized" if greater European cohesion in defense led to the creation of an internal caucus within NATO.[5]

Following further warnings issued by Deputy Assistant Secretary of State James Dobbins on visits to European capitals and expressions of concern by Secretary of Defense Dick Cheney, the US approach to European defense integration appeared to have settled on five main points: the United States supported the development of common European foreign, security, and defense policies; NATO must remain the essential forum for consultations and venue for agreement on all policies bearing on the security and defense commitments of its members under the North Atlantic Treaty; NATO should retain its integrated military structure; the United States supports the European right to take common military action outside Europe to preserve its interests or ensure the respect of international law; and European members of NATO that do not belong to the European Union should not be excluded from European defense policy deliberations.[6]

Toward the end of 1991, the United States backed away from overt protests about a European defense identity, even though substantial ambiguity remained regarding what the United States really wanted from Europe. Tactically, US policymakers concentrated on diplomatic efforts to ensure that the definition of that identity emerging from the NATO summit in Rome and the EU summit in Maastricht, the

Netherlands, would be consistent with US interests in NATO as the primary European security institution.

As discussed in Chapter 8, NATO's 1991 new strategic concept established three areas of particular emphasis for future NATO policies. First, the allies said that, as part of a "broader" approach to security, they would actively seek cooperation and dialogue among all European states and particularly with the former Warsaw Pact adversaries (discussed in Chapter 6). Second, they declared that NATO's nuclear and nonnuclear military forces would be reduced and that remaining forces would be restructured to take into account the need for militaries that could handle crisis management tasks (such as the one that later developed in Bosnia in the 1990s and the even more demanding ones in Afghanistan after the 9/11 attacks on the United States) as well as collective defense. Third, the allies agreed that the European members of NATO would assume greater responsibility for their own security. Specifically, the NATO leaders judged that "the development of a European security identity and defense role, reflected in the further strengthening of the European pillar within the alliance, will reinforce the integrity and effectiveness of the Atlantic Alliance." At that time, there was absolutely no concept for how this should come about, particularly when the allies were almost universally focused on how to cut defense expenditures in light of the reduced threats to produce a peace dividend for domestic spending programs.

And in an important footnote to the support for a stronger European pillar, the leaders reiterated that NATO is "the essential forum for consultation among its members and the venue for agreement on policies bearing on the security and defense commitments of Allies under the Washington [North Atlantic] Treaty."[7]

In December 1991, in the wake of NATO's new strategic concept, the members of the European Community signed the Maastricht Treaty, transforming the European Community into the European Union and setting the goal of establishing a monetary union and a common currency, the Euro. The treaty importantly included, as part of that Union, a commitment to "define and implement a common foreign and security policy" that would eventually include "framing of a common defence policy, which might in time lead to a common defence." The key articles that followed set the path for enhancement of the role that defense and security would play in the future development of European unification:

Article J.1
The Member States shall support the Union's external and security policy actively and unreservedly in a spirit of loyalty and mutual solidarity. They shall refrain from any action which is contrary to the interests of the Union or likely to impair its effectiveness as a cohesive force in international relations. The Council shall ensure that these principles are complied with.

Article J.2
1. Member States shall inform and consult one another within the Council on any matter of foreign and security policy of general interest in order to ensure

that their combined influence is exerted as effectively as possible by means of concerted and convergent action.

2. Whenever it deems it necessary, the Council shall define a common position. Member States shall ensure that their national policies conform to the common positions.

3. Member States shall coordinate their actions in international organizations and at international conferences. They shall uphold the common positions in such fora. In international organizations and at international conferences where not all the Member States participate, those which do take part shall uphold the common positions.[8]

The treaty designated the Western European Union (WEU) as the organization responsible for implementing defense aspects of the European Union's decisions on foreign and security policy. The WEU members subsequently agreed (at Petersberg, Germany, in 1992) that they would use WEU military forces for joint operations in humanitarian and rescue missions, peacekeeping, crisis management, and peace enforcement—the so-called Petersberg tasks.

The outcomes in Rome and Maastricht appeared to resolve the conceptual differences between the United States and France about how a European defense identity should relate to the transatlantic alliance, but they really just papered them over. This became patently clear in the first half of 1992, when the United States issued strong warnings to the German and French governments concerning their plans to create a Franco-German military corps of some 35,000 troops. American officials reportedly expressed reservations about the degree to which the corps would displace NATO as the focus of European defense efforts and undermine domestic support in the United States for a continuing US presence in Europe. National Security Adviser Brent Scowcroft was said to have sent a "strongly worded" letter to the German government suggesting that the Germans were not taking a firm enough position against what Scowcroft interpreted as French efforts to undermine cooperation in NATO.[9] The controversy reflected continuing differences between the US and French governments about the requirements for future European security organization.

US policy toward European defense has always been set within a broader US concept of its role in the world and the way in which allies relate to that world. During the George H. W. Bush administration, internal administration studies that suggested the United States should establish and sustain unquestioned superpower status raised questions in Europe as well as in the United States. Concern arose when a draft of the US Department of Defense "defense guidance" memorandum was leaked to the press early in 1992.[10] The document's vision of far-flung US military requirements in the post-Cold War era, apparently designed to ensure that the United States remained the only global superpower, provoked an outcry from a wide variety of observers who saw the draft plan as seriously out of touch with contemporary political and economic realities.

The reaction among the European allies was that the Pentagon approach seemed to view Europe as a potential adversary rather than an ally. The implication was that the United States should undermine efforts at closer European unity to ensure that no European rival emerged to "balance" the US role in the world. White House and State Department officials characterized the draft as "a 'dumb report' that in no way or shape represents US policy,"[11] suggesting that, even within the Bush administration, there was no consensus on the US role in the world to serve as *political* guidance for the Department of Defense's strategy.

Following the strong reactions to the leaked draft, a new version was produced that reportedly eliminated most of what the European allies and other observers found objectionable.[12] Nonetheless, the controversial draft, by framing one clear perspective on the future US role in the world, made an important and provocative contribution to the ongoing discussion.

Because the American people clearly wanted the United States to focus its energies on economic and social problems at home, the 1992 election campaign produced very little light on the definition of the future US role in the world. President Bill Clinton's administration came to office against the backdrop of an election in which those voting sent a clear message calling for more attention to domestic issues, including the still-mounting federal deficit.

The Clinton administration hoped to dispel any residual impression that the United States did not want the Europeans to take on more burdens and responsibilities in the alliance. As noted in Chapter 6, at least one of Clinton's foreign policy advisers had even argued that withdrawal of US forces from Europe would signal US willingness to envision "Europeanization" of NATO. Less radical approaches prevailed, however, and in January 1994, at Clinton's first opportunity for major initiatives on NATO issues, the NATO Brussels summit acknowledged the important role that a European Security and Defense Identity (ESDI) could play in the evolving European security system.

The January 1994 NATO summit meeting in Brussels approved the idea, initially proposed by the United States, of creating Combined Joint Task Force (CJTF) headquarters as part of NATO's integrated command structure. The CJTF initiative, as discussed in Chapter 8, was designed to give NATO's command structure additional flexibility to accomplish a variety of objectives, including facilitating the dual use of NATO forces and command structures for alliance operations and/or those run by the Western European Union. The purpose was to encourage European nations to undertake missions with forces that are "separable but not separate" from NATO in the context of an emerging ESDI.

The Brussels summit yielded multiple references in the allied declaration to the importance of European-level cooperation and the constructive role played by the Western European Union. (The declaration included no fewer than eight references to the Western European Union, seven references each to the ESDI and European Union, and two each to the Maastricht Treaty on European Union and the Union's Common Foreign and Security Policy goal.)

NATO's work to implement the January 1994 agreements in principle moved ahead slowly but remained hampered by different US and French visions of the future. Many French analysts and officials had interpreted the summit outcome as a US vote for Europeanization of the alliance. In fact, the administration had not intended to go so far and wanted only to open the way toward a stronger European role in the alliance. The perceptual split was suggested by the way each looked at CJTF. The French and some other Europeans saw CJTF primarily as a way for the European allies to engage in more autonomous military actions. The United States saw this as one of the functions of CJTF but regarded the concept's first role as making it possible for NATO itself to operate in more flexible formations and combinations.

In the second half of 1995, the British government began actively searching for ways to create an ESDI within the framework of the alliance and in a fashion that would facilitate France's return to full military integration. Early in 1996, the French and British governments proposed what became known as the "Deputies proposal."[13] NATO forces in Europe have always been commanded by an American officer who occupied the position of Supreme Allied Commander, Europe (SACEUR). The British and French suggested that the Deputy SACEUR, traditionally a senior European officer, and other European officers in the NATO command structure wear WEU command hats as well as their NATO and national command hats. This multiple-hatting procedure would, without duplication of resources and personnel, permit the WEU countries to use the NATO command structure to organize and command a military operation under largely European auspices.

The Deputies proposal reportedly raised serious issues for the US Joint Chiefs of Staff and SACEUR General George Joulwan. Senior US military commanders were concerned that the WEU command arrangements might weaken the European commitment to the NATO structure as well as lessen the American commitment to NATO. However, other US officials, including senior officials at the White House, believed that a continued active US role in the alliance depended on being able to demonstrate to Congress and the American public that the European allies were willing and able to take on greater responsibility for military missions both inside Europe and beyond.[14] The re-involvement of France in the alliance, with its willingness and ability to participate in military interventions beyond national borders, was seen as the key to the construction of a meaningful and coordinated European contribution to post-Cold War security concerns. The spring 1996 session of NATO ministers, scheduled to be held in Berlin, Germany, emerged as the opportunity to tie the loose ends together. In a discussion prior to that session with a key administration diplomat responsible for NATO policy, I asked whether he would support the Deputies proposal. His answer was, "I'll support it as soon as General Joulwan does," suggesting the depth of resistance from the SACEUR and the Joint Chiefs of Staff more generally. Just days prior to the Berlin meeting, US uniformed military leaders were still resisting the transformation of the Deputy SACEUR position. Senior advisers to the president realized that the time had come for a deal, and the White House overruled the Joint Chiefs—a step not easily taken by a president whose credentials with the military were so suspect.[15] As a consequence, the 1994 summit goals were transformed at Berlin into a plan to build a European defense pillar inside the NATO alliance despite objections from the Joint Chiefs.

In Berlin, NATO foreign ministers agreed to move ahead with implementation of the CJTF concept. In addition, they agreed that an ESDI would be created within the alliance by making NATO "assets and capabilities" available for future military operations commanded by the Western European Union. Such decisions would be made by consensus on a case-by-case basis. To facilitate such operations, European officers in the NATO structure would, when appropriate, shift from their NATO responsibilities to WEU command positions.

The allies determined that adaptation of the alliance should be guided by three fundamental objectives: to ensure the alliance's military effectiveness and ability to perform its traditional mission of collective defense while undertaking new military roles, to preserve the transatlantic link by strengthening NATO as a forum for political consultation and military cooperation, and to support development of an ESDI by creating the possibility for NATO supported task forces to perform missions under the direction of the WEU nations.

The Berlin ministerial marked a watershed in the development of US and NATO policy toward creation of a more coherent European role in the alliance. The Clinton administration had clearly gone on the record as supporting a stronger European pillar, but when it came to making significant structural changes in NATO to help bring the concept to fruition, there was profound resistance in the US policy community.

Even after Berlin, the question was what military operations the European allies could actually take on within the framework of the new arrangements. During the intervening years, it was demonstrated that they did not have the combination of military resources and political will to take on operations such as the Implementation Force (IFOR) or Stabilization Force (SFOR) in Bosnia, and the United States provided most of the key resources for the air war against Serbia over Kosovo. In 1997, when impending chaos in Albania threatened to destabilize southeastern Europe, the Europeans were not even able to agree on organizing an intervention under the Western European Union but rather sent in an ad hoc coalition force under Italian command. All these experiences led observers to bemoan the fact that Europe did not have the military capacity required to maintain stability on the borders of EU/WEU member states, to say nothing of the capacity to project significant force beyond the Balkans. As Michael Brenner has written,

> The cumulative record of EU failure and NATO's recovery (in the Balkans) sharpened the issue of whether an ESDI built within NATO on the CJTF principle was satisfactory. For the European allies, the record could be read two ways: as making a compelling case for them to take more drastic measures to augment their military resources and to cement their union, or as providing telling evidence that the quest for an autonomous ESDI was futile. Few drew the first conclusion.[16]

In June 1997, the members of the European Union, in the process of updating and strengthening the Maastricht Treaty, approved the Treaty of Amsterdam. In the area of common defense policy, the Treaty of Amsterdam included a reference to the Petersberg tasks and authorized the adoption of EU common strategies. It also created the position of High Representative for the Common Foreign and Security Policy, one that was not filled until September 1999, when former NATO Secretary General Javier Solana took on the job. Solana had performed well as NATO secretary general and had won admiration in Washington—no small accomplishment for a Spanish socialist who had opposed his country's membership in NATO in the early 1980s. Solana's selection clearly was intended to reassure the United States. In retrospect, the question may be whether Solana's new job was more important than the one he gave up. In fact, it probably was. It would be important for the European Union to move into NATO's exclusive reserve in a way that did not create too much choppy water across the Atlantic, and Solana had a reputation not only for hard work but also for his diplomatic skills—skills that he surely would need in his new job.

An "Autonomous" European Security and Defense Policy

In the autumn of 1998, the shape of the discussion on European defense was changed profoundly by British Prime Minister Tony Blair's decision to make a major push for an EU role in defense. Blair first tried out his ideas at an EU summit in Pörtschach, Austria, in October 1998 and then reaffirmed his approach on November 3 in a major address to the North Atlantic Assembly's annual session[17] in Edinburgh, Scotland. Blair bemoaned the fact that Europe's ability for autonomous military action was so limited and called for major institutional and resource innovations to make Europe a more equal partner in the transatlantic alliance. Blair's initiative may also have betrayed some uncertainty concerning NATO's future.[18]

Traditionally, Great Britain had been the most reliable, predictable partner of the United States when it came to dealing with defense issues. The British had shared US skepticism regarding initiatives that might create splits between the United States and Europe in the alliance, particularly those with roots in French Neo-Gaullist philosophy. The fact that Blair was moving out in front on this issue produced mixed reactions in the United States.

On the one hand, the United States believed that it still could trust Great Britain not to do anything that would hurt the alliance, and Blair claimed that his goal was to strengthen NATO by improving Europe's ability to share security burdens in the twenty-first century. On the other hand, Blair's initiative sounded "too French" to skeptics, and even those who were hopeful were concerned about the political setting for Blair's initiative. It was said that Blair wanted to demonstrate commitment to Europe at a time when the United Kingdom was not going to join in the inauguration of the Euro, the European Union's common currency. Questions about the seriousness of the initiative were also raised by the fact that the proposal seemed to come out of nowhere. In discussions with British foreign office official minutes after the Edinburgh speech was delivered, the author was told that the initiative until then consisted of the two speeches and that on their return to London, they would begin putting meat on the bones of the approach.

At the Edinburgh meeting, Blair and British officials got a foretaste of one of the key aspects of American reactions to the initiative. A report released at the meeting by US Senator William V. Roth Jr. said,

> The United States should give every possible help and encouragement to the continuing consolidation of European defense efforts. But the United States must not be held accountable for the inability of European states to develop a more coherent European role in the Alliance. It is the responsibility of the European Allies to develop the European Security and Defense *Capabilities* to give real meaning to a European Security and Defense *Identity*.[19]

Any doubts about the serious nature of the Blair initiative were removed when Blair met with President Jacques Chirac at Saint-Malo early in December 1998. The declaration, named for this French resort town, envisioned the creation of a Common European Security and Defense Policy (CESDP) with the means and mechanisms to permit the EU nations to act "autonomously" should NATO not decide to act in some future scenario requiring military action. The French delegation reportedly had lined up support from German Chancellor Gerhard Schroeder prior to the meeting, giving the declaration even more weight. The statement included the following key elements:

1. The European Union needs to be in a position to play its full role on the international stage.
2. On the basis of intergovernmental decisions, the Union must have the capacity for autonomous action, backed up by credible military forces, the means to decide to use them and a readiness to do so, in order to respond to international crises.
3. The NATO and WEU collective defense commitments of the EU members must be maintained, obligations to NATO honored, and the various positions of European states in relation to NATO and otherwise must be respected.
4. The Union must be given appropriate structures and a capacity for analysis of situations, sources of intelligence and a capability for relevant strategic planning, without unnecessary duplication.
5. Europe needs strengthened armed forces that can react rapidly to the new risks, and which are supported by a strong and competitive European defense industry and technology.[20]

US administration officials said the Blair initiative was given the benefit of the doubt.[21] The administration thought that British motivations were solid, even if they remained concerned about those of the French. When the Saint-Malo statement emerged, however, administration officials felt that the British had not been 100 percent transparent about the likely outcome. The administration's formal reaction took the traditional form of the "yes, but" approach characterized earlier. Secretary of State Madeleine Albright, presenting themes originally developed as an opinion piece for publication by National Security Adviser Sandy Berger, formally declared the administration's support *but* cautioned the Europeans against "the three Ds": duplication, decoupling, and discrimination. Secretary Albright emphasized these concerns at the December 1998 ministerial meetings in Brussels, just days after the Saint-Malo meeting.

According to Albright, the allies should not duplicate what already was being done effectively in NATO. This would be a waste of defense resources at a time when defense spending in most European nations was in decline. More fundamentally, the new European initiative should not in any way "decouple" or "delink" the United States from Europe in the alliance or the European defense efforts from those coordinated through NATO. This could result from a lack of candor and transparency that the United States feared might be an intended or unintended consequence of the new European approach. A process that would encourage European allies to "gang up" on the United States or even its perception on the US side of the Atlantic could surely spell the end of the alliance. Finally, Albright's article insisted there be no discrimination against NATO allies who were not members of the European Union. This point applied in particular to Turkey but also to European allies Norway, Iceland, the Czech Republic, Hungary, and Poland, as well as Canada and the United States on the North American side of the alliance.

The "three Ds" accurately summarized the administration's main concerns and hearkened back to the George H. W. Bush administration's earlier warnings in reaction to the Franco-German development of the Euro-corps. Despite these footnotes to US support for the initiative, it moved ahead in parallel with NATO's conduct of the air campaign over Kosovo intended to wrest the province from Serbian control and allow Kosovo refugees to return to their homes in peace. The campaign, which threatened to cast a dark shadow over NATO's fiftieth-anniversary summit meeting in Washington, also added impetus to the Blair approach. When the numbers were toted up at the end of the air campaign, the United States had conducted nearly 80 percent of the sorties.

From the US perspective, the fact that the allies for the most part were not able to contribute to such a high-tech, low-casualty campaign suggested the wisdom of the Defense Capabilities Initiative (DCI). The DCI, adopted at the Washington summit, was designed to stimulate European defense efforts to help them catch up with the US Revolution in Military Affairs. From the European perspective, the Kosovo experience clearly demonstrated Europe's (undesirable and growing) military dependence on the United States and the need to get together to do something about it. Even if Washington saw a more assertive European role as a challenge to American leadership, more capable European military establishments could relieve the United States of some of its international security burdens, improving the burden-sharing equation and thereby strengthening, not weakening, transatlantic ties.

The Washington summit communiqué and the strategic concept for NATO agreed upon at the meeting reflected transatlantic agreement that European defense capabilities needed a serious shot in the arm and that it had to be done in ways consistent with the US "three Ds." However, although the Saint-Malo accord was endorsed by all EU members at meetings in Cologne (June 1999) and Helsinki

(December 1999), over the course of the year there were growing rumbles and signs of dissatisfaction on the American side. According to one former administration official, as the initiative took shape, British officials came to Washington regularly prior to each major stage of negotiations with France and the other EU members to reassure US officials that they agreed completely with American perspectives. However, the Saint-Malo outcome and its subsequent implementation at Cologne and Helsinki gave much more emphasis to "autonomy" than the administration would have liked. This official noted that British reassurances throughout this period were often followed by outcomes that reflected compromises with French positions that were not entirely to the liking of administration officials, raising concerns about the eventual impact of a "European caucus" on transatlantic cooperation.

On the European side, NATO and government officials chafed under the impression left by the "three Ds" that the US superpower was putting too much emphasis on the negative. European experts and officials openly cautioned US State and Defense officials at transatlantic discussions of defense issues not to allow this negative approach to capture US policy. Former British Minister of Defense George Robertson, after succeeding Javier Solana as NATO secretary general, offered a more positive approach. Addressing the forty-fifth annual session of the NATO Parliamentary Assembly, Robertson said, "For my part, I will ensure that ESDI is based on three key principles, the three I's: *improvement* in European defense capabilities; *inclusiveness* and transparency for all Allies, and the *indivisibility* of transatlantic security, based on shared values (emphasis added)." Moving from "Ds" to "Is," Robertson tried to put a positive spin on the American concerns that would make the same points but in a fashion less offensive to the Europeans.

By the end of 1999, the European Union had tied a major package together based on the guidelines of the Saint-Malo statement. The EU members agreed that Javier Solana, in addition to serving as the Union's High Representative for the Common Foreign and Security Policy, would become WEU secretary general to help pave the way for implementation of the decision confirmed at Cologne to merge the Western European Union within the European Union. In Helsinki, the EU members declared their determination "to develop an autonomous capacity to take decisions and, where NATO as a whole is not engaged, to launch and conduct EU-led military operations in response to international crises." They noted that the process "will avoid unnecessary duplication and does not imply the creation of a European army." The EU members continued to reiterate that collective defense remained a NATO responsibility and would not be challenged by the new EU arrangements. They agreed on a series of substantial steps, called the "Helsinki Headline Goals," required to implement their political commitment, including the following:

1. To establish by 2003 a corps-size intervention force of up to 60,000 persons from EU member-state armed forces capable of deploying within sixty days and being sustained for at least one year;
2. to create new political and military bodies to allow the European Council to provide political guidance and strategic direction to joint military operations;

3. to develop modalities for full consultation, cooperation, and transparency between the European Union and NATO, taking into account the "needs" of all EU member states (particularly the fact that four EU members—Austria, Ireland, Finland, and Sweden—are not NATO members);
4. to make "appropriate" arrangements to allow non-EU European NATO members and others to contribute to EU military crisis management;
5. to establish a nonmilitary crisis management mechanism to improve coordination of EU and member-state political, economic, and other nonmilitary instruments in ways that might mitigate the need to resort to the use of force or make military actions more effective when they become necessary.

The EU members moved quickly to implement the goals. By March 2000, the Political and Security Committee (PSC, also known by the French acronym COPS), the European Union Military Committee (EUMC), and the EU Military Staff (EUMS) started functioning as interim organizations. The PSC was to be the political decision-making body for CESDP, preparing decisions for EU Council consideration on foreign policy and crisis situations and implementing decisions of the EU members. The EUMC, like the NATO Military Committee, was designed to provide military advice and recommendations to the PSC and to implement the military aspects of EU decisions. The EUMS was to support the work of the Military Committee.

The most immediate task was to prepare a catalog of forces that would be made available to actions authorized under the CESDP. This work resulted in the European Union Capabilities Commitment Conference, which convened November 20–21, 2000. The conference produced an impressive inventory of resources, including about 100,000 soldiers, 400 combat aircraft, and 100 ships, including two aircraft carriers. In addition, non-EU NATO members and EU associate partners pledged capabilities that could join in future EU operations. One well-informed commentator has emphasized that there were "certain realities" about the pledging operations that were missed by some observers. According to former high-level British defense official Michael Quinlan,

> First, there was no suggestion that the forces to be contributed by countries towards the Goals would be entirely new and additional ones created for that purpose; they would be existing ones though . . . much improvement or redesign might be required. Second, there was no suggestion that they would be separate from forces declared to NATO. European countries in the integrated military structure already customarily declared all that they could to NATO; there was no separate reservoir of similar forces available beyond those. Nothing in the CESDP concept rested on hypotheses of extensive autonomous EU action at a time when NATO itself needed to employ forces, and alternative earmarking did not therefore entail illegitimate or confusing double-count (any more than did the long-familiar fact that almost all Alliance members had sometimes used their NATO-declared forces for national or U.N. purposes). Third, the capability was not intended as a European Army—a description specifically rejected in EU

utterances—or even a European Rapid Reaction force in the customary usage of that term in NATO.[22]

The main issue during 2000, however, was how these new EU institutions would relate to their NATO counterparts. The problem grew out of the strong desire of some in the European Union, particularly in French diplomatic and political circles, for an "autonomous" EU approach, less vulnerable to US influence. This conflicted with the hope in NATO that the European Union's role in defense would be integrated as fully as possible within the overall transatlantic alliance.

A New NATO-EU Relationship

Until the beginning of the new millennium, the relationship between NATO and the European Union had been informal and lacking much substance. Even though these two organizations constituted the core of intra-European and Euro-Atlantic relations, they largely existed as separate, disconnected organizations with bureaucracies and political cultures, particularly on the EU side, that were interested primarily in keeping a safe distance from one another. Because the United States had in so many ways been the dominant influence in NATO, EU national and international officials historically feared that too close a relationship with the alliance would bring too much US influence into European councils. In the 1990s, former US Ambassador to NATO Robert Hunter frequently lamented the lack of any working communication and coordination channels between NATO and the European Union. During Hunter's years at NATO in the mid-1990s, NATO Secretary General Javier Solana met informally with the president of the European Commission, the European Union's top official. And the NATO Berlin decisions of 1996, intended to give life to NATO's support for development of an ESDI, led to closer coordination between NATO officials and those from the Western European Union. But a huge gap remained between NATO and the European Union.

With the proclaimed EU goal of establishing an "autonomous" CESDP, a more formal NATO-EU relationship clearly was required. The process was slow in developing, partly because of the residual concern among a few EU governments, particularly the one in Paris, that the construction of CESDP not be overly influenced by the United States. For the first half of 2000, this view led the French government to argue that CESDP institutions should be developed prior to serious discussions of how the European Union's decision-making process would relate to NATO. However, according to NATO Secretary General Lord Robertson, by September 2000 the process of linking NATO and EU institutions was well under way and moving in positive directions. Speaking to the SACLANT Symposium in Reykjavik, Iceland, on September 6, 2000, Robertson noted that

already, NATO and the EU are working together closely—meeting together to decide on how to share classified information and drawing on NATO's experience to help the EU flesh out the requirements of its headline goal. . . . Put simply, NATO-friendly European defence is finally taking shape—and it is taking the right shape.[23]

In September 2000, NATO's North Atlantic Council (NAC) and the European Union's "Interim" Political and Security Committee (COPSI) began meeting to work out details of the arrangement and to establish a pattern and format for cooperation. The first joint NAC/COPSI meeting took place on September 19, 2000, followed by a second meeting on November 9, 2000. Meanwhile, four EU-NATO working groups began to work on their assigned issues: security of sensitive information, Berlin-plus (ESDI initiatives designed to facilitate more coherent European contributions within the NATO framework), military capabilities, and permanent EU-NATO institutional arrangements. In addition, Robertson and his predecessor, Javier Solana, actively collaborated to ensure that the NATO-EU liaison worked effectively.

In the Clinton administration's last major initiative regarding EU-NATO relations, Secretary of Defense William Cohen on October 10, 2000, delivered informal but important remarks to a meeting of NATO defense ministers in Birmingham, United Kingdom.[24] Cohen strongly endorsed the development of CESDP, saying that "we agree with this goal—not grudgingly, not with resignation, but with wholehearted conviction." At the same time, Cohen dismissed the logic sometimes used to provide a rationale for CESDP, saying, "The notion that Europe must begin to prepare for an eventual American withdrawal from Europe has no foundation in fact or in policy."

In addition, Secretary Cohen suggested that it was hard to imagine a future case in which the United States and the European Union would diverge dramatically on whether a crisis situation warranted a joint response. According to Secretary Cohen,

It is overwhelmingly likely that in any situation where any ally's involvement on a significant scale is justified, and where there is a consensus in Europe to undertake a military operation, the United States would be part of the operation. In addition, it is difficult to imagine a situation in which the United States was prepared to participate, but our European Allies would prefer to act alone.

With regard to the question of whether the European Union should establish its own military planning capacity, Cohen argued for a NATO-EU approach that would be "unitary, coherent, and collaborative." He suggested that NATO and the European Union should create a "European Security and Defense Planning System" that would involve all NATO and EU countries. In Cohen's judgment, "It would be highly ineffective, seriously wasteful of resources, and contradictory to the basic principles of close NATO-EU cooperation that we hope to establish if NATO and the EU were to proceed along the path of relying on autonomous force planning structures."

Cohen concluded,

The NATO-EU relationship, Ministerial Guidance, and implementation of DCI [an initiative agreed to at the NATO Washington summit in 1999 designed to improve allied defense capabilities] are not separate, parallel processes that we can allow to proceed in isolation from one another. Rather, they are all vital strands in the powerful and enduring fabric of Euro-Atlantic security.

Secretary Cohen's remarks made it clear how important it would be to ensure that NATO and EU military planning move forward hand in hand in whatever institutional construct proved acceptable to all parties. In the best case, NATO and EU military planners would in fact be largely the same people working toward the same ends, whether they wore NATO or EU hats. It was also hoped that the dynamics created by the European Union's defense objectives might help reinvigorate and give new sense of direction to the NATO planning process.

The fact that the Cohen proposal for resolution of the planning issue was not received enthusiastically by the European Union (particularly by the French) led the secretary of defense, at his last NATO meeting in December 2000, to put more emphasis on the "but" side of the "yes, but" equation. Cohen warned that CESDP could, if handled incorrectly, turn NATO into a "relic of the past."[25]

At the end of the year, the NATO-EU negotiations came close to agreement on how to work together in the future. During the December 14–15 meeting of the NAC, the NATO allies were able to note that progress had been made in the four working groups. They welcomed the European Union's agreement at its summit in Nice, France, earlier in December that there should be a "regular pattern" of meetings at all levels between the European Union and NATO. According to the NAC communiqué, "Meetings between the North Atlantic Council and the Political and Security Committee outside times of crisis should be held not less than three times, Ministerial meetings once, per EU Presidency (in other words, every six months); either organization may request additional meetings as necessary."[26]

The communiqué also noted favorably the European Union's agreement that consultation would be intensified in times of crisis. In addition, the allies welcomed the Nice provisions for inviting the NATO secretary general, the chairman of the Military Committee, and the Deputy SACEUR to EU meetings. NATO reciprocated by agreeing to invite the EU presidency and secretary general/high representative to NATO meetings and providing that the chairman of the EUMC or his representative would be invited to meetings of the NATO military committee.

The allies also stated their intention to make arrangements for

assured EU access to NATO planning capabilities able to contribute to military planning for EU-led operations; the presumption of availability to the EU of pre-identified NATO capabilities and common assets for use in EU-led operations;

the identification of a range of European command options for EU-led operations, further developing the role of DSACEUR in order for him to assume fully and effectively his European responsibilities; and the further adaptation of the Alliance's defence planning system, taking account of relevant activities in and proposals from the European Union. Allies will be consulted on the EU's proposed use of assets and capabilities, prior to the decision to release these assets and capabilities, and kept informed during the operation.[27]

However, at the end of the day, the government of Turkey blocked consensus to permit the European Union "assured access" to NATO planning and therefore prevented final agreement on the whole NATO-EU package. Ankara had wanted the European Union to grant the Turkish government veto power over the Union's deployment of a military force under circumstances that could affect Turkey's security. That, of course, was a nonstarter with the European Union.

When the George W. Bush administration came to office in 2001, most details of the NATO-EU arrangement had been agreed to, but it was left to the new administration in Washington to help find a way around the EU-Turkish impasse and perhaps also to review aspects of the NATO-EU agreement that it found of concern.

NATO/EU Relations during the George W. Bush Administration

The Bush administration faced a mix of European fears and expectations as it confronted relations with the NATO allies. Candidate Bush had made some statements suggesting the United States should begin to pull back from some of its overseas commitments, but the overall thrust of administration policy was in unilateralist, not isolationist, directions, at least as seen by most Europeans.

The first foreign policy actions of the Bush administration tended to raise warning flags for European governments. Unilateral US decisions not to join in the International Criminal Court, to remain outside the Kyoto Protocol on green house gas emissions, and to terminate the Anti-Ballistic Missile Treaty with Russia were all seen as signs that the United States was heading in new directions based almost exclusively on short-term US policy choices and with no regard for their impact on the views or interests of its closest allies.

After 9/11, the approach taken by the Bush administration during the early stages of the war against terrorism, beginning with the campaign in Afghanistan, produced mixed reactions. On the one hand, the administration's strategy was based on building a broad international coalition against terrorism. The rhetoric and formal approach of US policy remained true to this goal. On the other hand, the United States conducted the campaign with little reference to offers from the allies to help out and without making much institutional use of the NATO framework.

US management of alliance relations during George W. Bush's first term, discussed in more detail in Chapter 11, suggested that when the United States appears to be overbearing in its relations with other countries, it may find it difficult to build international consensus on behalf of its policies. Early Bush administration policy toward allies and NATO in its first term demonstrated that there are costs associated with policies that build coalitions by trying to use overpowering political force rather than by consultation, persuasion, and compromise.[28]

The new Bush administration was alert to any signs that CESDP might be undermining NATO. British Prime Minister Blair hurried to Washington to reassure President Bush. In his meetings with Blair in February 2001, President Bush accepted on good faith that CESDP would not hurt NATO. Following Camp David discussions with Blair, the president said,

> He [Blair] assured me that NATO is going to be the primary way to keep the peace in Europe. And I assured him that the United States will be actively engaged in NATO, remain engaged in Europe with our allies. But he also assured me that the European defense would no way undermine NATO. He also assured me that there would be a joint command, that the planning would take place within NATO, and that should all NATO not wish to go on a mission, that would then serve as a catalyst for the defense forces moving on their own. And finally, I was very hopeful, when we discussed the prime minister's vision, that such a vision would encourage our NATO allies and friends to bolster their defense budgets, perhaps. And so, I support what the prime minister has laid out. I think it makes a lot of sense for our country.[29]

Some observers speculated that Bush had endorsed CESDP in return for Blair's support for the new administration's missile defense goals, but it seems more likely that the two issues were considered on their own merits by both sides. The reaffirmation of US support for the initiative was necessary because the incoming administration was known to have concerns similar to those expressed earlier by the Clinton administration and by private experts outside the administration—some of whom were appointed to positions of influence inside the new administration.[30]

Even among Euro-enthusiasts, there was lingering concern that CESDP would produce rhetoric, promises, and institutions but no additional capabilities. The EU pledge to create a 60,000-troop intervention force with 400 aircraft and 100 ships was impressive. But, there was little evidence that European governments were increasing defense spending to buy the strategic lift and other assets required to make the force credible. On balance, the Europeans still lagged well behind the United States in deployed military capabilities for force projection, intervention, and high-tech warfare.

Following President Bush's meeting with Prime Minister Blair, the new administration appeared to settle into a relatively passive approach toward CESDP, perhaps in the belief that nothing dramatic affecting US interests was likely to happen in the near term. The more urgent priority in the first half of 2001 was to develop US policy toward ballistic missile defense and sell it to the allies, Russia and China, as well as to reform and repair the US defense establishment.

Another priority—the war against terrorism—displaced all others on September 11, 2001, when terrorists killed almost 3,000 Americans and citizens of more than 80 other countries by hijacking four civilian passenger aircraft and flying them into the World Trade Center in New York, the Pentagon outside Washington, D.C., and the Pennsylvania countryside (the implications for the alliance of the terrorist attacks and the war in Iraq are discussed in Chapter 11).

As the United States, Europe, and the world turned their eyes toward the threat posed by international terrorism, important questions remained unanswered about the relationship between the United States and Europe in the alliance.

The Bush administration, despite the Blair reassurances, seemed wary of the potential for CESDP to create artificial distinctions among NATO allies, undermining NATO's political cohesion. The CESDP process and the demands of its institutional creations could encourage "we/they" distinctions between Europeans and the United States and even among European members of NATO. The Clinton administration was quite restrained in its response to French diplomatic initiatives in Eastern and central Europe that appeared designed to convince states that were candidates for EU membership that they should line up with EU positions in the ongoing negotiations with NATO concerning the EU-NATO relationship.[31]

During 2002, while the allies were enmeshed in the divisive debate over Iraq, the EU/Turkey problem was resolved and cooperative arrangements between NATO and the European Union were quietly put in place. On December 16, NATO Secretary General Lord George Robertson and EU foreign policy chief Javier Solana issued the "EU-NATO Declaration on ESDP,"[32] elaborating the principles that underlie the NATO-EU strategic partnership in crisis management.

Tensions in the US relationship with those allies who opposed the Iraq war escalated in April 2003 when the leaders of Belgium, France, Germany, and Luxembourg held a meeting in Brussels to discuss developing a European defense union that would be independent of NATO. The four European leaders said they were not trying to weaken NATO but to strengthen the European pillar of the alliance and to give the EU the ability to become a strong partner of the United States. Many of the proposals they issued built on existing plans for an EU defense force and proposals for strengthening European defense cooperation being developed by the European constitutional convention. Their four-page declaration also included plans for their own rapid-reaction force centered on the Franco-German brigade and two new European military institutions: "a multinational deployable force headquarters" for operations that do not involve NATO and a "nucleus of collective capability for planning and conducting operations for the European Union."

This "rump" European meeting was ill-timed and disruptive both in transatlantic relations and inside Europe, irritating many EU governments that were not invited to participate in the session. Dutch Foreign Minister Jaap de Hoop Scheffer explained his country's decision not to participate, saying "Belgium and France will not guarantee our security. . . . Germany will not guarantee the security of the Netherlands. I cannot imagine world order built against the United States."[33] In the meantime, getting the NATO-EU relationship right was becoming even more important, as the EU constitutional convention moved ahead. The shape of the NATO-EU relationship at the end of 2003 would likely provide a critical part of the foundation on which the EU constitution's provisions on defense would be constructed.

Late in 2003, Tony Blair, seeking to find some common ground on which the UK, France, and Germany could restore a degree of unity following their split on Iraq, worked out a compromise giving the green light for the EU to develop a small defense planning capability. Reacting to the development at a meeting of the North Atlantic Council on October 16, the US Permanent Representative Nicholas Burns, presumably under instructions from Washington, told fellow ambassadors that the European Union's pursuit of greater military autonomy posed "one of the greatest dangers to the transatlantic relationship."[34] In the end, however, the United States backed away from Burns' warning and accepted the approach. It hasn't been proven, but US acquiescence may well have been at least a partial payoff to Blair for his support on Iraq.

On December 12, 2003, EU leaders, meeting in Brussels, agreed to create a small EU military planning cell. British Prime Minister Tony Blair said the final accord fully met London's requirements not to do harm to NATO, telling reporters, "What this gives us is the opportunity to keep the transatlantic American alliance very strong, but make sure that in circumstances where America is not engaged in an operation, and where the vital European interests are involved, that Europe can act, and that is exactly what we wanted, and doing it in a way that is completely consistent with NATO as the cornerstone of our alliance."[35] The unit is co-located with the EU's military staff in Brussels. A separate EU unit attached to SHAPE, NATO's military headquarters in Mons, Belgium, was also made permanent.

Once again, Blair's leadership on the question of how European defense cooperation should relate to the transatlantic defense relationship was crucial. The Iraq war debate had badly split the NATO allies (see the discussion of the Iraq war divisions in Chapter 11), but was equally devastating to the image of foreign policy unity among current and future EU members. Blair's success in finding a solution to the EU planning cell issue not only helped find a transatlantic compromise but also promoted the process of healing the wounds to EU unity.

What did the Bush administration's acquiescence in the EU planning cell demonstrate? President Bush undoubtedly saw it as a reward for Blair's cooperation on Iraq. Pentagon Euro-skeptics perhaps decided it really didn't make much difference, given their low expectations about the EU, NATO, and the "old" Europeans. Some at the Department of State may have seen it as a signal of US moderation and reason, opening the way for European countries and the EU to take over more responsibility for the defense and security of Europe.

During 2004 it appeared that the relationship between NATO and the European Union was developing constructively. The Atlanticist and Europeanist requirements had more or less been compromised in the new NATO/EU cooperative arrangements. Those arrangements carried forward the practical elements of the 1996 Berlin Accords while acknowledging the need for a degree of autonomy in development of an EU military capability.

Perhaps most importantly, the Europeans demonstrated their willingness to take on more responsibility in the transatlantic security relationship. In August 2004, the

Euro-corps took command of the NATO-led International Security Assistance Force (ISAF) in Afghanistan for a six-month rotation. Then, in December 2004, the European Union took over from NATO in Bosnia and Herzegovina. On December 2, a ceremony in Sarajevo, Bosnia and Herzegovina, marked the end of NATO's Stabilization Force (SFOR) mission and the beginning of the European Union's follow-on EUFOR. The EUFOR mission was organized under the "Berlin Plus" arrangements for NATO to support European Union missions and represented the first major operational test of those arrangements.

Beyond the Transatlantic Battles

Transatlantic relationships during the Bush administration's first term suggested that if the United States and its allies do not manage the NATO-EU relationship effectively, it could intrude dramatically on a wide range of issues in which their common interests are likely served by pragmatic cooperation rather than conflict inspired by current international power realities.

This reality was modestly reflected in the second term of President George W. Bush, during which Bush and other officials attempted to repair relations with American allies, particularly European states. Early in 2005, both Secretary of State Condoleezza Rice and President Bush visited European capitals explicitly seeking to repair some of the damage done by the administration in its first term, and most particularly by the decision to go to war against Iraq. The administration made few formal changes in its policies toward the alliance, and many of the same officials whose statements had seriously damaged relations with the allies remained in place. But there was a change toward more conciliatory and less confrontational approaches to the allies. The new US attitude notably included support for NATO taking over command of the International Security Assistance force in Afghanistan.

Following a NATO summit meeting in February 2005, President Bush praised the alliance saying "NATO is the most successful alliance in the history of the world. . . . Because of NATO, Europe is whole and united and at peace. . . . NATO is an important organization, and the United States of America strongly supports it."[36]

During the question and answer period, one reporter suggested that Europeans remained skeptical about administration intentions, particularly as Secretary of Defense Donald Rumsfeld was still suggesting "the mission should determine the coalition." The reporter asked what the United States would do to improve transatlantic relations. The President's answer was relatively straight-forward: we had a major difference with some allies over Iraq and now we need to put that issue behind us.

For the most part, European governments did appear to put the issue behind them, by agreeing to disagree about the wisdom of invading Iraq, but accepting the new more NATO-friendly US attitude as reaffirmation of US support for the alliance. Few Europeans were convinced that the administration's words and actions could be undone simply by a "charm offensive" by the President and his Secretary of State, but the more productive Euro-Atlantic relationship suggested that attitudes do matter. The new US approach also seemed to take some of the drive out of the European temptation to try to develop the European Union as a "pole" with which they could balance American power.

As for the EU's role as an international security actor, early in 2009, Javier Solana, the EU High Representative for the Common Foreign and Security Policy, told the European Parliament that the EU had in recent years been very active in contributing to international security challenges: " . . . more than 20 civilian and military operations are or have been deployed on almost every continent, from Europe to Asia, from the Middle East to Africa. Thousands of European men and women are engaged in these operations, ranging from military to police, from border guards to monitors, from judges to prosecutors, a wide range of people doing good for the stability of the world."[37] Solana also pointed to the fact that EU actions under the ESDP have been guided by the European Security Strategy of 2003, as updated by a new report in December 2008.

As impressive and helpful as the EU's operations have been, they have been limited in many ways. The failures of the EU Constitution and then the Lisbon Treaty temporarily blocked some of the consolidating and streamlining measures that were intended to give stronger leadership to the Common Foreign and Security Policy and the ESDP. Those failures reflected the fact that divisions among and within EU members remain substantial, and that national sovereignty on foreign and defense policy issues remains closely guarded by EU member states. It also reflected the fact that the EU has neither the command structures and military capabilities nor the political will to conduct military operations that are particularly demanding. Moreover, the agreement on a European Security Strategy, defining threats and desirable responses from a purely European perspective, has failed to generate additional European military capabilities.[38]

Looking Ahead

With the inauguration of President Barack H. Obama in 2009, the United States was presented with an opportunity for a new beginning with American allies. Obama, having achieved something close to rock star status in Europe during the 2008 presidential campaign, came to office explicitly acknowledging the importance to US interests of allies, alliances and international cooperation and organizations more generally.

In addition, the decision by French President Nicolas Sarkozy that brought France back into full participation in NATO's integrated command structure in 2009 mitigated suspicions in Washington about French intentions and the potential for a competing European pole in international relations. Part of the deal for France's return called for appointment of a senior French officer as the new commander of Allied Command Transformation. The move rewarded France for its return to the Integrated Command Structure and also symbolized France's commitment to intensified cooperation in the transatlantic framework.

Photo 10.1: EU High Representative for the Common Foreign and Security Policy (and former NATO Secretary General 1995-99), Javier Solana and NATO Secretary General, Jaap de Hoop Scheffer meet in October 2008 in the context of a joint session of NATO's North Atlantic Council and the EU's Political and Security Committee

Source: NATO.

These political developments enhance the prospects for a more effective alliance, but do not guarantee transatlantic tranquility. For example, a continuing challenge is in the area of defense industrial relations. There remains a danger that US unilateralism combined with the EU desire for "autonomy" could increase transatlantic trade and industrial tensions by supporting development of a "fortress Europe" mentality in defense procurement. This is an area where the United States can take much of the blame for the lack historically of a "two-way street" in transatlantic armaments trade and failure to devise ways of sharing new technologies with the European allies to help them participate in the "Revolution in Military Technology." ESDP does not necessarily require that Europe increase protectionism or favoritism for its own defense industries. Lagging far behind American defense firms in adjusting to post-Cold War market conditions, the necessary mergers and consolidations are finally beginning to rationalize the European defense industrial base. The next logical step is for rationalization of the *transatlantic* industrial base through a variety of means. This next step would have to be facilitated by governments, and both the United States and the EU members would have to make alliance solidarity and cooperation a high priority to overcome existing barriers to transatlantic armaments cooperation. An EU that puts a higher priority on developing ESDP could easily put new obstacles in the way of alliance cooperation in armaments, and particularly in the way of purchasing US systems.[39]

One strong but critical supporter of the European Union, Charles Grant, has assessed the progress of the development of EU foreign and security policy capabilities and found them wanting. Grant observes that:

> In 2004 the EU launched the idea of "battlegroups." In theory the EU should be able to send up to two battlegroups to a crisis zone at any time. Each of these is a rapid reaction force of some 1,500 troops provided by a single member-state or a group of them. But no battle group has yet been deployed. In 2008 the UN asked the EU to send battlegroups to eastern Congo, Britain and Germany were "on call" to provide their battlegroups, but refused to send them. Some of the battlegroups that exist on paper are probably not useable: unfortunately, each government—rather than an independent body—is allowed to verify whether its battlegroup is operational.[40]

According to Grant, the EU's shortcomings in the areas of foreign policy and defense have multiple causes, not the least of which is the strong desire of member states to retain ultimate control over these core aspects of their sovereignty. In addition, the member states come from very different histories and experiences, meaning that today they have no common strategic culture. EU states simply look at foreign and defense issues through very different prisms, and come up with national assessments and conclusions that make common positions impossible on many issues.

On balance, the European Union of 2009 was far advanced from the European Community of 1973, when the author drafted the first US intelligence estimate of the European integration process.[41] But the even-more solidified core of the process remains seriously hedged by its member states. The European Union is much more of an international actor than it was in 1973, although it is still misleading to speak of "Europe" as if it consisted of like-minded, similarly-thinking and acting, states and citizens. It perhaps was never that "united," but the EU's post-Cold War enlargement has made creation of a unitary European actor across the entire range of international relations even more problematic. And, Europe's "identity" remains clouded by questions about future expansion, particularly whether or not Turkey should be brought into the European fold or left with tenuous European moorings.

The unilateralist character of US foreign and defense policy under George W. Bush led some Europeans to favor using integration in the European Union to "balance" US power in the international system. This multi-polar temptation, like the US unilateral temptation, threatened trans-Atlantic cooperation and therefore international stability. François Heisbourg, director of the French Fondation pour la Recherche Stratégique, has argued persuasively that his nation's government should avoid the divisive rhetoric of multipolarity and pursue a multilateral agenda of cooperation with the United States and others.[42] Real world developments have reinforced such perspectives, and President Sarkozy seems to have heeded Heisbourg's advice.

The failure of the EU Constitution to win approval in France and The Netherlands undermined the argument that Europe could effectively balance US power, and strengthened the case for building Europe in parallel with maintenance of a cooperative transatlantic relationship—a position favored by several EU members led by the U.K. and many of Europe's new democracies.

The "Reform Treaty," a more modest version of the EU Constitution that took effect in December 2009, confirms the continuity of the process of integration. But it also confirms the judgment that the emergence of anything like a United States of Europe remains for future generations to manage. As the respected German commentator Theo Sommer has observed, ". . . the United States of Europe is a long way off. But the United Europe of States is a realistic short-term goal."[43] French President Sarkozy still talks about a multi-polar world, but makes it clear that this neither requires Europe to balance American power nor France to submerge its sovereignty in an EU framework.[44]

Perhaps now it would be more appropriate to talk about a "multi-player" international system, in which the European Union is an important player in many policy areas. Advocating a "multi-polar" system implies competition, shifting alliances and balance of power politics—a system that would serve neither American nor European interests. The European Union is already an important participant in a multi-player world. A continuing trend back toward a position of a "pillar" in the transatlantic relationship and away from "polar" pretensions would augur well for both the United States and Europe.

For the next period of history, the European Union will neither be transformed into a United States of Europe nor fall apart at the seams. It will most likely continue to evolve toward a "United Europe of States," as suggested by Theo Sommer. Someday, the members of the European Union may decide to create a unitary political state but, until that day, the member states will retain ultimate control over their foreign and defense policies. The basic transatlantic bargain will not be forced to react to revolutionary developments in the process of European integration. The prospect that cooperation at the European level will enhance the transatlantic relationship, rather than compete with it, has brightened considerably.

A key question about ESDP and NATO remains that of what additional military responsibilities the European allies are capable of taking on in the near future. According to Michael Quinlan, one should be encouraged by the fact that "most European countries now accept that their forces should in the future be configured, equipped, trained, and available much more than before for expeditionary or similar use, in support of international order, rather than for direct homeland defense against massive aggression."[45] It seems unlikely that the European allies will find substantially more resources to devote to defense. The question, therefore, is whether they will find ways to make current levels of spending more effective.

The return of France to full participation in the alliance helps make the point that European integration and transatlantic cooperation can and should be compatible and mutually reinforcing. The tactics of European and US policymakers down the road may occasionally lead to further bouts of NATO-EU competition, particularly as central and Eastern European states try to adjust to the demands of membership in both organizations. The challenge will be to keep the competitive instincts of policymakers on both sides of the Atlantic under control in the interest of NATO-EU convergence. Management of the issue will therefore be a continuing challenge for US and European officials for many years to come.

Notes

1. Michael Brenner, *Terms of Engagement: The United States and the European Security Identity,* The Washington Papers no. 176, Center for Strategic and International Studies (Westport, Conn.: Praeger, 1998), 23.
2. Stanley R. Sloan, *NATO's Future: Toward a New Transatlantic Bargain* (Washington, D.C.: National Defense University Press, 1985), 191.
3. Sean Kay, *NATO and the Future of European Security* (Lanham, Md.: Rowman & Littlefield, 1998), 149.
4. This discussion draws on the author's examination of US attitudes toward European defense where he first described the "yes, but" nature of US policy. See: Stanley R. Sloan, "The United States and European Defence," *Chaillot Paper* no. 36 (Paris: Western European Union Institute for Security Studies, April 2000).
5. Catherine Guicherd, "A European Defense Identity: Challenge and Opportunity for NATO," Congressional Research Service Report 91478 (Washington, D.C.: Congressional Research Service, June 12, 1991). For the text of the "Bartholemew Telegram" of February 20, 1991, see Willem van Eekelen, *Debating European Security, 1948–1998* (The Hague: Sdu Publishers, 1998), 340–44.
6. Guicherd, "A European Defense Identity," 60–61.
7. Rome Declaration on Peace and Cooperation, Issued by the Heads of State and Government Participating in the Meeting of the North Atlantic Council in Rome on November 7–8, 1991.
8. Single European Act, Title V: Provisions on a Common Foreign and Security Policy, Articles J 1, 2.
9. Frederick Kempe, "US, Bonn Clash over Pact with France," *Wall Street Journal,* May 27, 1992, A9.
10. Patrick E. Tyler, "Senior US Officials Assail Lone-Superpower Policy," *New York Times,* March 11, 1992, A6.
11. Tyler, "Senior US Officials Assail Lone-Superpower Policy," 6.
12. Barton Gellman, "Pentagon Abandons Goal of Thwarting US Rivals," *Washington Post,* May 24, 1992, A1.
13. This concept was developed in a Congressional Research Service report originally prepared for Senator William V. Roth Jr. (R-Del.). See Stanley R. Sloan, "NATO's Future: Beyond Collective Defense," Congressional Research Service Report 95–979 S (Washington, D.C.: Congressional Research Service, September 15, 1995), 21–24, 30–32. French officials subsequently acknowledged that the report contributed to what eventually became a British-French initiative. British

officials have suggested that London was beginning to think along similar lines when the report appeared.

14. Discussions with administration officials in 1996.
15. This point is based on interviews with US officials involved in the decision.
16. Brenner, *Terms of Engagement*, 35.
17. In the course of that session, the Assembly renamed itself the NATO Parliamentary Assembly to emphasize its role as the parliamentary component of the transatlantic alliance.
18. Jolyon Howorth, *European Integration and Defence: The Ultimate Challenge?* (Paris: Western European Union Institute for Security Studies, 2001), 108.
19. William V. Roth Jr., *NATO in the 21st Century* (Brussels: North Atlantic Assembly, September 1998), 57.
20. "Statement on European Defence" (text of a joint statement by the British and French governments, Franco-British summit, Saint-Malo, France, December 4, 1998).
21. Interviews conducted with Clinton administration officials.
22. Michael Quinlan, *European Defense Cooperation: Asset or Threat to NATO?* (Washington, D.C.: Woodrow Wilson Center Press, 2001), 38.
23. Lord Robertson, "NATO's New Agenda: More Progress Than Meets the Eye" (remarks at the SACLANT Symposium, Reykjavik, Iceland, September 6, 2000).
24. William Cohen, "Meeting the Challenges to Transatlantic Security in the 21st Century: A Way Ahead for NATO and the EU" (remarks at the Informal Defense Ministerial Meeting, Birmingham, United Kingdom, October 10, 2000).
25. Reuters News Service, "Cohen Warns Europe That NATO Could Become 'Relic,'" *International Herald Tribune*, December 6, 2000, 7.
26. Final Communiqué, Ministerial Meeting of the North Atlantic Council held at NATO Headquarters, Brussels, December 1415, 2000, para. 31.
27. Final Communiqué, para 33.
28. For a more extended treatment of this issue see Stanley R. Sloan, Robert G. Sutter, and Casimir A. Yost, *The Use of U.S. Power, Implications for U.S. Interests* (Washington, D.C.: Institute for the Study of Diplomacy, Georgetown University, 2004). More recently, see Fareed Zakaria, "The Future of American Power, How the United States Can Survive the Rise of the Rest," *Foreign Affairs*, 87(3), May/June 2008, p. 41, and Richard Haass, "The Age of Nonpolarity, What Will Follow U.S. Dominance," *Foreign Affairs*, 87(3), May/June 2008, p. 56.
29. Transcript of President Bush and British Prime Minister Tony Blair's news conference following their first meeting at Camp David, February 23, 2001.
30. For example, Peter Rodman, who had written and commented widely on CESDP from his position at the Nixon Center, moved into a senior policy position at the Department of Defense; Robert Zoellick, a supporter of European defense cooperation, became the US trade representative; and John Bolton, a strong skeptic, moved to a position at the National Security Council.

31. The perception among many Eastern and central European officials was that this was the intent of French diplomacy for a period early in 2000, even though it has been denied by French officials.
32. During 2001 the EU members dropped the word "Common" and began referring to the policy as the "European Security and Defense Policy (ESDP)."
33. John Vinocur, "4 Nations Agree to Set up Autonomous Europe Defense Body," *International Herald Tribune*, April 30, 2003. Jaap de Hoop Scheffer's clear statement may have served as a leading credential for his appointment as NATO Secretary General in 2004.
34. Judy Dempsey, "NATO Urged to Challenge European Defence Plan," *The Financial Times*, October 17, 2003.
35. Transcript of remarks to journalists released by the Prime Minister's office. See www.number10.gov.uk/output/Page4990.asp [accessed July 8, 2009].
36. President and Secretary General Hoop de Scheffer Discuss NATO meeting, White House Press Release, February 22, 2005.
37. Javier Solana, "EU High Representative for the CFSP, addresses the European Parliament on the EU common security and defence policy," Council of the European Union, Brussels, February 18, 2009.
38. For an excellent, albeit perhaps excessively optimistic, assessment of the process of developing security and defense policy competence in the EU, see: Jolyon Howorth, *Security and Defence Policy in the European Union*, The European Union Series (New York: Palgrave MacMillan, 2007).
39. For an excellent survey of transatlantic defense industrial issues see Burkard Schmitt editor, with Gordon Adams, Christophe Cornu, and Andrew D. James, "Between Cooperation and Competition: The Transatlantic Defence Market," *Chaillot Papers*, Number 44, Western European Union Institute for Security Studies, January 2001. For additional background see Gordon Adams, Alex Ashbourne, et al., *Europe's Defence Industry: A Transatlantic Future* (London: Centre for European Reform, 1999) and Robert P. Grant, "Transatlantic Armament Relations under Strain," *Survival* 39(1), Spring 1997, 111–37.
40. Charles Grant, *Is Europe doomed to fail as a power?* Centre for European Reform essays, July 2009.
41. In April 1973, National Security Advisor Henry Kissinger gave a speech entitled "The Year of Europe," which led to European concern and speculation about Kissinger's "agenda." The questions Kissinger raised about how transatlantic relations would be affected by the process of European integration undoubtedly gave rise to the US intelligence community's decision to prepare an estimate on the development of a "common" European approach.

Many of the issues raised in 1973 are still open today, and the overall conclusion in the estimate remains reasonably accurate. The draft approved in the interagency review process noted that the United States should think in terms of a "uniting Europe," observing that European integration was a long historical process, with no clear outcome foreordained. The estimate concluded that as integration advanced, and as more common policies were decided, a "uniting Europe" would nonetheless present a mixed picture to the outside world, a blend between areas in which the central institutions had been given authority over key decisions and implementation of community policies and areas in which national identities, interests and prerogatives still prevailed.

42. François Heisbourg, "Chirac should be more cynical," *Financial Times*, June 4, 2003.
43. Theo Sommer, "Not a Cinch, but a Success," *The Atlantic Times*, 4(7), July 2007, p. 1.
44. See, for example, President Sarkozy's answers to questions on his visit to Iraq on February 10, 2009. The text can be found at http://www.ambafrance-uk.org/President-Sarkozy-s-visit-to-Iraq.html#sommaire_1 [accessed April 7, 2009].
45. Quinlan, *European Defense Cooperation*, 54.

CHAPTER 11

Implications of the Bush, 9/11, and Iraq Shocks for the Transatlantic Bargain

"We are All Americans"

—*Headline in* Le Monde *(Paris) September 12, 2001*

The September 11 Challenge

This reassuring, and surely misleading, headline in *Le Monde* after the terrorist attacks on the United States suggested the extent to which terrorism would affect the future of the transatlantic bargain. The event was traumatic for Americans and Europeans alike. The *Le Monde* headline was indicative of European empathy and support for the United States. But Americans, led by the George W. Bush administration, adopted a war mentality, whose perpetuation Bush officials actively encouraged through the November 2004 elections. Europeans, acting more like Europeans, were inclined to see September 11 as a major event in the struggle against terror, but not the beginning of a war whose outcome would be determined anytime soon.

In any case, on September 11, 2001, the challenges to transatlantic relations became much more complex and demanding. The terrorist attacks on the United States, organized by the al Qaeda radical Islamic group led by Osama bin Laden, left some three thousand people dead. Bands of terrorists hijacked four civilian airliners, crashing them into both towers of the World Trade Center in New York and the Pentagon in Washington, D.C. A fourth hijacked aircraft, perhaps headed for the White House or the US Capitol, crashed in a field in Pennsylvania after passengers learned of the other three hijackings and decided to try to wrest control of the aircraft from the terrorists.

US President George W. Bush declared a "global war on terrorism (GWOT)" in response to the attacks. The United States prepared to mount a campaign against the Taliban leadership and forces in Afghanistan that had hosted and supported the al Qaeda organization and bin Laden, and had refused to turn bin Laden and his associates over to the United States for prosecution.

Within 24 hours the attack on the United States was addressed by the North Atlantic Council in Brussels, which decided to invoke Article 5 of the North Atlantic Treaty if it was determined that the attack was the responsibility of a foreign source, and not domestic terrorism, from which many allies had suffered but which does not fall under the collective defense provisions of the Treaty. On September 12, the NAC declared:

> The Council agreed that if it is determined that this attack was directed from abroad against the United States, it shall be regarded as an action covered by Article 5 of the Washington Treaty, which states that an armed attack against one or more of the allies in Europe or North America shall be considered an attack against them all.
>
> The commitment to collective self-defence embodied in the Washington Treaty was first entered into in circumstances very different from those that exist now, but it remains no less valid and no less essential today, in a world subject to the scourge of international terrorism. When the Heads of State and Government of NATO met in Washington in 1999, they paid tribute to the success of the alliance in ensuring the freedom of its members during the Cold War and in making possible a Europe that was whole and free. But they also recognized the existence of a wide variety of risks to security, some of them quite unlike those that had called NATO into existence. More specifically, they condemned terrorism as a serious threat to peace and stability and reaffirmed their determination to combat it in accordance with their commitments to one another, their international commitments, and national legislation.
>
> Article 5 of the Washington Treaty stipulates that in the event of attacks falling within its purview, each ally will assist the Party that has been attacked by taking such action as it deems necessary. Accordingly, the United States' NATO allies stand ready to provide the assistance that may be required as a consequence of these acts of barbarism.[1]

On October 2, 2001, NATO Secretary-General Lord Robertson announced the allies had concluded the attacks had been directed from abroad and they therefore would be regarded as covered by Article 5. The United States had made it clear that, even though it appreciated the alliance's declaration of an Article 5 response, it would conduct military operations itself, with ad hoc coalitions of willing countries. Initially this included only the United Kingdom among NATO allies. The United States decided not to ask that military operations be conducted through the NATO integrated command structure. Such a request would have created serious political dilemmas for many allies. The discussion of NATO's area of operation had basically been put aside since the debates leading up to the 1999 strategic concept, and there was no enthusiasm for reopening these debates in the middle of this crisis. Furthermore, the United States obviously preferred to keep tight control of any military operations.

Nonetheless, NATO was asked to provide a number of services on behalf of the war against terrorism. On October 4, NATO allies agreed to

> enhance intelligence sharing and cooperation, both bilaterally and in the appropriate NATO bodies, relating to the threats posed by terrorism and the actions to

be taken against it; provide, individually or collectively, as appropriate and according to their capabilities, assistance to Allies and other states which are or may be subject to increased terrorist threats as a result of their support for the campaign against terrorism; take necessary measures to provide increased security for facilities of the United States and other Allies on their territory; back-fill selected Allied assets in NATO's area of responsibility that are required to directly support operations against terrorism; provide blanket overflight clearances for the United States and other Allies' aircraft, in accordance with the necessary air traffic arrangements and national procedures, for military flights related to operations against terrorism; provide access for the United States and other Allies to ports and airfields on the territory of NATO nations for operations against terrorism, including for refueling, in accordance with national procedures.[2]

The North Atlantic Council also agreed that the alliance was prepared to deploy elements of its Standing Naval Forces to the eastern Mediterranean in order to provide a NATO presence and demonstrate resolve and that NATO was ready to deploy elements of its Airborne Early Warning force to support operations against terrorism. In fact, on October 8 it was announced that NATO AWACS aircraft would be deployed to the United States to help patrol US airspace. The move freed up US assets for use in the air war against Taliban forces in Afghanistan. Just as NATO had invoked Article 5 for the first time ever, the dispatch of NATO forces to protect US territory, according to NATO's Supreme Allied Commander General Joseph Ralston, the Supreme Allied Commander Europe, was "the first time NATO assets will have been used in direct support of the continental United States."[3]

NATO's reaction to the terrorist attacks was quick and unequivocal. The reaction was initially applauded by the Bush administration. Two months after the attacks, the US ambassador to NATO, R. Nicholas Burns, argued that NATO had responded strongly to the terrorist challenge, and that the response demonstrated NATO's continuing relevance: "With the battle against terrorism now engaged, it is difficult to imagine a future without the alliance at the core of efforts to defend our civilization."[4]

Preparing for and conducting operations in Afghanistan, the US administration sought help from the allies mainly through bilateral channels, not through NATO. In the weeks following the attacks, some Pentagon officials privately dismissed NATO's formal invocation of the alliance's mutual defense provision and complained that the alliance was not relevant to the new challenges posed by the counter-terror campaign. Meanwhile, some NATO allies were led to believe that the United States did not value or want contributions that they might make in the battle against terrorism. The Italians, for example, were embarrassed by their exclusion from British-French-German talks about counterterrorist operations held on the fringes of a European Union summit in Ghent, Belgium, combined with rumors, apparently from French sources, that the United States had rejected Italian offers of military assistance.[5]

By November, many allies, including Germany, had pledged forces to the counterterrorist campaign, and their offers had been explicitly welcomed by the administration. As the campaign stretched into 2002, more NATO country forces were brought to bear on the conflict. Many allies pledged forces for post-conflict peacekeeping duties. Several Danish and German soldiers were killed trying to destroy Taliban munitions. Canadian forces saw combat against al Qaeda and Taliban elements in the eastern Afghan mountains, and the British deployed a force of some 1,700 Royal Marines to join in the fight against residual al Qaeda and Taliban forces.

In the aftermath of the terrorist attacks and the US reactions, one British expert judged that the US choice not to use NATO to run the military operations against terrorist targets in Afghanistan means "It's unlikely the Americans will ever again wish to use NATO to manage a major shooting war."[6] The Bush administration did not initially ask that NATO run the military actions in Afghanistan because they did not want to repeat the Kosovo experience, where the conduct of military operations was complicated by allied criticism of US targeting strategy. Specifically, the French government on several occasions vetoed targets that had been identified by US planners. Complaints by Bush administration Pentagon officials about NATO's limited utility apparently were registered without the administration even asking the allies to give the alliance a more substantial role.

With regard to the other US partner to the transatlantic bargain, the US Congress, the traditional burden-sharing debate took on a new and pointed direction. Leading members of the US Senate argued strongly that Europe's failure to take the war on terrorism seriously could undermine the US commitment to NATO and destroy the alliance altogether. At the Thirty-eighth Annual Munich Conference on Security Policy, defense expert Senator John McCain (R-Ariz.) joined leading Bush administration officials stressing "the need for the European allies to acquire better capabilities for their armed forces so that they can cope with sudden terrorist threats and possibly join US troops in a campaign to overthrow Saddam Hussein in Iraq."[7] This argument came in the wake of President Bush's State of the Union address in which he argued that Iraq, Iran, and North Korea constituted an "axis of evil" that could be the target of US preemptive strikes.[8]

Senator Richard G. Lugar (R-Ind), longtime NATO supporter and leading commentator on the alliance, hit hard in a speech to the US-NATO Missions Annual Conference in Brussels on January 19, 2002, arguing that a division of labor in which the United States did the war fighting and Europe did the peacekeeping was unacceptable. Senator Lugar summed up his view saying,

America is at war and feels more vulnerable than at any time since the end of the Cold War and perhaps since World War II. The threat we face is global and existential. We need allies and alliances to confront it effectively. Those alliances can no longer be circumscribed by artificial geographic boundaries. All of America's alliances are going to be reviewed and recast in light of this new challenge, including NATO. If NATO is not up to the challenge of becoming effective in the new war against terrorism, then our political leaders may be inclined to search for something else that will answer this need.[9]

On the European side, allied officials complained that, after showing their support and willingness to contribute, the United States largely proceeded with a strategy focusing on dividing, not sharing, responsibilities. According to press reports, the situation "irritated European leaders. Behind their unflagging public political support for Washington are private complaints about the constant risk of being caught flatfooted by the US refusal to limit its own options by revealing its plans. Accustomed to being consulted about or at least alerted to US moves, these leaders are now embarrassed."[10] One French official reportedly observed that the message from the United States was "We'll do the cooking and prepare what people are going to eat, then you will wash the dirty dishes."[11] It subsequently became popular to observe that the new formula for international security management was "the US fights, the UN feeds, and the EU finances and does peacekeeping."

To some extent, the situation can be attributed to factors for which the Europeans themselves are to blame. First, they did not, for the most part, have significant military assets to contribute to the first phase of the Afghan campaign, which relied heavily on air-delivered precision-guided munitions. Second, officials in the Bush administration were fully aware of past NATO-nation resistance to involving the alliance in military operations beyond their borders, to say nothing of beyond Europe.

On the other hand, it appeared that the United States missed an opportunity to move the NATO consensus well beyond the 1999 strategic concept following the September 11 events. Given invocation of Article 5 and the explicit willingness of many NATO allies to contribute military capabilities to the war against terrorism, a political consensus existed that perhaps could have been used to expand NATO's horizons and establish a mechanism for NATO contributions in the future. For example, the allies could have taken NATO's involvement at least one step further by creating a NATO Counterterrorism Combined Joint Task Force.[12] Creation of a special task force would have provided the organizational focus required for a serious NATO contribution to the counterterrorist campaign. It would have provided a reliable framework for allied involvement in the campaign, built on the foundation of NATO's integrated command structure, for as long as such support was required.

Implications for NATO

The terrorist attacks on the United States and the nature of the US response had a major impact on US-European relations. The attacks left fundamentally different impressions on Americans and Europeans. The "war mentality" adopted by the Bush administration seemed to warrant all necessary steps to defend the country, irrespective of the views of other countries or the accepted norms of international law. Europeans, although shocked and sympathetic, did not see the attacks as changing global realities in any profound way. They remained convinced that international

Photo 11.1: NATO Team

Source: Courtesy of Kevin KAL Gallagher.

cooperation and law were vitally important foundations for international stability and, indeed, for a struggle against international terrorism.

The actions required to respond militarily to the terrorist attacks nonetheless demonstrated in many ways the wisdom of the allied approach to adaptation of the alliance that began in the early 1990s. NATO never abandoned the critical Article 5 commitment, but it began preparing for the new kind of security challenges alliance members thought likely in the twenty-first century. The implications for force structure were clear: NATO needed more forces capable of being moved quickly to conflicts beyond national borders and prepared to fight as allies in a variety of topographic and climatic conditions in coalitions using a synergistic mix of conventional and "high-tech" weaponry. Even though the September 11 attacks constituted a clear case for invocation of Article 5, the response required the kinds of forces and philosophies that the allies had been seeking to develop for so-called "non-Article 5 contingencies."

Unfortunately, the directions suggested by NATO strategy documents and incorporated in the 1999 Defense Capabilities Initiative had not been taken seriously by most European governments. This was a major factor encouraging the cynicism of Bush administration and Pentagon officials concerning the utility of NATO and European military forces. NATO acknowledged allied shortcomings in December 2001 when allied defense ministers in a special statement observed that

Efforts to improve NATO's ability to respond to terrorism must be an integral, albeit urgent, part of the more general ongoing work to improve Alliance military capabilities. There has been some progress in this wider regard since our last meeting, but a great deal more needs to be done. We are especially concerned about persistent longstanding deficiencies in areas such as survivability, deployability, combat identification, and intelligence, surveillance, and target acquisition. The full implementation of DCI is essential if the Alliance is to be able to carry out its missions, taking into account the threat posed by terrorism.[13]

In 1999, the allies had finessed the issue of whether or not NATO could be used for military operations beyond Europe. The United States had argued strongly that most applications of allied cooperation in the future would likely be well beyond allied borders. If given the mandate, NATO could have begun assessing allied forces that could be used in different conditions of weather and terrain and the means available for delivering them to zones of operation. But most European allies had opposed any open-ended commitment to employ NATO on a more global basis. As the war on terrorism unfolded in Afghanistan, far from Europe, the alliance had no agreement in principle concerning where NATO could be used. Legally, they needed no such agreement once they had declared the attacks on the United States to fall under NATO's collective defense provisions. But the lack of a commitment to and planning for operations far from NATO's borders meant alliance activities, mindsets, and force structures were not oriented toward being helpful in such contingencies.

In spite of such handicaps and the Bush administration's initial reluctance to involve NATO in the war on terrorism, many allies ultimately contributed forces to post-conflict peacekeeping duties in Afghanistan. In 2003, as discussed in Chapter 9, NATO itself took command of the peacekeeping part of military operations there. NATO command of the International Security Assistance Force (ISAF), a UN-mandated force initially responsible for providing security in and around Kabul, became NATO's first mission beyond the Euro-Atlantic area.

The Iraq Crisis in Transatlantic Relations

Immediately following the 9/11 attacks, if not before, some key officials in the Bush administration began to act on the assumption that Saddam Hussein was part of the terrorist problem that should, and could, be eliminated. By early 2002, it seemed clear that the United States was intent on bringing about a regime change in Iraq.

While the United States was laying the groundwork for an attack against Saddam Hussein's Iraq, the European allies were not prepared to come to the same conclusions reached already by Bush administration officials. Europeans generally agreed that Hussein was a problem and that his regime was in clear violation of international law. Further, they shared some of the US frustration that international sanctions had done much to hurt the Iraqi people but little to undermine Saddam's rule.

However, most Europeans and many European governments reacted strongly to the Bush administration's determination to go to war against Iraq no matter what other countries thought, irrespective of how unilateral action might affect the future of international cooperation, and with little regard for the impact on international law.

The unilateral US approach to Iraq was the instigating event for the crisis in US-European relations, but French President Jacques Chirac and German Chancellor Gerhard Schroeder helped ensure that the crisis would produce deep divisions among Europeans as well as between many Europeans and the United States. Given German public opinion in the summer of 2002, Chancellor Schroeder undoubtedly needed to take a stand against attacking Iraq in order to be returned as chancellor in the fall elections. But Schroeder disappointed many Americans, and surely President Bush, by failing to soften his opposition after the election. France's criticism of the US stance was seen in Washington, and across the country, as typical Gaullist grandstanding designed to show France's flag and to rein in the US hegemon. As in the case of Germany, however, US expectations concerning French behavior ultimately led to disappointment and even anger.

Many Americans expected France to be with the United States when the time came to use force, to ensure that France would have a say in the important post-conflict period in Iraq. Damage to the transatlantic alliance and to European solidarity, already serious, was aggravated when France not only remained opposed but happily took on the role of leader of the opposition. France's attitude, supported by French and broader European public opinion, nonetheless was highly divisive in the European framework, particularly when President Chirac "derided those Central and East European countries that have signed letters expressing their support for the United States as 'childish,' 'dangerous,' and missing 'an opportunity to shut up.'"[14]

For its part, the Bush administration further fanned the flames of European concern when, in September 2002, the White House released a policy statement on the "National Security Strategy of the United States." The paper focused on "those terrorist organizations of global reach and any terrorist or state sponsor of terrorism which attempt to gain or use weapons of mass destruction (WMD) or their precursors." With regard to such threats, the document laid out an unambiguous strategy of preemption, saying "as a matter of common sense and self-defense, America will act against such emerging threats before they are fully formed." It then added that "while the United States will constantly strive to enlist the support of the international community we will not hesitate to act alone, if necessary, to exercise our right of self-defense by acting preemptively against such terrorists."[15] Even though much of what the document said reflected realities of the contemporary security environment, it was widely interpreted as a unilateral assertion of rights beyond the accepted norms of international law, which could be misused by the United States or copied by other countries with destabilizing results.

The Irony of Success in Prague

Just as Kosovo had been the uninvited guest at the 1999 Washington Summit, Iraq was the new dark cloud shadowing alliance leaders when they met in Prague, the Czech Republic, in November 2002. The Prague meeting fortuitously fell at a time when the United States, the UK, France, and Germany were still trying to develop a common approach to Iraq through the United Nations. This brief lull in the Iraq controversy helped produce a better environment for the Prague meeting. Somewhat ironically, the Prague Summit yielded significant steps forward for the alliance at a time when political relations in the alliance were headed for new lows. One suspects that the Bush administration and the European allies wanted to show that their differences over how to deal with Iraq would not prevent them from making the Prague Summit a success. Not only did the allies invite seven new members (Bulgaria, Estonia, Latvia, Lithuania, Romania, Slovakia, and Slovenia) to join the alliance—another major step toward a Europe "whole and free"—but they also took giant strides toward making NATO an important player in security well beyond Europe.

In anticipation of the summit, Czech Republic President Vaclav Havel wrote that for "the Alliance to define clearly the role it wants to play in the global campaign against terrorism, the Prague Summit will have to involve a fundamental re-examination of the way in which NATO operates. Moreover, it will have to set in motion a still more radical transformation of the Alliance in order for NATO to reaffirm its position as a key pillar of international security."[16]

Havel's goals for the summit were largely met. The leaders confirmed the decision to create a NATO Response Force (NRF) intended to be capable of taking on virtually any military mission anywhere in the world. They approved reform of NATO's command structure to move away from its old geographic focus into a new functional approach organized around a command for "operations" and another for "transformation." (See Chapter 8 for more detail on the evolution of NATO organization and missions.)

As a result of decisions taken at Prague and after, NATO was given a mandate and some of the instruments required to play a meaningful role in dealing with twenty-first-century security challenges. It began using these new tools with the International Security Assistance Force in Afghanistan in 2003 and in Iraq, where it supported NATO ally Poland's role there, and in 2004 began helping train Iraqi security forces.

In addition, the agreements between NATO and the European Union known as "Berlin Plus" designed to facilitate cooperation between the two organizations finally were agreed upon and implemented. The accords did not guarantee smooth sailing in the NATO-EU relationship, particularly given the suspicions about the purposes of European defense integration still harbored by key Bush administration officials. But their implementation did provide a new and constructive foundation on which NATO-EU relations could develop. (See Chapter 10 for more detail on the NATO-EU relationship.)

Crisis over Ensuring Turkey's Security

Even with the successful Prague meeting, the Iraq issue continued to plague the alliance. Early in 2003, the question of whether to begin planning defensive assistance to Turkey should it be attacked by Iraq during a presumptive US-led coalition attack on Saddam Hussein's regime exploded, threatening the very underpinnings of the alliance. On January 15, US Deputy Secretary of Defense Paul Wolfowitz formally asked NATO allies to consider what supporting roles they might play in case of a US-led war on Iraq. Six areas of assistance were discussed, including sending Patriot missiles and AWACS surveillance planes to defend Turkey, the only NATO country that borders Iraq; sending naval forces to help protect ships in the eastern Mediterranean; providing personnel to help protect US military bases in Europe; access to airspace, ports, bases, and refueling facilities in Europe; backfilling US forces that are sent to the Gulf; and deploying NATO troops to Iraq after a possible war to help rebuild and govern the country.

After considerable discussion within the North Atlantic Council, Belgium, France, and Germany publicly announced their opposition to allowing NATO to begin planning to provide military assistance to Turkey. The three recalcitrant allies said they were not opposed to aiding Istanbul but believed that planning for such action was premature while UN arms inspectors were still seeking to disarm Iraq peacefully. The initiative was seen as an attempt by the United States to get preemptive NATO support for a military action that was not sanctioned by the UN Security Council. Once before, in the case of Kosovo, NATO had acted without a Security Council mandate. In that case, however, all the allies agreed that Russia and China should not be allowed to block a military action in Europe deemed necessary by the NATO allies. In this case, the three allies wanted to make it clear that a NATO mandate would not be sufficient to justify military action against Iraq. The choices of the United States to put the issue before the alliance and of the three allies to block the requested planning brought existing political differences over Iraq into NATO in a way that put NATO's mutual defense commitment on the line.

To break the stalemate, NATO Secretary-General Robertson and some member states suggested bringing the issue before the Defense Planning Committee (DPC), in which France, at that time, still chose not to participate. Agreement was finally reached in the French-less DPC when Belgium and Germany dropped their opposition to beginning planning possible military aid to Turkey.

The scenario illustrated to what extent the Iraq issue had frayed political bonds among the allies. It also demonstrated that NATO remained an alliance of sovereign states, and that it works only when serious efforts have been made to build a political consensus behind a course of action, particularly when that action requires the use of military force.

The Bush administration worked hard to get as many European governments as possible on board in support of the war. In addition to the Blair government, the most responsive European governments were those that had been liberated from

Soviet control by the successful end of the Cold War. For many of these countries, the goal of eliminating one of the world's most despotic dictators undoubtedly seemed more compelling than for those countries which for decades had experienced peace, democracy, and financial well-being.[17] The list of European countries that supported the war effort in principle was substantial.[18] The UK contributed combat troops and played a significant role in the attack on Iraq and in the postwar occupation. Poland took charge of a postwar military region in Iraq, and Spain and Italy contributed paramilitary and intelligence units. However, even in countries whose governments supported the war, public opinion remained strongly critical.

The initial war against Hussein's regime in Iraq was militarily successful, resulting in the overthrow of Hussein and the eventual capture of the former leader and elimination or capture of most of his top lieutenants. But Europeans remained unconvinced. In the summer of 2003, when asked "was the war in Iraq worth the loss of life and other costs," 70 percent of all Europeans polled answered "no," while only 25 percent said "yes." Even in states whose government supported the war effort, majorities answered in the negative, including the UK (55 percent); Poland (67 percent); Italy (73 percent); Portugal (75 percent); and the Netherlands (59 percent). In the two leading European opponents of the war, the results were more emphatic: France (87 percent) and Germany (85 percent).[19]

An in-depth analysis of European public opinion following the Iraq war came to the conclusion that opposition to the war was at least partly rooted in the perception that the United States was acting unilaterally, and without reference to international opinion. According to this analysis, "it makes a significant difference whether a potential military action involved a unilateral US move or one supported by NATO or the U.N. In Europe support increases from 36% for the U.S. acting alone to 48% for an action under a U.N. mandate."[20]

After the initial hostilities in Iraq, one influential European commentator who had earlier defended the US role as a benign hegemon cautioned the Bush administration and other Americans not to sacrifice the good will and cooperation that had for decades constituted part of the foundation for American power. Pro-American commentator Josef Joffe responded to the growing US unilateralist tendencies by observing that the United States would remain the dominant force in international affairs for some time to come, and that no traditional power balance would be provided by another power or combination of powers. However, in Joffe's view, US self-interest would not be well served by a strategy based on a "with us or against us" philosophy like that deployed by President Bush following the 9/11 attacks. Rather, according to Joffe, the United States should assume the inevitable costs that are associated with international leadership:

> Primacy does not come cheap, and the price is measured not just in dollars and cents, but above all in the currency of obligation. Conductors manage to mold 80 solo players into a symphony orchestra because they have fine sense for everybody else's quirks and qualities—because they act in the interest of all; their labour

is the source of their authority. . . . Power exacts responsibility, and responsibility requires the transcendence of narrow self-interest. As long as the United States continues to provide such public goods, envy and resentment will not escalate into fear and loathing that spawn hostile coalitions.[21]

Late in 2003, when it appeared the Bush administration was attempting to broaden the base of international support for Iraqi stabilization and reconstruction, and just before George W. Bush was scheduled to call the leaders of Germany, France, and Russia to ask them to forgive old Iraqi debt, the administration took another unilateral step that surprised and angered the European governments that had opposed the war. A directive from Deputy Secretary of Defense Paul Wolfowitz— cleared by the White House—was posted on the Pentagon website making it clear that only Iraq coalition members would be eligible to serve as prime contractors for US-financed reconstruction projects in Iraq. This eliminated three key countries Bush was about to ask for Iraqi debt relief and others, including Canada. The predictable reaction was immediate. German foreign minister Joschka Fischer said that the move would "not be acceptable" to Germany" And it wouldn't be in line with the spirit of looking to the future together and not into the past."[22] The move undermined the diplomatic efforts of Secretary of State Colin Powell to build international support for Iraqi debt relief. Russian defense minister Sergei Ivanov spoke out in opposition to forgiveness of Iraq's $120 billion debt, $8 billion of which is owed to Russia. Ivanov remarked, "Iraq is not a poor country."[23]

Just prior to release of the contracting decision, former Secretary of State James Baker had been asked to travel to Europe to convince key allied states to forgive Iraqi debt as a contribution to Iraqi recovery from the war. Baker found a cool reception in Paris, Berlin, and Moscow, but the three key governments all agreed to negotiate some package of debt reductions. Irritated by the US contracting decision, French President Chirac, German Chancellor Schroeder, and Russian President Putin all decided to handle the debt reduction issue via normal diplomatic channels, which in this case would be through the "Paris Club, a group of 19 industrialized nations that have collaborated since 1956 on easing financial burdens of heavily indebted nations."[24]

In the first half of 2004, the international character and political depth of the US-led coalition in Iraq took a serious hit. On March 14, national elections in Spain removed the party of Prime Minister Jose Maria Aznar from power. Voters apparently blamed Aznar's support of the US-led war in Iraq for the terrorist bombings that killed just under two hundred people in Madrid on March 11 and rebuffed the government's attempt to blame the bombings on Basque nationalists. Voters overwhelmingly endorsed candidates from the opposition Socialist Party, whose leader, Jose Luis Rodriguez Zapatero, had promised to withdraw Spain's 1,300 troops from Iraq, move Spain's foreign policy away from such close links to the United States, and restore good relations with European allies France and Germany that had opposed the Iraq war. Zapatero moved quickly and, as promised, all Spanish troops were out of Iraq by the end of May.

As the United States struggled to move Iraq from a war in progress toward self-rule and democratic elections, the allies softened their reaction to the requests for assistance from the United States but stopped far short of providing the kind of help the United States wanted. At the NATO Istanbul Summit in June 2004 the allies agreed that NATO's mission in Iraq could be expanded beyond backing up the Polish command there to include training for Iraqi forces. The allies were careful, however, to avoid giving President Bush any "victory" that he could use to good effect in his reelection campaign. This reluctance was reinforced by the fact that Bush administration claims about Iraqi weapons of mass destruction and ties to terrorist groups, used to justify the war, were not supported by the evidence, validating European reticence about participating in the conflict.

Following the November 2 elections that returned George W. Bush for another four-year term, the Europeans almost immediately moved to begin the process of rebuilding bridges to Washington. British Prime Minister Tony Blair, who had stood behind the Bush administration on Iraq in spite of strong opposition to the war at home as well as around Europe, flew to Washington to try to get US-European relations back on track. Blair seized on the death of Palestinian leader Yasir Arafat as a possible opening for US and European diplomacy to cooperate in making another push for an Israeli-Palestinian peace accord. During Blair's White House talks, President Bush responded to Blair's efforts by acknowledging that "the world is better off, America is better off, Europe is better off when we work together."[25]

The European countries responded to the Bush victory by compromising on Iraqi debt, agreeing to forgive much of that debt, in spite of Iraq's potential future oil income.[26] But French President Chirac continued to call for a multi-polar world,[27] and President Bush said he would use the "capital" he earned in the elections in support of his policy preferences. These positions left questions about how quickly US-European relations would recover from the Iraq and 9/11 traumas.

In addition, the allies agreed at the December 2004 ministerial meetings in Brussels to expand NATO's Baghdad training presence from sixty to some three hundred officers. Six countries—France, Germany, Belgium, Greece, Spain, and Luxembourg—while not blocking the initiative, refused to assign officers to the training program. US Secretary of State Powell and NATO Secretary-General Jaap de Hoop Scheffer both expressed their concern that officers from these countries, serving on NATO's International Military Staff, would not be allowed to participate in the program.[28]

The bottom line early in 2005 was that US prestige in Europe had dropped to an all-time low, by almost any measure. The image of US intelligence capabilities, brought low by US claims that Saddam Hussein had an active weapons of mass destruction program, had suffered as well. Would the United States be able to convince European governments to follow its lead on some future issue that relied on US intelligence capabilities and judgments? The Euro-Atlantic debates over Iraq had left obvious scars on transatlantic relations as well as on intra-European ties.

Many European governments remained supportive of US policy even though all European governments faced public opinion that opposed the war and thought little of US leadership in general. Additional members of the Iraq war coalition were preparing to pull their troops back from Iraq, making very little difference in the capabilities of the "coalition" but further exposing the fact that the United States, with the exception of Tony Blair's loyal support, was carrying most of the burden of maintaining security there. George Bush's "fence mending" trip to Europe in February 2005 helped establish a better atmosphere for the US-European dialogue, and even made some progress toward coordination of US and European approaches to Iran and other issues. Good will was evident on both sides. But many underlying suspicions and unresolved issues remained.

How and Why Did NATO Survive the Crisis?

The case could be made that NATO will, in fact, not survive for long and that the issues that came to a head in the crisis instigated by the policies of George W. Bush's administration will return to undermine the alliance down the road. If, however, "survival" is defined by the will of the member states to sustain the alliance relationship, the alliance appears to be recovering from this most recent in a long line of crises in the relationship.

The fact that NATO moved past this confluence of events cannot be explained in terms of the need for a response to an existential threat. Such a threat from the Soviet Union had been history for a decade before George W. Bush came to office, and had not been reconstituted. It also cannot be explained by the Bush administration's post-9/11 argument—an argument not accepted by most Europeans—that the United States and its allies were at war with radical Islamic extremism.

Even though the Bush administration carried unilateralism to new levels, the European allies had already experienced a taste of it in the alliance-friendly Clinton administration. The Bush administration's actions, however, on top of the Clinton experiences, convinced many Europeans that US unilateralism and hegemonic behavior were becoming the norm in transatlantic relations. The suggestion by some that Bush administration behavior was an American anomaly was undermined by the fact that in 2004 the American people re-elected George Bush for a second term.

These European perceptions increased support for building up the European Union (EU) as a counterbalance to US power. They fed support for the European Constitution agreed by EU governments in 2003. Such attitudes toward US behavior also led to the "rump" meeting of France, Germany, Belgium and Luxembourg in April 2003 that produced agreement on establishing a separate EU military planning cell independent of NATO, which US Ambassador to NATO Nicholas Burns subsequently called "the most significant threat to NATO's future."

What could have been seen as a reason for European states to get used to America's hegemonic behavior, started to turn into a dynamic that could have led to the end of alliance. Why did it not? The paragraphs that follow discuss some of the possible explanations.

The Bush administration in its second term recognized the need for allies and the importance of NATO in mustering allied contributions to security and made serious efforts to show that the United States remained committed to the alliance.

The Bush administration in its second term mounted a campaign to win back the trust and cooperation of European governments. Both Secretary of State Condoleezza Rice and President Bush visited European capitals early in 2005 explicitly seeking to repair some of the damage done by the administration in its first term, and most particularly by the decision to go to war against Iraq.

The shift perhaps reflected the Bush administration's acceptance that more traditional approaches to dealing with its allies would be to the US advantage. In the late 1990s, German commentator Joe Joffe had argued that the United States was different from previous dominant powers: "It irks and domineers, but it does not conquer. It tries to call the shots and bend the rules, but it does not go to war for land and glory." Further, he argued, the dominating US position is based on "soft" as well as "hard" power: "This type of power—a culture that radiates outward and a market that draws inward—rests on pull, not on push; on acceptance, not on conquest."[29] In its second term, the Bush administration tried to rely more on these natural strengths of the United States, and to push more gently.

Failure of the EU Constitution to win popular acceptance implied that arguments being made for the EU to become a "balancer" of US power internationally could not be sustained by reality, at least not in the near term.

The failure of the European Union Constitution to win approval in 2005 referenda in France and the Netherlands did not signify popular rejection of the "balancer" argument. Decisions in France and the Netherlands were based far more on the desire to preserve national identities and cultures and on concerns about economic consequences than on any grand strategic arguments.

But this failure did squelch talk about the EU as a "balancer," and led to serious introspection among EU governments. How could one imagine the EU counterbalancing the United States if even the most "Gaullist" of European countries, whose government had promoted the concept of making the EU an international pole of power, could not win popular approval for a document that would establish the platform for such a role?

New European democracies in Eastern and Central Europe were strongly committed to NATO's continuation, particularly because their historical and geographic proximity to Russian power and influence convinced them that NATO provided an essential link to US power that was not provided by EU membership.

Former Soviet satellites in central and eastern Europe and three former Soviet Republics (Latvia, Lithuania and Estonia) had worked hard to adopt "western" political and economic systems. They wanted to align with the United States and to protect themselves against Russian influence. They wanted to be EU and NATO members to ensure that they are fully part of Europe with strong links to the United States.

Those who wanted the EU to become a "balancer" of American power were disappointed and even angered by the fact that the new democracies wanted a form of European unity that remained compatible with transatlantic alliance. The net impact, however, was to reaffirm the importance of the transatlantic link and NATO.

European governments simply had no alternative to remaining in alliance with the United States, and NATO was still the most important symbol and operational component of the relationship.

Even before the EU Constitution went down in defeat, there were serious questions about the EU balancer concept. In a new balance of power system, the EU would have been required to align itself with Russia and China from time to time in response to disagreements with the United States. One presumes this also could mean that the United States would be free to align with other countries, let's say India and Japan, or even Russia or China, against the European Union. It doesn't take much imagination to envision how unstable international relations could become in such an environment.

Moreover, how comfortable would Europeans feel about aligning themselves with autocratic or even authoritarian states against the American democracy? Somehow this model of international relations never made much sense.

One answer, of course, is that the EU could be a "soft" balancer, simply opposing US policies as necessary and acting as a friendly critic of the United States and not formally aligning itself with any other power. This, however, is not much different from the current state of transatlantic relations. A healthy dialogue over differing points of view is in the interests of democracies on both sides of the Atlantic.

West European governments remained split concerning the future construction of Europe, and the default position (of European integration within the broader context of transatlantic cooperation) was sufficiently compelling to discourage other options.

The debate in Europe over the US invasion of Iraq reflected the fact that there were very different attitudes and assumptions concerning the relationship with the United States. While some European states opposed the US action based on their judgment that the case for war had not been made, others lined up in support. Among some traditional NATO allies, the United States was supported by several governments led by conservative parties. In the United Kingdom, the powerful influence of the "special relationship" in the hands of Prime Minister Tony Blair aligned the United Kingdom with its American ally.

The divisions among allies and even within allied governments were based not just on the merits of the case for war but also on differing images of Europe's future. When the model of the EU as a balancer fell apart, the idea of a uniting Europe with the framework of continued transatlantic cooperation reasserted itself.

In addition, the change of leaders in two key countries—France and Germany—substantially improved the dynamics of their bilateral and alliance relations with the United States. When Christian Democrat Angela Merkel assumed the chancellorship in Germany in 2005 she consciously sought to repair some of the damage to Germany's relations with the United States, and to make NATO "a high priority for German foreign policy."[30]

Similarly, when Nicolas Sarkozy won the French presidency in 2007 he brought with him a fundamentally changed attitude toward NATO and relations with the United States. Sarkozy's intent to return France to NATO's integrated military command and to develop the European Union's Security and Defense Policy in NATO-friendly directions was welcomed by the Bush administration.[31]

The fact is that, in spite of differences over Iraq and international relations generally, the United States and its European allies still share an impressive collection of values and interests.

For those who argued in the 1990s and into the 2000s that Europe and the United States were inevitably drifting apart, the standard assertion of common Euro-Atlantic values appeared undermined by the many issues on which there seemed to be serious differences: the death penalty, global warming, abortion, gun control, and when to use military force, among others. However, in spite of these differences, what made the transatlantic alliance special was the fact that it still stood in defense of core values such as individual liberty, democracy, and the rule of law. The validity of this value foundation was strongly reaffirmed by the former members of the Warsaw Pact and former Soviet Republics that put these values at the heart of their new democratic systems.

The financial and economic fortunes of the United States and Europe had become so mutually interdependent that a political/security break with the United States could put vital European and American interests at risk.

In addition to shared political values, the United States and EU member states have market-based economic systems in which competition drives the market but is governed by democratically approved rules and regulations. European and American market economies are the essential core of the global economic system.[32] The European Union is the largest US partner in the trade of goods and services. The members of the EU have over $860 billion of direct investment in the United States. The United States has some $700 billion invested in EU states.

The EU and the United States together account for more than 40 percent of world trade and represent almost 60 percent of the industrialized world's gross domestic product. Joseph P. Quinlin concluded in his excellent 2003 study of US-European mutual economic interdependence that: "In sum, the years since the fall of the Berlin Wall have witnessed one of the greatest periods of transatlantic economic integration in history. Our mutual stake in each other's prosperity has grown dramatically since the end of the Cold War. We ignore these realities at our peril."[33]

Finally, in 2008, developments in Russian policy starkly highlighted what could return as another reason why NATO will survive the Bush administration crisis in transatlantic relations.

Since the end of the Cold War, NATO's members have attempted to develop cooperative political, economic and security relations with Russia. This has not stopped the allies from taking steps that they saw as warranted by their own values and interests, such as admitting former Warsaw Pact allies and Soviet republics to alliance membership. However, other dynamics have been working on Russian policies.

After the collapse of the Soviet Union, there was a chance that Russia itself would fall apart, as the Chechen separatist movement seemed to suggest. It was therefore not a surprise that Russia moved into a new, perhaps prolonged, period of authoritarian tendencies designed to keep the country from disintegrating.

As noted in Chapter 7, when Russia invaded Georgia in August 2008, NATO states clearly did not want the affair to destroy the potential for a cooperative relationship with Russia over the long run. However, the short-term effect was to provide more evidence for the arguments being made in the states that had only recently escaped from Russian domination that they still needed protection against that threat. NATO, and the vital link it provided to American power, remained the most reliable guarantee of their security that they could imagine.

Lessons That Should Be Learned

The United States with which European leaders and states will have to deal in the foreseeable future will remain a *de facto* hegemon with the capacity to do much good or much harm in terms of their interests and international stability. "Europe" will remain a work in progress, acting united in many areas but with EU members acting very much like nation-states particularly in the areas of foreign and defense policy. This will be a "uniting Europe of states" more than a "United States of Europe."

At the end of the day, the Bush crisis in alliance relations seems to have demonstrated that the United States, Canada and the European states cannot afford to go it alone internationally, even if future differences might tempt them to do so again. If the allies wish to avoid or mitigate similar crises in the future, what lessons need to be learned?

Lesson: As long as the United States retains such a strong international presence, it must learn how to be a hegemonic power without acting like one. In spite of its overwhelming military power, it nonetheless needs cooperation with allies and international institutions to legitimize use of force, win the peace.

The United States will have to "speak more softly," as US President Teddy Roosevelt famously recommended. Everyone knows that the United States already carries the "biggest stick." And, future US administrations will be required to be more constructive and creative in the use of international institutions and multilateral cooperation.

United States needs NATO. Ad hoc coalitions sometimes are necessary, but they can't replace NATO cooperation. Even when the NATO integrated command structure is not directly in play, the day-to-day political/military cooperation among allies and partners provides the experience and habits of cooperation necessary to make ad hoc coalitions viable.

Particularly in conflicts like the current one with al Qaeda leaders who use terrorist tactics on behalf of their radical ideology, the United States cannot "win" simply by the use of military force. It desperately needs the political legitimacy and assistance that is provided by allies and partners who share in the risks and take on military and non-military responsibilities. The bottom line is that the United States should not give the impression through its words or actions that it does not value the contribution the NATO alliance makes to its interests.

Lesson: If European states do not develop more substantial international military capabilities, familiar burden-sharing tensions with the United States and among European countries will resurface as possible sources of new crises.

As we have seen, the strongly held view in the first Bush administration that the European allies and NATO had little to contribute to America's security interests was a key factor behind events leading to the crisis in alliance relations. The fact that Europe was perceived as having little to offer also suggested that the United States did not need to pay attention to European views or preferences. If this circumstance is not altered, the same sort of crisis could re-occur in the future.

Lesson: Europeans need NATO as a source of involvement in international security and influence on US decisions affecting European interests.

A bigger European stick, with longer reach, will produce a more effective European voice in the alliance. Europeans will have to bring more resources and capabilities to the transatlantic security table. Europe's speaking softly while carrying a big carrot simply won't cut it. The US–European relationship needs a better balance in terms of both authority and capability. However, it is not up to the United States to "give" Europe more authority. European nations and the European Union will wield greater influence in Washington and internationally based on their will and ability to contribute to solutions of international security problems.

Lesson: Dealing with terrorism and other challenges requires US-European soft- as well as hard-power cooperation.

The experience in Afghanistan so far contains many potential lessons, but one of the key ones is that both the United States and Europe will need a variety of non-military capabilities and programs to deal with this and future security problems arising from failed states. More extensive and coordinated US and European, NATO and EU, cooperation on the use of non-military instruments of security policy could help keep transatlantic perceptions of security requirements and required policies closer to consensus approaches.

A number of suggestions are already on the table for ways to improve transatlantic security cooperation without undermining the important roles of NATO and the European Union.[34] So far, such proposals have not been sufficiently compelling to override resistance to change, including bureaucratic preferences for muddling through rather than taking chances on new approaches, and institutional insecurities leading to fears that new ways of doing business might undermine the EU, NATO or the United Nations. The question of whether NATO is sufficient for the security needs of its member states is discussed in Chapter 12.

Lesson: As much as the allies believe in democracy as the value foundation for their alliance, one of the lessons from Iraq should be that it is much easier to support democratic systems that have been freely chosen by other countries than to try to superimpose them on a base not yet fully prepared for them.

The fact that the United States seemed to many Europeans to be on a crusade to establish democratic political systems across the Middle East was one source of transatlantic differences over policies toward Iraq. Trying to impose democracy on populations that either do not want it or are not prepared to implement it is a costly enterprise that should be undertaken only if the entire community of democracies is prepared to support the process.

Lesson: Do not divide responsibilities between the United States and its allies, as this only deepens divergence in perceptions.

Given the current disparities between US and European military capabilities, some have suggested dividing responsibilities in the alliance. It does make sense for individual nations, or groups of nations, to take on specific tasks within the overall framework of transatlantic cooperation. In fact, the special capacities that European allies have for managing stabilization and reconstruction activities could be usefully combined with the potent US ability for war fighting to develop a full spectrum of pre-conflict, conflict, and post-conflict coalition activities. This would require closer political and strategic cooperation and better integrated planning, including the will to imagine and project reactions to a wide range of contingencies.

However, any formal division of responsibilities (hard power tasks for the United States, soft power jobs for the Europeans) would be a disaster for US–European relations. In a world of divided Euro-Atlantic responsibilities, responses to every future security challenge would have to overcome growing divergences in appreciation of the problem before effective cooperation could even be imagined.

The bottom line is that there should be a practical division of tasks among the transatlantic partners, but not a formal division of labor across the Atlantic. Ideally, both American and European forces should be engaged in the high intensity and lower intensity ends of future conflicts, sharing responsibility for the strategies required for the entire continuum.

Lesson: In the near term, the allies need to prepare a new strategic concept that will take into account both these lessons and the experiences of the decade that has passed since the last strategic concept was prepared.

Former NATO Secretary General Jaap de Hoop Scheffer for over two years called for preparation of a new Strategic Concept for the alliance. With the advent of a new administration in Washington, the time arrived for the task. Such concepts seldom break dramatic new ground, but they do consolidate realities in ways that provide guidance for future actions. This one, now scheduled to be completed in 2010, could effectively mark the end of the Bush administration NATO crisis and the opening of a new spirit of cooperation that is sorely needed to deal with the challenges now facing the alliance.

Lesson: Perceptions do matter.

The ways that the United States and the allies perceive each other's intentions and actions have an important impact on the functioning of the alliance. Moreover, because all the allies are democracies, the way that publics on both sides of the Atlantic perceive the value of allies and the alliance can profoundly affect its future.

NATO's public information services perform an important function in providing material about NATO that can then be used by commentators, teachers, and governments. Over the long run, the way that the alliance is portrayed on op ed pages and in classrooms will have an important effect on perceptions. This is even more important now that substantially fewer Americans serve in European countries on NATO duty resulting in substantially diminished person-to-person contacts that have in the past helped sustain transatlantic cooperation.

In the near term, European and American governments need to take care that the impressions they give to their publics about the value of these relationships are consistent with their interests. And, if they believe that NATO is important to their interests, they need to be pro-active in shaping public opinion in supportive ways.

The Bottom Line

The transatlantic alliance faces a complex and demanding set of issues, including: what will be required to succeed in Afghanistan; how can international terrorism best be confronted and contained; how should the allies deal with a Russia that is reconsolidating and reasserting its power and influence; should NATO remain a regional alliance with global partnerships and missions, or should it become a global alliance; and how can the allies best accommodate internal political and economic dynamics among European countries and within the overall Atlantic community?

The allies cannot afford another crisis like the one the alliance has just survived. Perhaps this is the bottom line lesson: *preserving cooperation among democratic states, of which the transatlantic allies are the essential core, is vitally important for the future security and well-being of them all.* For that matter, such cooperation is essential to the effective functioning of the international system more broadly. Dealing with the challenges of the past decade presumably has convinced allied governments that putting that cooperation at risk is unlikely to be the best answer to any imaginable future security issues.

That said, there are many different ideas in Europe and the United States about whether NATO is up to the task at hand or if it needs to be replaced, changed, or supplemented. Suggestions for future organization of Euro-Atlantic security relations are examined in the next chapter.

Notes

1. Statement by the North Atlantic Council, NATO Press Release (2001) 124, September 12, 2001.
2. George Robertson, NATO Secretary-General, statement to the press on the North Atlantic Council Decision on Implementation of Article 5 of the Washington Treaty following the September 11 attacks against the United States, October 4, 2001.

3. "NATO Airborne Early Warning Aircraft Begin Deploying to the United States," SHAPE News Release, October 9, 2001.

4. R. Nicholas Burns, "NATO Is Vital for the Challenges of the New Century," *International Herald Tribune*, November 10–11, 2001, 8.

5. Not-for-attribution discussion with Italian government officials in October 2001.

6. Charles Grant, "Does This War Show That NATO No Longer Has a Serious Military Role," The *Independent*, October 16, 2001.

7. Joseph Fitchett, "Pentagon in a League of Its Own," *International Herald Tribune*, February 4, 2002, 3.

8. George W. Bush, State of the Union Address, The White House, January 29, 2002.

9. Richard G. Lugar, "NATO Must Join War on Terrorism," speech to the US-NATO Missions Annual Conference, January 19, 2002.

10. Joseph Fitchett, "US Allies Chafe at 'Cleanup' Role," *International Herald Tribune*, November 26, 2001, 1.

11. Fitchett, "US Allies Chafe at 'Cleanup' Role," 1.

12. As discussed in Chapter 6, NATO in 1994 accepted the US idea of creating Combined Joint Task Force (CJTF) headquarters as a means of making the alliance's command structure more flexible to deal with new threats to security. A NATO Counterterrorism Task Force would not have been designed to run military operations against terrorist targets. However, such a task force could have been developed as a support mechanism for Afghanistan and future operations. In addition to military officers, the task force could have involved participation by representatives from the foreign and finance ministries of task force countries to bring to bear the wide range of resources needed to wage the campaign. One of the beneficial attributes of the CJTF structure is that non-NATO allies can be invited to participate. In addition, a Counterterrorism Task Force would have provided a framework for enhanced NATO-Russia cooperation. Russia could have been represented in the task force command and support counterterrorist operations even if it did not join openly in attacks on terrorist targets.

 The author recommended such an initiative following the September 11, 2001, terrorist attacks, first in an October 7, 2001, presentation to the Political Committee of the NATO Parliamentary Assembly, during the Assembly's annual meeting in Ottawa, Canada, entitled "A Perspective on the Future of the Transatlantic Bargain," in a lecture at the NATO Defense College on October 22, 2001, and then in the *International Herald Tribune*: Stanley R. Sloan, "Give NATO a Combined Task Force against Terrorism," *International Herald Tribune*, November 13, 2001, 8.

13. NATO North Atlantic Council in Defence Ministers Session, "Statement on Combating Terrorism: Adapting the Alliance's Defence Capabilities," NATO Press Release (2001) 173, December 18, 2001.

14. Craig S. Smith, "Chirac Upsets East Europe by Telling It to 'Shut Up' on Iraq," *The New York Times*, February 19, 2003.

15. US Government, the White House, "The National Security Strategy of the United States," September 2002.

16. Vaclav Havel, "Prague Predictions," *NATO Review*, Spring 2002. Text available at: www.nato.int/docu/review/2002/issue1/english/art1.html [accessed July 8, 2009].

17. The White House even noted in a press release on March 20, 2003, "it is no accident that many member nations of the Coalition recently escaped from the boot of a tyrant or have felt the scourge of terrorism. All Coalition member nations understand the threat Saddam Hussein's weapons pose to the world and the devastation his regime has wreaked on the Iraqi people."

18. On April 3, 2003, almost two weeks after the opening of hostilities in Iraq, the White House listed some 49 Iraq Coalition members, including the following 23 European (including former Soviet republics) states: Albania, Azerbaijan, Bulgaria, Czech Republic, Denmark, Estonia, Georgia, Hungary, Iceland, Italy, Latvia, Lithuania, Macedonia, the Netherlands, Poland, Portugal, Romania, Slovakia, Spain, Turkey, Ukraine, United Kingdom, and Uzbekistan.

19. Data quoted are from Ronald Asmus, Philip P. Everts, and Pierangelo Isernia, "Power, War and Public Opinion: Thoughts on the Nature and Structure of the Trans-Atlantic Divide," *Transatlantic Trends 2003*, a project of the German Marshal Fund of the United States and the Compagnia di San Paolo.

20. Asmus, Everts, and Isernia, "Power, War and Public Opinion," 12.

21. Josef Joffe, "Gulliver Unbound: Can America Rule the World?" the Twentieth Annual John Bonython Lecture, The Centre for Independent Studies, Sydney, Australia, August 5, 2003.

22. Erin E. Arvedlund, "Allies Angered at Exclusion from Bidding," nytimes.com, December 11, 2003. 12.

23. Arvedlund, "Allied Angered at Exclusion from Bidding."

24. Craig S. Smith, "France Gives Baker Lukewarm Commitment on Iraqi Debt," nytimes.com, December 16, 2003.

25. Richard W. Stevenson and Steven R. Weisman, "Bush Says U.S. Will Push Hard on Peace Plan," nytimes.com, November 13, 2004.

26. Craig S. Smith, "Major Creditors in Accord to Waive 8% of Iraq Debt," nytimes.com, November 22, 2004.

27. In a speech sponsored by the International Institute for Strategic Studies in London on November 18, 2004, Chirac observed "It is by recognizing the new reality of a multi-polar and interdependent world that we will succeed in building a sounder and fairer international order." Patrick E. Tyler, "Chirac Hints France Will Help Rebuild Iraq," nytimes.com, November 19, 2004. The day before Chirac left for London, he told interviewers that "To a certain extent Saddam Hussein's departure was a positive thing. But it also provoked reactions, such as the mobilization in a number of countries of men and women of Islam,

which has made the world more dangerous." Craig S. Smith, "Chirac Says War in Iraq Spreads Terrorism," nytimes.com, November 18, 2004.

28. Joel Brinkley, "NATO Agrees to Expansion of Forces Training Soldiers in Iraq," *The New York Times*, December 10, 2004.

29. Josef Joffe, "How America Does It," *Foreign Affairs*, September/October 1997, 16.

30. Christian Hacke, "The Merkel Miracle? The Promising Beginnings of a Readjusted German Foreign Policy," American Institute for Contemporary German Studies Analyses, Washington, D.C., March 17, 2006, http://www.aicgs.org/analysis/c/hacke031706one.aspx.

31. See, for example, Leo Michel, "Getting to Oui," *Internationale Politik*, German Council on Foreign Relations, Berlin, Summer 2008, http://www.ip-global.org/archiv/2008/summer2008/getting-to-oui.html.

32. See Joseph P. Quinlin, "Drifting Apart or Growing Together? The Primacy of the Transatlantic Economy," Center for Transatlantic Relations [Washington] March 2003.

33. Joseph P. Quinlin, "Drifting Apart or Growing Together?" xi.

34. The suggestions include this author's proposals in the past decade for an Atlantic Community Treaty Organization that would serve as a framework for coordination of NATO and European Union member state policies and efforts on the non-military aspects of security. Other advocacies for broader cooperation among democratic states have included proposals from Simon Serfaty and the Center for Strategic and International Studies in Washington, the Princeton Project on National Security, Senator John McCain, and former French Prime Minister Edouard Balladur, all of which are discussed in Chapter 12.

PART III

Permanent Alliance?

CHAPTER 12

Is NATO Necessary but Not Sufficient?

As the transatlantic bargain stretched into the first decade of the twenty-first century, the Euro-Atlantic allies increasingly saw the alliance as necessary, but not sufficient, for their security requirements. This chapter examines a few of the alternatives to NATO that have been offered as better ways to guarantee Euro-Atlantic security and others that have been suggested to improve and keep NATO while expanding options for the members of the EU and NATO. Of course, there are those who have argued that NATO is not even necessary, and, for the sake of accuracy, we make note of those arguments up front.

"NATO Is Not Necessary" Arguments

1. NATO is too much a Cold War institution.

This argument was heard immediately after the end of the Cold War, when the dissolution of the Warsaw Pact and the Soviet Union removed the threat that had stimulated NATO's creation and, until then, apparently ensured its continuity. It seemed logical to many observers that an organization that had lost its purpose should not be sustained at considerable cost to its members. Some experts speculated that the Organization for Security and Europe (OSCE) could provide the framework for European security cooperation in a post-Cold War setting.

The OSCE-centered option for European security was a popular vision for many Europeans in the early days of the post-Cold War era. That popularity faded quickly, however, partly because the first Bush administration in the early 1990s made it clear that the United States was not prepared to see the OSCE (then the CSCE) take the lead away from NATO and, in part, because the OSCE became seen increasingly as an unwieldy operational instrument for military cooperation.

When NATO began moving toward enlargement of its membership in the mid-1990s, some opponents of the move argued that NATO was too tainted by its anti-Soviet/Russian character, and could not be a successful basis for organization of European security. One such opponent of enlargement, American analyst Charles Kupchan, argued that NATO and the Article 5 commitment had outlived their utility and recommended the creation of a broadly based "Atlantic Union" to take over from both NATO and the EU. According to Kupchan,

> The solution to the West's troubles is an Atlantic Union (au) that would subsume both organizations. The EU would abandon its federal aspirations and concentrate

on the extension of its single market east to Central Europe and west to North America. NATO would become the new group's defense arm, but its binding commitments to the collective defense of state borders would give way to more relaxed commitments to uphold collective security through peace enforcement, peacekeeping, and preventive diplomacy. The au could then open its doors to the new democracies of Central Europe in a manner acceptable to both Russia and the commitment-weary electorates of the current NATO countries. Once democracy takes root in Russia and the other states of the former Soviet Union, the au would include them in its security structures and single market.[1]

This approach, Kupchan explained, would be a looser set of Atlantic and European organizational ties, but one more compatible with Russia's emergence as a liberal democratic state: "Because NATO is a traditional military alliance—a concentration of power against a common external threat—its extension would impel Russia to marshal a countervailing coalition. NATO enlargement would resurrect, not erase, the dividing line between Europe's east and west."[2] More recently, Kupchan hedges his bets, arguing that "Atlantic relations are still in a transitional phase; it is far too soon to determine what type of order will constitute a stable and durable equilibrium." He nonetheless leans away from viewing transatlantic security cooperation as a key element of the future for Europe or America, writing ". . . the Atlantic community has already passed through a historical breakpoint and that close-knit security partnership of the past five decades is in all likelihood gone for good."[3]

It now is Russia's leadership that makes the complaint voiced in the 1990s by Kupchan and others. Russian President Medvedev's 2008 proposal for a new European security system criticized Atlanticism and NATO as remnants of the Cold War. Medvedev told an audience in Berlin in June 2008:

> It is my conviction that Atlanticism as a sole historical principle has already had its day. We need to talk today about unity between the whole Euro-Atlantic area from Vancouver to Vladivostok. . . . NATO has also failed so far to give new purpose to its existence. It is trying to find this purpose today by globalising its missions, including to the detriment of the UN's prerogatives, which I mentioned just before, and by bringing in new members. But this is clearly still not the solution.[4]

The sentiment that NATO is too compromised by its Cold War history undoubtedly is shared in some non-Russian quarters on both sides of the Atlantic. However, Russia's proposal for an alternative arrangement has raised as much suspicion as it has interest, particularly among former Warsaw Pact nations and Soviet republics that sought NATO membership as insurance against future Russian domination.

2. Global security should be handled by the United Nations, not NATO.

Russian President Medvedev's complaint about NATO displacing the United Nations has been heard from Russian leaders for over a decade. Starting with NATO's peace enforcement role in the Balkans in the 1990s and continuing particularly in

NATO's use of force to drive Serbian forces out of Kosovo, Russia has complained that NATO's growing global role has been usurping the prerogatives and responsibilities of the UN Security Council. Russia's criticism is consistent with its interests because, to the extent that NATO acts without a mandate from the Security Council, as it did in 1999 over Kosovo, Russian influence is diminished. As Medvedev told his audience in Berlin,

> The founders of this system, the founders of the UN, showed great foresight and established the UN as an organisation in which countries would cooperate on an equal basis. There is no other such organisation in the world and the coming years are not likely to produce one. Attempts to replace the UN with 'exclusive format' groups [i.e., NATO] (such as is sometimes proposed) would have a totally destructive effect on the current world order.[5]

Today, NATO's command of the International Security Assistance Force in Afghanistan raises questions about whether NATO will take on even more non-European security challenges in the future, and if this will undercut the intended role of the United Nations. The ISAF, of course, is operating under a mandate from the UN Security Council, but Russia (and China) clearly would prefer to have more control over such operations than they do when NATO and the United States are in charge.

3. European security should be managed by Europeans; NATO is too much US and not enough Europe.

This complaint is heard on both sides of the Atlantic, particularly since the end of the Cold War. From the US side, many Americans see NATO as an organization in which the United States has always carried the largest burden and in which European states have been essentially "free riding" to ensure their security. The "burden-sharing" question, of course, is as old as the Euro-Atlantic alliance, as earlier chapters in this volume made clear. But particularly in difficult economic times, many Americans would like to see allied governments relieving the United States of some of its burdens for maintaining international security.

The complaint is also heard from the European side of the alliance, but with a very different set of assumptions. The discussion in Chapter 10 made it clear that one strong motivation for European defense cooperation during the Cold War, and for the European Security and Defense Initiative (ESDI) and the European Security and Defense Policy (ESDP) in the years since, was the European desire to have a larger say in the transatlantic alliance, and even to replace the alliance with a security system based on European resources and not so dependent on the United States.

At the end of the Cold War, many Europeans thought that the reduced threat conditions would provide a perfect opportunity for "Europeanization" of the alliance. In fact, in the mid-1990s the French government misread the intentions of the Clinton administration and apparently believed that Clinton was opening the door for Europeanization of NATO. This led to serious misunderstandings and disagreements that persisted for several years.

The unilateralist approach taken by the George W. Bush administration during the first decade of the twenty-first century brought a revival to this European motivation for "autonomous" defense efforts in the framework of the ESDP. However, as was discussed in Chapter 11, a number of factors have led back to a situation where Americans still believe Europe should do much more and many Europeans believe Europe should be more autonomous in defense and foreign policy, but in which neither outcome appears easy or likely in the near term.

"NATO Is Necessary but Insufficient" Arguments

1. NATO's membership is too limited.
   The fact that NATO's enlargement process has been limited to European states (limited to this class of states by Article 10 of the North Atlantic Treaty) that wish to join has become a source of concern and advocacy for some American analysts, one of whom in 2009 began serving as President Obama's ambassador to NATO. US and NATO efforts in Afghanistan have been supported in particular by several democratic states from outside the Euro-Atlantic region. A few, in fact, have arguably made more important contributions than some NATO allies.[6]
   This led to a suggestion that such countries should perhaps be offered partnership with or even membership in NATO, to give them justifiable influence over decisions that they were helping implement. In a provocative article in *Foreign Affairs*, Ivo Daalder [now US Ambassador to NATO] and James Goldgeier argued that NATO had moved in the right direction by thinking about strengthening partnership to global partners, including Australia, New Zealand, South Korea and Japan. In fact, the Bush administration and the UK in 2006 tabled a proposal at NATO for establishing a Global Partnership project. But Daalder and Goldgeier wanted the alliance to go further. Reflecting on the fact that NATO's Partnership for Peace had led to many of the partners becoming members, they suggested

   > NATO's new global-partnership project should play a similar role by preparing the alliance to transform itself from a transatlantic entity into a global one. NATO need not decide in advance which countries it would invite to join its ranks; it need only decide that membership should in principle be open to non-European countries.[7]

   The US/UK global partnership ran into serious resistance among many NATO members. Some were reluctant to expand NATO's reach and responsibilities as far as global partnerships would imply. Others, particularly those with continuing concerns about Moscow's intentions, did not want the Article 5 collective defense guarantee to be re-focused to another part of the globe. The Daalder/Goldgeier suggestion went much too far for many of the European allies.

2. NATO should be part of a broader global arrangement for cooperation among democracies.

Another variant on this complaint has led some commentators to suggest that all democratic states should work together to establish a union of all democratic states. In the United States, the idea of bringing new forms of cooperation to bear on international security problems has emerged from sources as diverse as Senator John McCain's concept of a "League of Democracies" and the Princeton University's Project on National Security's proposal for a "Concert of Democracies." McCain put his concept forward as part of his run for the presidency in 2008, suggesting "We need to strengthen our transatlantic alliance as the core of a new global compact—a League of Democracies—that can harness the great power of the more than 100 democratic nations around the world to advance our values and defend our shared interests."[8] In McCain's view, the new League would be built on the foundation provided by the Euro-Atlantic alliance.

The Princeton Project on National Security, released in September 2006, recommended expansion of cooperation among democracies on a global scale, with a reformed NATO as an instrument of the new structure:

> While pushing for reform of the United Nations and other major global institutions, the United States should work with its friends and allies to develop a global "Concert of Democracies"—a new institution designed to strengthen security cooperation among the world's liberal democracies. This Concert would institutionalize and ratify the "democratic peace." If the United Nations cannot be reformed, the Concert would provide an alternative forum for liberal democracies to authorize collective action, including the use of force, by a supermajority vote. Its membership would be selective, but self-selected. Members would have to pledge not to use or plan to use force against one another; commit to holding multiparty, free-and-fair elections at regular intervals; guarantee civil and political rights for their citizens enforceable by an independent judiciary; and accept the responsibility to protect.
>
> The United States must also: revive the NATO alliance by updating its grand bargains and expanding its international partnerships . . . [9]

These proposals came at an awkward time. When the Bush administration's claims that Iraq had weapons of mass destruction and was actively supporting international terrorism were contradicted by the facts, President Bush began describing Iraq as a democratization project. As a result, the concept of organizing the international community around the concept of democracy building was tarnished by association with an increasingly unpopular war.

3. The Atlantic Community needs more than NATO.

The idea that there is an "Atlantic Community" of democratic nations sharing deeply held commitments to common values and shared interests has been around for many decades. The North Atlantic Treaty acknowledges these special bonds in its preamble (see the text of the Treaty in the Appendix). But the idea of going beyond the military cooperation in NATO has persisted from the 1950s until now.

The most ambitious plan was advocated by Clarence Streit. Streit had written a volume in 1939 advocating a federal union of democratic states and their colonies to defend against the emergence of totalitarianism in Germany, Italy and Japan.[10] His idea gave rise to the "Federal Union" initiative and attracted significant elite support on both sides of the Atlantic. According to the Streit Council, an organization in Washington, D.C. that carries forward the goals of cooperation among democratic states, "In 1949 Federal Union members spawned the Atlantic Union Committee, a political action group that played a significant role in the creation of NATO. The AUC's officers included US Supreme Court Justice Owen J. Roberts, Secretary of War Robert Patterson, Under Secretary of State Will Clayton and Elmo Roper of Roper Polls. Prime Minister of Canada Lester Pearson was a strong supporter, as were many leaders in Europe."[11]

Clarence Streit's dedication to the goal of a federal Atlantic union was largely regarded as idealistic in its time, in spite of support the idea attracted from important elite voices. Most proposals that have been tabled since have been more modest, but many of them grow from similar inspirations.

Following World War II, the United States provided many of the ideas and critical resources to help reconstruct Europe (through the Marshall Plan), encourage the process of European integration (promoting the development of what now is the European Union), and deploy a defense system against Soviet power through NATO. The post-World War II phase of institution-building created a web of European and transatlantic organizations that, taken together, constituted a loosely knit cooperation and security community among the United States, Canada, and the West European allies.

Some other North American and European advocates in the 1950s and 1960s picked up the Streit arguments and sought to extend the process of cooperation to build a full-fledged transatlantic community that would bring together the many strands of common political, cultural, economic, and security interests between North America and Western Europe. From the late 1940s through the 1970s, a number of proponents urged creation of an "Atlantic Union," and the US Congress considered a variety of proposals aimed at stimulating this process. Representative Paul Findley, a liberal Republican from Illinois and a prominent Atlantic Union advocate, argued in 1973 that "all is not well with our present institutional methods for dealing with problems confronting the Atlantic community."[12] However, the idea of a transatlantic federation as proposed by Findley and others never received serious intergovernmental consideration. There was little official enthusiasm in Washington for such an initiative. And in Paris and elsewhere in Europe, a formalized "Atlantic Community," presumably dominated by the United States, was seen as a threat to the autonomous development of the European integration process.

In spite of continuing resistance on both sides of the Atlantic, at the February 1995 Wehrkunde Conference in Munich, Germany, foreign and defense ministers from Britain, France, and Germany put forward complementary proposals to replace the existing transatlantic bargain with a new "contract" or "covenant." The result would be a new "Atlantic Community."

The 1995 proposals were aimed at something more modest than a federal organization of transatlantic relations but more ambitious than proposals for a treaty between the United States and the European Union. No country would give up sovereignty in the arrangement, but all would pledge their individual and joint efforts to promote common interests. The ideas, as put forward, sought to capture all aspects of transatlantic relationships in a single cooperative framework. The officials offered two main arguments for their suggestions. First, they said they believed that the current institutions were inadequate to meet the needs of US-European cooperation in the post-Cold War world. The German Christian Democrat Volker Rühe, then serving as defense minister, put it simply: "The foundation for transatlantic relations has changed. NATO as the sole institutional basis is no longer sufficient."[13] British Minister of Defense Malcolm Rifkind agreed, saying, "Defense issues alone do not offer a broad enough foundation for the edifice we need."[14] Alain Juppé, then serving as French foreign minister, suggested a similar motivation when he argued that "the end of the cold war and the political assertion of Europe will force us to think through the terms of a renewed partnership if we want to prevent an insidious disintegration of the transatlantic link."[15]

Second, these officials were concerned that the United States was drifting away from its close Cold War ties to Western Europe—a worry expressed during the Clinton administration that was not in any way laid to rest in the Bush administration. Foreign Minister Juppé observed that the United States might increasingly act unilaterally rather than in concert with its allies, saying, "Across the Atlantic . . . there is a temptation . . . not to draw back, but rather to act unilaterally."[16] Rühe concluded that the Euro-Atlantic partnership "must be given fresh impetus so that states on both sides of the Atlantic are not tempted to go their own ways."[17]

The 1995 proposals provoked very little official reaction and no governmental action. One US official observed that "the vision is important" for the future,[18] but it was clear that the administration's plate was already full with NATO enlargement, relations with Russia, and the difficult situation in Bosnia. In France, policy officials were focused primarily on how the European Union could develop an autonomous military and security role within the overall framework of the transatlantic alliance but not subordinate to it.

Discussions at the February 2001 Munich Conference on Security Policy (formerly known as the Wehrkunde Conference) once again demonstrated the persistence of the Atlantic community theme. The conference focused on the burgeoning transatlantic divisions that had been exacerbated by the EU's desire to form an "autonomous" defense capability and the new Bush administration's initiatives aimed at accelerating US national missile defense programs, despite European concerns. Following the meeting, some experts and officials were attracted to the idea of negotiating a "grand bargain" in which the United States would support the

European Union's European Security and Defense Policy (ESDP) and the Europeans would accept the validity of the US approach to missile defenses.

Despite the superficial attractions of this approach, it was recognized that consummating such a deal would have been a disservice to the transatlantic relationship, giving a green light to unilateralist tendencies on both sides of the Atlantic. The exchange on this issue demonstrated that, despite the close US-European relationship, serious mutual misperceptions and misunderstandings remained, distressingly so among high-level US and European officials. Perhaps most important, the discussions revealed the need to revitalize the foundations of the transatlantic relationship.

This need has been explicitly acknowledged by a number of scholars and former officials, including Henry Kissinger, who has written that "NATO will no longer prove adequate as the sole institutional framework for Atlantic cooperation."[19] Kissinger goes on to caution,

> It is not an exaggeration to say that the future of democratic government as we understand it depends on whether the democracies bordering the North Atlantic manage to revitalize their relations in a world without Cold War and whether they can live up to the challenges of a global world order. If the Atlantic relationship gradually degenerates into the sort of rivalry that, amidst all its great achievements, spelled the end of Europe's preeminence in world affairs, the resulting crisis would undermine those values the Western societies have cherished in common.[20]

In his provocative book *The Clash of Civilizations and the Remaking of World Order*, Samuel P. Huntington argues, "If North America and Europe renew their moral life, build on their cultural commonality, and develop close forms of economic and political integration to supplement their security collaboration in NATO, they could generate a third Euro-American phase of Western economic affluence and political influence."[21] Huntington, like Kissinger, concludes with a warning: "The futures of both peace and Civilization depend upon understanding and cooperation among the political, spiritual, and intellectual leaders of the world's major civilizations. In the clash of civilizations, Europe and America will hang together or hang separately."[22]

Convincing Americans and Europeans to expand the Euro-Atlantic relationship beyond NATO and bilateral US-EU ties would not be an easy task. For most Americans, NATO is perceived as *the* transatlantic relationship. But that relationship is more than just NATO, even though NATO has effectively carried most of the burden of multilateral transatlantic relations for more than sixty years. It also involves much more than is represented by the growing US relationship with the European Union, which increasingly seeks to express Europe's political and security perspectives as well as economic policies in dealings with the United States. But the European Union does not yet include all European democracies, and different views

Photo 12.1: NATO leaders at 2009 Strasbourg/Kehl 60th Anniversary Summit (British Prime Minister Brown, US President Obama, NATO Secretary General Jaap de Hoop Scheffer, German Chancellor Merkel, French President Sarkozy)

Source: NATO Photos.

of Europe's future among its members suggest that it will be years, if not decades, before the European Union equals "Europe" in all its aspects.

Against this background, it has become clear that the challenges faced by the Euro-Atlantic allies cannot be managed effectively within NATO's narrow confines or even in a treaty between the United States and members of the European Union (EU), which would leave out Canada and important European allies, such as Norway and Turkey. Furthermore, the US-EU bilateral relationship has a distinctly functional nature—it is primarily concerned with the technical details of the US-EU relationship and has very little political prominence or association with broader goals and values.

As NATO moved beyond collective defense and into the world of crisis management—first in the Balkans and now in Afghanistan—the allies discovered that the alliance did not have all the assets required to deal with complex political, economic and social realities in defeated or failed states. This is not to say that NATO member states did not have sufficient assets or competence, but rather that NATO, as an organization, had neither the mandate nor the organizational means to deal on its own with the diverse challenges posed by terrorist threats and failed or defeated states.

The expertise and organization to deal with these non-military aspects of security rests in a great variety of institutions. The United Nations, for one, has a wide array of institutional structures that can respond to the needs of societies and states that are being re-constructed or even re-constituted. The Organization for Security and Cooperation in Europe (OSCE) has been filling a number of gaps in this field, but its area of operations does not extend beyond the organization's membership. Many diverse and capable non-governmental organizations (NGOs) are effective in dealing with specific needs, whether they be humanitarian assistance, development, education, or a variety of other fields. The European Union, which includes many NATO members, has proven itself to be able to call on a wide variety of non-military tools that can be helpful in dealing with turbulent conditions in Europe or beyond.

The problem is the absence of any coordinated approach to the use of these institutions and resources. NATO has acknowledged the need for better coordination, and has in recent ministerial and summit declarations articulated the need for a "comprehensive approach" to security. The 2009 Strasbourg/Kehl Summit Declaration reiterated that "Experience in the Balkans and Afghanistan demonstrates that today's security challenges require a comprehensive approach by the international community, combining civil and military measures and coordination." This assertion was followed by statements about progress made in this regard in coordination with the United Nations and the European Union.

However, NATO does not seek the role of "coordinator" for such a comprehensive approach, nor would other organizations want the alliance to take on such a leadership role. NATO is perceived by key players at the United Nations as a US-dominated organization, and they therefore do not want UN programs subordinated to NATO. In some respects, the same dynamic applies in the European Union, where some officials have been reluctant to expand the non-military role of the EU in Afghanistan—where help is sorely needed—because they do not want the EU to be working under a dominant NATO and US role. Non-governmental organizations largely believe that their effectiveness is enhanced by the absence of any hierarchical relationships with governments or intergovernmental organizations. These attitudes may have been mitigated to some extent by the end of the George W. Bush administration and the more reconciliatory posture of the Obama presidency, but they by no means have disappeared completely.

On the other hand, most NATO members would not want the alliance's military programs to fall under control of either the United Nations or the European Union. The difficult experience with an ineffectual UN in the Balkans in the 1990s is still a vivid memory for NATO members. The United States and other NATO members would object to any dominant EU role that affected NATO's missions.

The Case for a Reinforced Atlantic Community

While it is widely acknowledged that contemporary security challenges cannot be met with military responses alone, nobody has found the silver bullet for a "comprehensive approach." The dilemma deepens when one considers that effective performance by non-military operations (intergovernmental or non-governmental organizations) in countries such as Afghanistan or other areas of conflict rely on a degree of protection from NATO, the United States, or some other friendly entity. This frequently means that non-military assistance does not appear when needed, or is eventually chased off by violence against the providers (as happened dramatically with the United Nations in Iraq).

The United Nations some day may provide an answer to this problem, depending on the political evolution of two key Security Council members: Russia and China. Today, however, it appears that the best chance for effective coordination would be among the members of NATO and the European Union, in spite of the fact that there are well-documented obstacles to making that connection effective.

In recent years, proposals have emerged for such a step. At the 2006 Munich security conference, NATO Secretary General Jaap de Hoop Scheffer in his keynote address concluded "We must build a true strategic partnership between NATO and the EU."[23]

Early in 2006, US analyst Francis Fukuyama argued that the neo-conservative moment had passed, having failed to create a sustainable basis for US foreign and security policy. Fukuyama accepted the neo-con critique of the United Nations, but argued that "The United States needs to come up with something better than 'coalitions of the willing' to legitimate its dealings with other countries." According to Fukuyama, " . . . creating new organizations that will better balance the dual requirements of legitimacy and effectiveness will be the primary task for the coming generation."[24]

More recently, a study prepared by the Center for Strategic and International Studies suggested that "The formal establishment of a council, including all EU and NATO members, as well as the EU itself . . . would create the appropriate forum for the discussion of the critical challenges to the 21st century Euro-Atlantic Community."[25]

NATO remains politically important as the commitment the allies have made to cooperate in dealing with security challenges together and functionally as an instrument to facilitate that cooperation. There is nothing else in the world comparable to NATO's Integrated Command Structure which helps perpetuate the "habits of cooperation" that are essential to the operations of military coalitions, whether under a NATO flag, EU banner, or in an ad hoc formation led by a NATO member state.

However necessary NATO remains for contemporary security requirements, it is by no means sufficient for the security needs of the United States and Europe. Following the Iraq crisis in US-European relations, the United States and Europe needed a major initiative to help restore mutual confidence in transatlantic cooperation. It will be up to the Obama administration to shape any such initiative. Functionally, the Euro-Atlantic nations need a broader cooperative framework for security, one that includes all NATO and EU members and which concentrates on all areas of non-military cooperation—areas that are currently beyond NATO's mandate and those of other transatlantic bodies.

The Obama administration in the United States and its counterparts in Europe could make it a high priority to create such a framework. According to one proposal, they could do so by directing the preparation of a New Atlantic Community Treaty to be signed by all NATO and EU members.[26] The new treaty then could be opened for signature by all democratic states that can subscribe to and defend treaty values and goals. For example, democratic states that currently contribute to the NATO-led International Security Assistance Force in Afghanistan and other efforts intended to promote international stability, such as Australia, New Zealand, Japan and South Korea, could be invited to join. In this sense, the idea would incorporate the arguments being made (see above) for broadening the community of like-minded democracies working together on security issues.

According to this appoach, the treaty would create an Atlantic Community Treaty Organization for non-military security cooperation that would complement, not compete with, NATO and the EU. Such a structure would be ideally suited for dealing with the complex issues raised by globalization and the post-September 11 terrorist and security challenges. Regular consultations would take place among all NATO and EU members following patterns already established in both organizations.

Operation of a new Atlantic Community could include the organization of twice-yearly summit meetings among all community members as well as observers from all countries recognized as candidates for membership in those two bodies. The meetings could be scheduled in conjunction with the regular NATO and EU summits and would supplant the current US–EU summit meetings. A permanent council and ad hoc working groups would support the summit framework by discussing issues as they develop between summit sessions. This framework could usefully include a "Non-military Operations Group" that could coordinate non-military responses to security challenges, in coordination with NATO and national military responses.

To give the Community a representative dimension, the NATO Parliamentary Assembly—which owes its founding to the efforts in the early 1950s of Clarence Streit—could be transformed into the Atlantic Community Assembly, including representatives from all member states in the Community, with the mandate to study and debate the entire range of issues in the transatlantic relationship.

To help reduce institutional overlap and heavy meeting schedules for transatlantic officials, all items currently on the US–EU agenda could be transferred to the new forum, covering virtually all aspects of transatlantic relations and including all countries with interests in the relationship, unlike the more narrow US–EU consultations. When specific US–EU issues arise, they could be handled in bilateral US–EU talks. Atlantic Community institutions could be established in or near Brussels, Belgium, to facilitate coordination with NATO and EU institutions.

It might be beneficial to address some other consolidation issues at the same time. The Euro-Atlantic Partnership Council (EAPC) in NATO has never established itself as a uniquely useful forum for dialogue and cooperation. At the same time, the Organization for Security and Cooperation in Europe (OSCE) could be strengthened as the body that would bring together the members of the new Atlantic Community and all the other states in Europe that do not qualify for or do not seek Atlantic Community membership, including, most important, Russia and Ukraine. Shifting all relevant EAPC functions to the OSCE framework would be a useful consolidation of European structures. The main responsibility of the OSCE would be to provide the "collective security" function for relations among states in Europe, helping build peace and cooperation across the Continent through confidence building and arms control measures, early warning, conflict prevention, crisis management, and post-conflict rehabilitation activities.

Approaching problems and issues from the broad perspective offered by an Atlantic Community framework would open up possibilities for consideration of and action on issues that are discussed unofficially among allied representatives at NATO but are not within NATO's formal mandate. In an Atlantic Community forum, there would be a better opportunity for a dynamic problem-solving synergy to develop when all aspects of issues can be put on the table. This would be a dynamic and inclusive "comprehensive approach."

Reaction to the 2001 terrorist attacks on the United States makes a good example. If there had been an Atlantic Community Council on September 11, it could immediately have established working groups to address all aspects of the campaign against sources of international terror. The North Atlantic Council would not have been required to wait for the Atlantic Community Council to act and could have invoked Article 5 on September 12 just as it did. However, in the meantime, discussions in the Atlantic Community Council could have been coordinating the response of police authorities in Community countries, discussing actions to cut off sources of financial support to terrorists, developing public diplomacy themes to accompany military and diplomatic action, and beginning consideration of long-term strategies designed to undermine support for terrorist activities. The Non-military Operations Group could have begun developing international actions and coordinating national responses.

A new Atlantic Community would embrace, not replace, NATO in the overall framework of transatlantic relations. Because it would be a consultative forum only, it would not threaten the "autonomy" of the European Union or undermine NATO's Article 5 collective defense commitment. In fact, it could help bridge the current artificial gap between NATO discussions of security policy and US–EU consultations on economic issues, which have important overlapping dimensions.

Because an Atlantic Community would encourage members to address issues that NATO does not tackle, the new structure would provide added value beyond that offered by the traditional alliance. It might also provide some additional options for shaping coalitions willing to deal with new security challenges in cases where using the NATO framework might not be acceptable to all allies and where action could be blocked by a single dissenting member.

Such an initiative would admittedly face some tough questions. Diplomats are reluctant to open the transatlantic relationship for review and revision, fearing with some justification that the outcome might be worse than the status quo. Some critics might ask what another "talk shop" among the Western democracies would accomplish. Would consultations in the Atlantic Community framework eventually take precedence over those in NATO's North Atlantic Council? Would such a forum have avoided Euro-Atlantic differences over Bosnia and Kosovo or Iraq? Would discussions in such a forum contribute to the settlement of transatlantic economic issues? Would US participation in such a setting simply add to the expense of US international involvement at a time when some want to reduce the scope and cost of the US role in the world? Some might question whether the proposal is an attempt to substitute process (more consultations) for a diminishing substance (common interests) in the relationship. Others might charge that such a community would threaten the independence of the European Union, others that the United States would be sacrificing sovereignty.

The answer to all these questions is that no one outcome is guaranteed, and all such questions would have to be answered by the choices made by participating governments. Some in Europe and in the United States might prefer to move away from alliance and toward something more like a "handshake relationship" in which cooperation continues but in a more ad hoc, less institutionalized, setting. This formula might yield greater freedom of maneuver for the United States and a uniting Europe but would also likely produce more tensions and frictions, given the lack of a solemn commitment to cooperation as a frame of reference.

To advance a framework for non-military security cooperation like the one discussed above, Europe would have to show a greater willingness to blend its impressive soft power capabilities with hard power to provide coherent answers to tomorrow's challenges. And the United States would have to build a better balance between soft and hard power instruments in its foreign and security policy tool kit—a process that has begun under the Obama administration. In the long run, the effective marriage of US and European soft and hard power capabilities would help prevent some problems from becoming military challenges, and enhance the ability of the world community to deal with post-conflict scenarios in ways that promote stability.

These questions and issues should all be considered in a debate on the need for a new Atlantic Community. The point, however, is that such a debate is required. No consultative arrangement will guarantee that the United States and Europe will be able to solve all problems between them. But without a renewed commitment to community and without the necessary institutional settings for dialogue and cooperation, the foundations of the transatlantic relationship could be at risk.

In sum, the diverse nature of twenty-first-century issues affecting allied interests suggests the need for a new initiative designed to broaden the context of the transatlantic relationship. The point of doing so would be to give form and substance to the apparent belief of all allied governments that, even in the absence of a Soviet threat and in the face of new terrorist challenges, they continue to share—and need to defend—many values, goals, and interests.

Even if such an initiative remains beyond the realm of the "politically possible," it is nonetheless remarkable that this transatlantic bargain has continued to survive crisis after crisis through its 60-plus years—not one country has left NATO, many have joined, and others wait outside the door. Is this Euro-Atlantic arrangement becoming the "permanent alliance" against which America's founding fathers warned, and which others have denied could exist? We conclude with discussion of this issue in the next chapter.

Notes

1. Charles A. Kupchan, "Reviving the West: For an Atlantic Union," *Foreign Affairs* 75(3) (May/June 1996), 93.
2. Kupchan, "Reviving . . . ," 97.
3. Charles A. Kupchan, "Atlantic Orders: The Fundamentals of Change," in Geir Lundestad, ed. *Just another Major Crisis: The United States and Europe Since 2000.* Oxford, UK: Oxford University Press, 2008, 54.
4. Dmitry Medvedev, "President of Russia Dmitry Medvedev's Speech at Meeting with German Political, Parliamentary and Civic Leaders, Berlin, June 5, 2008," Ministry of Foreign Affairs of the Russian Federation, Press and Information Department, June 6, 2008.
5. Medvedev, Berlin speech.
6. Australia, in particular, has taken on demanding and dangerous missions in Afghanistan.
7. Ivo Daalder and James Goldgeier, "Global NATO," *Foreign Affairs* 85(5) (September/October 2006), 110.
8. John McCain, "America must be a good role model, *Financial Times,* March 18, 2008 http://www.ft.com/cms/s/0/c7e219e2-f4ea-11dc-a21b-000077b07658.html?nclick_check=1 [accessed July 27, 2009].
9. *Final Report of the Princeton Project on National Security,* (PDF version) 11.
10. Clarence Streit, *Union Now, A Proposal for a Federal Union of the Democracies of the North Atlantic* (New York: Harper and Brothers, 1939).
11. The Streit Council, "A Brief History," http://www.streitcouncil.org/content/about_us/History/brief_history.html [accessed July 27, 2009].
12. For further details, see US House Committee on Foreign Affairs, Subcommittee on International Organizations and Movements, Hearing on H.J. Res. 205, 206, 213, 218, 387, H. Cong. Res. 39, 67, 93rd Cong., 1st sess., March 26, 1973.
13. Volker Rühe, "Europe and America—A New Partnership for the Future" (speech to the annual Wehrkunde Conference, Munich, Germany, February 1995).
14. Joseph Fitchett, "Western European Proposes New Trans-Atlantic Pact," *International Herald Tribune,* February 7, 1995, 1.
15. M. Alain Juppé (speech on the occasion of the twentieth anniversary of the Centre d'analyse et de prévision, Paris, January 30, 1995).

16. Juppé (speech).
17. Rühe, "Europe and America."
18. Fitchett, "Western European Proposes New Trans-Atlantic Pact," 1.
19. Henry Kissinger, *Does America Need a Foreign Policy? Toward a Diplomacy for the 21st Century* (New York: Simon & Schuster, 2001), 80.
20. Kissinger, *Does America Need a Foreign Policy?* 81–82.
21. Samuel P. Huntington, *The Clash of Civilizations: Remaking of World Order* (New York: Simon & Schuster, 1996), 308.
22. Huntington, *The Clash of Civilizations*, 321.
23. Jaap de Hoop Scheffer, "Speech at the 42nd Munich Conference on Security Policy," February 4, 2006.
24. Francis Fukuyama, "After Neoconservatism," *The New York Times*, February 19, 2006, NYTimes.com [accessed May 17, 2007].
25. Franklin D. Kramer and Simon Serfaty, "Initiative for a Renewed Transatlantic Partnership," Center for Strategic and International Studies, February 1, 2007.
26. A suggested draft of such a treaty can be found in Stanley R. Sloan, *NATO, the European Union and the Atlantic Community: The Transatlantic Bargain Challenged* (Lanham, Md.: Rowman and Littlefield, 2005).

CHAPTER 13

Permanent Alliance?

With NATO, we are all Europeanists; we are all Atlanticists.

—*Lawrence S. Kaplan*[1]

Perhaps the biggest threat to the viability of the transatlantic bargain has been the tension between Atlanticist and Euro-centric perspectives in the alliance. Lawrence Kaplan's assertion may be somewhat optimistic, but it appears increasingly true. Acceptance of the fact that American and European values and interests create a unique sense of community has spread, and officials on both sides of the Atlantic now are more focused on how to make the processes of European integration and transatlantic cooperation work in complementary rather than competitive ways.

This emerging reality raises the question of whether or not the transatlantic alliance has become a "permanent alliance" between the North American and European democracies, one that is providing the core for broader cooperation among democratic states around the globe.

No Entangling Alliances

As noted in the first chapter of this volume, America's founding fathers had seen enough of European intrigues and involvement in attempts to establish the United States of America. In 1796, George Washington announced in his "Farewell Address" that he would not run for a third term, which at that time the constitution permitted. Most of Washington's address was dedicated to domestic questions, but his words on foreign relations linger as the most memorable. Washington cautioned

> [T]he great rule of conduct for us in regard to foreign nations is in extending our commercial relations, to have with them as little political connection as possible. So far as we have already formed engagements, let them be fulfilled with perfect good faith. Here let us stop. Europe has a set of primary interests which to us have none, or a very remote relation. Hence she must be engaged in frequent controversies, the causes of which are essentially foreign to our concerns . . .
>
> . . . Why, by interweaving our destiny with that of any part of Europe, entangle our peace and prosperity in the toils of European ambition, rivalship, interest, humor or caprice?

It is our true policy to steer clear of permanent alliances with any portion of the foreign world; so far, I mean, as we are now at liberty to do it; for let me not be understood as capable of patronizing infidelity to existing engagements ...

Taking care always to keep ourselves by suitable establishments on a respectable defensive posture, we may safely trust to temporary alliances for extraordinary emergencies.

Thomas Jefferson, in his 1801 inaugural address, added his own exclamation point to Washington's warning, proclaiming that the United States should seek "peace, commerce, and honest friendship with all nations, entangling alliances with none." This early policy of non-interventionism reflected the fact that this was a young democracy, filled with potential, wary of the ways of the "old world" and concerned about potential threats from stronger European powers. Washington's and Jefferson's pleas for peace and commerce with other nations but no involvement in power balances or alignments accurately reflected the national interests of this revolutionary American project.

This policy proved incredibly persistent, largely because subsequent experiences with European powers, particularly Great Britain, confirmed the potential threat and the need for commerce and peace with all other nations to allow the dynamic process of growth and expansion to take place from America's Atlantic coast to the Pacific. As one author has suggested, "It became more than a policy; it became an expression of a national point of view about ourselves and our place in the world, a view which contrasted the simple virtues of our Republic with the subtle and complex qualities (some said corruptions) of Europe."[2]

Very little that happened in Europe in the nineteenth century suggested that the founding fathers had been wrong. The United States kept clear of the European alliance machinations and wars. British Foreign Secretary Lord Palmerston seemed to confirm the wisdom of the American choice when he declared that "Nations have no permanent friends or allies, they only have permanent interests."

In the twentieth century, the United States was forced by events to abandon non-intervention in European affairs as it joined the fight against the axis powers in World War I. However, the continuing strength of isolationism was demonstrated when President Woodrow Wilson was unable to convince the US Senate to give its advice and consent to ratification of the League of Nations treaty. Three decades later, America's critical involvement in World War II convinced a majority of Americans that the United States could no longer stand aside from international affairs. The Senate approved the United Nations Charter and then, facing the perceived threat from a communist Soviet Union, gave its advice and consent to the North Atlantic Treaty, not only involving the United States in a treaty with European powers, but installing it as the leader of the coalition.

For many Senators who voted in support of the North Atlantic Treaty, the commitment presumably was viewed as consistent with George Washington's loophole: that the United States could engage in foreign commitments "for extraordinary emergencies." Over sixty years later, however, the "emergency" is certainly over, but the alliance continues. Does this suggest that the transatlantic bargain has become an unbreakable Euro-Atlantic contract?

A Unique Alliance

What is it about the transatlantic bargain that has ensured its survival? The Soviet threat provided the main rationale and explanation until the Warsaw Pact disbanded and the Soviet Union disintegrated. In 1989, with the fall of the Berlin Wall, that explanation began to disappear, and the allies were left to assert in the early 1990s that unspecified threats and risks could require allied military cooperation in the future.

Those assertions by NATO governments were not credible to many experts who predicted the demise of an alliance whose founding rationale had gone away. Even during the Cold War, the transatlantic alliance had been said to be in crisis or disarray on a continuing basis, whether caused by the US failure to support the British and French invasion of the Suez in 1956, France's departure from NATO's Integrated Command Structure in 1966, differences over how to deal with the 1979 Soviet invasion of Afghanistan, deployment of intermediate-range nuclear missiles in Europe in the 1980s, or other causes of friction and debate. Why wouldn't such differences in the future lead the allies to abandon the cooperation that had seemed so essential during the Cold War?

One expert, Wallace J. Thies, has provided a detailed and compelling answer to this question. According to Thies, NATO is different from previous alliances in at least two key ways. First, it was established not just to meet a specific threat or serve a narrow purpose, but was designed to have much more lasting utility. Second, NATO was an alliance among liberal democracies, with a value foundation that previous alliances had lacked. On the first point, Thies argues that

> . . . pre-1939 alliances were often little more than temporary arrangements created to address a particular need—typically to launch an attack or repel one—after which they were disbanded or rendered inoperative. The Atlantic Alliance, in contrast, was intended to be both permanent and open ended, as evidenced by the deliberate omission of a terminal date from the North Atlantic Treaty and the permissively worded provisions for consultations in Articles 4 and 9.[3]

Regarding the unique nature of the alliance, Thies writes,

> The Atlantic Alliance . . . was intended to promote cooperation among its members that would be both intensive and extensive, as symbolized by the commitment in Article 3 to "continuous and effective self-help and mutual aid" and the inclusion of Article 2 with its provisions for cooperation in nonmilitary endeavors . . . The Atlantic Alliance . . . was formed by members sharing

a common heritage, common values, and common interests, backed by a willingness to pool their resources in peacetime as well as wartime for the sake of defending and advancing those common values and interests.[4]

Thies maintains that evidence usually offered to suggest impending doom for the alliance—". . . critical comments, rude behavior, mutual exasperation and even anger . . ."[5]—can be misleading. The evidence summoned by Thies suggests that when the allies appear to be on the verge of a deal-breaking dispute, they usually make the most serious efforts to find common ground, make compromises, or work around issues. He concludes, "Unlike many pre-1939 alliances, which collapsed at the first hint of troubles among the members, the democracies that make up the Atlantic Alliance have shown a willingness to do whatever it takes—even outright policy reversals—to heal a rift in the Alliance.[6]

The frequent difficult periods described by many of us over the years as "crises" in the alliance, were in fact difficult circumstances that might have brought a less solid alliance to an end. Some Sinologists have argued that the Chinese characters for "crisis" do not translate into "danger creating opportunity," as it has been popular to say.[7] However, it is true that while each crisis has left marks on the alliance, most of the wounds healed quickly and the alliance members refused to let their differences bring the alliance down. More often than not, the perception of a crisis helped provide the stimulus for resolution or at least management of the issue at hand. The transatlantic bargain is, without question, an alliance of commitment, not just convenience.

At the end of the Cold War some observers speculated that, without an existential threat to keep the allies together, the natural economic frictions among the allies would lead to their strategic divorce. During the Cold War, the allies fought over a wide variety of economic issues—ranging from debates over imports of chickens (the "chicken war"[8]) to subsidies for European farmers (the European Union's Common Agricultural Policy). It seemed natural to some analysts that the predictable trade and financial frictions between the United States and Europe would threaten cooperation on broader political and security relations. This did not happen. In fact, the end of the Cold War witnessed a dramatic expansion of transatlantic trade and economic interdependence. The international economic system accommodated the inclusion of many new and important players, but continued to revolve around the relatively stable core of transatlantic cooperation.

The reality is that it was not the Soviet threat that kept economic differences from destroying the alliance during the Cold War, it was the nature of the international economic system. That system is based on a complex and imperfect set of rules and regulations. The natural interaction of competition among trading states produces frictions which can lead to trade disputes and bilateral tensions. However, the system also relies on resolution of such conflicts through negotiations and adoption of new rules and new financial and economic relationships. All trading partners know this. They understand that their interests require eventual settlement of disputes. They also understand that new competition and conflicts will arise, and will require the same process of negotiation and compromise to return to cooperation. The system, in this general sense, was self-regulating during the Cold War, and is so today. It does not require an external threat to function effectively.

Permanent Alliance?

Does this all suggest that the transatlantic bargain, with NATO at its heart, has become a permanent alliance? If we acknowledge that nothing in life lasts forever, the transatlantic bargain between the United States, Canada and its European allies appears as close to a permanent international alliance as has ever been fashioned by sovereign independent states. Its appearance of permanence is based on the fact that it is founded on shared values and interests and that the arrangement does not attempt to impose supranational constraints on its members. It respects, honors and defends their sovereignty and independence.

The question for the foreseeable future may not be whether the alliance will persist, but whether or not it will be of increasing or diminishing value to the participants. It is, after all, the perceptions of the member states, their leaders and publics that will determine how well or poorly the alliance works in the future.

What, then, are the most important challenges to the effective functioning of this arrangement? At this writing, based on recent experience, a few challenges in particular stand out.

Challenges

The first decade of the twenty-first century revealed how unilateral behavior on both sides of the Atlantic can limit the effectiveness of the alliance. The most important characteristic of the new international system remains the emergence of the United States as the only true global superpower—not omnipotent, but more powerful than any other nation or organized group of nations on this earth. Having been subjected to a brutal terrorist attack on innocent civilians at this critical point in its national history left the United States a more intense and less predictable international actor. How the United States decides to use its power and influence will have a major impact on the future of the alliance that it still leads. Will it continue to move away from the unilateralism and paranoia that irritated and alienated even its best allies in order to find a way to be a confident and effective leader? The bottom line is that, for the transatlantic alliance to thrive in the future, the United States will have to find ways to balance the advantages of multilateral cooperation and burden sharing against the temptations and attractions of unilateralism.

How the European allies react to US leadership is also important. Most European nations appear prepared to follow a benign US hegemon on most major issues. Will the incredible power and capabilities of the United States convince the allies to follow, even when the United States leads with a clumsy hand? Or will the allies revolt, periodically, individually, or as a group, in response to heavy-handed US unilateralism? In terms of capabilities, will the allies respond to US leadership by creating the capabilities required to make serious military contributions to global military operations? Will they decide to take the "easy road" of concentrating on their soft-power resources and allow the United States to take most responsibility for military capabilities? Or will they build up significant European military capabilities intended to give Europe more leverage over US decisions? If the EU's European Security and Defense Policy is to be taken seriously in Washington, the EU members will have to demonstrate that the new aspect of the unification process adds capabilities to the transatlantic inventory of security tools, not just institutions and acronyms.

At the national level, for Europe to play its part in maintaining a positive transatlantic dynamic, Germany will be required to find a new balance in its policies that serves two old masters—Europeanism and Atlanticism—while responding to its rediscovered, redefined, and reenergized sense of national interests. France will have to give more weight to the transatlantic dimension of its interests, as President Sarkozy appears to have done. Great Britain will be required to be a "good European" while remaining Washington's trusted partner.

The attitudes and capabilities the United States and Europe bring to the NATO table in the years immediately ahead will determine whether the alliance will become part of the answer to problems of global instability. If NATO—meaning, of course, the NATO nations—successfully manages the stabilization effort in Afghanistan, it will establish its credentials as a serious and constructive device for multilateral security cooperation for the international community. Of course, failure in any mission the members assign to the alliance could have disastrous consequences for NATO's credibility and future utility.

In addition, demographic challenges could complicate the alliance's future. In past years, many Europeans worried that America's demographic shift away from its Anglo-Saxon population base toward a more Asian and Hispanic one could refocus US priorities in relations with Europe. However, as those changes slowly work their way into the American system, it seems that it is the acceptance of the American system of government that is the key variable, not one's ancestry. Belief in and defense of democracy, individual liberty and the rule of law is arguably the glue holding the United States together.

Now, there is concern about Europe's changing demographic base. One American analyst has argued that demographic trends in Europe could create some severe problems for the alliance in the near future. Jeffrey Simon argues that a number of troubling factors are at work.[9] Native populations in most European NATO countries are declining, and average ages are increasing, diminishing the pool of young individuals available for military service. Smaller European populations will also mean less economic weight and reduced influence on the international scene. In addition, immigration and reproductive trends in Europe are steadily increasing the percentage of the population that is of Muslim origin, raising questions about the values that this growing part of European electorates will follow.

The demographic challenge could, on the one hand, force Europe to cooperate even more closely with the United States. On the other hand, a shrinking European economic and military contribution to the alliance could raise further burden-sharing problems. The big question, however, will be whether or not the allies continue to value the importance of democracy, individual liberty and rule of law for the future of their societies. Perhaps the demographic trends will create further pressures for bringing other democracies into the bargain to help defend those values against threats posed by radical groups, unstable governments and authoritarian regimes.

Outlook

At the end of the day, there are two basic requirements for NATO to be perceived as important enough for the member states to ensure its survival. Put most simply, the United States must be convinced that political and military cooperation with the European allies makes an important net contribution to US interests. On the other side of the coin, Europeans must believe that contributing to international security efforts alongside the United States will produce influence for Europe over US decisions that affect their security. These are the fundamental terms for continuation of a vital, productive transatlantic bargain.

In fact, the twenty-first century NATO is not "your father's NATO." It has prospered by adapting to new international conditions, including political changes inside the alliance itself. It will have to continue the process of change in order to ensure its "permanence."

Expansion of membership in the alliance has brought with it not only predictions of deadlock among a larger number of allies but also proposals for adding supranational aspects to the alliance's decision-making process. Following the divisive debate over aid to Turkey, the US Senate passed a resolution in May 2003 suggesting the United States look for ways to enable NATO to act without a full consensus and to suspend difficult members from alliance decision making.[10] Proponents argued that a NATO that had grown to 26 members and was likely to have more in the future might have an increasingly difficult time reaching a meaningful consensus. As superficially attractive as such proposals might appear, neither is likely or desirable. NATO is an alliance of sovereign states based on cooperation, not supranational integration. The requirement for consensus has been constructively bent in the past, for example when the Netherlands took footnotes to language about NATO nuclear policy in the 1980s, Greece abstained constructively (not supporting but not blocking) on NATO's attack on Serbian forces in Kosovo, and when, in the 2003 Turkish case, the decision was moved to the Defense Planning Committee to avoid a French veto in the North Atlantic Council.

It seems quite unlikely that the NATO members—least of all the United States—will want the alliance to become a supranational body rather than a cooperative framework among sovereign states. In such a case, the consensus process clearly will need to be flexed from time to time, as it has been in the past, but it seems unlikely to be "fixed."[11]

One important "flexing" of NATO's consensus procedure could be to ensure that NATO commanders are delegated sufficient authority to run a military operation without frequent resort to the North Atlantic Council for detailed guidance, as was the case in the air war against Serbia over Kosovo. If there is a compelling case for NATO to act, effective diplomacy and leadership on both sides of the Atlantic in most cases will produce a consensus or at least a situation where no country will veto. Perhaps a good example in this regard was provided by the initial refusal of six allies to provide military officers to staff NATO's training facility in Iraq but their willingness to allow the operation to go ahead with officers provided by the other allies.

On the question of suspending troublesome members, simply considering such a procedure would be divisive in the extreme and not worth the trouble. If NATO is not able to function in the future because of the obstinacy of one or more members then the alliance would be in danger of slipping toward irrelevance. Chances are, if the United States and the European allies continue to see transatlantic security cooperation as in their interest, they will find ways to compromise on difficult issues and to move ahead, using ad hoc coalition approaches when absolutely necessary to get around opposition to making an operation a formal NATO mission.

Respect for the sovereign decisions of member states has, of course, been the underlying problem with NATO's operation of the International Security Assistance Force (ISAF) in Afghanistan. As discussed in Chapter 9, ISAF's effectiveness was handicapped by the fact that some countries were unwilling to allow their troops to operate in parts of Afghanistan and in circumstances that would put them at greater risk. It is well understood that political realities and historical experiences have determined the approaches that nations have taken to this issue. The eventual evaluation of NATO's performance in Afghanistan will undoubtedly reflect such problems, even if the long run produces a relatively successful outcome. Assessing the mission's effectiveness will become part of the process of adapting the alliance to future security challenges.

Will the NATO members continue to find NATO cooperation to their advantage, even with a difficult experience in Afghanistan? Only time will tell. However, history suggests that, in spite of their differences, the United States and Europe will try to keep their act together. And today, NATO remains an important part of the script for that routine. Dealing with the threats posed by terrorism and managing most other aspects of transatlantic relations demand more effective transatlantic cooperation in political, economic, financial, and social as well as military aspects of the relationship.

The bottom line, therefore, is that the transatlantic bargain will survive Afghanistan. The alliance has already shown its resilience during the early twenty-first century when decisions by the Bush administration put alliance cooperation under severe pressure.

The bargain will survive in part because the security of the member states cannot be ensured through national measures alone. It will survive because the member states will continue to recognize that imperfect cooperation serves their interests better than no cooperation at all. NATO will be adapted to meet new challenges. And the value foundation of the transatlantic bargain will persist, in spite of differences over specific issues and shifting patterns of member state interests.

It will survive in part because the bargain is not just NATO. In fact, recent trends suggest that there is much more creative thought and political momentum behind enhancing transatlantic cooperation rather than diminishing it. As Lawrence S. Kaplan has observed, "The transatlantic bargain still resonates in the twenty-first century."[12] As a result, this bargain in the hearts and minds of the member states has become as close as one could imagine to being a "permanent alliance."

Notes

1. Lawrence S. Kaplan, "Atlanticists vs. Europeanists in NATO," in *NATO and the European Union, Confronting the Challenges of European Security and Enlargement*, S. Victor Papacosma and Pierre-Henri Laurent, eds. (Kent, Ohio: Lyman Lemnitzer Center for NATO and European Union Studies, 1999), 17.
2. David Fromkin, "Entangling Alliances," *Foreign Affairs* 48 no. 4 (July 1970): 688.
3. Wallace J. Thies, *Why NATO Endures* (New York: Cambridge University Press, 2009), 288.
4. Thies, *Why NATO Endures*.
5. Thies, *Why NATO Endures*, 306–07.
6. Thies, *Why NATO Endures*, 207.
7. Victor H. Mair, "danger + opportunity ≠ crisis, How a misunderstanding about Chinese characters has led many astray," Pīnyīn.info, http://www.pinyin.info/chinese/crisis.html [accessed August 17, 2009].
8. In 1962 the European Economic Community (EEC—precursor to the European Union) raised tariffs on imports of chicken. The new levels denied US producers access to the EEC poultry market. The United States retaliated by increasing tariffs on four European exports: potato starch, dextrin, brandy, and light trucks. This trade dispute became known as "the chicken war."
9. Jeffrey Simon, "NATO's Uncertain Future: Is Demography Destiny," National Defense University, US National Defense University Strategic Forum, No. 236, October 2008.
10. US Congress, Congressional Record—Senate, May 8, 2003, S5882.
11. For an excellent study of the issue see Leo G. Michel, "NATO Decisionmaking: Au Revoir to Consensus?" National Defense University, US National Defense University Strategic Forum, No. 202, August 2003. http://www.ndu.edu/inss/strforum/SF202/SF202.pdf [accessed August 17, 2009].
12. Lawrence S. Kaplan, *NATO 1948, The Birth of the Transatlantic Alliance*, (Lanham, Md.: Rowman & Littlefield, 2007), 242.

APPENDIX

The North Atlantic Treaty: Washington D.C.—April 4, 1949

The Parties to this Treaty reaffirm their faith in the purposes and principles of the Charter of the United Nations and their desire to live in peace with all peoples and all governments.

They are determined to safeguard the freedom, common heritage and civilisation of their peoples, founded on the principles of democracy, individual liberty and the rule of law. They seek to promote stability and well-being in the North Atlantic area.

They are resolved to unite their efforts for collective defence and for the preservation of peace and security. They therefore agree to this North Atlantic Treaty:

Article 1

The Parties undertake, as set forth in the Charter of the United Nations, to settle any international dispute in which they may be involved by peaceful means in such a manner that international peace and security and justice are not endangered, and to refrain in their international relations from the threat or use of force in any manner inconsistent with the purposes of the United Nations.

Article 2

The Parties will contribute toward the further development of peaceful and friendly international relations by strengthening their free institutions, by bringing about a better understanding of the principles upon which these institutions are founded, and by promoting conditions of stability and well-being. They will seek to eliminate conflict in their international economic policies and will encourage economic collaboration between any or all of them.

Article 3

In order more effectively to achieve the objectives of this Treaty, the Parties, separately and jointly, by means of continuous and effective self-help and mutual aid, will maintain and develop their individual and collective capacity to resist armed attack.

Article 4

The Parties will consult together whenever, in the opinion of any of them, the territorial integrity, political independence or security of any of the Parties is threatened.

Article 5

The Parties agree that an armed attack against one or more of them in Europe or North America shall be considered an attack against them all and consequently they agree that, if such an armed attack occurs, each of them, in exercise of the right of individual or collective self-defence recognised by Article 51 of the Charter of the United Nations, will assist the Party or Parties so attacked by taking forthwith, individually and in concert with the other Parties, such action as it deems necessary, including the use of armed force, to restore and maintain the security of the North Atlantic area.

Any such armed attack and all measures taken as a result thereof shall immediately be reported to the Security Council. Such measures shall be terminated when the Security Council has taken the measures necessary to restore and maintain international peace and security.

Article 6[1]

For the purpose of Article 5, an armed attack on one or more of the Parties is deemed to include an armed attack:

- on the territory of any of the Parties in Europe or North America, on the Algerian Departments of France,[2] on the territory of or on the Islands under the jurisdiction of any of the Parties in the North Atlantic area north of the Tropic of Cancer;
- on the forces, vessels, or aircraft of any of the Parties, when in or over these territories or any other area in Europe in which occupation forces of any of the Parties were stationed on the date when the Treaty entered into force or the Mediterranean Sea or the North Atlantic area north of the Tropic of Cancer.

Article 7

This Treaty does not affect, and shall not be interpreted as affecting in any way the rights and obligations under the Charter of the Parties which are members of the United Nations, or the primary responsibility of the Security Council for the maintenance of international peace and security.

Article 8

Each Party declares that none of the international engagements now in force between it and any other of the Parties or any third State is in conflict with the provisions of this Treaty, and undertakes not to enter into any international engagement in conflict with this Treaty.

Article 9

The Parties hereby establish a Council, on which each of them shall be represented, to consider matters concerning the implementation of this Treaty. The Council shall be so organised as to be able to meet promptly at any time. The Council shall set up such subsidiary bodies as may be necessary; in particular it shall establish immediately a defence committee which shall recommend measures for the implementation of Articles 3 and 5.

Article 10

The Parties may, by unanimous agreement, invite any other European State in a position to further the principles of this Treaty and to contribute to the security of the North Atlantic area to accede to this Treaty. Any State so invited may become a Party to the Treaty by depositing its instrument of accession with the Government of the United States of America. The Government of the United States of America will inform each of the Parties of the deposit of each such instrument of accession.

Article 11

This Treaty shall be ratified and its provisions carried out by the Parties in accordance with their respective constitutional processes. The instruments of ratification shall be deposited as soon as possible with the Government of the United States of America, which will notify all the other signatories of each deposit. The Treaty shall enter into force between the States which have ratified it as soon as the ratifications of the majority of the signatories, including the ratifications of Belgium, Canada, France, Luxembourg, the Netherlands, the United Kingdom and the United States, have been deposited and shall come into effect with respect to other States on the date of the deposit of their ratifications. ([3])

Article 12

After the Treaty has been in force for ten years, or at any time thereafter, the Parties shall, if any of them so requests, consult together for the purpose of reviewing the Treaty, having regard for the factors then affecting peace and security in the North Atlantic area, including the development of universal as well as regional arrangements under the Charter of the United Nations for the maintenance of international peace and security.

Article 13

After the Treaty has been in force for twenty years, any Party may cease to be a Party one year after its notice of denunciation has been given to the Government of the United States of America, which will inform the Governments of the other Parties of the deposit of each notice of denunciation.

Article 14

This Treaty, of which the English and French texts are equally authentic, shall be deposited in the archives of the Government of the United States of America. Duly certified copies will be transmitted by that Government to the Governments of other signatories.

Notes

1. The definition of the territories to which Article 5 applies was revised by Article 2 of the Protocol to the North Atlantic Treaty on the accession of Greece and Turkey signed on 22 October 1951.
2. On January 16, 1963, the North Atlantic Council noted that insofar as the former Algerian Departments of France were concerned, the relevant clauses of this Treaty had become inapplicable as from July 3, 1962.
3. The Treaty came into force on 24 August 1949, after the deposition of the ratifications of all signatory states.

Select Bibliography

For basic NATO information refer to *The NATO Handbook* (Brussels: NATO Office of Information and Press, July 2002). Information beyond this digital handbook can be found under "issues" and other headings at www.nato.int. European Union information, including a chronology of developments from 1945 to the present day, is on the Europa website at http://europa.eu/abc/history/index_en.htm. On many of the topics covered in this volume, the Congressional Research Service produces and updates objective and non-partisan reports. Most of the CRS reports cannot be obtained directly from CRS but fortunately can be accessed at www.opencrs.com. The London Centre for European Reform produces excellent analyses of issues affecting the process of European integration. Other very useful websites include that of the EU Institute for Security Studies, at www.iss-eu.org, where the Chaillot Papers are located; the Atlantic Council of the United States, at www.acus.org; the Atlantic Initiative (Berlin) at http://www.atlantic-community.org,and the author's Atlantic Community Initiative, at www.AtlanticCommunity.org, where a "living history" of the Atlantic Community that supplements the information in this volume can be found.

Acheson, Dean. *Present at the Creation: My Years in the State Department.* New York: W. W. Norton, 1969.

Asmus, Ronald D., Richard L. Kugler, and F. Stephen Larrabee. "Building a New NATO." *Foreign Affairs,* September–October 1993, 28–40.

Baker, James A. *The Politics of Diplomacy: Revolution, War and Peace, 1989–1992.* New York: G. P. Putnam's Sons, 1995.

Balladur, Edouard. *For a Union of the West between Europe and the United States.* Stanford, Ca: Hoover Intitution, 2009.

Bannerman, Edward, Steven Everts, Heather Grabbe, Charles Grant, and Alasdair Murray. *Europe after September 11th.* London: Centre for European Reform, 2001.

Binnendijk, Hans and Cordero, Gina, eds. *Transforming NATO: An NDU Anthology.* Washington, D.C.: Center for Technology and National Security, National Defense University, 2008.

Boniface, Pascale. "The Specter of Unilateralism," *Washington Quarterly,* summer 2001, 155–62.

Boxhoorn, Bram, Niklaas Hoekstra, and Rob de Wijk, eds. *NATO after Kosovo.* Breda, the Netherlands: Royal Netherlands Military Academy, 2000.

Braun, Aurel, ed. *NATO-Russia Relations in the Twenty-First Century.* Abingdon: Routledge, 2008.

Brenner, Michael. *Terms of Engagement: The United States and the European Security Identity.* The Washington Papers no. 176. Center for Strategic and International Studies. Westport, Conn.: Praeger, 1998.

Brenner, Michael, and Guillaume Parmentier. *Reconcilable Differences: U.S.-French Relations in the New Era.* Washington, D.C.: Brookings Institution Press, 2002.

Buchan, Alistair. *NATO in the 1960s: The Implications of Interdependence.* New York: Praeger, 1963.

Bush, George, and Brent Scowcroft. *A World Transformed.* New York: Knopf, 1998.

Clark, Wesley K. *Waging Modern War: Bosnia, Kosovo, and the Future of Combat.* New York: Public Affairs, 2001.

Cleveland, Harlan. *NATO: The Transatlantic Bargain.* New York: Harper & Row, 1970.

Cole, Alistair. *François Mitterrand: A Study in Political Leadership.* New York: Routledge, 1994.

Cook, Don. *Forging the Alliance.* New York: Arbor House, 1989.

Daalder, Ivo H. *Getting to Dayton: The Making of America's Bosnia Policy.* Washington, D.C.: Brookings Institution Press, 2000.

Daalder, Ivo H., and Goldgeier, James. "Global NATO." *Foreign Affairs*, September/October 2006.

Daalder, Ivo H., and Michael E. O'Hanlon. *Winning Ugly: NATO's War to Save Kosovo.* Washington, D.C.: Brookings Institution Press, 2000.

de Wijk, Rob. *NATO on the Brink of the New Millennium: The Battle for Consensus.* London: Brassey's, 1997.

Dean, Jonathan. *Watershed in Europe: Dismantling the East-West Military Confrontation.* Lexington, Mass.: Lexington Books, 1987.

Deni, John R. *Alliance Management and Maintenance, Restructuring NATO for the 21st Century.* Aldershot, UK: Ashgate, 2007.

Dinan, Desmond, ed. *Encyclopedia of the European Union.* Boulder, Colo.: Lynne Rienner, 1998.

Drew, Nelson S. *NATO from Berlin to Bosnia: Trans-Atlantic Security in Transition.* Washington, D.C.: National Defense University Press, 1987.

Everts, Steven, Lawrence Freedman, Charles Grant, Francois Heisbourg, Daniel Keohane, and Michael O'Hanlon. *A European Way of War.* London: Centre for European Reform, 2004.

Friend, Julius. *The Long Presidency: France in the Mitterrand Years, 1981–1995.* Boulder, Colo.: Westview, 1998.

Genscher, Hans Dietrich. *Rebuilding a House Divided.* New York: Broadway Books, 1998.

Gnesotto, Nicole, ed. *EU Security and Defence Policy: The First Five Years (1999–2004).* Paris: Institute for Security Studies, 2004.

Goldgeier, James M. *Not Whether but When: The U.S. Decision to Enlarge NATO.* Washington, D.C.: Brookings Institution Press, 1999.

Golino, Louis R. "Europe, the War on Terrorism, and the EU's International Role." *Brown Journal of World Affairs* (winter 2002): 61–72.

Goodman, Elliot R. *The Fate of the Atlantic Community.* New York: Praeger, 1975.

Gordon, Phillip H., and James B. Steinberg. *NATO Enlargement: Moving Forward.* Washington, D.C.: Brookings Institution Press, 2001.

Gow, James. *Triumph of the Lack of Will: International Diplomacy and the Yugoslav War.* New York: Columbia University Press, 1997.

Grant, Charles. *Is Europe doomed to fail as a power?* London: Centre for European Reform, 2009.

Halle, Louis J. *The Cold War as History.* New York: Harper & Row, 1967.

Hamilton, Daniel S., ed. *Transatlantic Transformations: Equipping NATO for the 21st Century.* Washington, D.C.: Center for Transatlantic Relations, 2004.

Harrison, Michael M. *The Reluctant Ally: France and Atlantic Security.* Baltimore: The Johns Hopkins University Press, 1981.

Hendrickson, Ryan C. *Diplomacy and War at NATO: The Secretary General and Military Action after the Cold War* Columbia, Mo: University of Missouri Press, 2006.

Heisbourg, François, Nicole Gnesotto, Charles Grant, Karl Kaiser, Andrez Karkoszka, Tomas Ries, Maartje Rutten, Stafano Silvestri, Alvaro Vasconcelos, and Rob de Wijk. *European Defence: Making It Work*. Chaillot Paper no. 42. Paris: Western European Union Institute for Security Studies, 2000.

Hill, Roger. *Political Consultation in NATO*. Toronto: Canadian Institute of International Affairs, 1978.

Hodes, Cyrus, and Mark Sedra. *The Search for Security in Post-Taliban Afghanistan*. Abingdon: Routledge for the International Institute for Strategic Studies, 2007.

Hoffman, Stanley. "The Crisis in the West." *New York Review of Books*, July 17, 1980.

Holbrooke, Richard. *To End a War*. New York: Random House, 1998.

Howorth, Jolyon. *Security and Defence Policy in the European Union*. New York: Palgrave MacMillan, 2007.

Ireland, Timothy P. *Creating the Entangling Alliance: The Origins of the North Atlantic Treaty Organization*. Westport, Conn.: Greenwood, 1981.

Jalali, Ali A. "Afghanistan: regaining momentum." *Parameters* 37.4 (Winter 2007): 5(15).

Joffe, Josef. "How America Does It." *Foreign Affairs* (September–October 1997): 13–27.

—*The Limited Partnership: Europe, the United States and the Burdens of Alliance*. Cambridge, Mass.: Ballinger, 1987.

Jones, Seth G. *Counterinsurgency in Afghanistan*: RAND Counterinsurgency Study—Volume 4. Arlington: RAND Corporation, 2008.

Kagan, Robert. *Of Paradise and Power: America and Europe in the New World Order*. New York: Knopf, 2003.

Kaim, Markus. "Germany, Afghanistan, and the future of NATO.(Canada-Germany relations)(Report)." *International Journal* 63(3) (Summer 2008), 607(17).

Kamp, Karl-Heinz and Yost, David, eds. *NATO and 21st Century Deterrence*. Rome: NATO College Research Directorate, May 2009.

Kaplan, Lawrence S., ed. *The United States and NATO: The Formative Years*. Lexington: University Press of Kentucky, 1984.

—*American Historians and the Atlantic Alliance*. Kent, Ohio: Kent State University Press, 1991.

—*NATO and the United States: The Enduring Alliance*. New York: Twayne, 1994.

—"Atlanticists vs. Europeanists in NATO." In *NATO and the European Union: Confronting the Challenges of European Security and Enlargement*. Edited by S. Victor Papacosma and Pierre-Henri Laurent. Kent, Ohio: Lyman Lemnitzer Center for NATO and European Union Studies, 1999.

—*The Long Entanglement: NATO's First Fifty Years*. Westport, Conn.: Praeger, 1999.

—*NATO Divided, NATO United: The Evolution of an Alliance*. Westport, Conn.: Praeger, 2004.

—*NATO 1948, The Birth of the Transatlantic Alliance*. Lanham, Md.: Rowman and Littlefield, 2007.

Kaplan, Lawrence S., and Robert W. Clawson, eds. *NATO after Thirty Years*. Wilmington, Del.: Scholarly Resources, 1981.

Katzman, Kenneth. "Afghanistan: Government Formation and Performance," Congressional Research Service Report for Congress, RL30508, June 2009.

Kay, Sean. *NATO and the Future of European Security*. Lanham, Md.: Rowman & Littlefield, 1998.

Kelleher, Catherine. *The Future of European Security*. Washington, D.C.: Brookings Institution Press, 1995.

Korski, Daniel. *Afghanistan: Europe's Forgotten War (Policy Paper)*. European Council on Foreign Relations, 2008.

Kupchan, Charles A. The *End of the American Era: U.S. Foreign Policy and the Geopolitics of the Twenty-First Century*. New York: Knopf, 2002.

Larson, Jeffrey A., and Kurt J. Klingenberger, eds. *Controlling Non-Strategic Nuclear Weapons: Obstacles and Opportunities*. Colorado Springs, Colo.: USAF Institute for National Security Studies, 2001.

Leurdijk, Dick A. *The United Nations and NATO in Former Yugoslavia: Partners in International Cooperation*. The Hague: Netherlands Atlantic Commission, 1994.

Lundestad, Geir. *The United States and Western Europe Since 1945*. Oxford: Oxford University Press, 2003.

—ed. *Just Another Major Crisis? The United States and Europe since 2000*. London: Oxford, 2008.

Lunn, Simon. *The Modernization of NATO's Long-Range Theater Nuclear Forces*. Report prepared for the US House Committee on Foreign Affairs. Washington, D.C.: Congressional Research Service, Library of Congress, 1981.

—*Burdensharing in NATO*. London: Royal Institute of International Affairs, 1983.

Menon, Anand. "Empowering paradise? The ESDP at ten." *International Affairs* 85(2) 2009, 227–46.

Michel, Leo G. "NATO Decisionmaking: Au Revoir to the Consensus Rule?": Strategic Forum No. 202, Institute for National Strategic Studies, National Defense University, August 2003.

—"Defense Transformation *à la française* and U.S. Interests." Strategic Forum No. 233, Institute for National Strategic Studies, National Defense University, September 2008.

Moens, Alexander. "American Diplomacy and German Unification." *Survival* (November–December 1991), 531–45.

Molenaar, Arnout. *[Dis]Organising European Security*. The Hague: Netherlands Atlantic Association, 2007.

Morelli, Vincent and Paul Belkin. "NATO in Afghanistan: A Test of the Transatlantic Alliance," Congressional Research Service Report RL33627, July 2009.

Myers, Kenneth A., ed. NATO—*The Next Thirty Years: The Changing Political, Economic, and Military Setting*. Boulder, Colo.: Westview, 1980.

North Atlantic Treaty Organization, *Afghanistan Report 2009*. Brussels: NATO Public Diplomacy Division, 2009.

Nye, Joseph S. *The Paradox of American Power: Why the World's Only Superpower Can't Go It Alone*. Oxford: Oxford University Press, 2002.

Ortega, Martin. *Military Intervention and the European Union*. Paris: Western European Union Institute for Security Studies, 2001.

Osgood, Robert. *NATO: The Entangling Alliance*. Chicago: University of Chicago Press, 1962.

Papacosma, S. Victor, Sean Kay, and Mark R. Rubin, eds. *NATO after Fifty Years*. Wilmington, Del.: Scholarly Resources, 2001.

Peters, John E., Stuart Johnson, Nora Bensahel, Timothy Liston, and Traci Williams. *European Contributions to Operation Allied Force: Implications for Transatlantic Cooperation*. Washington, D.C.: Rand, 2001.

Pond, Elizabeth. *The Rebirth of Europe*. Washington, D.C.: Brookings Institution Press, 1999.

Quinlan, Michael. *European Defense Cooperation: Asset or Threat to NATO?* Washington, D.C.: Woodrow Wilson Center Press, 2001.

Raj, Christopher S. *American Military in Europe*. New Delhi: ABC Publishing House, 1983.

Reyn, Sebastian. *Allies or Aliens? George W. Bush and the Transatlantic Crisis in Historical Perspective*. The Hague: Netherlands Atlantic Commission, 2004.

Roth, William V. Jr. *NATO in the 21st Century*. Brussels: North Atlantic Assembly, September 1998.

Rühle, Michael. "Imagining NATO 2011." *NATO Review* (autumn 2001): 18–21.

Rutten, Maartje, ed. *From St. Malo to Nice, European Defence: Core Documents*. Chaillot Paper no. 47. Paris: Western European Union Institute for Security Studies, 2001.

Rynning Sten. *NATO Renewed: The Power and Purpose of Transatlantic Cooperation*. New York: Palgrave Macmillan. 2005.

Sarotte, Mary Elise. *German Military Reform and European Security*. Oxford: Oxford University Press, 2001.

Schmitt, Burkard, ed., with Gordon Adams, Christophe Cornu, and Andrew D. James. *Between Cooperation and Competition: The Transatlantic Defence Market*. Paris: Western European Union Institute for Security Studies, January 2001.

Schweigler, Gebhard. "A Wider Atlantic?" *Foreign Policy* (September–October 2001), 87–88.

Serfaty, Simon. *The Vital Partnership: Power and Order, American and Europe beyond Iraq*. Lanham, Md.: Rowman and Littlefield, 2007.

—*Architects of Delusion: Europe, America and the Iraq War*. Philadelphia: University of Pennsylvania, 2008.

Simon, Jeffrey. *Central European Civil–Military Relations and NATO Expansion*. Washington, D.C.: National Defense University Press, 1996.

—*Roadmap to NATO Accession: Preparing for Membership*. Washington, D.C.: Institute for National Strategic Studies, National Defense University, October 2001.

—"NATO's Uncertain Future: Is Demography Destiny?" Strategic Forum No. 236, Institute for National Strategic Studies, National Defense University, October 2008.

Sloan, Stanley R. *NATO's Future: Toward a New Transatlantic Bargain*. Washington, D.C.: National Defense University Press, 1985.

—ed. *NATO in the 1990s*. Washington, D.C.: Pergamon-Brassey's, 1989.

—*NATO's Future: Beyond Collective Defense*. Washington, D.C.: National Defense University Press, 1996.

—*The United States and European Defence*. Chaillot Paper no. 36. Paris: Western European Union Institute for Security Studies, 2000.

—*NATO, the European Union, and the Atlantic Community: The Transatlantic Bargain Challenged*. Lanham, Md.: Rowman and Littlefield, 2005.

—*How and Why Did NATO Survive the Bush Doctrine?* Rome: NATO College Research Directorate, 2008.

Sloan, Stanley, and Peter van Ham. *What Future for NATO?* London: Centre for European Reform, 2002.

Sperling, James, and Mark Webber. "NATO: from Kosovo to Kabul.(Report)." *International Affairs* 85(3) (May 2009), 491(21).

Stuart, Douglas, and William Tow. *The Limits of Alliance: NATO Out-of-Area Problems since 1949*. Baltimore: The Johns Hopkins University Press, 1990.

Szabo, Stephen F. *The Diplomacy of German Unification.* New York: St. Martin's, 1992.

Szayna, Thomas S. *NATO Enlargement 2000–2015: Determinants and Implications for Defense Planning and Shaping.* Santa Monica, Calif.: Rand, 2001.

Thies, Walter J. *Friendly Rivals: Bargaining and Burden-Shifting in NATO.* Armonk, N.Y.: Sharpe, 2003.

—*Why NATO Endures.* New York: Cambridge University Press, 2009.

Toje, Asle. *America, the EU and Strategic Culture: Renegotiating the Transatlantic Bargain.* Abingdon: Routledge, 2008.

—*The EU, NATO and European Defence—A Slow Train Coming.* Brussels: European Union Institute for Security Studies, 2008.

Treverton, Gregory R., ed. *The Shape of the New Europe.* New York: Council on Foreign Relations, 1992.

US Government. Department of State. *Foreign Relations of the United States* (series).

US Senate Committee on Foreign Relations. Subcommittee on European Affairs. *NATO at 40.* Report prepared by the Congressional Research Service, Library of Congress, May 1989 (includes extensive annotated bibliography).

Van Eeckelen, Willem. *Debating European Security, 1948–1998.* The Hague: Sdu Publishers, 1998.

—*From Words to Deeds: The Continuing Debate on European Security.* Brussels: Centre for European Policy Studies, 2006.

Van Heuven, Marten, and Gregory F. Treverton. *Europe and America: How Will the United States Adjust to the New Partnership?* Santa Monica, Calif.: Rand, 1998.

Van Oudenaren, John. *Uniting Europe: An Introduction to the European Union.* 2nd edn Lanham, Md.: Rowman and Littlefield, 2005.

Williams, Phil. *The Senate and U.S. Troops in Europe.* London: Macmillan, 1985.

Yost, David S. *NATO Transformed, The Alliance's New Roles in International Security.* Washington, D.C.: United States Institute of Peace Press, 1998.

Zelikow, Philip, and Condoleezza Rice. *Germany Unified and Europe Transformed: A Study in Statecraft.* Cambridge, Mass.: Harvard University Press, 1995.

Zoellick, Robert B. "The Lessons of German Unification." *The National Interest* (fall 2000), 17–28.

About the Author

Stanley R. Sloan is the founding director of the Atlantic Community Initiative (www.AtlanticCommunity.org), president of VIC-Vermont, a visiting scholar and winter term professor at Middlebury College, and an independent lecturer and writer. He is a Woodrow Wilson Foundation Visiting Fellow and a member of the Fulbright Specialists Program. In 2006, he was named an Honorary Ancien of the NATO Defense College.

Before retiring from 32 years of government service, he was the senior specialist in international security policy at the Congressional Research Service (CRS) of the Library of Congress, where he previously served as head of the Office of Senior Specialists, division specialist in US alliance relations, and head of the Europe/Middle East/Africa section, among other positions. Prior to joining CRS, he was a commissioned officer in the US Air Force and held a number of analytical and research management positions at the Central Intelligence Agency, including Deputy National Intelligence Officer for Western Europe. In 1973, he served as a member of the US Delegation to Negotiations on Mutual and Balanced Force Reductions.

He has published a large number of CRS Reports for Congress, as well as journal articles, book chapters and opinion editorials in major US and European publications on international security topics, US foreign policy, and European security. His books and monographs include *NATO's Future: Toward a New Transatlantic Bargain* (1985), *NATO in the 1990s* (1989), *NATO's Future: Beyond Collective Defense* (1995), *The U.S. Role in the Twenty-first Century World: Toward a New Consensus* (1997), *The United States and European Defence* (2000), *NATO and Transatlantic Relations in the 21st Century: Crisis, Continuity or Change?* (2002), *The Use of U.S. Power: Implications for U.S. Interests* (2004) (coauthor), and *NATO, the European Union, and the Atlantic Community: The Transatlantic Bargain Challenged* (2005). He was rapporteur and study director for the North Atlantic Assembly's report on "NATO in the 1990s" (1988) and "NATO in the 21st Century" (1998). He lectures widely on international security topics in the United States and Europe.

Sloan received his B.A. from the University of Maine and his masters in international affairs from the Columbia University School of International Affairs; he completed all but his dissertation for a Ph.D. at the School of International Service, American University; and is a distinguished graduate of the USAF Officers Training School.

Index